Seventh Edition

Business Essentials

Ronald J. Ebert

Ricky W. Griffin

Prentice Hall
Upper Saddle River

VP/Publisher: Natalie E. Anderson
Executive Editor: Jodi McPherson
Director, Product Development: Pamela Hersperger
Editorial Project Manager: Kristen Kaiser, KMK Editorial Services
Editorial Assistant: Rosalinda Simone
AVP/Executive Editor, Media: Richard Keaveny
AVP/Executive Producer: Lisa Strite
Editorial Media Project Manager:
Production Media Project Manager: Lorena Cerisano
Senior Marketing Manager: Maggie Moylan
Marketing Assistant: Justin Jacob
Senior Managing Editor: Cynthia Zonneveld
Associate Managing Editor: Camille Trentacoste
Production Project Manager: Lynne Breitfeller
Manager of Rights & Permissions: Charles Morris
Senior Operations Specialist: Nick Sklitsis

Operations Specialist: Natacha Moore
Senior Art Director: Jonathan Boylan
Interior Design: Words & Numbers
Cover Design: Words & Numbers
Cover Illustration/Photo: www.shutterstock.com, www.istockphoto.com, Getty Images
Cover Visual Research and Permissions: Karen Sanatar
Director, Image Resource Center: Melinda Patelli
Manager, Rights and Permissions: Zina Arabia
Manager: Visual Research: Beth Brenzel
Image Permission Coordinator: Ang'John Ferrari
Photo Researcher: Kathy Ringrose
Composition: GEX Publishing Services
Full-Service Project Management: GEX Publishing Services
Printer/Binder: Courier Kendaville
Typeface: Helvetica 10/12

Credits and acknowledgments borrowed from other sources and reproduced, with permission, in this textbook appear on appropriate page within text (or on page 259).

Microsoft, Windows, Word, PowerPoint, Outlook, FrontPage, Visual Basic, MSN, The Microsoft Network, and/or other Microsoft products referenced herein are either trademarks or registered trademarks of the Microsoft Corporation in the U.S.A. and other countries. Screen shots and icons reprinted with permission from the Microsoft Corporation. This book is not sponsored or endorsed by or affiliated with the Microsoft Corporation.

Pearson Education Ltd., London
Pearson Education Singapore, Pte. Ltd
Pearson Education, Canada, Ltd
Pearson Education–Japan
Pearson Education Australia PTY, Limited

Pearson Education North Asia Ltd
Pearson Educación de Mexico, S.A. de C.V.
Pearson Education Malaysia, Pte. Ltd.
Pearson Education, Upper Saddle River, New Jersey

Prentice Hall
is an imprint of

www.pearsonhighered.com

10 9 8 7 6 5 4 3 2 1
ISBN-13: 978-0-13-607076-4
ISBN-10: 0-13-607076-0

*Dedicated with gratitude to my long-time friend
Don Mullikin—a talented humorist, devoted family
man, and unwavering patriot.   R.J.E.*

*With love and admiration to my mother-in-law
Nora Lee May—a selfless, devoted, steadfast, and
inquisitive feminist.   R.W.G.*

BRIEF CONTENTS

CONTENTS

Contents   xi

How to Use This Book

Welcome to the new edition of *Business Essentials!* This revision builds upon what you have always loved and what has made this book the number-one brief Introduction to Business text.

As instructors across the country have confirmed in reviews and focus groups, current world events are calling for a changed emphasis within the Introduction to Business course and text. The focus on practical skills, knowing the basics, and highlighting important developments in business makes for a brief book but a rich experience. Taking your comments seriously, we have made the following changes to the seventh edition of *Business Essentials*:

New!

Look and Feel

The book's new design and improved art help students who are visual learners better process and understand chapter content.

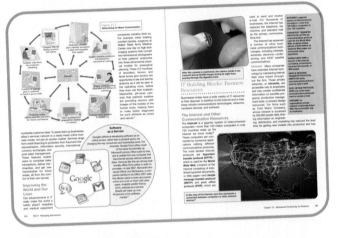

New!

"Managing Finances" Chapter

You asked for more finance content, and we've responded with an all-new chapter on managing finances, both business and personal. From basic principles, we push forward to explore debt and equity financing, risk, and maximizing capital growth. We also delve into securities markets and the opportunities they present to businesses and individuals.

New!

MyBizLab

The seventh edition features robust online support at **www.mybizlab.com**. Students will find links to informative and exciting supplemental text and media, as well as practice what they've learned through interactive exercises that give instant feedback.

In addition, your favorite case studies and features from the last edition, including the popular video exercises, can now be easily accessed at **www.mybizlab.com**, so you don't have to worry about missing the features you loved in the past.

New!

Glindex

In addition to the key terms sidebars you loved from previous editions, the seventh edition also features a combined glossary and index to make it even easier to find the definitions of key terms and where they are referenced in the text.

Updated!

Chapter Case Vignettes

We've updated or completely replaced the chapter-opening cases, keeping them fresh, relevant, and up-to-date. Covering companies from Facebook to eBay to Apple, these chapter case vignettes pique students' interest at the beginning of the chapter and reinforce concepts they've learned throughout the chapter at the end.

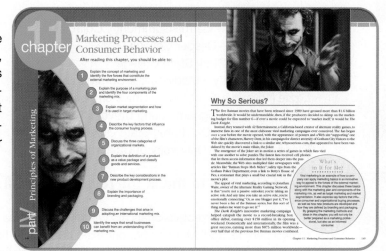

Updated!

"Entrepreneurship and New Ventures" Features

Whether working for a large corporation or starting their own business, students need to be both entrepreneurial and intrapreneurial. These now updated popular boxed features touch on entrepreneurs who have really made a difference.

Updated!

"Say What You Mean" Features

Updated "Say What You Mean" boxed features sensitize students to cultural differences and teach them to communicate more effectively, both orally and in writing.

Acknowledgments

Although two names appear on the cover of the book, we could never have completed the seventh edition without the assistance of many fine individuals. First, we would like to thank all the professionals who took time from their busy schedules to review materials for *Business Essentials*:

We'd like to thank the reviewers of the seventh edition:

Kate Demarest – Carroll Community College
Gary Donnelly – Casper College
Pam Janson – Stark State College
David W. Murphy – Madisonville Community College
Lizzie Ngwenya-Scoburgh – University of Northwestern Ohio
Mary Nygren – Brigham Young University, Idaho
Glenda Orosco – Oklahoma State University
David Robinson – University of California, Berkeley

We'd also like to thank the reviewers of all our previous editions.

A number of other professionals also made substantive contributions to the text. We are most indebted to two people. Jodi McPherson, our executive editor, has instilled a continuing commitment to elevate the quality and profile of this book, and to help us maintain and enhance our leadership position in this highly competitive market. Kristen Kaiser also joined us as our project manager in what was truly a team effort. Kristen competently coordinated the activities of our many contributors, and consistently challenged us in working together for quality and timeliness. We'd also like to acknowledge the professional contributions of Words & Numbers, a partnering company whose creative resources have added so much to the development of the seventh edition's design and content.

Of course, this edition also builds on past successes. Hence, we would be remiss not to acknowledge Shannon LeMay-Finn and Ron Librach, the development editors on our previous editions. We'd also like to thank the reviewers of the previous edition whose contributions have strengthened this seventh edition.

Our colleagues at the University of Missouri-Columbia and Texas A&M University also deserve recognition. Each of us has the good fortune to be a part of a community of scholars who enrich our lives and challenge our ideas. Finally, we want to acknowledge the people who are the foundation of our lives. We take pride in the accomplishments of our wives, Mary and Glenda, and draw strength from the knowledge that they are there for us to lean on. And we take joy from our children, Matt, Kristen, and Brayer, and Ashley, Dustin, and Matt. Thanks to all of you for making us what we are.

Ronald J. Ebert
Ricky W. Griffin

What's in it for you?

If you're like many students, you may be starting this semester with some questions about why you're here. Whether you're taking this course at a two-year college, at a four-year university, or at a technical school, in a traditional classroom setting or online, you may be wondering just what you're supposed to get from this course and how it will benefit you. In short, you may be wondering, "What's in it for me?"

First, regardless of what it may be called at your school, this is a survey course designed to introduce you to the many exciting and challenging facets of business, both in the United States and elsewhere. The course is designed to fit the needs of a wide variety of students. You may be taking this course as the first step toward earning a degree in business, you may be thinking about business and want to know more about it, or you may know you want to study business but are unsure of the area you want to pursue. You may plan to major in another field but want some basic business background and are taking this course as an elective. Or you may be here because, frankly, this course is required or is a prerequisite to another course.

For those of you with little work experience, you may be uncertain as to what the business world is all about. If you have a lot of work experience, you may even be a bit skeptical as to what you can actually learn about business from an introductory course. One of our biggest challenges as authors is to write a book that meets the needs of such a diverse student population, especially when we acknowledge the legitimacy of your right to ask "What's in it for me?" We also want to do our best to ensure that you find the course challenging, interesting, and useful.

The world today is populated with a breathtaking array of businesses and business opportunities. Big and small business, established and new businesses, broad-based and niche businesses, successful and unsuccessful businesses, global and domestic businesses—throughout this book we'll discuss how they get started and how they work, why they grow and why some fail, and how they affect you. Regardless of where your future plans take you, we hope that you look back on this course as one of your first steps.

Going forward, we also urge you to consider that what you get out of this course—what's in it for you—is shaped by at least three factors. One factor is this book and the various learning aids that accompany it. Another factor is your instructor. He or she is a dedicated professional who wants nothing more than to help you grow and develop intellectually and academically.

The third factor? You. Learning is an active process that requires you to be a major participant. Simply memorizing the key terms and concepts in this book may help you achieve an acceptable course grade. But true learning requires that you read, study, discuss, question, review, experience, and evaluate as you go along. While tests and homework may be a "necessary evil," we believe we will have done our part if you finish this course with new knowledge and increased enthusiasm for the world of business. We know your instructor will do his or her best to facilitate your learning. The rest, then, is up to you. We wish you success.

Seventh Edition

Business Essentials

chapter 1

The U.S. Business Environment

After reading this chapter, you should be able to:

1 Define the nature of U.S. business and identify its main goals and functions.

2 Describe the external environments of business and discuss how these environments affect the success or failure of any organization.

3 Describe the different types of global economic systems according to the means by which they control the factors of production.

4 Show how markets, demand, and supply affect resource distribution in the United States.

5 Identify the elements of private enterprise and explain the various degrees of competition in the U.S. economic system.

6 Explain the importance of the economic environment to business and identify the factors used to evaluate the performance of an economic system.

What Goes Up . . . Can Go Even Higher!

The sign in front of a Texas Mobil gasoline station summed it up nicely: The "prices" for the three grades of gasoline sold at the station were listed as "an arm," "a leg," and "your first born." While the sign no doubt led to a few smiles from motorists, its sentiments were far from a laughing matter. The stark reality was that in mid-2008, retail gasoline prices in the United States were at an all-time high, hovering around $4.00 per gallon. The upward price spiral that began in mid-2004 has left consumers, government officials, and business leaders struggling to find answers.

What made this gas crisis unusual was that it began with an unusual mix of supply, demand, and global forces. In the past, gas prices generally increased only when the supply was reduced. But the circumstances underlying the increases that started in 2004 and continued through 2008 were much more complex. First, global supplies of gasoline have been increasing at a rate that has more than offset the steady decline in U.S. domestic production of gasoline since 1972. As a result, the United States has been relying more on foreign producers and is, therefore, subject to whatever prices those producers want to charge. Second, demand for gasoline in the United States has continued to rise as a result of a growing population, the continued popularity of large gas-guzzling vehicles, and a strong demand for other petroleum-based products.

Another major piece of the puzzle has been a surging global economy that has caused a higher demand for oil and gasoline. More people are buying cars, and petroleum refiners work around the clock to help meet the unprecedented demand for gasoline. China, in particular, has become a major consumer of petroleum, passing Japan in 2005 to trail only the United States in total consumption.

The price increases led to a wide array of consequences. Automobile manufacturers stepped up their commitment to making more fuel-efficient cars. Refiners posted record profits (indeed, some critics charged that the energy companies were guilty of price gouging). And even local police officers were kept busy combating a surge in gasoline theft, yet another indication that gas was becoming an increasingly valuable commodity![1]

What's in It for Me?

The gas crisis is an example of how external environments, a global economy, and supply and demand affect business and distribution in the United States. In addition to these factors, this chapter will discuss the nature and purpose of a business and the elements of private enterprise and competition. It will also prepare you to analyze how different factors affect a business's success or failure and to evaluate the performance of an economic system in the context of business.

The Concept of Business and the Concept of Profit

● ● ● ● ● ● ● ● ● ● ● ● ● ● ● ● ● ● ● ●

What do you think of when you hear the word *business*? Does it conjure up images of successful corporations, such as General Electric? Or are you reminded of smaller firms, such as your local supermarket, or family-owned operations, such as your neighborhood pizzeria?

All these organizations are **businesses**—organizations that provide goods or services that are then sold to earn profits. Indeed, the prospect of earning **profits**—the difference between a business's revenues and its expenses—is what encourages people to open and expand businesses. After all, profits are the rewards owners get for risking their money and time. The right to pursue profits distinguishes a business from those organizations—such as most universities, hospitals, and government agencies—that run in much the same way but that generally don't seek profits.[2]

Consumer Choice and Demand   In a capitalistic system, such as that in the United States, businesses exist to earn profits for owners; an owner is free to set up a new business, grow that business, sell it, or even shut it down. But consumers also have freedom of choice. In choosing how to pursue profits, businesses must take into account what consumers want and/or need. No matter how efficient, a business won't survive without a demand for its goods or services. Neither a snowblower shop in Florida nor a beach-umbrella store in Alaska is likely to do well.

Opportunity and Enterprise   If enterprising businesspeople can spot a promising opportunity and then develop a good plan for capitalizing on it, they can succeed. The opportunity always involves goods or services that consumers need and/or want—especially if no one else is supplying them or if existing businesses are doing so inefficiently or incompletely.

The Benefits of Business   Businesses produce most of the goods and services we consume, and they employ most working people. They create most new innovations and provide a vast range of opportunities for new businesses, which serve as their suppliers. A healthy business climate also contributes to the quality of life and standard of living of people in a society. Business profits enhance the personal incomes of millions of owners and stockholders, and business taxes help to support governments at all levels. Many businesses support charities and provide community leadership. However, some businesses also harm the environment, and their decision makers sometimes resort to unacceptable practices for their own personal benefit.

The External Environments of Business

● ●

All businesses, regardless of their size, location, or mission, operate within a larger external environment. This **external environment** consists of everything outside an organization's boundaries that might affect it. (Businesses also have an *internal environment*, more commonly called *corporate culture*, which is discussed in Chapter 5.) Managers must have a complete and accurate understanding of the external environment and strive to operate and compete within it or their organizations will not survive. Table 1.1 describes the external environment for the clothing retailer Urban Outfitters.

Domestic Business Environment
The **domestic business environment** refers to the environment in which a firm conducts its operations and derives its revenues. In general, businesses seek to be close to their customers, to establish strong relationships with their suppliers, and to distinguish themselves from their competitors.

Global Business Environment
The **global business environment** refers to the international forces that affect a business. Factors affecting the global environment at a general level include international trade agreements, international economic conditions, political unrest, and so forth. At a more immediate level, any given business is likely to be affected by international market opportunities, suppliers, cultures, competitors, and currency values.

Technological Environment
The **technological environment** generally includes all the ways by which firms create value for their constituents. Technology includes human knowledge, work

methods, physical equipment, electronics and telecommunications, and various processing systems that are used to perform business activities.

Political-Legal Environment

The **political-legal environment**, which reflects the relationship between business and government, is important for several reasons. The legal system defines and regulates many aspects of what an organization can and can't do, including advertising practices, safety and health considerations, and acceptable standards of business conduct. Pro- or anti-business sentiment in government and political stability are also important considerations, especially for international firms.

Sociocultural Environment

The **sociocultural environment** includes the customs, mores, values, and demographic characteristics of the society in which an organization functions. Sociocultural processes also determine the goods and services, as well as the standards of business conduct, that a society is likely to value and accept.

Economic Environment

The **economic environment** refers to relevant conditions that exist in the economic system in which a company operates. For example, if an economy is doing well enough that most people have jobs, a growing company may find it necessary to pay higher wages and offer more benefits in order to attract workers from other companies. But if many people in an economy are looking for jobs, a firm may be able to pay less and offer fewer benefits.

Economic Systems

· · · · · · · · · · · · ·

The economic system of a firm's *home country*—the nation in which it does most of its business—is a key factor is determining how a firm operates. An **economic system** is a nation's system for allocating its resources among its citizens, both individuals and organizations.

Factors of Production

A basic difference between economic systems is the way in which a system manages its **factors of production**—the resources that a country's businesses use to produce goods and services. Economists focus on five factors of production. Note that the concept of factors of production can also be applied to the resources that an individual organization *manages* to produce goods and services.

Labor Sometimes called **human resources**, **labor** includes the physical and intellectual contributions people make to a business while engaged in economic

Table 1.1 The External Environments of Business: Urban Outfitters

Domestic Business Environment	Global Business Environment	Technological Environment	Political-Legal Environment	Sociocultural Environment	Economic Environment
• Initially located stores near urban college campuses; now has locations in more upscale neighborhoods as well • Strong network of suppliers • Wholesale supplier to other retailers through its Free People division • Competing with Gap and Abercrombie & Fitch for customers and market share	• Global presence with stores in Belgium, Canada, Denmark, Ireland, Sweden, and United Kingdom as well as an online presence in Japan • Many suppliers are foreign companies	• Sophisticated information system that tracks sales and inventory levels, allowing for quick response to customers • Successful e-commerce Web sites	• Subject to a variety of political and legal forces, including product identification and local zoning requirements • Actively protects assets by monitoring copyright infringement by competition	• Pulled items after unfavorable publicity in 2003 for Monopoly-like game called Ghettopoly that was criticized for making light of poverty and social problems • Discontinued sale of Jesus Dress Up magnets in 2004 after pressure from family activist groups	• Employee opportunities are desirable, with competitive salaries and a strong benefits package

production. Starbucks, for example, employs over 194,000 people,[3] including baristas who prepare coffees for customers, store managers, regional managers, coffee tasters, quality-control experts, coffee buyers, marketing experts, financial specialists, and other specialized workers and managers.

Capital Obtaining and using labor and other resources requires **capital**—the financial resources needed to start a business, operate it, and keep it growing. For example, Howard Schultz used personal savings and a loan to finance his acquisition of the fledgling Starbucks coffee outfit back in 1987. As Starbucks grew, he came to rely more on its profits and eventually sold stock to other investors to raise even more money. Today, Starbucks continues to rely on a blend of current earnings and both short- and long-term debt to finance its operations and fuel its growth.

Entrepreneurs An **entrepreneur** is a person who accepts the risks and opportunities entailed in creating and operating a new business. Howard Schultz was willing to accept the risks associated with retail growth and, after buying Starbucks, he capitalized on the market opportunities for rapid growth. Had his original venture failed, Schultz would have lost most of his savings. Most economic systems encourage entrepreneurs, both to start new businesses and to make the decisions that allow them to create new jobs and make more profits for their owners.

Physical Resources **Physical resources** are the tangible things that organizations use to conduct their business. They include natural resources and raw materials, offices, storage and production facilities, parts and supplies, computers and peripherals, and a variety of other equipment. For example, Starbucks relies on coffee beans and other food products, the equipment it uses to make its coffee drinks, paper products for packaging, and other retail equipment, as well as office equipment and storage facilities for running its business at the corporate level.

Information Resources The production of tangible goods once dominated most economic systems. Today, **information resources**—data and other information used by businesses—play a major role. Information resources that businesses rely on include market forecasts, the specialized knowledge of people, and economic data. In turn, much of what they do results either in the creation of new information or the repackaging of existing information for new users. For example, Starbucks uses various economic statistics to decide where to open new outlets. It also uses sophisticated forecasting models to predict the future prices of coffee beans. And consumer taste tests help the firm decide when to introduce new products.

Types of Economic Systems

The various types of economic systems differ in how they manage these factors of production and make decisions about production and allocation. In some systems, all ownership is private; in others, all factors of production are owned or controlled by the government. Most systems, however, fall between these extremes.

Planned Economies A **planned economy** relies on a centralized government to control all or most factors of production and to

Starbucks uses various factors of production, including labor such as these baristas.

Say What You Mean

The Culture of Risk

Risk taking has been a defining feature of U.S. business culture for a long time. From the early pioneers and prospectors heading west to the would-be dot-com billionaires of the 1990s, Americans are known not only for their readiness to try out new ideas, but also for their willingness to risk everything for the chance to make it big. Risk taking has become an important part of California's business culture, especially in the entertainment and high-tech industries, and New York is home to high rollers in the world of finance. Risk taking in the United States differs by industry and size of company. Small companies are more likely to make risky decisions than large companies, where elaborate approval processes may slow things down. Likewise, publicly traded companies whose stockholders usually keep a close eye on investments are less likely to take big risks than privately held firms.

In contrast, many foreign cultures inhibit risk taking by businesses. In Japan, for example, business failure carries with it significant social stigma—a loss of "face." As a result, entrepreneurs there are slow to expand their businesses until they are certain they will succeed. Likewise, in countries like Russia and Poland, where up until a few years ago most businesses were government-owned, many managers today remain cautious and are reluctant to go too far out on a limb for a new opportunity.

COMMUNISM political system in which the government owns and operates all factors of production

MARKET ECONOMY economy in which individuals control production and allocation decisions through supply and demand

MARKET mechanism for exchange between buyers and sellers of a particular good or service

political system. Today, North Korea, Vietnam, and the People's Republic of China are among the few nations with openly communist systems. Even in these countries, however, planned economic systems are making room for features of the free enterprise system.

Market Economies In a **market economy**, individual producers and consumers control production and allocation by creating combinations of supply and demand. A **market** is a mechanism for exchange between the buyers and sellers of a particular good or service. (Like *capital*, the term *market* can have multiple meanings.) Market economies rely on capitalism and free enterprise to create an environment in which producers and consumers are free to sell and buy what they choose (within certain limits). As a result, items produced and prices paid are largely determined by supply and demand.

To understand how a market economy works, consider what happens when you go to a fruit market to buy apples. While one vendor is selling apples for $1 per pound, another is charging $1.50. Both vendors are free to charge what they want, and you are free to buy what

make all or most production and allocation decisions. There are two basic forms of planned economies: *communism* (discussed here) and *socialism* (discussed as a mixed market economy).

As envisioned by nineteenth-century German economist Karl Marx, **communism** is a system in which the government owns and operates all factors of production. Under such a system, the government would assign people to jobs, own all business, and control all business decisions—what to make, how much to charge, and so forth. Marx proposed that individuals would contribute according to their abilities and receive benefits according to their needs. He also expected government ownership of production factors to be temporary: Once society had matured, government would wither away, and workers would take direct ownership of the factors of production.

The former Soviet Union and many Eastern European countries embraced communism until the end of the twentieth century. In the early 1990s, one country after another renounced communism as both an economic and a

Free Enterprise in China?

Once strictly synonymous with the Maoist communist regime, China is slowly demonstrating internal change. Fundamental events, such as the 2008 Olympics in Beijing, gradually alter the way domestic commerce is conducted as the demand for goods and services drastically increases. The changes will still not affect much of the population, but free enterprise is fragmentarily affecting certain businesses. Although not always the rule, as a country becomes richer, its economy is likely to become less rigid.

CAPITALISM system that sanctions the private ownership of the factors of production and encourages entrepreneurship by offering profits as an incentive

MIXED MARKET ECONOMY economic system featuring characteristics of both planned and market economies

PRIVATIZATION process of converting government enterprises into privately owned companies

SOCIALISM planned economic system in which the government owns and operates only selected major sources of production

Despite becoming a territory of the communist People's Republic of China in 1997, Hong Kong remains one of the world's freest economies. In Hong Kong's Lan Kwai Fong district, for example, traditional Chinese businesses operate next door to standard U.S. chains.

you choose. If both vendors' apples are of the same quality, you will buy the cheaper ones. If the $1.50 apples are fresher, you may buy them instead. In short, both buyers and sellers enjoy freedom of choice.

Individuals in a market system are free to not only buy what they want but also to work where they want and to invest, save, or spend their money in whatever manner they choose. Likewise, businesses are free to decide what products to make, where to sell them, and what prices to charge. This process contrasts markedly with that of a planned economy, in which individuals may be told where they can and cannot work, companies may be told what they can and cannot make, and consumers may have little or no choice in what they purchase or how much they pay. The political basis of market processes is called **capitalism**, which allows the private ownership of the factors of production and encourages entrepreneurship by offering profits as an incentive.

Mixed Market Economies In reality, there are no "pure" planned or "pure" market economies. Most countries rely on some form of **mixed market economy** that features characteristics of both planned and market economies. Even a market economy that strives to be as free and open as possible, such as the U.S. economy, restricts certain activities. Some products can't be sold legally, others can be sold only to people of a certain age, advertising must be truthful, and so forth. And the People's Republic of China, the world's most important planned economy, is increasingly allowing and overseeing certain forms of private ownership and entrepreneurship.

When a government is making a change from a planned economy to a market economy, it usually begins to adopt market mechanisms through **privatization**—the process of converting government enterprises into privately owned companies. The Netherlands, for example, has privatized its TNT Post Group N.V., transforming it into one of the world's most efficient post-office operations. Generally speaking, privatizing enterprises can reduce payroll expenses and boost efficiency, productivity, and profits.

In the partially planned system called **socialism**, the government owns and operates selected major industries. In such mixed market economies, the government may control banking, transportation, or industries producing such basic goods as oil and steel. Smaller businesses, such as clothing stores and restaurants, are privately owned. Many Western European countries, including England and France, allow free market operations in most economic areas but keep government control of others, such as health care.

The Economics of Market Systems

Understanding the complex nature of the U.S. economic system is essential to understanding the environment in which U.S. businesses operate.

Demand and Supply in a Market Economy

A market economy consists of many different markets that function within that economy. As a consumer, for instance, the choices you have and the prices you pay for goods and services are all governed by different sets of market forces. Businesses also have many different choices about buying and selling their products. Managers make decisions about inventory levels, prices, and distribution. Literally billions of exchanges take place every day between businesses and individuals; between businesses; and among individuals, businesses, and governments. Moreover, exchanges conducted in one area often affect exchanges elsewhere. For instance, the high cost of gas may also lead to prices going up for other items, ranging from food to clothing to delivery services, because of the reliance on gas for transportation.

The Laws of Demand and Supply On all economic levels, decisions about what to buy and what to sell are determined primarily by the forces of demand and supply.[4] **Demand** is the willingness and ability of buyers to purchase a product (a good or a service). **Supply** is the willingness and ability of producers to offer a good or service for sale. Generally speaking, demand and supply follow basic laws:

■ The **law of demand**: Buyers will purchase (demand) *more* of a product as its price *drops* and *less* of a product as its price *increases*.

■ The **law of supply**: Producers will offer (supply) *more* of a product for sale as its price *rises* and *less* of a product as its price *drops*.

The Demand and Supply Schedule To appreciate these laws in action, consider the market for pizza in your town. If everyone is willing to pay $25 for a pizza (a relatively high price), the town's only pizzeria will produce a large supply. But if everyone is willing to pay only $5 (a relatively low price), it will make fewer pizzas. Through careful analysis, we can determine how many pizzas will be sold at different prices. These results, called a **demand and supply schedule**, are obtained from marketing research, historical data, and other studies of the market. Properly applied, they reveal the relationships among different levels of demand and supply at different price levels.

Demand and Supply Curves The demand and supply schedule can be used to construct demand and supply curves for pizza in your town. A **demand curve** shows how many products—in this case, pizzas—will be demanded (bought) at different prices. A **supply curve** shows how many pizzas will be supplied (baked or offered for sale) at different prices.

Figure 1.1 shows demand and supply curves for pizzas. As you can see, demand increases as price decreases; supply increases as price increases. When demand and supply curves are plotted on the same graph, the point at which they intersect is the **market price** (also called the **equilibrium price**)—the price at

which the quantity of goods demanded and the quantity of goods supplied are equal. In Figure 1.1, the equilibrium price for pizzas in our example is $10. At this point, the quantity of pizzas demanded and the quantity of pizzas supplied are the same: 1,000 pizzas per week.

Surpluses and Shortages What if the pizzeria decides to make some other number of pizzas—if the owner tried to increase profits by making *more* pizzas to sell or if the owner *reduced* the number of pizzas offered for sale to lower overhead and cut back on store hours? In either case, the result would be an inefficient use of resources and lower profits. For instance, if the pizzeria supplies 1,200 pizzas and tries to sell them for $10 each, 200 pizzas will not be bought. Our demand schedule shows that only 1,000 pizzas will be demanded at this price. The pizzeria will therefore have a **surplus**—a situation in which the quantity supplied exceeds the quantity demanded. It will lose the money that it spent making those extra 200 pizzas.

Conversely, if the pizzeria supplies only 800 pizzas, a **shortage** will result. The quantity demanded will be greater than the quantity supplied. The pizzeria will "lose" the extra profit that it could have made by producing 200 more pizzas. Even though consumers may pay more for pizzas because of the shortage, the pizzeria will still earn lower total profits than if it had made 1,000 pizzas. It will also risk angering customers who cannot buy pizzas and encourage other entrepreneurs to set up competing pizzerias to satisfy unmet demand. Businesses should seek the ideal combination of price charged and quantity supplied so as to maximize profits, maintain goodwill among

DEMAND the willingness and ability of buyers to purchase a good or service

SUPPLY the willingness and ability of producers to offer a good or service for sale

LAW OF DEMAND principle that buyers will purchase (demand) more of a product as its price drops and less as its price increases

LAW OF SUPPLY principle that producers will offer (supply) more of a product for sale as its price rises and less as its price drops

DEMAND AND SUPPLY SCHEDULE assessment of the relationships among different levels of demand and supply at different price levels

DEMAND CURVE graph showing how many units of a product will be demanded (bought) at different prices

SUPPLY CURVE graph showing how many units of a product will be supplied (offered for sale) at different prices

MARKET PRICE (EQUILIBRIUM PRICE) profit-maximizing price at which the quantity of goods demanded and the quantity of goods supplied are equal

SURPLUS situation in which quantity supplied exceeds quantity demanded

SHORTAGE situation in which quantity demanded exceeds quantity supplied

PRIVATE ENTERPRISE economic system that allows individuals to pursue their own interests without undue governmental restriction

COMPETITION vying among businesses for the same resources or customers

customers, and discourage competition. This ideal combination is found at the equilibrium point.

Our example involves only one company, one product, and a few buyers. The U.S. economy—indeed, any market economy—is far more complex. Thousands of companies sell hundreds of thousands of products to millions of buyers every day. In the end, however, the result is much the same: Companies try to supply the quantity and selection of goods that will earn them the largest profits.

Private Enterprise and Competition in a Market Economy

Market economies rely on a **private enterprise** system—one that allows individuals to pursue their own interests with minimal government restriction. In turn, private enterprise requires the presence of four elements:

1 *Private property rights.* Ownership of the resources used to create wealth is in the hands of individuals.

2 *Freedom of choice.* Individuals can choose which employers to sell their labor to and which products to buy, and producers can choose whom to hire and what to produce.

3 *Profits.* The lure of profits (and freedom) leads some people to abandon the security of working for someone else and to assume the risks of entrepreneurship. Anticipated profits also influence individuals' choices of which goods or services to produce.

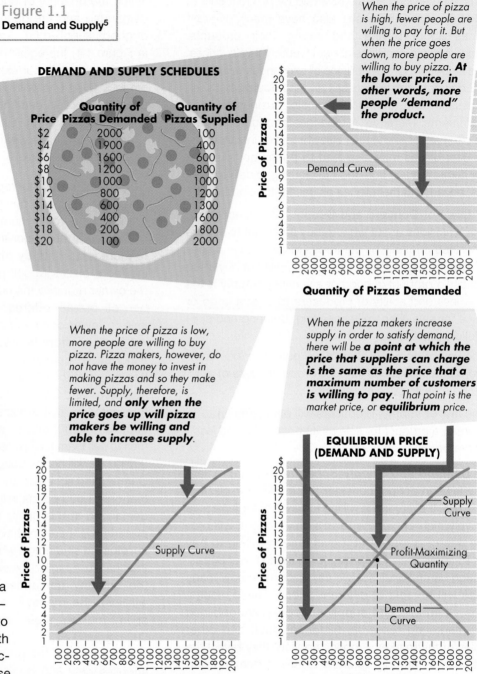

Figure 1.1
Demand and Supply[5]

DEMAND AND SUPPLY SCHEDULES

Price	Quantity of Pizzas Demanded	Quantity of Pizzas Supplied
$2	2000	100
$4	1900	400
$6	1600	600
$8	1200	800
$10	1000	1000
$12	800	1200
$14	600	1300
$16	400	1600
$18	200	1800
$20	100	2000

When the price of pizza is high, fewer people are willing to pay for it. But when the price goes down, more people are willing to buy pizza. **At the lower price, in other words, more people "demand" the product.**

Demand Curve

Quantity of Pizzas Demanded

When the price of pizza is low, more people are willing to buy pizza. Pizza makers, however, do not have the money to invest in making pizzas and so they make fewer. Supply, therefore, is limited, and **only when the price goes up will pizza makers be willing and able to increase supply**.

Supply Curve

Quantity of Pizzas Supplied

When the pizza makers increase supply in order to satisfy demand, there will be **a point at which the price that suppliers can charge is the same as the price that a maximum number of customers is willing to pay**. *That point is the market price, or* **equilibrium** *price.*

EQUILIBRIUM PRICE (DEMAND AND SUPPLY)

Supply Curve

Profit-Maximizing Quantity

Demand Curve

Quantity of Pizzas

4 *Competition.* If profits motivate individuals to start businesses, competition motivates them to operate those businesses efficiently. **Competition** occurs when two or more businesses vie for the same resources or customers. To gain an advantage over competitors, a business must produce its goods or services efficiently and be able to sell at a reasonable profit by convincing customers that its products are either better or less expensive than those of its competitors. Competition, therefore, forces all businesses to make products better or cheaper. A company that produces inferior, expensive products is likely to fail.

Table 1.2 **Degrees of Competition**

Characteristic	Perfect Competition	Monopolistic Competition	Oligopoly	Monopoly
Example	Local Farmer	Stationery Store	Steel Industry	Public Utility
Number of Competitors	Many	Many, but fewer than in perfect competition	Few	None
Ease of Entry into the Industry	Relatively easy	Fairly easy	Difficult	Regulated by government
Similarity of Goods/Services Offered by Competing Firms	Identical	Similar	Can be similar or different	No directly competing goods or services
Level of Control over Price by Individual Firms	None	Some	Some	Considerable

PERFECT COMPETITION market or industry characterized by numerous small firms producing an identical product

MONOPOLISTIC COMPETITION market or industry characterized by numerous buyers and relatively numerous sellers trying to differentiate their products from those of competitors

OLIGOPOLY market or industry characterized by a handful of (generally large) sellers with the power to influence the prices of their products

Degrees of Competition Even in a free enterprise system, not all industries are equally competitive. Economists have identified four degrees of competition in a private enterprise system: *perfect competition*, *monopolistic competition*, *oligopoly*, and *monopoly*. Note that these are not always truly distinct categories but actually tend to fall along a continuum; perfect competition and monopoly anchor the ends of the continuum, with monopolistic competition and oligopoly falling in between. Table 1.2 summarizes the features of these four degrees of competition.

Perfect Competition For **perfect competition** to exist, two conditions must prevail: (1) all firms in an industry must be small, and (2) the number of firms in the industry must be large. Under these conditions, no single firm is powerful enough to influence the price of its product. Prices are, therefore, determined by such market forces as supply and demand.

In addition, these two conditions also reflect four principles:

1 The products of each firm are so similar that buyers view them as identical to those of other firms.

2 Both buyers and sellers know the prices that others are paying and receiving in the marketplace.

3 Because each firm is small, firms can easily enter or leave the market.

4 Going prices are set exclusively by supply and demand and accepted by both sellers and buyers.

U.S. agriculture is a good example of perfect competition. The wheat produced on one farm is the same as that from another. Both producers and buyers are aware of prevailing market prices. It is relatively easy to start producing wheat and relatively easy to stop when it's no longer profitable.

Monopolistic Competition In **monopolistic competition**, there are numerous sellers trying to make their products at least seem to be different from those of competitors. While there are many sellers involved in monopolistic competition, there tend to be fewer than in pure competition. Differentiating strategies include brand names, design or styling, and advertising.

Product differentiation also gives sellers some control over prices. For instance, even though Target shirts may have similar styling and other features, Ralph Lauren polo shirts can be priced with little regard for lower Target prices. But the large number of buyers relative to sellers applies potential limits to prices: Although Ralph Lauren might be able to sell shirts for $20 more than a comparable Target shirt, it could not sell as many shirts if they were priced at $200 more. Monopolistically competitive businesses may be large or small, but they can still enter or leave the market easily. For example, many small clothing stores compete successfully with larger apparel retailers, such as Abercrombie & Fitch and Banana Republic. A good case in point is bebe stores. The small clothing chain controls its own manufacturing facilities and can respond just as quickly as firms like the Gap to changes in fashion tastes.

Oligopoly When an industry has only a handful of sellers, an **oligopoly** exists. As a general rule, these sellers are quite large. The entry of new competitors is hard because large capital investment is needed. Thus, oligopolistic industries tend to stay that way—for example, only Boeing and Airbus make large commercial aircraft. Furthermore, as the trend toward globalization continues, most experts believe that oligopolies will become increasingly prevalent.

Oligopolists have more control over their strategies than monopolistically competitive firms, but the actions of one firm can significantly affect the sales of every other firm in the industry. When an airline announces new fare discounts, others adopt the same strategy almost immediately. Just as quickly, when discounts end for one airline, they usually end for everyone else. Therefore, the prices of comparable products are usually similar.

Monopoly A **monopoly** exists when an industry or market has only one producer (or else is so dominated by one producer that other firms cannot compete with it). A sole supplier enjoys nearly complete control over the prices of its products. Its only constraint is a decrease in consumer demand due to increased prices or government regulation. In the United States, laws, such as the Sherman Antitrust Act (1890) and the Clayton Act (1914), forbid many monopolies and regulate prices charged by **natural monopolies**—industries in which one company can most efficiently supply all needed goods or services.[6] Many electric companies are natural monopolies because they can supply all the power needed in a local area. Duplicate facilities—such as two power plants and two sets of powerlines—would be inefficient.

Economic Indicators

Because economic forces are so volatile and can be affected by so many things, the performance of a country's economic system varies over time. Sometimes it gains strength and brings new prosperity to its members; other times it weakens and damages their fortunes. But knowing how an economy is performing is useful for both business owners and investors alike. Most experts look to various **economic indicators**—statistics that show whether an economic system is strengthening, weakening, or remaining stable—to help assess the performance of an economy.

Economic Growth, Aggregate Output, and Standard of Living

At one time, about half the population of this country was involved in producing the food that we needed. Today, less than 2.5 percent of the U.S. population works in agriculture, and this number is expected to decrease slightly over the next decade.[7] But agricultural efficiency has improved because better ways of producing products have been devised, and better technology has been

Entrepreneurship and New Ventures

Business...and Pleasure

Americans are multitaskers. We sip lattes while driving, we walk the dog while checking stock quotes, and we pay our bills online while watching TV; it is no surprise that this trend has taken on bigger dimensions. Business and entertainment are no longer considered two separate entities. Entertainment used to be defined as amusement parks, miniature golf, baseball games, and movies. Business was business: work, dine, shop, etc. But now, in a slowing market economy, industries feel even more pressure to mix business with entertainment. The brightly colored play structures in McDonald's and the first mall roller coaster paved the way for this upsurge of integration that is now almost impossible to avoid.

In September of 2007, Apple and Starbucks announced a partnership that allows customers to preview millions of Apple iTunes while waiting in line. The customers also have the option to buy or download music onto their iPod touch, iPhone, PC, or Mac. JetBlue partnered with XM Radio to offer passengers a sample of the new wave of satellite radio. Select Wal-Mart stores host live broadcasts of concerts enticing shoppers to linger just a little longer. This growing trend is not likely to change anytime soon. But businesses should be wary of new business cycles created in the entertainment realm. Entertainment-driven corporations are always at a high risk of deflation when the economy falters. Those businesses that rely on partnerships with these high-risk firms may not be as grounded as they seem.

Table 1.3 **U.S. GDP and GDP Per Capita**[8]

Gross Domestic Product (GDP) ($ Trillion)	GDP: Real Growth Rate (%)	GDP per Capita: Purchasing Power Parity
$13.86	2.2	$46,000

invented for getting the job done. We can say that agricultural productivity has increased because we have been able to increase total output in the agricultural sector.

We can apply the same concepts to a nation's economic system, although the computations are more complex. Fundamentally, how do we know whether an economic system is growing or not? Experts call the pattern of short-term ups and downs (or, better, expansions and contractions) in an economy the **business cycle**. The primary measure of growth in the business cycle is **aggregate output**—the total quantity of goods and services produced by an economic system during a given period.[9]

To put it simply, an increase in aggregate output is growth (or economic growth). When output grows more quickly than the population, two things usually follow:

■ Output per capita—the quantity of goods and services per person—goes up.

■ The system provides more of the goods and services that people want.

When these two things occur, people living in an economic system benefit from a higher **standard of living**, which refers to the total quantity and quality of goods and services that they can purchase with the currency used in their economic system. To know how much your standard of living is improving, you need to know how much your nation's economic system is growing (see Table 1.3).

Gross Domestic Product The first number, **gross domestic product (GDP)**, refers to the total value of all goods and services produced within a given period by a national economy through domestic factors of production. GDP is a measure of aggregate output. Generally speaking, if GDP is going up, aggregate output is going up; if aggregate output is going up, the nation is experiencing *economic growth*.

Sometimes, economists also use the term **gross national product (GNP)**, which refers to the total value of all goods and services produced by a national economy within a given period regardless of where the factors of production are located. What, precisely, is the difference between GDP and GNP? Consider a General Motors automobile plant in Brazil. The profits earned by the factory are included in U.S. GNP—but not in GDP—because its output is not produced domestically (that is, in the United States). Conversely, those profits are included in Brazil's GDP—but not GNP—because they are produced domestically (that is, in Brazil). Calculations quickly

become complex because of different factors of production. The labor, for example, will be mostly Brazilian but the capital mostly American. Thus, wages paid to Brazilian workers are part of Brazil's GNP even though profits are not.

Real Growth Rate GDP and GNP usually differ by less than 1 percent, but economists argue that GDP is a more accurate indicator of domestic economic performance because it focuses only on domestic factors of production. With that in mind, let's look at the middle column in Table 1.3. Here we find that the real growth rate of U.S. GDP—the growth rate of GDP *adjusted for inflation and changes in the value of the country's currency*—is 2.2 percent. How good is that rate? Remember that *growth depends on output increasing at a faster rate than population*. The U.S. population is growing at a rate of 0.90 percent per year.[10] The *real growth rate* of the U.S. economic system, therefore, seems quite healthy, and the U.S. standard of living should be improving.

GDP per Capita The number in the third column of Table 1.3 is a reflection of the standard of living: *GDP per capita* means GDP per person. We get this figure by dividing total GDP ($13.86 trillion) by total population, which happens to be about 301 million.[11] In a given period (usually calculated on an annual basis), the United States produces goods and services equal in value to $46,000 for every person in the country. Figure 1.2 shows both GDP and GDP per capita in the United States between 1950 and 2004. GDP per capita is a better measure than GDP itself of the economic well-being of the average person.

Real GDP Real GDP means that GDP has been adjusted to account for changes in currency values and price changes. To understand why adjustments are

---

BUSINESS CYCLE short-term pattern of economic expansions and contractions

AGGREGATE OUTPUT the total quantity of goods and services produced by an economic system during a given period

STANDARD OF LIVING the total quantity and quality of goods and services people can purchase with the currency used in their economic system

GROSS DOMESTIC PRODUCT (GDP) total value of all goods and services produced within a given period by a national economy through domestic factors of production

GROSS NATIONAL PRODUCT (GNP) total value of all goods and services produced by a national economy within a given period regardless of where the factors of production are located

REAL GDP gross domestic product (GDP) adjusted to account for changes in currency values and price changes

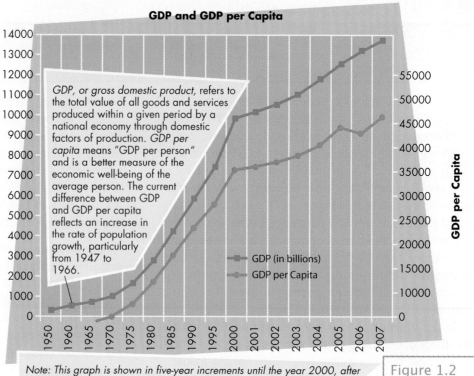

GDP and GDP per Capita

GDP, or gross domestic product, refers to the total value of all goods and services produced within a given period by a national economy through domestic factors of production. GDP per capita means "GDP per person" and is a better measure of the economic well-being of the average person. The current difference between GDP and GDP per capita reflects an increase in the rate of population growth, particularly from 1947 to 1966.

— GDP (in billions)
— GDP per Capita

Note: This graph is shown in five-year increments until the year 2000, after which it is shown in one-year increments so as to provide more detail for recent periods. Hence, the curve artificially "flattens" after 2000.

Figure 1.2
GDP and GDP Per Capita[12]

necessary, assume that pizza is the only product in a hypothetical economy. In 2005, a pizza cost $10; in 2006, a pizza cost $11. In both years, exactly 1,000 pizzas were produced. In 2005, the local GDP was $10,000 ($10 × 1,000); in 2006, the local GDP was $11,000 ($11 × 1,000). Has the economy grown? No. Because 1,000 pizzas were produced in both years, *aggregate output* remained the same. The point is to not be misled into believing that an economy is doing better than it is. If it is not adjusted, local GDP for 2006 is **nominal GDP**—GDP measured in current dollars or with all components valued at current prices.[13]

Purchasing Power Parity In the example, *current prices* would be 2006 prices. On the other hand, we calculate real GDP when we adjust GDP to account for changes in *currency values and price changes*. When we make this adjustment, we account for both GDP and **purchasing power parity**—the principle that exchange rates are set so that the prices of similar products in

Figure 1.3
The Big Mac Index[14]
One interesting method for comparing purchasing power in different countries is the Big Mac Index—a comparison of the costs of a McDonald's hamburger in different countries.

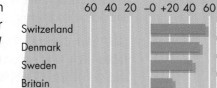

Under (−)/over (+) valuation against the dollar, %

	Big Mac Price*, $
Switzerland	5.05
Denmark	4.84
Sweden	4.59
Britain	3.90
Euro area	3.82†
United States	3.22‡
Thailand	1.78
Indonesia	1.75
Malaysia	1.57
Hong Kong	1.54
China	1.41

Note: *At market exchange rate (January 31, 2007)
† Weighted average of member countries
‡ Average of four cities

different countries are about the same. Purchasing power parity gives us a much better idea of *what people can actually buy with the financial resources allocated to them by their respective economic systems*. In other words, it gives us a better sense of standards of living across the globe. Figure 1.3 illustrates a popular approach to see how purchasing power parity works in relation to a Big Mac. For instance, the figure pegs the price of a Big Mac in the United States at $3.22. Based on currency exchange rates, a Big Mac would cost $3.90 in Britain and $5.05 in Switzerland. But the same burger would cost only $1.54 in Hong Kong and $1.78 in Thailand.

Productivity A major factor in the growth of an economic system is **productivity**, which is a measure of economic growth that compares how much a system produces with the resources needed to produce it. Let's say that it takes 1 U.S. worker and 1 U.S. dollar to make 10 soccer balls in an 8-hour workday. Let's also say that it takes 1.2 Saudi workers and the equivalent of 1.2 riyals, the currency of Saudi Arabia, to make 10 soccer balls in the same 8-hour workday. We can say that the U.S. soccer-ball industry is more productive than the Saudi soccer-ball industry. The two factors of production in this extremely simple case are labor and capital.

If more products are being produced with fewer factors of production, the prices of these products go down. As a consumer, therefore, you would need less of your currency to purchase the same quantity of these products. In short, your standard of living—at least with regard to these products—has improved. If your entire economic system increases its productivity, then your overall standard of living improves. In fact, *standard of living improves only through increases in productivity*.[15] Real growth in GDP reflects growth in productivity.

Productivity in the United States is increasing, and as a result, so are GDP and GDP per capita. Ultimately, increases in these measures of growth mean an improvement in the standard of living. However, things don't always proceed so smoothly. Several factors can inhibit the growth of an economic system, including *balance of trade* and the *national debt*.

Balance of Trade A country's **balance of trade** is the economic value of all the products that it exports minus the economic value of its imported products. The principle here is quite simple:

- A *positive* balance of trade results when a country exports (sells to other countries) more than it imports (buys from other countries).

- A *negative* balance of trade results when a country imports more than it exports.

A negative balance of trade is commonly called a *trade deficit*. In 2007, the U.S. trade deficit exceeded $700 billion for the third year in a row. The United States is a *debtor nation* rather than a *creditor nation*. Recent trends in the U.S. balance of trade are shown in Figure 1.4.

Trade deficit affects economic growth because the amount of money spent on foreign products has not been paid in full. Therefore, it is, in effect, borrowed money, and borrowed money costs more in the form of interest. The money that flows out of the country to pay off the deficit can't be used to invest in productive enterprises, either at home or overseas.

National Debt Its **national debt** is the amount of money that the government owes its creditors. As of this writing, the U.S. national debt is over $9.4 trillion. You can find out the national debt on any given day by going to any one of several Internet sources, including the U.S. National Debt Clock at **www.brillig. com/debt_clock**.

How does the national debt affect economic growth? While taxes are the most obvious way the government raises money, it also sells *bonds*—securities through which it promises to pay buyers certain amounts of money by specified future dates. (In a sense, a bond is an IOU with interest.)[17] These bonds are attractive investments because they are extremely safe: The U.S. government is not going to default on them (that is, fail to make payments when due). Even so, they must also offer a decent return on the buyer's investment, and they do this by paying interest at a competitive rate. By selling bonds, therefore, the U.S. government competes with every other potential borrower for the available supply of loanable money. The more money the government borrows, the less money is available for the private borrowing and investment that increase productivity.

Economic Stability

Stability is a condition in which the amount of money available in an economic system and the quantity of goods and services produced in it are growing at about the same rate. A chief goal of an economic system, stability can be threatened by certain factors.

BALANCE OF TRADE the economic value of all the products that a country exports minus the economic value of all the products it imports

NATIONAL DEBT the amount of money the government owes its creditors

STABILITY condition in which the amount of money available in an economic system and the quantity of goods and services produced in it are growing at about the same rate

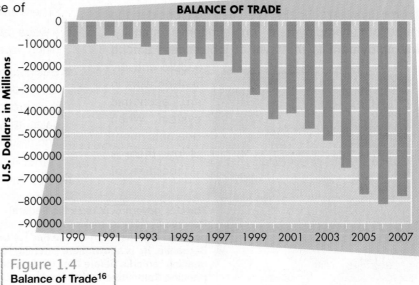

BALANCE OF TRADE

U.S. Dollars in Millions

Figure 1.4
Balance of Trade[16]

Inflation Inflation occurs when an economic system experiences widespread price increases. Instability results when the amount of money injected into an economy exceeds the increase in actual output, so people have more money to spend but the same quantity of products available to buy. As supply and demand principles tell us, as people compete with one another to buy available products, prices go up. These high prices will eventually bring the amount of money in the economy back down. However, these processes are imperfect—the additional money will not be distributed proportionately to all people, and price increases often continue beyond what is really necessary. As a result, purchasing power for many people declines.

Keeping in mind that our definition of inflation is the occurrence of widespread price increases throughout an economic system, it stands to reason that we can measure inflation by measuring price increases. Price indexes such as the **consumer price index (CPI)** measure the prices of typical products purchased by consumers living in urban areas.[18]

Unemployment Finally, we need to consider the effect of unemployment on economic stability. **Unemployment** is the level of joblessness among people actively seeking work in an economic system. When unemployment is low, there is a shortage of

The U.S. government uses the Federal Reserve System to implement its monetary policies. The chairman of "the Fed" is Ben Bernanke. He is shown here listening to opening remarks before the U.S. Senate Banking Committee in Washington, D.C.

McCAIN'S WAR PLAN | DEATH IN PAKISTAN | NERD GIRLS

Newsweek

A New Kind Of **RECESSION**

DANIEL GROSS AND FAREED ZAKARIA

Rising unemployment and gas prices, combined with slumping housing prices and sluggish GDP growth, led many analysts to fear a recession in 2008.

labor available for businesses to hire. As businesses compete with one another for the available supply of labor, they raise the wages they are willing to pay. Then, because higher labor costs eat into profit margins, they raise the prices of their products. Although consumers have more money to inject into the economy, this increase is soon undone by higher prices, so purchasing power declines.

There are at least two related problems:

■ If wage rates get too high, businesses will respond by hiring fewer workers and unemployment will go up.

■ Businesses could raise prices to counter increased labor costs, but they won't be able to sell as many of their products at higher prices. Because of reduced sales, they will cut back on hiring and, once again, unemployment will go up.

What if the government tries to correct this situation by injecting more money into the economic system—say by cutting taxes or spending more money? Prices in general may go up because of increased consumer demand. Again, purchasing power declines and inflation may set in.[19]

Recessions and Depressions   Unemployment is sometimes a symptom of a system-wide disorder in the economy. During a downturn in the business cycle, people in different sectors may lose their jobs at the same time. As a result, overall income and spending may drop. Feeling the pinch of reduced revenues, businesses may cut spending on the factors of production—including labor. Yet more people will be put out of work, and unemployment will only increase further. Unemployment that results from this vicious cycle is called *cyclical unemployment.*

If we look at the relationship between unemployment and economic stability, we are reminded that when prices get high enough, consumer demand for goods and services goes down. We are also reminded that when demand for products goes down, producers cut back on hiring and, not surprisingly, eventually start producing less. Consequently, aggregate output decreases. When we go through a period during which aggregate output declines, we have a recession. During a *recession*, producers need fewer employees—less labor—to produce products. Unemployment, therefore, goes up.

To determine whether an economy is going through a recession, we start by measuring aggregate output. Recall that this is the function of real GDP, which we find by making necessary adjustments to the total value of all goods and services produced within a given period by a national economy through domestic factors of production. A **recession** is more precisely defined as a period during which aggregate output, as measured by real GDP, declines. A prolonged and deep recession is a **depression**.

Managing the U.S. Economy

The government acts to manage the U.S. economic system through two sets of policies: fiscal and monetary. It manages the collection and spending of its revenues through **fiscal policies**. Tax rates, for example, can play an important role in fiscal policies helping to manage the economy.

Monetary policies focus on controlling the size of the nation's money supply. Working primarily through the Federal Reserve System (the nation's central bank, often referred to simply as "the Fed"), the government can influence the ability and willingness of banks throughout the country to lend money.[20]

Taken together, fiscal policy and monetary policy make up **stabilization policy**—government economic policy whose goal is to smooth out fluctuations in output and unemployment and to stabilize prices.

> **For additional topics related to this material and end-of-chapter exercises and practices, please visit www.mybizlab.com.**

Questions for Review

1 What are the factors of production? Is one factor more important than the others? If so, which one? Why?

2 What is a demand curve? A supply curve? What is the term for the point at which they intersect?

3 What is GDP? Real GDP? What does each measure?

4 Why is inflation both good and bad? How does the government try to control it?

Questions for Analysis

5 In recent years, many countries that previously used planned economies have moved to market economies. Why do you think this has occurred? Can you envision a situation that would cause a resurgence of planned economies?

6 Cite an instance in which a surplus of a product led to decreased prices. Cite an instance in which a shortage led to increased prices. What eventually happened in each case? Why?

7 Explain how current economic indicators, such as inflation and unemployment, affect you personally. Explain how they may affect you as a manager.

8 At first glance, it might seem as though the goals of economic growth and stability are inconsistent with one another. How can you reconcile this apparent inconsistency?

Application Exercises

9 Visit a local shopping mall or shopping area. List each store that you see and determine what degree of competition it faces in its immediate environment. For example, if there is only one store in the mall that sells shoes, that store represents a monopoly. Note those businesses with direct competitors (two jewelry stores) and show how they compete with one another.

10 Interview a business owner or senior manager. Ask this individual to describe for you the following: (1) how demand and supply affect the business, (2) what essential factors of production are most central to the firm's operations, and (3) how fluctuations in economic indicators affect his or her business.

chapter 2

Business Ethics and Social Responsibility

After reading this chapter, you should be able to:

1 Explain how individuals develop their personal codes of ethics and why ethics are important in the workplace.

2 Distinguish social responsibility from ethics, identify organizational stakeholders, and characterize social consciousness today.

3 Show how the concept of social responsibility applies both to environmental issues and to a firm's relationships with customers, employees, and investors.

4 Identify four general approaches to social responsibility, and describe the four steps that a firm must take to implement a social responsibility program.

5 Explain how issues of social responsibility and ethics affect small business.

Under the Guise of Green

Oil companies aren't usually known for their environmentally responsible reputations. Global energy giant BP, however, has made an effort to market an environmentally friendly image. For the most part, this strategy has worked—leading many to overlook the facts suggesting that BP is not entirely the environmentally responsible exception it claims to be.

For the past several years, BP has committed environmental offenses almost annually. In 2000, the company was convicted of an environmental felony for failing to report that its subcontractor was dumping hazardous waste in Alaska. In 2005, BP allegedly ignored knowledge that its Texas City refinery was unsafe in a cost-cutting effort that led to an explosion, 15 deaths, and even more injuries. The following year, BP's negligence at its Prudhoe Bay oil field caused a 200,000-gallon oil spill and misdemeanor violation of the Clean Water Act. Then, in 2007, BP lobbied Indiana regulators for an exemption allowing it to increase its daily release of ammonia and sludge into Lake Michigan.

Despite these misdeeds, BP maintains its image as a "green" company. The Natural Resource Defense Council has even praised it for being a leader in the industry's move toward renewable energy. Indeed, true to the tag line, "Beyond Petroleum," that accompanies its green logo, BP's 2007 Sustainability Report projects spending $8 billion over the next ten years on renewable energy products. Its Web site even offers a carbon footprint calculator that lets visitors see how their own choices affect the environment.

BP risks compromising its green image by engaging in what Greenpeace calls the "greatest climate crime" in history—extracting oil from the tar sands of Alberta, Canada. The project is energy- and water-intensive, produces excessive amounts of greenhouse gases, destroys acres of forest, and harms indigenous communities, but it comes at a time when oil prices are high and western consumers are dependent on Middle Eastern oil. It remains to be seen whether BP's seemingly socially responsible ends can justify their environmentally damaging means.[1]

What's in It for Me?

To make an informed judgment about a company's social responsibility, it's important to understand how individual codes of ethics develop and play a role in the workplace, to distinguish between ethics and social responsibility, and to understand social consciousness. In addition to these elements, this chapter will explore the ethical and social responsibility issues that businesses face in terms of their customers, employees, investors, and immediate and global communities. In addition, it will look at general approaches to social responsibility, the steps businesses must take to implement social responsibility programs, and issues of social responsibility and ethics in small businesses.

Ethics in the Workplace

Ethics are beliefs about what's right or wrong and good or bad based on an individual's values and morals, plus a behavior's social context. In other words, **ethical behavior** conforms to individual beliefs and social norms about what's right and good. **Unethical behavior** conforms to individual beliefs and social norms about what's wrong or bad. **Business ethics** refers to ethical or unethical behaviors by employees in the context of their jobs.

Individual Ethics

Because ethics are based on both individual beliefs and social concepts, they vary among individuals, situations, and cultures. People may develop personal

Tax Revenues Disappear into Bermuda Triangle

The epidemic of scandals that dominated business news over the past decade shows how willing people can be to take advantage of potentially ambiguous situations—indeed, to create them. For example, in 1997, Tyco sold itself to the smaller ADT Ltd. Because its new parent company was based in the tax haven of Bermuda, Tyco no longer had to pay U.S. taxes on its non-U.S. income. In 2000 and 2001, Tyco's subsidiaries in such tax-friendly nations doubled, and the company slashed its 2001 U.S. tax bill by $600 million. "Tyco," complained a U.S. congressman, "has raised tax avoidance to an art," but one tax expert replies that Tyco's schemes "are very consistent with the [U.S.] tax code."[2] Even in the face of blistering criticism and the indictment of its former CEO, Tyco retains its offshore ownership structure.[3]

codes of ethics reflecting a wide range of attitudes and beliefs without violating general standards. Thus, some ethical and unethical behaviors are widely agreed upon, while others fall into gray areas.

Ambiguity, the Law, and the Real World Societies generally adopt formal laws that reflect prevailing ethical standards or social norms. We try to make unambiguous laws, but interpreting and applying them can still lead to ethical ambiguities. It isn't always easy to apply statutory standards to real-life behavior. For instance, during the aftermath of Hurricane Katrina in 2005, desperate survivors in New Orleans looted grocery stores for food and other essentials. While few people criticized this behavior, such actions were technically illegal.

Individual Values and Codes The ethics of business start with the ethics of individuals—managers, employees, and other legal representatives. Each person's personal code of ethics is determined by a combination of factors that are formed and refined throughout our lives.

Business and Managerial Ethics

Managerial ethics are the standards of behavior that guide individual managers in their work.[5] Although managerial ethics can affect business in any number of ways, it's helpful to classify them into three broad categories.

Behavior Toward Employees This category covers such matters as hiring and firing, wages and working conditions, and privacy and respect. Ethical and legal guidelines suggest that hiring and firing decisions should be based solely on the ability to perform a job.

Wages and working conditions, while regulated by law, are also controversial. Consider a manager who pays a worker less than he deserves because the manager knows that the employee can't afford to quit or

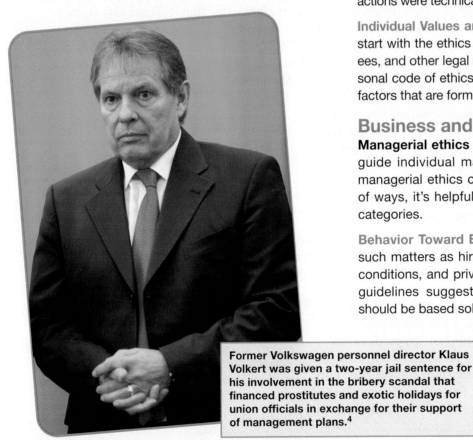

Former Volkswagen personnel director Klaus Volkert was given a two-year jail sentence for his involvement in the bribery scandal that financed prostitutes and exotic holidays for union officials in exchange for their support of management plans.[4]

The Ethical Soft-Shoe

To bribe or not to bribe? That is the question. Although the textbook answer is a nonnegotiable "no" regardless of the business environment, culture, or country you're in, the real-world answer is much less clear. To varying degrees, complicated business dealings that ignore the strict letter of the law—offering or accepting incentives to get things done, extracting a personal favor or two, using the power and influence of people we know—happen all the time.

In fact, in some cultures ethically ambiguous practices are hallmarks of business culture. Brazilians, for example, apply the philosophy of *jeitinho*—"to find a way"—in which there's always another way to get something done—using personal connections, bending the rules, making a "contribution," or simply approaching the problem from a different angle. If you need an official document, for instance, you might set out determined to take all the proper bureaucratic steps to get it. However, when you find yourself in a maze of rules and regulations, you're likely to resort to *jeitinho*. *Jeitinho* almost never involves butting heads with authority, but is rather a complex dance that enables individuals to go around problems instead of having to go through them.

Even if you're operating in a country like Brazil, in which sidestepping the rules is business as usual, you don't *have* to do an ethical soft-shoe. Many global companies have strict ethical guidelines for doing business: International

U.S. business practices, for example, are regulated by the Foreign Corrupt Practices Act. The key to dancing with a foreign partner is understanding the culture—observing the way business is conducted and preparing yourself for any challenges—before you get out on the dance floor.

In Brazil, someone pressed for time might invoke the philosophy of *jeitinho* when facing a long wait in line. The philosophy allows for rule-bending like cutting in line if fairness and practicality are overriding factors.

risk his job by complaining. While some see the behavior as unethical, others see it as a smart business move.

Behavior Toward the Organization Employee behavior toward employers involves ethical issues in such areas as conflict of interest, confidentiality, and honesty. A *conflict of interest* occurs when an activity may benefit the individual to the detriment of his or her employer. To avoid even the appearance of bribery or favoritism, most companies have policies that forbid buyers from accepting gifts from suppliers. Businesses in highly competitive industries—software and fashion apparel, for example—have safeguards, such as nondisclosure agreements, against designers selling company secrets to competitors. Relatively common problems in the general area of honesty include stealing supplies and padding expense accounts.

Behavior Toward Other Economic Agents Advertising, bargaining and negotiation, financial disclosure, ordering and purchasing—ethical ambiguity is possible in just about every activity businesses conduct with *primary agents of interest*—mainly customers, competitors, stockholders, suppliers, dealers, and unions.

Global variations can complicate ethical business practices. For example, while U.S. law forbids bribes, many countries incorporate them into normal business

practices. A U.S. power-generating company recently lost a $320 million contract in the Middle East because it refused to pay bribes that a Japanese firm was willing to pay to get the job. Chapter 4 discusses more ways that social, cultural, and legal differences affect international business.

"From a purely business viewpoint, taking what doesn't belong to you is usually the cheapest way to go."

Assessing Ethical Behavior

The following steps set a simplified course for applying ethical judgments to ethically subjective and ambiguous business situations:

1. Gather the relevant factual information.

2. Analyze the facts to determine the most appropriate moral values.

3. Make an ethical judgment based on the rightness or wrongness of the proposed activity or policy.

The process may not work this smoothly, though; facts may not be clear-cut, and moral values may not be agreed upon. Nevertheless, a judgment and a decision must be made in order to maintain trust, an indispensable element in any business transaction.

Consider a complex dilemma faced by managers with expense accounts to cover work-related expenses when they're traveling for business or entertaining clients for business purposes. If a manager takes a client to a $150 dinner, submitting a $150 reimbursement receipt for that dinner is accurate and appropriate. But suppose that this manager has a $150 dinner the next night with a friend for purely social purposes. Submitting that receipt for reimbursement would be unethical. But some employees would disagree, rationalizing that they're underpaid, so submitting this receipt as well is just a means of "recovering" income due to them.

Consider the following ethical *norms*, which Figure 2.1 incorporates into a model of ethical judgment making that can be applied in cases like this:[6]

1. *Utility.* Does a particular act optimize the benefits to those who are affected by it? (That is, do all relevant parties receive equally useful benefits?)

2. *Rights.* Does it respect the rights of all individuals involved?

3. *Justice.* Is it fair?

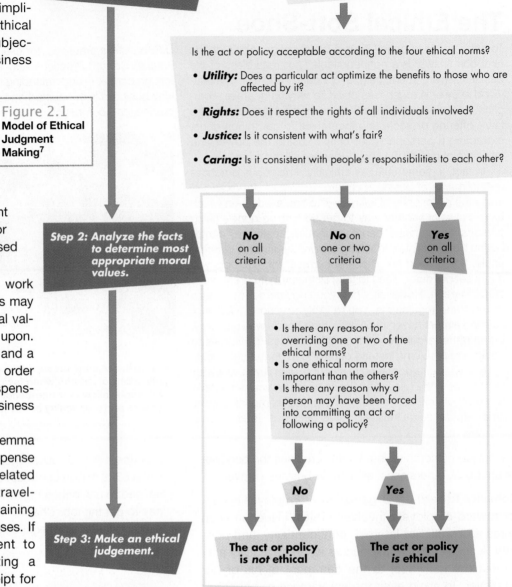

Figure 2.1
Model of Ethical Judgment Making[7]

4. *Caring.* Is it consistent with people's responsibilities to one another?

While the utility norm acknowledges that the manager benefits from a padded account, others, such as coworkers and owners, don't. Most would also agree that the act doesn't respect the rights of others (such as investors, who have to foot the bill). Moreover, it's clearly unfair and compromises the manager's responsibilities to others. This particular act, then, appears to be clearly unethical.

Figure 2.1, however, also provides mechanisms for dealing with unique circumstances that make ethical issues more or less clear-cut. Suppose, for example, that our manager loses the receipt for the legitimate dinner but retains the receipt for the social dinner. Some will now argue that it's okay to submit the illegitimate receipt because the manager is only doing so to get proper reimbursement. Others, however, will reply that submitting the alternative receipt is wrong under any circumstances.

Company Practices and Business Ethics

To discourage unethical and illegal activities, companies have taken formal steps, such as setting up codes of conduct, developing clear ethical positions, and perhaps most effectively, demonstrating upper-management support of ethical standards. These policies contribute to a corporate culture that values ethical standards and announce that the firm is equally concerned with good citizenship and profits.

Two of the most common approaches to formalizing top management commitment to ethical business practices are *adopting written codes* and *instituting ethics programs*.

Adopting Written Codes
Many companies have written codes that formally announce intent to do business ethically. The number of such companies has risen dramatically in the last three decades, and today almost all major corporations have written codes of ethics. Even Enron had a code of ethics, but managers must follow the code if it's going to work. On one occasion, Enron's board of directors voted to set aside the code in order to complete a deal that would violate it; after the deal was completed, they then voted to reinstate the code!

Instituting Ethics Programs
Many examples suggest that ethical responses can be learned through experience. In the classic 1982 case of a corporate saboteur who poisoned Tylenol capsules and caused the deaths of several consumers, employees at Johnson & Johnson, the maker of Tylenol, didn't wait for instructions or a company directive before informing retailers and pulling the product from shelves. In retrospect, they reported simply knowing that this was what the company would want them to do. Business schools are important players in ethics education, but most analysts agree that companies must take the chief responsibility for educating employees.

More and more firms, like ExxonMobil and Boeing, require managers to go through periodic ethics training

Do No Evil

Although strategies, practices, and objectives can change, an organization's core principles and values should remain steadfast. For example, Google must be flexible enough to adapt its strategies and practices to meet the challenges posed by the rapidly evolving technology industry. Google's core principle is simple: "Don't be evil." Google's code of conduct is built around this idea—ethical responsibility is central to Google's identity, which is especially important for a company that has access to vast amounts of private and sensitive information.

to remind them of the importance of ethical decision making and to update them on current laws and regulations. Others, such as Texas Instruments, have ethics hotlines that employees may call to discuss the ethics of a particular problem or situation or to report unethical behavior or activities by others.

Social Responsibility
● ● ● ● ● ● ● ● ● ● ● ● ●

While ethics affect individual behavior in the workplace, **social responsibility** refers to the overall way in which a business attempts to balance its commitments to relevant groups and individuals in its social environment. These groups and individuals who are directly affected by the practices of an organization and have a stake in its performance are **organizational stakeholders**.[8]

The Stakeholder Model of Responsibility
Most companies that strive to be responsible to their stakeholders concentrate first and foremost on *customers*, *employees*, *investors*, *suppliers*, and *local communities*. They may then select other stakeholders who are particularly relevant or important to the organization and try to address their needs and expectations as well.

> **SOCIAL RESPONSIBILITY** the attempt of a business to balance its commitments to groups and individuals in its environment, including customers, other businesses, employees, investors, and local communities
>
> **ORGANIZATIONAL STAKEHOLDERS** those groups, individuals, and organizations that are directly affected by the practices of an organization and who therefore have a stake in its performance

Apple has maintained a strong customer service reputation with features like the Apple Store's "Genius Bar," where Mac specialists answer questions for Mac users.

The Electronic Equivalent of Paper Shredding

In virtually every major corporate scandal of the last few years, the best-laid plans of managerial miscreants have come unraveled, at least in part, when e-mail surfaced as key evidence. For example, Citigroup analyst Jack Grubman changed stock recommendations in exchange for favors from CEO Sandy Weill and confirmed the arrangement via e-mail. Investigators found that David Duncan, Arthur Andersen's head Enron auditor, had deleted incriminating e-mails shortly after the start of the Justice Department's investigation. After Tim Newington, an analyst for Credit Suisse First Boston, refused to give in to pressure to change a client's credit rating, an e-mail circulated on the problem of Newington's troublesome integrity: "Bigger issue," warned an upper manager, "is what to do about Newington in general. I'm not sure he's salvageable at this point."

Many corporations are nervous about the potential liability that employee e-mails may incur. Software developer Omniva Policy Systems saw this concern as an opportunity. Their e-mail software allows users to send encrypted messages, specify an expiration date after which they can no longer be decrypted, and prevent resending or printing. In the event of a lawsuit or investigation, administrators can hit a "red button" that prevents any e-mail from being deleted.

"Our goal," says Omniva CEO Kumar Sreekanti, "is to keep the honest people honest . . . We help organizations comply with regulations automatically so they don't have to rely on people to do it."

E-mails like Jack Grubman's often provide investigators with a smoking gun.

Customers Businesses that are responsible to their customers treat them fairly and honestly, charge fair prices, honor warranties, meet delivery commitments, and stand behind product quality. Apple, Wegmans Food Markets, UPS, and Lexus are among those companies with excellent reputations in this area.[9]

Employees Businesses that are socially responsible in their dealings with employees treat workers fairly, make them part of the team, and respect their dignity and basic human needs. Many of these firms are also committed to hiring and promoting qualified minorities.

Investors A socially responsible stance toward investors means following proper accounting procedures, providing appropriate information about financial performance, and protecting shareholder rights and investments. Accurate and candid assessments of future growth and profitability are also important, as is avoiding even the appearance of impropriety in such sensitive areas as insider trading, stock-price manipulation, and the withholding of financial data.

Suppliers Relations with suppliers should also be managed with care, and firms should recognize the importance of mutually beneficial partnerships.

A large corporation might easily take advantage of suppliers by imposing unrealistic delivery schedules and pushing for lower prices. Instead, it should keep suppliers informed about future plans, negotiate mutually agreeable delivery schedules and prices, and so forth.

Local and International Communities Most businesses try to be socially responsible to local communities by contributing to local programs, getting involved in charities, and minimizing negative impact on communities. Target stores, for example, give over $2 million each week to local neighborhoods, programs, and schools.[10]

Starbucks helps local farmers gain access to credit, works to develop and maintain sustainability of the coffee crop, and is building farmer support centers in Costa Rica, Ethiopia, and Rwanda to provide local farmers with agricultural and technical education and support.[11]

An organization should also recognize international stakeholders. The actions of international businesses affect their suppliers, employees, and customers in multiple countries. International businesses must also address their responsibilities in areas such as wages, working conditions, and environmental protection across different countries with varying regulatory laws and norms.

Contemporary Social Consciousness

Social consciousness and views toward social responsibility have been evolving since entrepreneurs such as John D. Rockefeller, J.P. Morgan, and Cornelius Vanderbilt raised concerns about abuses of power and led to the nation's first laws regulating basic business practices. In the 1930s, many blamed the Great Depression on a climate of business greed and lack of restraint. Out of this economic turmoil emerged new laws that dictated an expanded role for business in protecting and enhancing the general welfare of society, formalizing the concept of *accountability*.

In the 1960s and 1970s, business was again characterized negatively. Some charged that defense contractors had helped promote the Vietnam War to spur their own profits. Eventually, increased social activism prompted increased government regulation that led to changes such as health warnings on cigarette packaging and stricter environmental protection laws.

The general economic prosperity of the 1980s and 1990s led to another period of laissez-faire attitudes toward business. For the most part, business was viewed as a positive force. Many businesses continue to operate in enlightened and socially responsible ways: Wal-Mart and Target have policies against selling weapons, GameStop refuses to sell Mature-rated games to minors, and Anheuser-Busch promotes the concept of responsible drinking in its advertising.

Unfortunately, the recent spate of corporate scandals may revive negative attitudes toward business and result in increased control and constraint of business practices by the government.[12] As just a single illustration, widespread moral

outrage erupted when some of former Tyco CEO Dennis Kozlowski's extravagant perquisites were made public. In addition to the almost $300 million he made between 1998 and 2001 in salary, bonuses, and stock proceeds, his perks included a $50 million Florida mansion, an $18 million New York apartment, $11 million for antiques and furnishings, and a $2.1 million birthday party in Italy for his wife. In 2005, Kozlowski was sentenced to 25 years in prison for misappropriating Tyco funds.[13]

Areas of Social Responsibility

When defining its sense of social responsibility, a firm typically confronts four areas of concern: responsibilities toward the *environment*, *customers*, *employees*, and *investors*.

Responsibility Toward the Environment

The devastating effects of increasing carbon dioxide (Figure 2.2) and other greenhouse gas emissions have begun to reveal themselves in the shrinking Arctic ice cap and the increase in severe weather incidents. With

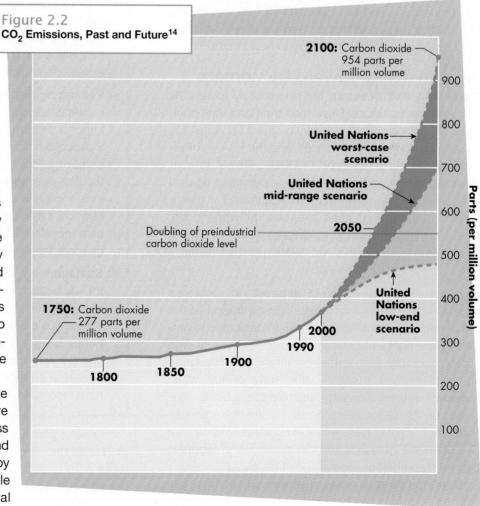

Figure 2.2
CO_2 Emissions, Past and Future[14]

2100: Carbon dioxide 954 parts per million volume

United Nations worst-case scenario

United Nations mid-range scenario

Doubling of preindustrial carbon dioxide level

2050

United Nations low-end scenario

1750: Carbon dioxide 277 parts per million volume

2000

1990

1900

1800   1850

Parts (per million volume)

increased attention to global climate change comes pressure on business, both from governments and consumers, to control negative environmental impact.

Many socially responsible companies go beyond what government regulations require. For example, in addition to developing hydrogen fuel technologies, Honda reduced its own CO_2 emissions by five percent between 2000 and 2005 and has pledged to reduce them another five percent by 2010.[15] Although cost concerns have created reluctance to "go green," the opportunity to make money by marketing green products to environmentally conscious consumers is becoming increasingly apparent.

Not all businesses make a sincere effort to adopt green policies and procedures. Some are guilty of **greenwashing**—using advertising to project a green image without adopting substantive environmentally friendly changes. In January 2008, the U.S. Federal Trade Commission (FTC) began a series of hearings to determine the veracity of many green marketing claims. No companies have been censured for false advertising as a result of these hearings, but increased regulation will likely result as the FTC catches up to new trends.[16]

Responsibility Toward Customers

A company that does not act responsibly toward its customers will ultimately lose their trust and their business. To encourage responsibility, the FTC regulates advertising and pricing practices, and the FDA enforces labeling guidelines for food products. These government regulating bodies can impose penalties against violators, who may also face civil litigation. For example, in 2006, the FTC fined the social networking site Xanga $1 million for allowing children under the age of 13 to create accounts in clear violation of the Children's Online Privacy Protection Act.[17]

Consumer Rights Current interest in business responsibility toward customers can be traced to the rise of **consumerism**—social activism dedicated to protecting the rights of consumers in their dealings with businesses. The first formal declaration of consumer rights protection came in the early 1960s when President John F. Kennedy identified four basic consumer rights. Since then, general agreement on two additional rights has emerged; these rights are described in Figure 2.3. The Consumer Bill of Rights is backed by numerous federal and state laws.

Merck provides an instructive example of what can happen to a firm that violates one or more of these

Green marketing (also environmental or ecological marketing)—the marketing of environmentally friendly goods—encompasses a wide variety of business strategies and practices.

- **Production Processes** Businesses, like Ford Motors and General Electric, modify their production processes to limit the consumption of valuable resources like fossil fuels by increasing energy efficiency and reduce their output of waste and pollution by cutting greenhouse gas emissions.

- **Product Modification** Products can be modified to use more environmentally friendly materials, a practice S.C. Johnson encourages with its Greenlist of raw materials classified according to their impact on health and the environment. Committed to only using the safest materials on this list, S.C. Johnson eliminated 1.8 million pounds of volatile organic compounds from its glass cleaner Windex.[18]

- **Carbon Offsets** Many companies are committed to offsetting the CO_2 produced by their products and manufacturing processes. In 2007, Volkswagen began a program of planting trees (which consume CO_2 during photosynthesis) in the so-called VW Forest in the lower Mississippi alluvial valley to offset the CO_2 emissions of every car they sell.[19]

- **Packaging Reduction** Reducing and reusing materials used in packaging products is another important strategy of green marketing, which Starbucks has pioneered. In 2004 the U.S. Food and Drug Administration gave the coffee retailer the first-ever approval to use recycled materials in its food and beverage packaging. Starbucks estimates that using cups composed of 10 percent recycled fibers reduces its packaging waste by more than five million pounds per year.[20]

- **Sustainability** Using renewable resources and managing limited resources responsibly and efficiently are important goals for any business pursuing a green policy. For example, Whole Foods Market is committed to buying food from farmers who use sustainable agriculture practices that protect the environment and agricultural resources, like land and water.

consumer rights. For several years the firm aggressively marketed the painkiller Vioxx, which it was forced to recall in 2004 after clinical trials linked it to an increased risk of heart attacks and strokes. After the recall was announced, it was revealed that Merck had known about

The U.S.-based environmental group Nature Conservancy has recently teamed up with Indonesian logging company Sumalindo Lestari Jaya to help local villagers log a forest in a remote area of Indonesia. Why? The group believes that by working together with the company, it can better enforce sustainable practices.

Korean Air Lines were heavily fined, but in exchange for turning them in, Virgin and Lufthansa were not penalized.[22]

Firms can also come under attack for *price gouging*—responding to increased demand with overly steep (and often unwarranted) price increases. For example, during threats of severe weather, people often stock up on bottled water and batteries. Unfortunately, some retailers take advantage of this pattern by marking up prices. Reports were widespread of gasoline retailers doubling or even tripling prices immediately after the events of September 11, 2001, and following the U.S. invasion of Iraq in 2003. Similar problems arose after hurricanes Katrina and Rita damaged oil refineries along the Gulf Coast in late 2005.

Ethics in Advertising In recent years, increased attention has been given to ethics in advertising and product information. Controversy arose when *Newsweek* magazine reported that Sony had literally created a movie critic who happened to be particularly fond of movies released by Sony's Columbia Pictures. When advertising its newest theatrical releases, the studio had been routinely using glowing quotes from a fictitious critic. After the story broke, Sony hastily stopped the practice and apologized.

Another issue concerns advertising that some consumers consider morally objectionable—for products such as underwear, condoms, alcohol, tobacco products, and firearms. Laws regulate some of this advertising (for instance, tobacco can no longer be promoted in television commercials, but can be featured in print ads in magazines), and many advertisers use common sense and discretion in their promotions. But some companies, such as Calvin Klein and Victoria's Secret, have come under fire for being overly explicit in their advertising.

> **COLLUSION** illegal agreement between two or more companies to commit a wrongful act
>
> **GREEN MARKETING** the marketing of environmentally friendly goods

these risks as early as 2000 and downplayed them so that they could continue selling it. In 2007, Merck agreed to pay $4.85 billion to individuals or families of those who were injured or died as a result of taking the drug.[21]

Unfair Pricing Interfering with competition can take the form of illegal pricing practices. **Collusion** occurs when two or more firms collaborate on such wrongful acts as price fixing. In 2007, the European airlines Virgin and Lufthansa admitted to colluding with rivals to raise the prices of fuel surcharges on passenger flights as much as 12 times the regular price between August 2004 and January 2006. British Airways and

**Figure 2.3
Consumer
Bill of Rights**

Consumer Bill of Rights

1 *Consumers have a right to safe products.*

2 *Consumers have a right to be informed about all relevant aspects of a product.*

3 *Consumers have a right to be heard.*

4 *Consumers have a right to choose what they buy.*

5 *Consumers have a right to be educated about purchases.*

6 *Consumers have a right to courteous service.*

Responsibility Toward Employees

Recruiting, hiring, training, promoting, and compensating are essential human resource

Because of controversies surrounding the potential misinterpretation of words and phrases, such as *light*, *reduced calorie*, *diet*, and *low fat*, food producers are now required to use a standardized format for listing ingredients on product packages.

management activities that provide the basis for social responsibility toward employees.

Legal and Social Commitments By law, businesses cannot discriminate against people in any facet of the employment relationship. For example, a company cannot refuse to hire someone because of ethnicity or pay someone a lower salary than someone else on the basis of gender. A company that provides its employees with equal opportunities without regard to race, sex, or other irrelevant factors is meeting both its legal and its social responsibilities. Firms that ignore these responsibilities risk losing good employees and leave themselves open to lawsuits.

Most would also agree that an organization should strive to ensure that the workplace is physically and socially safe. Companies with a heightened awareness of social responsibility also recognize an obligation to provide opportunities to balance work and life pressures and preferences, help employees maintain job skills, and, when terminations or layoffs are necessary, treat them with respect and compassion.

Ethical Commitments: The Special Case of Whistle-Blowers
Respecting employees as people also means respecting their behavior as ethical individuals. Ideally, an employee who discovers that a business has been engaging in illegal, unethical, or socially irresponsible practices should be able to report the problem to higher-level management and feel confident that managers will stop the questionable practices. However, if no one in the organization will take action, the employee might elect to drop the matter, or he or she may inform a regulatory agency or the media and become what is known as a **whistle-blower**—an employee who discovers and tries to put an end to a company's unethical, illegal, or socially irresponsible actions by publicizing them.[23]

DECEMBER 30, 2002 / JANUARY 6, 2003   SPECIAL DOUBLE ISSUE

PERSONS OF THE YEAR

TIME

The Whistleblowers

CYNTHIA COOPER OF WORLDCOM   COLEEN ROWLEY OF THE FBI   SHERRON WATKINS OF ENRON

www.time.com AOL Keyword: TIME

Enron's Sherron Watkins (right) reported concerns about the company's accounting practices well before the company's problems were made public, warning top management that Enron would "implode in a wave of accounting scandals." CEO Kenneth Lay commissioned a legal review of the firm's finances, but told his investigators not to "second-guess" decisions by Enron's auditor, accounting firm Arthur Andersen.[24]

Unfortunately, whistle-blowers may be demoted, fired, or, if they remain in their jobs, treated with mistrust, resentment, or hostility by coworkers. One recent study suggests that about half of all whistle-blowers eventually get fired, and about half of those who get fired subsequently lose their homes and/or families.[25] The law offers some recourse to employees who take action. The current whistle-blower law stems from the False Claims Act of 1863, which was designed to prevent contractors from selling defective supplies to the Union Army during the Civil War. With 1986 revisions to the law, the government can recover triple damages from fraudulent contractors. If the Justice Department does not intervene, a whistle-blower can proceed with a civil suit. In that case, the whistle-blower receives 25 to 30 percent of any money recovered.[26] Unfortunately, however, the prospect of large cash awards has generated a spate of false or questionable accusations.[27]

Responsibility Toward Investors

Managers can abuse their responsibilities to investors in several ways. As a rule, irresponsible behavior toward shareholders means abuse of a firm's financial resources so that shareholder-owners do not receive their due earnings or dividends. Companies can also act irresponsibly toward shareholder-owners by misrepresenting company resources.

Improper Financial Management Blatant financial mismanagement—such as paying excessive salaries to senior managers, sending them on extravagant "retreats" to exotic resorts, and providing frivolous perks—are unethical, but not necessarily illegal. In such situations, creditors and stockholders have few options for recourse. Forcing a management changeover is a difficult process that can drive down stock prices—a penalty that shareholders are usually unwilling to impose on themselves.

Insider Trading **Insider trading** is using confidential information to gain from the purchase or sale of stocks. Suppose, for example, that a small firm's stock is currently trading at $50 a share. If a larger firm is going to buy the smaller one, it might have to pay as much as $75 a share for a controlling interest. Individuals aware of the impending acquisition before it is publicly announced, such as managers of the two firms or the financial institution making the arrangements, could gain by buying the stock at $50 in anticipation of selling it for $75 after the proposed acquisition is announced.

Informed executives can also avoid financial loss by selling stock that's about to drop in value. Legally, stock can only be sold on the basis of public information available to all investors. Potential violations of this regulation were at the heart of the Martha Stewart scandal. Sam Waksal, president of ImClone, learned that the company's stock was going to drop in value and hastily tried to sell his own stock in 2001. He allegedly tipped off close friend Martha Stewart, who subsequently sold her stock as well. Stewart, who argued that she never received Waksal's call and sold her stock only because she wanted to use the funds elsewhere, eventually pled guilty to other charges (lying to investigators) and served time in prison. Waksal, meanwhile, received a much stiffer sentence because his own attempts to dump his stock were well documented.

Misrepresentation of Finances In maintaining and reporting its financial status, every corporation must conform to generally accepted accounting principles (GAAP; see Chapter 14). Unethical managers might project profits in excess of what they actually expect to earn, hide losses and/or expenses in order to boost paper profits, or slant financial reports to make the firm seem stronger than is really the case. In 2002, the U.S. Congress passed the *Sarbanes-Oxley Act*, which requires an organization's chief financial officer to personally guarantee the accuracy of all financial reporting (see Chapter 14).

Implementing Social Responsibility Programs

Opinions differ dramatically concerning social responsibility as a business goal. While some oppose any business activity that threatens profits, others argue that social responsibility must take precedence. Some skeptics fear that businesses will gain too much control over the ways social projects are addressed by society as a whole, or that they lack the expertise needed to address social issues. Still, many believe that corporations should help improve the lives of citizens because they are citizens themselves, often control vast resources, and may contribute to the very problems that social programs address.

> **INSIDER TRADING** illegal practice of using special knowledge about a firm for profit or gain
>
> **OBSTRUCTIONIST STANCE** approach to social responsibility that involves doing as little as possible and may involve attempts to deny or cover up violations
>
> **DEFENSIVE STANCE** approach to social responsibility by which a company meets only minimum legal requirements in its commitments to groups and individuals in its social environment

Approaches to Social Responsibility

Given these differences of opinion, it is little wonder that corporations have adopted a variety of approaches to social responsibility. As Figure 2.4 illustrates, the four stances that an organization can take concerning its obligations to society fall along a continuum ranging from the lowest to the highest degree of socially responsible practices.

Obstructionist Stance The few organizations that take an **obstructionist stance** to social responsibility usually do as little as possible to solve social or environmental problems, have little regard for ethical conduct, and will go to great lengths to deny or cover up wrongdoing. For example, IBP, a leading meat-processing firm, has a long record of breaking environmental protection, labor, and food processing laws and then trying to cover up its offenses.

Defensive Stance Organizations who take a **defensive stance** will do everything that is legally required, including admitting to mistakes and taking corrective actions, but nothing more. Defensive stance managers insist that their job is to generate profits and might, for example, install pollution-control equipment dictated by law but not higher-quality equipment to further limit pollution.

Tobacco companies generally take this position in their marketing efforts. In the United States, they are legally required to include product warnings and to limit advertising to prescribed media. Domestically, they follow these rules to the letter of the law, but in many Asian and African countries, which don't have these rules, cigarettes are heavily promoted, contain higher levels of tar and nicotine, and carry few or no health warning labels.

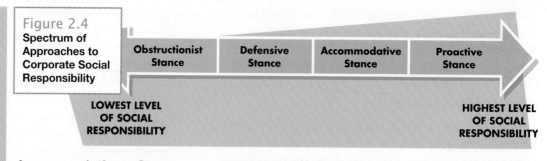

Figure 2.4
Spectrum of Approaches to Corporate Social Responsibility

| Obstructionist Stance | Defensive Stance | Accommodative Stance | Proactive Stance |

LOWEST LEVEL OF SOCIAL RESPONSIBILITY

HIGHEST LEVEL OF SOCIAL RESPONSIBILITY

ACCOMMODATIVE STANCE approach to social responsibility by which a company, if specifically asked to do so, exceeds legal minimums in its commitments to groups and individuals in its social environment

PROACTIVE STANCE approach to social responsibility by which a company actively seeks opportunities to contribute to the well-being of groups and individuals in its social environment

SOCIAL AUDIT systematic analysis of a firm's success in using funds earmarked for meeting its social responsibility goals

Accommodative Stance A firm that adopts an **accommodative stance** meets and, in certain cases exceeds, its legal and ethical requirements. Such firms will agree to participate in social programs if solicitors convince them that given programs are worthy of their support. Both Shell and IBM, for example, will match contributions made by their employees to selected charitable causes.

Proactive Stance Firms with the highest degree of social responsibility exhibit the **proactive stance**; they take to heart the arguments in favor of social responsibility, view themselves as citizens in a society, indicate sincere commitment to improve the general social welfare, and surpass the accommodative stance by proactively seeking opportunities to contribute. The most common—and direct—way to implement this stance is to set up a foundation for providing direct financial support for various social programs. An excellent example of a proactive stance is the McDonald's Corporation's Ronald McDonald House program. These houses, located close to major medical centers, can be used for minimal cost

by families while their sick children are receiving medical treatment nearby.

However, these categories are not sharply distinct: Organizations do not always fit neatly into one category or another. The Ronald McDonald House program has been widely applauded, but McDonald's has also been accused of misleading consumers about the nutritional value of its food products.

Managing Social Responsibility Programs

A full commitment to social responsibility requires a carefully organized and managed program and managers who take steps to foster a companywide sense of social responsibility:[29]

1 *Social responsibility must start at the top and be considered a factor in strategic planning.* No program can succeed without the support of top management, who must embrace a strong stand on social responsibility and develop a policy statement outlining that commitment.

2 *A committee of top managers must develop a plan detailing the level of management support.* Companies may set aside percentages of profits for social programs or set specific priorities, such as supporting the arts.

Table 2.1 **Top 10 Corporate Foundations**[28]

Foundation	State	Total Giving (In U.S. Dollars)	Fiscal Date
1 Aventis Pharmaceuticals Health Care Foundation	NJ	217,845,821	12/31/05
2 Wal-Mart Foundation	AR	155,073,614	1/31/06
3 The Bank of America Charitable Foundation, Inc.	NC	123,287,819	12/31/05
4 The JPMorgan Chase Foundation	MI	85,458,083	12/31/05
5 Citigroup Foundation	CA	80,764,000	12/31/05
6 Ford Motor Company Fund	TX	79,881,090	12/31/05
7 GE Foundation	NY	70,635,496	12/31/05
8 The Wells Fargo Foundation	NJ	65,007,124	12/31/05
9 ExxonMobil Foundation	NY	63,660,965	12/31/05
10 Verizon Foundation	CT	61,834,820	12/31/05

3 *One executive must be put in charge of the firm's agenda.* Whether a separate job or part of an existing one, the selected individual must monitor the program and ensure implementation consistent with the firm's policy statement and strategic plan.

4 *The organization must conduct occasional* **social audits**—*systematic analyses of its success in using funds earmarked for its social responsibility goals.* Consider the case of a company whose strategic plan calls for spending $200,000 to train 300 unemployed people and to place 275 of them in jobs. If, at the end of a year, the firm has spent $198,000, trained 305 people, and filled 270 jobs, a social audit will confirm the program's success. But if the program has cost $350,000, trained only 190 people, and placed only 40 of them, the audit will reveal the program's failure. Such failure should prompt a rethinking of the program's implementation and its priorities.

Social Responsibility and the Small Business

●●●●●●●●●●●●●●●●●●●●●●●●●●●●●●●●●

Small-businesses owners are faced with similar ethical questions, although they may largely be a question of individual ethics. As the owner of a garden supply store, how would you respond to a building inspector's suggestion that a cash payment will speed your building permit application? As a liquor store manager, would you sell alcohol to a customer whose identification card looks forged? As the owner of a small laboratory, would you verify the license of your medical waste disposal company? Who will really be harmed if you pad your small firm's income statement to get a much-needed bank loan?

What about questions of social responsibility? Can your small business afford a social agenda? Should you sponsor Little League teams and donate to the United Way? Do joining the chamber of commerce and supporting the Better Business Bureau cost too much? Clearly, all managers in all organizations have to make decisions about ethics and social responsibility. One key to business success is to decide in advance how to respond to the issues that underlie all questions of ethical and social responsibility.

For additional topics related to this material and end-of-chapter exercises and practices, please visit www.mybizlab.com.

Questions for Review

1 What basic factors should be considered in any ethical decision?

2 Who are an organization's stakeholders? Who are the major stakeholders with which most businesses must be concerned?

3 What are the major areas of social responsibility with which businesses should be concerned?

4 What are the four basic approaches to social responsibility?

5 In what ways do you think your personal code of ethics might clash with the operations of some companies? How might you try to resolve these differences?

Questions for Analysis

6 What kind of wrongdoing would most likely prompt you to be a whistle-blower? What kind of wrongdoing would least likely cause you to blow the whistle? Why?

7 In your opinion, which area of social responsibility is most important? Why? Are there areas other than those noted in the chapter that you consider important?

8 Identify some specific ethical or social responsibility issues that might be faced by small-business managers and employees in each of the following areas: environment, customers, employees, and investors.

Application Exercises

9 Develop a list of the major stakeholders of your college or university. How do you think the school prioritizes these stakeholders? Do you agree or disagree with this prioritization?

10 Using newspapers, magazines, and other business references, identify and describe at least three companies that take a defensive stance to social responsibility, three that take an accommodative stance, and three that take a proactive stance.

Entrepreneurship, New Ventures, and Business Ownership

After reading this chapter, you should be able to:

1 Define *small business*, discuss its importance to the U.S. economy, and explain popular areas of small business.

2 Explain entrepreneurship and describe some key characteristics of entrepreneurial personalities and activities.

3 Describe the business plan and the start-up decisions made by small businesses and identify sources of financial aid available to such enterprises.

4 Discuss the trends in small business start-ups and identify the main reasons for success and failure among small businesses.

5 Explain sole proprietorships, partnerships, and cooperatives and discuss the advantages and disadvantages of each.

6 Describe corporations, discuss their advantages and disadvantages, and identify different kinds of corporations.

7 Explain the basic issues involved in managing a corporation and discuss special issues related to corporate ownership.

Harvard Dropout Turned Billionaire

In 2004, Mark Zuckerberg created the Web site Facebook for his Harvard classmates. Just a few years later, the social networking site had not only expanded beyond the Harvard campus, it had close to 40 million active users. By 2008, Zuckerberg was widely thought to be the richest person in the world under the age of 25, with a net worth of over $1.5 billion, all due to Facebook's success.

Zuckerberg's vision goes beyond a simple student directory. Facebook, which was made available to anyone with a valid e-mail address in 2006, allows users to re-create their network of social relationships online and facilitates their streamlined communication by, for example, sending newsfeed-style bulletins to everyone in a person's network whenever they make a change to their page, such as adding a friend or uploading a photograph. This feature caused privacy concerns and wasn't very popular when first introduced. But Zuckerberg listened to users, admitted he could have handled the launch better, and provided opt-out options. Now News Feed is one of Facebook's most popular features, and the service's ability to create instant word-of-mouth buzz among networks of friends has attracted software developers and advertisers. In fact, the site has done so well that it's attracted the attention of big-name corporations. Viacom and Yahoo have both expressed interest in buying Facebook, offering as much as $1 billion. But at this point, Zuckerberg isn't selling.

It takes more than a good idea to become the richest 24-year-old in the world, however. Zuckerberg worked long hours and even dropped out of Harvard to make his vision for Facebook a reality. Flexibility has also been important in allowing him to tailor the site to suit its always-expanding audience. Zuckerberg has also had to learn managerial skills on the job, but his willingness to make and learn from mistakes has served him well and helped Zuckerberg make Facebook the second-most popular social networking site in the world.[1]

What's in It for Me?

Zuckerberg displayed many of the characteristics key to entrepreneurial success. This chapter will discuss these and additional elements important for starting and owning a business, including the business plan, reasons for success and failure, and the advantages and disadvantages of different kinds of ownership. First, we'll start by defining a small business and identifying its importance in the U.S. economy.

What Is a "Small" Business?

Locally owned and operated restaurants, dry cleaners, and hair salons are obviously small businesses, and giant corporations, such as Dell, Starbucks, and Best Buy, are clearly big businesses. But between these extremes fall thousands of companies that cannot be easily categorized.

The U.S. Department of Commerce and the **Small Business Administration (SBA)**, a government agency that assists small businesses, define the size of a business based on its industry and number of employees. According to SBA standards, a small business can have as many as 1,500 employees. Because strict numerical terms sometimes lead to contradictory classifications, we will consider a **small business** to be an independent (that is, not part of a larger business) business with relatively little influence in its market. A neighborhood

grocer would be small, assuming it is not part of a chain and that the prices it pays to wholesalers and charges its customers are largely set by market forces. Dell was a small business when founded by Michael Dell in 1984, but today it's number one in the personal computer market and by no means small. Hence, it can negotiate from a position of strength with its suppliers and can set its prices with less consideration for what others are charging.

Dell-ivering Innovation

Innovations are not always new products. Michael Dell didn't invent the PC; he developed an innovative way to build it (buy finished components and then assemble them) and an innovative way to sell it (directly to consumers, first by telephone and now via the Internet). Today, small businesses produce 13 times as many patents per employee as large patenting firms.[2]

The Importance of Small Business in the U.S. Economy

As Figure 3.1 shows, most U.S. businesses employ fewer than 100 people, and most U.S. workers are employed by small firms. The contribution of small business can be measured in terms of *job creation*, *innovation*, and *contributions to big business*.

Job Creation Small businesses are an important source of new (and often well-paid) jobs. In recent years, small businesses have accounted for 40 percent of all new jobs in high-technology sectors.[3] Small firms often hire at a faster rate than big firms and are generally the first to hire in times of economic recovery. However, they also tend to cut jobs at a higher rate than big firms, which are generally the last to lay off workers during downswings.

Innovation Major innovations are as likely to come from small businesses (or individuals) as from big ones. Small firms and individuals invented the personal

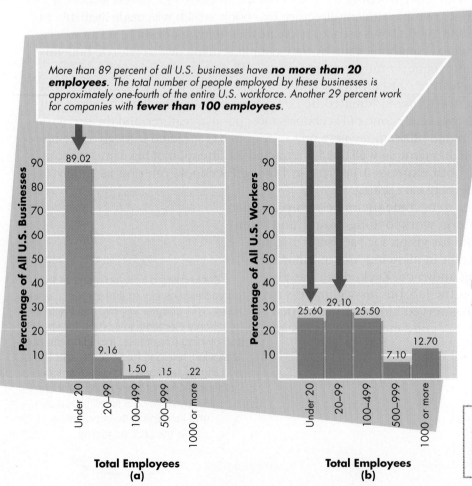

More than 89 percent of all U.S. businesses have **no more than 20 employees**. The total number of people employed by these businesses is approximately one-fourth of the entire U.S. workforce. Another 29 percent work for companies with **fewer than 100 employees**.

(a) Percentage of All U.S. Businesses vs. Total Employees: Under 20: 89.02; 20–99: 9.16; 100–499: 1.50; 500–999: .15; 1000 or more: .22

(b) Percentage of All U.S. Workers vs. Total Employees: Under 20: 25.60; 20–99: 29.10; 100–499: 25.50; 500–999: 7.10; 1000 or more: 12.70

Figure 3.1
The Importance of Small Business in the United States[4]

computer, the stainless-steel razor blade, the photocopier, the jet engine, and the self-developing photograph.

Contributions to Big Business Most of the products made by big businesses are sold to consumers by small businesses. For example, most dealerships that sell Fords, Toyotas, and Volvos are independently operated. Even as more shoppers turn to the Internet, many larger online retailers outsource the creation of their Web sites and the distribution of their products to small or regional firms. Smaller businesses also provide data-storage services, as well as other services and raw materials, for larger businesses. Microsoft, for instance, relies on hundreds of small firms to write most of its code.

Popular Areas of Small-Business Enterprise

Small businesses play a major role in services, retailing, construction, wholesaling, finance and insurance, manufacturing, and transportation. Generally, the more resources required, the harder a business is to start and the less likely an industry is dominated by small firms. Remember, too, that small is a relative term. The criteria (number of employees and total annual sales) differ among industries and are often meaningful only when compared with truly large businesses. Figure 3.2 shows the distribution of all U.S. businesses employing fewer than 20 people across industry groups.

Services About 50 percent of businesses with fewer than 20 employees are involved in the service industry, which ranges from marriage counseling to computer software, from management consulting to professional dog walking. Partly because they require few

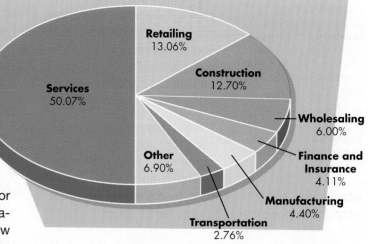

Figure 3.2
Small Business by Industry[5]

Services 50.07%
Retailing 13.06%
Construction 12.70%
Wholesaling 6.00%
Finance and Insurance 4.11%
Manufacturing 4.40%
Transportation 2.76%
Other 6.90%

resources, service providers are the fastest-growing segment of small business.

Retailing Retailers, which sell products made by other firms directly to consumers, account for about 13 percent of these firms. Usually, people who start small retail businesses favor specialty shops—big men's clothing or gourmet coffees—that let them focus limited resources on narrow market segments.

Construction About 13 percent are involved in construction. Because many construction jobs are small local projects, like a homeowner adding a garage or remodeling a room, local contractors are often best suited to handle them.

Wholesaling Small-business owners often do well in wholesaling, which accounts for about 6 percent of businesses with fewer than 20 employees. Wholesalers buy products in bulk from manufacturers or other producers and store them in quantities and locations convenient for selling them to retailers.

Finance and Insurance Financial and insurance firms account for about 4 percent. Most of these businesses, such as local State Farm Insurance offices, are affiliates of or agents for larger national firms.

Manufacturing More than any other industry, manufacturing lends itself to big business, but it still accounts for about 4 percent of firms with fewer than 20 employees. Indeed, small manufacturers sometimes outperform big ones in such innovation-driven industries as electronics, toys, and computer software.

There are many areas in which small businesses excel. This enterprising entrepreneur, for example, has a lucrative business as a dog walker. A small business is much more likely than a large business to succeed in such a venture.

Transportation About 3 percent of these small companies are in transportation and related businesses, including many taxi and limousine companies, charter airplane services, and tour operators.

Other The remaining 7 percent or so are in other industries, such as small research-and-development laboratories and independent media companies, like small-town newspapers and radio broadcasters.

Entrepreneurship

Entrepreneurs are people who assume the risk of business ownership. **Entrepreneurship** is the process of seeking business opportunities under conditions of risk. However, not all entrepreneurs have the same goals.

Many entrepreneurs are driven to launch new businesses by the goal of gaining independence from working for someone else and securing a financial future for themselves, but they may not aspire to grow their businesses beyond their capacities to run them. Consider Jack Matz, who opened a photocopy and print service business after losing his job as a corporate executive when his firm merged with another. His goal is to earn enough money to lead a comfortable life until he retires. The term *small business* is most closely associated with these kinds of enterprises.

Others strive to grow and expand their ventures into large businesses. Terms such as *new ventures* and *start-ups* are often used to refer to these kinds of businesses.

In some cases, an entrepreneur's goals may not always be clear in the early stages of business development. For instance, the founders of Google had no idea that their firm would grow to its present size. Others might start out with ambitious growth plans, but find that expected opportunities cannot be realized.

Entrepreneurial Characteristics

Many successful entrepreneurs share certain characteristics: resourcefulness, a concern for good customer relations, the ability to deal with uncertainty and risk, a desire to be their own bosses, to have greater control over their lives, and to build for their families.

Yesterday's entrepreneur was often stereotyped as "the boss"—self-reliant, male, and able to make quick,

---

Say What You Mean

The Wide World of Risk

Globalization and the expanded reach and power of multinational companies require corporations to innovate, grow, and adapt to new markets and economic circumstances. In a highly interconnected world, it's often hard to figure out the complex ownership and organizational structures of many global corporations. Branding strategies and management structures may lead people to think that companies are local when, in fact, the real source of corporate power may lie thousands of miles away. One thing's for sure: if you're going to be dealing with a company overseas, you'd better have a good idea of where and how decisions are made, and who has the real power to make them.

Remember, too, that different cultures have different attitudes when it comes to entrepreneurship. Some countries and cultures, like that of the United States, promote a lively entrepreneurial spirit. Businesspeople are open to taking risks, and if they fail, they tend to pick themselves up and move on to something else. In some Asian countries, the entrepreneurial spirit is often tempered by the need for consensus. This approach requires a lot of patience and the ability to compromise. Knowing the cultural forces that shape both a business organization and people's attitudes toward risk, success, and failure is an elementary but important component of international business.

firm decisions. Today's entrepreneur is seen more often as an open-minded leader, just as likely to be male or female, who relies on networks, business plans, and consensus. Past and present entrepreneurs also have different views on such topics as how to succeed, how to automate business, and when to rely on experience in the trade or on basic business acumen.[6]

Consider Yoshiko Shinohara, who had lost her father by the age of 8, was divorced by the age of 28, and never received a college education. At the age of 70, she is president of Tempstaff, a Japanese temp agency that she started out of her one-room apartment more than 30 years ago. Fueled by Japan's need for temps during a period of stagnation in the 1990s and Shinohara's ambition, Tempstaff is now a $1.5 billion company with a high-rise headquarters in Tokyo.[7]

Among other things, Shinohara's story illustrates what is almost always a key element in entrepreneurship: risk. Interestingly, most successful entrepreneurs seldom see what they do as risky. Whereas others may focus on possibilities for failure and balk at gambling everything on a new venture, most entrepreneurs are so passionate about their ideas and plans that they see little or no likelihood of failure. For example, when Shinohara started Tempstaff, few Japanese businesses understood or had even heard of the temporary-worker concept. But Shinohara felt that she "had nothing to lose anyway" and preferred taking that risk to ending up "serving tea or just being a clerical assistant."[8]

Starting and Operating a New Business

Now more than ever, the Internet has made setting up a small business easier and faster, has created more potential opportunities, and has heightened the ability to gather and assess information. Would-be entrepreneurs must still decide whether to buy an existing business or build from the ground up and must know when to seek expert advice and where to find financing.

Crafting a Business Plan

Before investing time and money, the starting point for virtually every new entrepreneur is a **business plan** in which the entrepreneur thoroughly develops and describes her or his business strategy and demonstrates how it will be implemented.[9]

Setting Goals and Objectives A business plan describes the match between the entrepreneur's abilities and experiences and the requirements for producing and/or marketing a particular product. It defines strategies for production and marketing, legal elements and organization, and accounting and finance. It should

specifically answer three questions: (1) What are the entrepreneur's goals and objectives? (2) What strategies will be used to obtain them? (3) How will these strategies be implemented?

Sales Forecasting Sales forecasts must be based on sound logic and research and demonstrate an understanding of the current market, the strengths and weaknesses of existing firms, and the means by which the new venture will compete. For example, simply asserting that the new venture will sell 100,000 units per month is not credible.

Financial Planning Financial planning refers to the entrepreneur's plan for turning all other activities into dollars. It generally includes an income statement, balance sheets, a breakeven chart, and a cash budget, which shows how much money is needed before the business opens and how much is needed to keep the business going before it starts earning a profit.[10]

Starting a Small Business

The first step to starting a new business is the individual's commitment to becoming a business owner. In preparing their business plans, entrepreneurs must come to understand the nature of the enterprises in which they are engaged.

"Eventually I'd like to have a business where the money rolls in and I wouldn't have to be there much."

Buying an Existing Business

Next, the entrepreneur must decide whether to buy an existing business or start from scratch. Because the odds are better, many experts recommend the first approach. If successful, an existing business has already proven its ability to attract customers and generate profit and has established relationships with lenders, suppliers, and other stakeholders. Moreover, potential buyers will have a much clearer picture of what to expect than any estimate of a start-up's prospects. For example, Ray Kroc bought McDonald's as an existing business, added entrepreneurial vision and business insight, and produced a multinational giant.

Franchising Most Subway, 7-Eleven, RE/MAX, and Blockbuster outlets are franchises operating under licenses issued by parent companies to local owners. A **franchise** agreement involves two parties, a *franchisee* (the local owner) and a *franchiser* (the parent company).

Franchisees benefit from the parent corporation's experience and expertise. The franchiser may pick the store location, negotiate the lease, purchase equipment, and supply financing. Franchises offer the benefit of brand recognition, which can make it easier to attract customers and reduce the costs of advertising as well as increase the likelihood of success.

Perhaps the most significant disadvantage in owning a franchise is the start-up cost, which varies widely. The fee for a Curves fitness center is between $31,400 and $53,500, but a McDonald's franchise costs $506,000 to $1.6 million,[11] and professional sports teams cost an average of $957 million dollars.[12] Franchisees may also be obligated to contribute a percentage of sales to parent corporations. From the perspective of the parent company, some firms, such as Starbucks, choose not to franchise in order to retain more control over quality and earn more profits for themselves.

Starting from Scratch Despite the odds, some people seek the satisfaction that comes from planting an idea and growing it into a healthy business. A new business

---

Entrepreneurs must study markets and answer the following questions:

- Who and where are my customers?
- How much will those customers pay for my product?
- How much of my product can I expect to sell?
- Who are my competitors?
- Why will customers buy my product rather than the product of my competitors?

The ability of an entrepreneur to obtain adequate financing is a critical component in the potential success of a new venture. Many entrepreneurs rely on SBA financial programs, venture capital companies, or small-business investment companies to launch their businesses.

doesn't suffer the ill effects of a prior owner's errors, and the start-up owner is free to make all the choices. Of all new businesses begun in the past decade, 64 percent were started from scratch. Dell, Wal-Mart, and Microsoft are among today's most successful businesses that were started from scratch by entrepreneurs.

However, new-business founders can only make projections about their prospects. Success or failure depends on identifying a genuine opportunity, such as a product for which many customers will pay well but which is currently unavailable.

Financing a Small Business

Although the choice of how to start a business is obviously important, it's meaningless without money. According to the National Federation of Independent Business, personal resources, including savings and money borrowed from friends and relatives, account for over two-thirds of all money invested in new small businesses, and one-half of that is used to purchase existing businesses. Getting money from banks, independent investors, and government agencies requires extra effort, like formulating business plans and meeting eligibility requirements. Moreover, lending institutions are more likely to help finance the purchase of an existing established business than a brand-new one.

Other Sources of Investment **Venture capital companies** are groups of small investors seeking to make profits on companies with rapid growth potential. Most of these firms do not lend money to start new businesses; they supply capital to fuel expansion of an existing firm in return for partial ownership, representation on boards of directors, and final approval of major decisions.

Small-business investment companies (SBICs) are federally licensed to borrow money from the SBA and to invest in or lend to small businesses with potential for rapid growth. Past beneficiaries of SBIC capital include Apple Computer, Intel, and FedEx. The government also sponsors *minority enterprise small-business investment companies (MESBICs)*, which target minority-owned businesses.

SBA Financial Programs Since its founding in 1953, the SBA has sponsored financing programs for small businesses that meet standards of size and independence and are unable to get private financing at reasonable terms. The most common form of SBA financing, its *7(a) loans programs*, allows small businesses to borrow from commercial lenders and guarantees to repay a maximum of 75 percent. The SBA's *special purpose loans* target businesses with specific needs, such as meeting international demands or implementing pollution-control measures. For loans under $35,000, the SBA offers the *micro-loan program*. The *Certified Development Company (504) program* offers fixed interest rates on loans from nonprofit community-based lenders to boost local economies.[13]

Other SBA Programs The SBA also helps entrepreneurs improve their management skills. The Service Corps of Retired Executives (SCORE) is made up of retired executives who volunteer to help entrepreneurs start new businesses. The **Small Business Development Center (SBDC)** program consolidates information from various disciplines and institutions for use by new and existing small businesses.

Trends, Successes, and Failures in New Ventures

For every Sam Walton, Russell Simmons, Donald Trump, or Steve Jobs—entrepreneurs who transformed small businesses into big ones—there are many who fail. Each year, between 600,000 and 650,000 new businesses are launched in the United States, and between 500,000 and 600,000 fail.[14] In this section, we will look at a few key trends in small-business start-ups and examine some of the reasons for their success and failure.

Trends in Small-Business Start-Ups

As noted previously, thousands of new businesses are started in the United States every year. Several factors account for this trend, and in this section, we focus on five of them.

Emergence of E-Commerce The most significant recent trend is the rapid emergence of electronic commerce. Because the Internet provides fundamentally new ways of doing business, savvy entrepreneurs have created and expanded new businesses faster and easier than ever before. Figure 3.3 underscores this point by summarizing the growth in online retail spending from 2003 through 2007.

Crossovers from Big Business More businesses are being started by people who have opted to leave big corporations and put their experience to work for themselves.[16] John Chambers spent several years working at IBM and Wang Laboratories/Wang Global before he signed on to help Cisco, then a small and struggling firm. Under his leadership and entrepreneurial guidance, Cisco has become one of the largest and most important technology companies in the world.

Opportunities for Minorities and Women More small businesses are also being started by minorities and women.[17] The number of businesses owned by African Americans increased by 48 percent during the most recent five-year period for which data are available and now totals about 1.2 million. The number of Hispanic-owned businesses has grown 31 percent and now totals about 1.6 million. Ownership among Asians has increased 24 percent and among Pacific Islanders 64 percent.[18]

Nearly 11 million businesses are now owned by women. Together, they generate a combined $2.5 trillion in revenue a year and employ 19 million workers.[19] Figure 3.4 shows some of the reasons women cite for starting their own businesses.

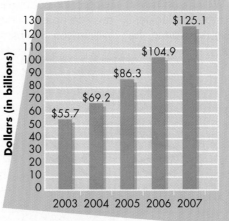

Figure 3.3
Growth of Online Retail Spending[15]

Bar chart: Dollars (in billions)
- 2003: $55.7
- 2004: $69.2
- 2005: $86.3
- 2006: $104.9
- 2007: $125.1

Figure 3.4
Reasons Women Give for Starting Businesses[20]

Pie chart: Gain control over my schedule 46%; Saw a market opportunity and decided to pursue it 24%; Frustrated with "glass ceiling" at big companies 23%; Other reasons 7%

Global Opportunities

Many entrepreneurs are also finding new opportunities in foreign markets. Doug Mellinger, founder and CEO of PRT Group, a software development company, had trouble finding trained programmers in the United States. So Mellinger set up shop on Barbados, where the government helps him attract foreign programmers. Today, PRT has customers and suppliers from dozens of nations.

Better Survival Rates   More people are encouraged to test their skills as entrepreneurs because the small-business failure rate has declined. During the 1960s and 1970s, fewer than half of all new start-ups survived more than 18 months; only one in five lasted 10 years. Now, however, 44 percent can expect to survive for at least four years.[21]

Reasons for Failure

Unfortunately, over half of all new businesses will not enjoy long-term success. Although no set pattern is a reliable predictor, four general factors contribute to failure:

1 *Managerial incompetence or inexperience.* Some entrepreneurs put too much faith in common sense, overestimate their own managerial skills, or believe that hard work alone ensures success. Success will likely elude managers who don't know how to make basic business decisions or understand basic management principles.

2 *Neglect.* Starting a small business demands an overwhelming commitment of time and effort. Owners aren't likely to see success if they try to launch ventures in their spare time or devote only limited time to new businesses.

3 *Weak control systems.* Effective control systems keep a business on track and alert managers to potential problems before they become serious. For instance, some businesses fail because they do a poor job of managing their credit-collection policies—anxious to grow, they may be too liberal in extending credit to their customers and then end up not being able to collect all the money that is owed to them.

4 *Insufficient capital.* Some entrepreneurs are overly optimistic about how soon they'll start earning profits. In most cases, it takes months or even years. Amazon.com didn't earn a profit for 10 years but obviously still required capital to pay employees and to cover other expenses. Experts say you need

---

Entrepreneurship and New Ventures

The Road to Recovery

A homeless heroin addict at 24, Bob Williamson never would have expected a car accident to be the luckiest thing that ever happened to him. While recovering, he decided it was time to turn his life around. Although he may not have seemed the ideal hire, Williamson already had a work ethic that would carry him to his current position as CEO of Horizon Software International: "First one in, last to leave."

He lived by this code even when his job was just putting labels on paint cans in the basement at Glidden, which ended up promoting him eight times in two years. After working for two other paint companies, Williamson had the know-how to create a new formula for his

airbrushing hobby. His formula was a hit, and he started his own company, which he spun out into several others. Williamson overcame hard times again when he nearly faced bankruptcy after discovering his accountant was embezzling money.

But luck wasn't far behind him. Williamson started Horizon using the software that he just so happened to be writing as the software industry was about to boom. Once Williamson realized the value of his software, he rode that opportunity wherever it took him, and soon the company was selling the software to colleges, military bases, and hospitals. Now a 61-year-old CEO, Williamson is still "first one in, last to leave."[22]

enough capital to operate at least six months to a year without earning a profit.[23]

Reasons for Success

Four basic factors are also typically cited to explain small-business success:

1 *Hard work, drive, and dedication.* Small-business owners must be committed to succeeding and willing to spend the time and effort to make it happen. When Gladys Edmunds, a single mother in Pittsburgh, wanted to open a travel agency, she washed laundry, made chicken dinners to sell to cab drivers, and sold fire extinguishers door to door to earn start-up money. Today, Edmunds Travel Consultants earns about $6 million a year.[24]

2 *Market demand for the products or services being provided.* Careful analysis of market conditions can help small-business owners assess the probable reception of their products. Attempts to expand restaurants specializing in baked potatoes, muffins, and gelato have largely failed, but hamburger and pizza chains continue to expand.

3 *Managerial competence.* Successful owners may acquire competence through training or experience or by drawing on the expertise of others. Most spend time in successful companies or partner with others to bring expertise to a new business.[25]

4 *Luck.* After Alan McKim started Clean Harbors, an environmental cleanup firm in New England, he struggled to keep his business afloat. Then the U.S. government committed $1.6 billion to toxic-waste cleanup—McKim's specialty. Had the government fund not been created at just the right time, McKim might well have failed. Instead, he landed several government contracts.

Noncorporate Business Ownership

All entrepreneurs must decide which form of legal ownership best suits their goals: *sole proprietorship*, *partnership*, or *corporation*. Table 3.1 compares the most important differences among the three major ownership forms.

Sole Proprietorships

A **sole proprietorship** is owned and usually operated by one person. They account for about 72 percent of all U.S. businesses but only about 5 percent of total revenues.

Advantages of Sole Proprietorships
Sole proprietors answer to no one but themselves and can sometimes open up shop just by putting a sign on the door. Low start-up costs, the simplicity of legal setup procedures, and tax benefits make this form appealing.

Disadvantages of Sole Proprietorships
A major drawback is **unlimited liability**: a sole proprietor is personally liable for all debts incurred by the business. Another disadvantage is lack of continuity: a sole proprietorship legally dissolves when the owner dies. Additionally, sole proprietors often find it hard to borrow money to start up or expand what many bankers see as risky businesses.

Partnerships

The most common type of partnership, the **general partnership**, is a sole proprietorship multiplied by the number of partner-owners. Partners may invest equal or unequal sums of money and may earn profits that bear no relation to their financial investments if, for instance, someone contributes a well-known name or special expertise.

Advantages of Partnerships
The most striking advantage of general partnerships is the ability to grow by adding new talent and money. Because banks prefer to make loans to enterprises that are not dependent on single individuals, partnerships find it relatively easy to borrow and can invite new partners to invest.

Partnerships must begin with some kind of agreement that details who invested what sums and who will

---

SOLE PROPRIETORSHIP business owned and usually operated by one person who is responsible for all of its debts

UNLIMITED LIABILITY legal principle holding owners responsible for paying off all debts of a business

GENERAL PARTNERSHIP business with two or more owners who share in both the operation of the firm and the financial responsibility for its debts

---

Table 3.1 **Comparative Summary: Three Forms of Business**

Business Form	Liability	Continuity	Management	Sources of Investment
Proprietorship	Personal, unlimited	Ends with death or decision of owner	Personal, unrestricted	Personal
General Partnership	Personal, unlimited	Ends with death or decision of any partner	Unrestricted or depends on partnership agreement	Personal by partner(s)
Corporation	Capital invested	As stated in charter, perpetual or for specified period of years	Under control of board of directors, which is selected by stockholders	Purchase of stock

receive profit shares, how responsibilities are assigned, how the partnership may be dissolved and assets distributed, and how surviving partners will be protected from claims of a deceased partner's heirs. In all but two states, the Revised Uniform Limited Partnership Act requires the filing of specific information about the business and its partners. Partners may also agree to bind themselves in ways not specified by law. However, partners are still taxed as individuals.

Disadvantages of Partnerships
Unlimited liability is the greatest drawback. Each partner may be liable for all business debts incurred by any of the partners. Partnerships also share with sole proprietorships the potential lack of continuity. When one partner dies or leaves, the original partnership dissolves, even if one or more of the others want it to continue. A related disadvantage

is difficulty in transferring ownership. No partner may sell out, retire, or transfer interest without the others' consent.

Alternatives to General Partnerships Because of these disadvantages, general partnerships are among the least popular forms of business. To resolve some of the problems inherent in general partnerships, some have tried alternative agreements. A **limited partnership** allows for **limited partners** who cannot take active roles in operations but invest money and are liable for debts only to the extent of their investments. For liability purposes, a limited partnership must have at least one **general (or active) partner** who runs the business and is responsible for its survival and growth.

Under a **master limited partnership**, an organization sells shares (partnership interests) to investors on public markets. Investors are paid back from profits. The master partner retains at least 50 percent ownership, runs the business, and provides detailed operating and financial reports to minority partners, who have no management voice.

Cooperatives
Groups of sole proprietorships or partnerships may agree to work together for their common benefit by forming **cooperatives**, which combine the freedom of sole proprietorships with the financial power of corporations. Although cooperatives make up only a minor segment of the U.S. economy, their role is still important in agriculture. Ocean Spray, the Florida Citrus Growers, and Cabot Creamery are among the best-known cooperatives.

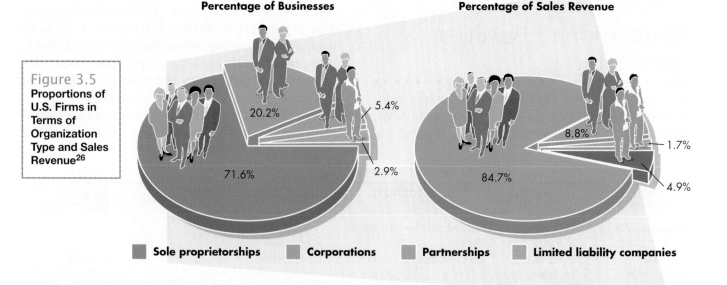

Figure 3.5
Proportions of U.S. Firms in Terms of Organization Type and Sales Revenue[26]

Percentage of Businesses

71.6%   20.2%   5.4%   2.9%

Percentage of Sales Revenue

84.7%   8.8%   1.7%   4.9%

■ **Sole proprietorships**   ■ **Corporations**   ■ **Partnerships**   ■ **Limited liability companies**

Corporations

• •

The 4.93 million corporations in the United States account for about 20 percent of all U.S. businesses but generate about 85 percent of all sales revenues.[27]

The Corporate Entity

The very word *corporation* inspires images of size and power. In reality, however, your corner newsstand has as much right to incorporate as a giant automaker, and they would share the characteristics of all **corporations**: legal status as separate entities, property rights and obligations, and indefinite life spans. As legal entities, like individuals, corporations can sue and be sued; buy, hold, and sell property; make and sell products; and commit crimes and be tried and punished for them.

Advantages of Incorporation The biggest advantage of corporations is **limited liability**: investor liability is limited to personal investment in the corporation. If, for example, you invest $1,000 in stock in a corporation that ends up failing, you may lose your $1,000, but no more.

Another advantage is continuity. Shares of stock may be sold or passed on to heirs, and most corporations also benefit from the continuity provided by professional management. Finally, corporations have advantages in raising money. By selling stock, they expand the number of investors and the amount of available funds, and lenders are more willing to grant loans.

Disadvantages of Incorporation Although a chief attraction is ease of transferring ownership, this same feature can create complications. For example, using a legal process called a **tender offer**—an offer to buy shares made by a prospective buyer directly to a corporation's shareholders—a corporation can be taken over against the will of its managers. Other disadvantages include heavy regulations, high start-up costs, and complex legal requirements.

The biggest disadvantage is **double taxation**. First, a corporation pays income taxes on company profits. Then, stockholders pay taxes on income returned by their investments. Thus, the profits earned by corporations are taxed twice—at both the corporate and ownership levels.

The advantages and disadvantages of corporate ownership have inspired laws establishing different kinds of corporations intended to take advantage of the benefits of the corporate model without assuming all the disadvantages.

Types of Corporations

Within the broad categories of *public* or *private* are several specific types of corporations, some of which are summarized in Table 3.2.

■ Most smaller firms are **closely held (or private) corporations**. Stock is held by only a few people and isn't available for public sale. The controlling group of stockholders may be a family, a management group, or even the firm's employees.[28]

■ Most large firms are **publicly held (or public) corporations**, in which shares are publicly issued.

■ An **S corporation** (*Subchapter S corporation*) is organized and operates like a corporation but treated like a partnership for tax purposes. S corporations must meet stringent eligibility requirements.

■ With a **limited liability corporation (LLC)**, owners are taxed like partners but also enjoy the benefits of limited liability. LLCs have grown in popularity in recent years, partially because of IRS rulings that allow corporations, partnerships, and foreign investors to be partial owners.

■ **Professional corporations** are most likely composed of doctors, lawyers, accountants, or other professionals. While the corporate structure protects from unlimited financial liability, members are not immune from unlimited liability. Professional negligence by a member can entail personal liability on the individual's part.

■ In a **multinational (or transnational) corporation**, stock may be traded on the exchanges of several countries, and managers are likely to be of different nationalities.

LIMITED LIABILITY legal principle holding investors liable for a firm's debts only to the limits of their personal investments in it

TENDER OFFER offer to buy shares made by a prospective buyer directly to a target corporation's shareholders, who then make individual decisions about whether to sell

DOUBLE TAXATION situation in which taxes may be payable both by a corporation on its profits and by shareholders on dividend incomes

CLOSELY HELD (OR PRIVATE) CORPORATION corporation whose stock is held by only a few people and is not available for sale to the general public

PUBLICLY HELD (OR PUBLIC) CORPORATION corporation whose stock is widely held and available for sale to the general public

S CORPORATION hybrid of a closely held corporation and a partnership, organized and operated like a corporation but treated as a partnership for tax purposes

LIMITED LIABILITY CORPORATION (LLC) hybrid of a publicly held corporation and a partnership in which owners are taxed as partners but enjoy the benefits of limited liability

PROFESSIONAL CORPORATION form of ownership allowing professionals to take advantage of corporate benefits while granting them limited business liability and unlimited professional liability

MULTINATIONAL (OR TRANSNATIONAL) CORPORATION form of corporation spanning national boundaries

Table 3.2 **Types of Corporations**

Type	Distinguishing Features	Examples
Closely Held	Stock held by only a few people	Blue Cross/Blue Shield
	Subject to corporate taxation	MasterCard
Publicly Held	Stock widely held among many investors	Dell Computer
	Subject to corporate taxation	Starbucks
		Texas Instruments
Subchapter S	Organized much like a closely held corporation	Minglewood Associates
	Subject to additional regulation	Entech Pest Systems
	Subject to partnership taxation	Frontier Bank
Limited Liability	Organized much like a publicly held corporation	Pacific Northwest Associates
	Subject to additional regulation	Global Ground Support
	Subject to partnership taxation	Ritz Ritz-Carlton
Professional	Subject to partnership taxation	Norman Hui, DDS & Associates
	Limited business liability	B & H Engineering
	Unlimited professional liability	Anderson, McCoy & Ortia
Multinational	Spans national boundaries	Toyota
	Subject to regulation in multiple countries	Nestlé
		General Electric

Managing a Corporation

A corporation must be managed on the principles of **corporate governance**—the roles of shareholders, directors, and other managers in corporate decision making and accountability. In this section, we discuss the principles of *stock ownership and stockholders' rights*, describe the role of *boards of directors*, and examine some special issues related to corporate ownership.

Corporate Governance

Corporate governance is established by a firm's bylaws and usually involves three distinct bodies: **stockholders (or shareholders)**, the *board of directors*, and *officers*.

Stock Ownership and Stockholders' Rights Corporations sell shares, called *stock*, to investors who then become stockholders, or shareholders. Profits are distributed among stockholders in the form of *dividends*, and corporate managers serve at stockholders' discretion.

Boards of Directors The governing body of a corporation is its **board of directors**, which reports to stockholders and other stakeholders and sets policy on dividends, major spending, and executive compensation. Boards of directors are legally responsible and accountable for corporate actions and are increasingly being held personally liable for them.

Presidents of four leading Japanese robot firms pose together to announce their joint venture to accelerate the market development of next generation robots.

Officers Although board members oversee operations, most do not participate in day-to-day management. Rather, they hire a team of **officers**, usually headed by the firm's **chief executive officer (CEO)**, who is responsible for overall performance. Other officers typically include a *president*, who is responsible for internal management, and *vice presidents*, who oversee various functional areas such as marketing and operations.

Special Issues in Corporate Ownership

In recent years, several issues have grown in importance in the area of corporate ownership, including *joint ventures* and *strategic alliances*, *mergers* and *acquisitions*, and *divestitures* and *spin-offs*.

Joint Ventures and Strategic Alliances In a **strategic alliance**, two or more organizations collaborate on a project for mutual gain. When partners share ownership of what is essentially a new enterprise, it is called a **joint venture**. The number of strategic alliances has increased rapidly in recent years on both domestic and international fronts.

Mergers and Acquisitions (M&As) A **merger** occurs when two firms combine to create a new company. In an **acquisition**, one firm buys another outright. In general, when the two firms are roughly the same size, the combination is usually called a merger even if one firm is taking control of the other. When the acquiring firm is substantially larger than the acquired firm, the deal is really an acquisition. So-called M&As are an important form of corporate strategy for increasing product lines, expanding operations, going international, and creating new enterprises.

Divestitures and Spin-offs Sometimes a corporation decides to sell a part of its existing business operations or set it up as a new and independent corporation. If a firm sells off an unrelated and/or underperforming businesses to focus more specifically on its core businesses, the sale is called a **divestiture**. When a firm sells part of itself to raise capital or because it deems a business unit more valuable as a separate company, the strategy is known as a **spin-off**. For example, in 2007, Morgan Stanley spun off its Discover Card division into a standalone company called Discover Financial Services. For every two shares of Morgan Stanley stock, shareholders received one share of Discover Financial Services. In effect, Morgan Stanley still owns Discover, but both companies are free to pursue separate and (hopefully) more profitable business strategies.[29]

> **For additional topics related to this material and end-of-chapter exercises and practices, please visit www.mybizlab.com.**

Questions for Review

1 Why are small businesses important to the U.S. economy?

2 Which industries are easiest for start-ups to enter? Which are hardest? Why?

3 Describe the key components of a business plan. Why is it important for a new start-up to create a business plan?

4 What are the primary reasons for new business failure and success?

5 What are the basic forms of noncorporate business ownership? What are the key advantages and disadvantages of each?

6 What are the types of corporations? What are the key advantages and disadvantages of incorporation?

Questions for Analysis

7 Why might a closely held corporation choose to remain private? Why might it choose to be publicly traded?

8 If you were going to open a new business, what type would it be? Why?

9 Would you prefer to buy an existing business or franchise, or start from scratch? Why?

10 Under what circumstances might it be wise for an entrepreneur to reject venture capital? Under what circumstances might it be advisable to take more venture capital than he or she actually needs?

Application Exercises

11 Interview the owner/manager of a sole proprietorship or a general partnership. What characteristics of that business form led the owner to choose it? Does he or she ever contemplate changing the form of the business? If yes, what form would the owner choose, and why would he or she change it?

12 Identify two or three of the fastest growing businesses in the United States during the last year. What role has entrepreneurship played in the growth of these firms?

chapter 4

The Global Context of Business

After reading this chapter, you should be able to:

1 Discuss the rise of international business and describe the major world marketplaces, trade agreements, and alliances.

2 Explain how differences in import-export balances, exchange rates, and foreign competition determine the ways in which countries and businesses respond to the international environment.

3 Discuss the factors involved in deciding to do business internationally and in selecting the appropriate levels of international involvement and organizational structure.

4 Describe some of the ways in which social, cultural, economic, legal, and political differences among nations affect international business.

A Truly Universal Studio

At first glance, 2007 was not a good year for the U.S. film industry centered in Hollywood, California. Although U.S. theaters sold nearly $9.7 billion in tickets, the total number of tickets sold fell for the fourth time in five years. Expensive, would-be blockbusters such as *Evan Almighty* and *The Golden Compass* failed to turn a profit, and much-hyped sequels like *Spider-Man 3*, *Shrek the Third*, and *Pirates of the Caribbean: At World's End* all grossed significantly less than their predecessors.

From a broader perspective, however, Hollywood had a very successful 2007. The take from domestic theaters is only half the story; the other half comes from foreign markets, where moviegoers spent a record $9.4 billion on films distributed by the six major studios (Warner Bros., Disney, Fox, Paramount, Sony, and Universal). Taking worldwide grosses into account, *Spider-Man 3* was the most successful *Spider-Man* film yet. In a similar trend, international sales accounted for over $300 million (81 percent) of *The Golden Compass's* total earnings and over $650 million (68 percent) of total earnings for *Pirates of the Caribbean: At World's End*.

The relationship between foreign markets and Hollywood's balance sheet is not a new one. With each new slate of releases, however, studio executives are reminded of the increasing importance of the international audience, which has set box office records in three of the past four years. The need to market a film to the broadest possible audience has even been blamed for what some perceive as a steady decline in the quality of Hollywood films. "What sells best overseas is a simple message, preferably one that is nonverbal and can be communicated with a single dominant image," argues Brooks Barnes of *The New York Times*. Whether this is itself an oversimplification remains debatable, but this much seems clear: the question of "what sells best overseas" will continue to generate lots of discussion in studio boardrooms.[1]

What's in It for Me?

Hollywood is hardly alone in its increasing awareness of the global marketplace. Businesses both large and small, across every industry, must understand how to reap the rewards and avoid the pitfalls of international trade. This chapter explores the various factors that influence a firm's decision to expand overseas, as well as the extent of that expansion. In turn, you will better understand how global forces affect you as both a customer and an employee, and you will be better equipped to assess how global opportunities and challenges can affect you as a business owner and an investor.

The Contemporary Global Economy

The total volume of world trade is immense—over $9 trillion in merchandise trade each year. As more firms engage in international business, the world economy is fast becoming an interdependent system—a process called **globalization**.

We often take for granted the diversity of products we can buy as a result of international trade. Your television, your shoes, and even your morning coffee or juice are probably **imports**—products made or grown abroad and sold domestically in the United States. At the same time, the success of many U.S. firms depends on **exports**—products made or grown here, such as machinery, electronic equipment, and grains, and shipped for sale abroad. Several forces have combined to spark and sustain globalization. For one thing, governments and businesses are more aware of the benefits of globalization to businesses and shareholders. These benefits include the potential for higher standards of living and improved business profitability. New technologies have made international travel, communication, and commerce faster and cheaper than ever before. Finally, there are competitive pressures: Sometimes, a firm must expand into foreign markets simply to keep up with competitors.

Globalization is not without its detractors. Some critics charge that globalization allows businesses to exploit workers in less developed countries and bypass domestic environmental and tax regulations. They also charge that globalization leads to the loss of cultural heritages and often benefits the rich more than the poor. As a result, many international gatherings of global economic leaders are marked by protests and demonstrations.

The Major World Marketplaces

Managers involved with international businesses need to have a solid understanding of the global economy, including the major world marketplaces. This section examines some fundamental economic distinctions between countries based on wealth and then looks at some of the world's major international marketplaces.

Distinctions Based on Wealth   The World Bank, an agency of the United Nations, uses per-capita income—average income per person—to make distinctions among countries. Its current classification method consists of four different categories of countries:[2]

1 *High-income countries.* Those with annual per-capita income greater than $11,115.

2 *Upper middle-income countries.* Those with annual per-capita income of $11,115 or less, but more than $3,595.

3 *Lower middle-income countries.* Those with annual per-capita income of $3,595 or lower, but more than $905.

4 *Low-income countries (often called developing countries).* Those with annual per-capita income of $905 or less.

Geographic Clusters   The world economy revolves around three major marketplaces: North America, Europe, and Pacific Asia. In general, these clusters include relatively more of the upper-middle and high-income nations, but relatively few low- and lower middle-income countries.

North America As the world's largest marketplace and most stable economy, the United States dominates the North American market. Canada also plays a major role in the international economy, and the United States and Canada are each other's largest trading partners.

Mexico has become a major manufacturing center, especially along the U.S.

Advocates of globalization argue that increased international commerce benefits all sectors of society and should be actively encouraged. But critics like these protestors argue that globalization benefits only big business and is eroding distinctive national cultures.

border, where cheap labor and low transportation costs have encouraged many firms from the United States and other countries to build factories. However, Mexico's role as a low-cost manufacturing center may have peaked. The emergence of China as a low-cost manufacturing center may lead companies to begin to shift their production from Mexico to China.[3]

Europe Europe is often regarded as two regions—Western and Eastern. Western Europe, dominated by Germany, the United Kingdom, and France, has long been a mature but fragmented marketplace. The transformation of this region via the European Union (discussed later) into an integrated economic system has further increased its importance. E-commerce and technology have also become increasingly important in this region. There has been a surge in Internet start-ups in southeastern England, the Netherlands, and the Scandinavian countries; Ireland is now one of the world's largest exporters of software; Strasbourg, France, is a major center for biotech start-ups; Barcelona, Spain, has many flourishing software and Internet companies; and the Frankfurt region of Germany is dotted with software and biotech start-ups.

Eastern Europe, once primarily communist, has also gained in importance, both as a marketplace and as a producer. Such multinational corporations as Daewoo, Nestlé, General Motors, and ABB Asea Brown Boveri have all set up operations in Poland. Ford, General Motors, Suzuki, and Volkswagen have all built new factories in Hungary. On the other hand, governmental instability has hampered development in parts of Russia, Bulgaria, Albania, Romania, and other countries.

Pacific Asia Pacific Asia is generally agreed to consist of Japan, China, Thailand, Malaysia, Singapore, Indonesia, South Korea, Taiwan, the Philippines, and Australia. Fueled by strong entries in the automobile, electronics, and banking industries, the economies of these countries grew rapidly in the 1970s and 1980s. After a currency crisis in the late 1990s that slowed growth in virtually every country of the region, Pacific

The growth in international commerce has led to the emergence of several major marketplaces. Much of the international commerce in these marketplaces, in turn, is generally managed from major cities. Traditional centers of international commerce include New York, London, Paris, Brussels, and Tokyo. In recent years, though, cities like Shanghai, Beijing, Hong Kong, Dubai, Vancouver, Bangalore, and Kuala Lumpur have taken on increased importance. For example, international business now defines the glittering skyline of Shanghai.

Asia is showing clear signs of revitalization. This is especially true of Japan, which—led by firms such as Toyota, Toshiba, and Nippon Steel—dominates the region. South Korea (home to firms Samsung and Hyundai, among others), Taiwan (owner of Chinese Petroleum and the manufacturing home of many foreign firms), and Hong Kong (a major financial center) are also successful players in the international economy.

China, the world's most densely populated country, has emerged as an important market and now boasts the world's third-largest economy, behind only the European Union and the United States.[4] Although its per-capita income remains low, the sheer number of potential consumers makes it an important market. India, though not part of Pacific Asia, is also rapidly emerging as one of the globe's most important economies.

As in North America and Europe, technology promises to play an increasingly important role in the future of this region. In some parts of Asia, however, poorly developed electronic infrastructures, slower adoption of computers and information technology, and a higher percentage of lower-income consumers hamper the emergence of technology firms.

Trade Agreements and Alliances

Various legal agreements have sparked international trade and shaped the global business environment. Indeed, virtually every nation has formal trade treaties with other nations. A *treaty* is a legal agreement that specifies areas

NORTH AMERICAN FREE TRADE AGREEMENT (NAFTA) agreement to gradually eliminate tariffs and other trade barriers among the United States, Canada, and Mexico

EUROPEAN UNION (EU) organization for economic, social, and security cooperation among European nations

ASSOCIATION OF SOUTHEAST ASIAN NATIONS (ASEAN) organization for economic, political, social, and cultural cooperation among Southeast Asian nations

GENERAL AGREEMENT ON TARIFFS AND TRADE (GATT) international trade agreement to encourage the multilateral reduction or elimination of trade barriers

WORLD TRADE ORGANIZATION (WTO) organization through which member nations negotiate trading agreements and resolve disputes about trade policies and practices

in which nations will cooperate with one another. Among the most significant treaties is the *North American Free Trade Agreement*. The *European Union*, the *Association of Southeast Asian Nations*, and the *World Trade Organization*, all governed by treaties, are also instrumental in promoting international business activity.

North American Free Trade Agreement The **North American Free Trade Agreement (NAFTA)** removes most tariffs and other trade barriers among the United States, Canada, and Mexico and includes agreements on environmental issues and labor abuses.

Most observers agree that NAFTA is achieving its basic purpose—to create a more active North American market. It has created several hundred thousand new jobs, although this number is smaller than NAFTA proponents had hoped. One thing is clear, though—the flood of U.S. jobs lost to Mexico predicted by NAFTA critics, especially labor unions, has not occurred.

The European Union The **European Union (EU)** includes most European nations, as shown in Figure 4.1. These nations have eliminated most quotas and set uniform tariff levels on products imported and exported within their group. In 1992, virtually all internal trade barriers went down, making the EU the largest free marketplace in the world.

The Association of Southeast Asian Nations (ASEAN) The **Association of Southeast Asian Nations (ASEAN)** was founded in 1967 as an organization for economic, political, social, and cultural cooperation. In 1995, Vietnam became the group's first Communist member. Figure 4.2 shows a map of the ASEAN countries. Because of its relative size, ASEAN does not have the same global economic significance as NAFTA and the EU.

The World Trade Organization The **General Agreement on Tariffs and Trade (GATT)** was signed in 1947. Its purpose was to reduce or eliminate trade barriers, such as tariffs and quotas. It did so by encouraging nations to protect domestic industries within agreed-upon limits and to engage in multilateral negotiations. The GATT proved to be relatively successful. So, to further promote globalization, most of the world's countries joined to create the **World Trade Organization (WTO)**, which began on January 1, 1995. (The GATT is the actual treaty that governs the WTO). The 152 member countries are required to open markets to international trade, and the WTO is empowered to pursue three goals:[6]

1 Promote trade by encouraging members to adopt fair trade practices.

2 Reduce trade barriers by promoting multilateral negotiations.

3 Establish fair procedures for resolving disputes among members.

Import-Export Balances

Although international trade has many advantages, it can also pose problems if a country's imports and exports don't maintain an acceptable balance. Table 4.1

Figure 4.1
The Nations of the European Union[5]

Figure 4.2
The Nations of the Association of Southeast Asian Nations (ASEAN)[7]

Trade Deficits and Surpluses When a country's imports exceed its exports—that is, when it has a negative balance of trade—it suffers a **trade deficit**. When exports exceed imports, the nation enjoys a **trade surplus**. Several factors, such as general economic conditions and the effect of trade agreements, influence trade deficits and surpluses. For example, higher domestic costs, greater international competition, and continuing economic problems among some of its regional trading partners have slowed the tremendous growth in exports that Japan once enjoyed. But rising prosperity in China and India has led to strong increases in both exports from and imports to those countries.

BALANCE OF TRADE economic value of all products a country exports minus the economic value of all products it imports

TRADE DEFICIT situation in which a country's imports exceed its exports, creating a negative balance of trade

TRADE SURPLUS situation in which a country's exports exceed its imports, creating a positive balance of trade

lists the United States' major trading partners. The top part of the table shows the ten largest markets for exported goods from the United States, while the bottom part of the table shows the ten largest markets that import goods into the United States. Note that nine of the ten countries on both lists are the same.

In deciding whether an overall balance exists, economists use two measures: *balance of trade* and *balance of payments*.

Balance of Trade A country's **balance of trade** is the total economic value of all the products that it exports minus the economic value of all the products that it imports. A *positive balance of trade* results when a country exports (sells to other countries) more than it imports (buys from other countries). A *negative balance of trade* results when a country imports more than it exports.

Relatively small trade imbalances are common and are unimportant. Large imbalances, however, are another matter. The biggest concern about trade balances involves the flow of currency. When U.S. consumers and businesses buy foreign products, dollars flow from the United States to other countries; when U.S. businesses are selling to foreign consumers and businesses, dollars flow back into the United States. A large negative balance of trade means that many dollars are controlled by interests outside the United States.

Table 4.1   **The Major Trading Partners of the United States[8]**

Top 10 U.S. Export Markets for Goods		
Rank	**Country**	**2007 Exports (in $ billions)**
1	Canada	248.9
2	Mexico	136.9
3	China	65.2
4	Japan	62.7
5	United Kingdom	50.3
6	Federal Republic of Germany	49.7
7	South Korea	34.7
8	Netherlands	33.0
9	France	27.4
10	Taiwan	26.4
Top 10 U.S. Import Suppliers for Goods		
Rank	**Country**	**2007 Imports (in $ billions)**
1	China	321.5
2	Canada	313.1
3	Mexico	210.8
4	Japan	145.5
5	Federal Republic of Germany	94.4
6	United Kingdom	56.9
7	South Korea	47.6
8	France	41.6
9	Venezuela	39.9
10	Taiwan	38.3

BALANCE OF PAYMENTS
the flow of all money into
or out of a country

Figures 4.3 and 4.4 highlight two series of events: (1) recent trends in U.S. exports and imports and (2) the resulting trade deficit. As Figure 4.3 shows, both U.S. imports and U.S. exports have, with minor variations, increased over the past eight years—a trend that's projected to continue.

Trade deficits between 2000 and 2007 are shown in Figure 4.4. There was a deficit in each of these eight years because more money flowed out to pay for foreign imports than flowed in to pay for U.S. exports. For example, in 2007, the United States exported $1,621.8 billion in goods and services and imported $2,333.4 billion in goods and services. Because imports exceeded exports, the United States had a *trade deficit* of $711.6 billion (the difference between exports and imports).

Balance of Payments The **balance of payments** refers to the flow of *money* into or out of a country. The money that a country pays for imports and receives for exports—its balance of trade—accounts for much of its balance of payments. Other financial exchanges are also factors. Money spent by tourists in a country, money spent by a country on foreign-aid programs, and money exchanged by buying and selling currency on international money markets affect the balance of payments.

For instance, suppose that the United States has a negative balance of trade of $1 million. Now, suppose that this year, U.S. citizens travel abroad as tourists and spend a total of $200,000 in other countries. This amount gets added to the balance of trade to form the balance of payments, which is now a negative $1.2 million dollars. Now, further suppose that tourists from other countries come to the United States and spend the equivalent of $300,000 while they are here.

This has the effect of reducing the negative balance of payments to $900,000. Then, further suppose that the United States then sends $600,000 in aid to help the victims of a tsunami-ravaged country in Asia. Because this represents additional dollars leaving the United States, the balance of payments is now a negative $1.5 million.

For many years, the United States enjoyed a positive balance of payments. Recently, however, the overall balance has become negative.

Figure 4.3
U.S. Imports and Exports[9]

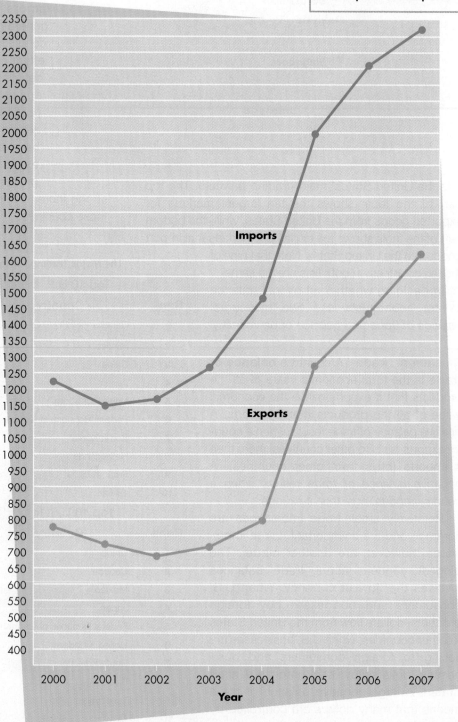

Exchange Rates

The balance of imports and exports between two countries is affected by the rate of exchange between their currencies. An **exchange rate** is the rate at which the currency of one nation can be exchanged for that of another. The exchange rate between U.S. dollars and British pounds has been hovering around $2 to £1. This means that it costs £1 to "buy" $2 or $1 to "buy" £0.5. Stated differently, £1 and $2 have the same purchasing power, or £1 = $2.

At the end of World War II, the major nations of the world agreed to set *fixed exchange rates*. The value of any country's currency relative to that of another would remain constant. The goal was to allow the global economy to stabilize. Today, however, *floating exchange rates* are the norm, and the value of one country's currency relative to that of another varies with market conditions. For example, when many British citizens want to spend pounds to buy U.S. dollars (or goods), the value of the dollar relative to the pound increases. Demand for the dollar is high, and a currency is strong when demand for it is high. It's also strong when there's high demand for the goods manufactured with that currency. On a daily basis, exchange rates fluctuate very little. Significant variations usually occur over longer time spans.

Exchange-rate fluctuation can have an important impact on balance of trade. Suppose you want to buy some English tea for £10 per box. At an exchange rate of $2 to £1, a box will cost you $20 (£10 × 2 = 20). But what if the pound is weaker? At an exchange rate of, say, $1.25 to £1, the same box would cost you only $12.50 (£10 × 1.25 = 12.50). If the dollar is strong in relation to the pound, the prices of all United States-made products will rise in England, and the prices of all English-made products will fall in the United States. The English would buy fewer U.S. products, and Americans would be prompted to spend more on English-made products. The result would probably be a U.S. trade deficit with England.

One of the most significant developments in foreign exchange has been the introduction of the **euro**—the common currency of the European Union. The euro was officially introduced in 2002 and has replaced other currencies, such as the German Deutsche Mark and the French franc. The EU anticipates that the euro will become as important as the dollar and the yen in international commerce. When the euro was first introduced, its value was pegged as being equivalent to the dollar: €1 = $1. But because the dollar has been relatively weak in recent years, its value has eroded relative to that of the euro. In June 2008, for example, $1 was worth only about €0.65.

Companies with international operations must watch exchange-rate fluctuations closely because changes affect overseas demand for their products and can be a major factor in competition. In general, when the value of a country's currency rises—becomes stronger—companies based there find it harder to export products to foreign markets and easier for foreign companies to enter local markets. It also makes it

> **EXCHANGE RATE** rate at which the currency of one nation can be exchanged for the currency of another nation
>
> **EURO** a common currency shared among most of the members of the European Union (excluding Denmark, Sweden, and the United Kingdom)

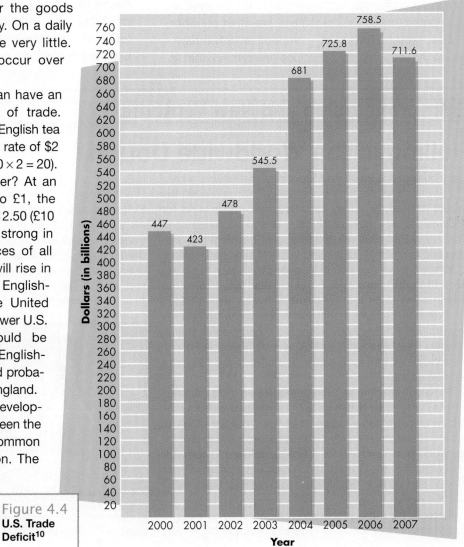

Figure 4.4
U.S. Trade Deficit[10]

Figure 4.5
Going International

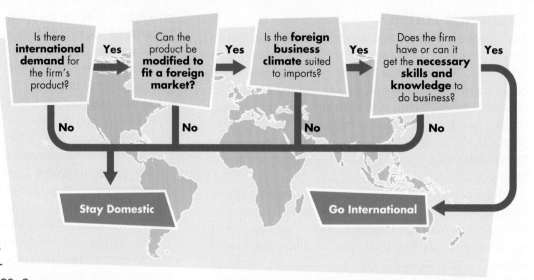

Is there **international demand** for the firm's product? — Yes → Can the product be **modified to fit a foreign market?** — Yes → Is the **foreign business climate** suited to imports? — Yes → Does the firm have or can it get the **necessary skills and knowledge** to do business? — Yes

No — No — No — No

Stay Domestic   **Go International**

more cost-efficient for domestic companies to move operations to lower-cost foreign sites. When the value of a currency declines—becomes weaker—the opposite occurs. As the value of a country's currency falls, its balance of trade usually improves because domestic companies should experience a boost in exports. There should also be less reason for foreign companies to ship products into the domestic market and less reason to establish operations in other countries.

Forms of Competitive Advantage

Before we discuss the fundamental issues involved in international business management, we must consider one last factor: forms of *competitive advantage*. Because no country can produce everything that it needs, countries tend to export what they can produce better or less expensively than other countries and use the proceeds to import what they can't produce as effectively. This principle doesn't fully explain why nations export and import what they do. Such decisions hinge partly on the advantages that a particular country enjoys regarding its abilities to create and/or sell certain products and resources.[11] Economists traditionally focused on absolute and comparative advantage to explain international trade. But because this approach

Entrepreneurship and New Ventures

Rolling in the Worldwide Dough

Is any business more confined to a local market than a bakery? Breads and pastries get stale quickly, and even the largest operations, such as those that make buns for McDonald's, only move products over short distances. But a bakery in Paris has refused to accept geographic limitations and is now selling its famous bread in global markets.

When Lionel Poilâne took over the family business more than 30 years ago, he was determined to return breadmaking to its roots. Poilâne built clay ovens based on sixteenth-century plans and technology, trained his breadmakers in ancient techniques, and began selling old-style dark bread with a thick, chewy, fire-tinged flavor. It quickly became a favorite in Parisian bistros, and demand soared.

To help meet demand, Poilâne built two more bakeries in Paris; today they sell over 15,000 loaves of bread a day. Poilâne also opened a bakery in London, but his efforts to expand to Japan were stymied: Local ordinances prohibited wood-burning ovens, and Poilâne refused to compromise. During the negotiation process, however, he realized that he didn't really *want* to build new bakeries all over the world.

Instead, he turned to modern technology to expand his old-fashioned business. The key was the big FedEx hub at Paris Roissy Charles de Gaulle Airport near Poilâne's largest Paris bakery. After launching a Web site, Poilâne started taking international orders. New orders are packaged as the bread cools and then picked up by FedEx. A quick warm-up in the customer's oven gives it the same taste as it had when it came out of Poilâne's oven. Today, a loaf of bread baked in Paris in the morning can easily be reheated for tomorrow night's dinner in more than 25 countries.[12]

focuses narrowly on such factors as natural resources and labor costs, a more contemporary view of national competitive advantage has emerged.

Absolute Advantage An **absolute advantage** exists when a country can produce something that is cheaper and/or of higher quality than any other country. Saudi oil, Brazilian coffee beans, and Canadian timber come close (because these countries have such abundant supplies of these resources), but examples of true absolute advantage are rare. For example, many experts say that the vineyards of France produce the world's finest wines. But the burgeoning wine business in California demonstrates that producers there can also make very good wine—wines that rival those from France but come in more varieties and at lower prices.

Comparative Advantage A country has a **comparative advantage** in goods that it can produce more efficiently or better than other nations. If businesses in a given country can make computers more efficiently than they can make automobiles, then that nation has a comparative advantage in computer manufacturing.

In general, both absolute and comparative advantages translate into competitive advantage. Brazil, for instance, can produce and market coffee beans knowing full well that there are few other countries with the right mix of climate, terrain, and altitude to enter the coffee bean market. The United States has comparative advantages in the computer industry (because of technological sophistication) and in farming (because of large amounts of fertile land and a temperate climate). South Korea has a comparative advantage in electronics manufacturing because of efficient operations and cheap labor. As a result, U.S. firms export computers and grain to South Korea and import DVD players from South Korea. South Korea can produce food, and the United States can build DVD players, but each nation imports certain products because the other holds a comparative advantage in the relevant industry.

National Competitive Advantage In recent years, a theory of national competitive advantage has become a widely accepted model of why nations engage in international trade.[13] **National competitive advantage** derives from four conditions:

1 *Factor conditions* are the factors of production we discussed in Chapter 1—*labor*, *capital*, *entrepreneurs*, *physical resources*, and *information resources*.

2 *Demand conditions* reflect a large domestic consumer base that promotes strong demand for innovative products.

3 *Related and supporting industries* include strong local or regional suppliers and/or industrial customers.

4 *Strategies*, *structures*, and *rivalries* refer to firms and industries that stress cost reduction, product quality, higher productivity, and innovative products.

When all attributes of national competitive advantage exist, a nation is likely to be heavily involved in international business. Japan, for instance, has an abundance of natural resources and strong domestic demand for automobiles. Its carmakers have well-oiled supplier networks, and domestic firms have competed intensely with one another for decades. These circumstances explain why Japanese car companies like Toyota and Honda are successful in foreign markets.

ABSOLUTE ADVANTAGE the ability to produce something more efficiently than any other country

COMPARATIVE ADVANTAGE the ability to produce some products more efficiently than others

NATIONAL COMPETITIVE ADVANTAGE international competitive advantage stemming from a combination of factor conditions, demand conditions, related and supporting industries, and firm strategies, structures, and rivalries

International Business Management

Wherever a firm is located, its success depends largely on how well it's managed. International business is so challenging because basic management tasks—planning, organizing, directing, and controlling—are much more difficult when a firm operates in markets scattered around the globe.

Managing means making decisions. In this section, we examine the three basic decisions that a company must make when considering globalization. The first decision is whether to go international at all. Once that decision has been made, managers must decide on the level of international involvement and on the organizational structure that will best meet the firm's global needs.

Going International

As the world economy becomes globalized, more firms are conducting international operations. U.S. firms are aggressively expanding abroad, while foreign companies such as BP and Nestlé continue to expand into foreign markets as well, including the U.S. market. This route, however, isn't appropriate for every company. If you buy and sell fresh fish, you'll find it more profitable to confine your activities to limited geographic areas because storage and transport costs may be too high to make international operations worthwhile. As Figure 4.5 shows, several factors affect the decision to go international.

OUTSOURCING the practice of paying suppliers and distributors to perform certain business processes or to provide needed materials or services

OFFSHORING the practice of outsourcing to foreign countries

EXPORTER firm that distributes and sells products to one or more foreign countries

IMPORTER firm that buys products in foreign markets and then imports them for resale in its home country

INTERNATIONAL FIRM firm that conducts a significant portion of its business in foreign countries

MULTINATIONAL FIRM firm that designs, produces, and markets products in many nations

Gauging International Demand

In considering international expansion, a company must consider whether there is a demand for its products abroad. Products that are successful in one country may be useless in another. Even when there is demand, advertising may still need to be adjusted. Market research and/or the prior market entry of competitors may indicate whether there's an international demand for a firm's products.

Adapting to Customer Needs

If its product is in demand, a firm must decide whether and how to adapt it to meet the special demands of foreign customers. For example, to satisfy local tastes, McDonald's sells wine in France, beer in Germany, and provides some vegetarian sandwiches in India.

Outsourcing and Offshoring

Outsourcing—the practice of paying suppliers and distributors to perform certain business processes or to provide needed materials or services—has become a very popular option for going international. It has become so popular because (1) it helps firms focus on their core activities and avoid getting sidetracked on secondary activities, and (2) it reduces costs by locating certain business functions in areas where relevant costs are low.[14]

The practice of outsourcing to foreign countries is more specifically referred to as **offshoring**. Many companies today contract their manufacturing to low-cost factories in Asia. Similarly, many service call centers today are outsourced to businesses located in India.

Levels of International Involvement

After deciding to go international, a firm must determine the level of its involvement. Several levels are possible: A firm may act as an exporter or importer, organize as an international firm, or (like most of the world's largest industrial firms) operate as a multinational firm.

Exporters and Importers An **exporter** makes products in one country to distribute and sell in others. An **importer** buys products in foreign markets and brings them home for resale. Both conduct most of their business in their home nations. Both entail the lowest level of involvement in international operations, and both are good ways to learn the fine points of global business. Many large firms entered international business as exporters. IBM and Coke, among others, exported to Europe for several years before setting up production sites there.

International Firms As exporters and importers gain experience and grow, many move to the next level of involvement. **International firms** conduct a good deal of their business abroad and may even maintain overseas manufacturing facilities. An international firm may be large, but it's still basically a domestic company with international operations. Hershey, for instance, buys ingredients for its chocolates from several foreign suppliers, but makes all of its products in the United States. Moreover, while it sells its products in approximately 50 other countries, it generates most of its revenues from its domestic market.[15]

Multinational Firms Most **multinational firms**—firms that design, produce, and market products in many nations—such as ExxonMobil, Nestlé, IBM, and Ford, don't think of themselves as having domestic and international divisions. Headquarters locations are almost irrelevant, and planning and decision making are

While Toyota markets five different sport-utility vehicles in the United States, it only sells its two smallest ones at home in Japan—crowded roads, narrow driveways, and scarce parking spaces make larger vehicles impractical.

Table 4.2 The World's Largest Multinationals[17]

Rank	Company	Revenues ($ millions)	Profits ($ millions)
1	Wal-Mart Stores	351,139.0	11,284.0
2	Exxon Mobil	347,254.0	39,500.0
3	Royal Dutch Shell	318,845.0	25,442.0
4	BP	274,316.0	22,000.0
5	General Motors	207,349.0	–1,978.0
6	Toyota Motor	204,746.4	14,055.8
7	Chevron	200,567.0	17,138.0
8	DaimlerChrysler	190,191.4	4,048.8
9	ConocoPhillips	172,451.0	15,550.0
10	Total	168,356.7	14,764.7

INDEPENDENT AGENT foreign individual or organization that agrees to represent an exporter's interests

LICENSING ARRANGEMENT arrangement in which firms choose foreign individuals or organizations to manufacture or market their products in another country

geared to international markets. The world's 10 largest multinationals in 2007 are shown in Table 4.2.

We can't underestimate the economic impact of multinational firms. Consider just the impact of the 500 largest multinationals: In 2007, these 500 firms generated $10.6 trillion in revenues and $645.2 billion in owner profits. They employed tens of millions of people, bought materials and equipment from literally thousands of other firms, and paid billions in taxes.[16] Moreover, their products affected the lives of hundreds of millions of consumers, competitors, investors, and even protestors.

International Organization Structures

Different levels of international involvement entail different kinds of organizational structure. A structure that would help coordinate an exporter's activities would be inadequate for those of a multinational. In this section, we consider the spectrum of organizational strategies, including *independent agents*, *licensing arrangements*, *branch offices*, *strategic alliances*, and *foreign direct investment*.

Independent Agents An **independent agent** is a foreign individual or organization that represents an exporter in foreign markets. Independent agents often act as sales representatives: They sell the exporter's products, collect payment, and make sure that customers are satisfied. They often represent several firms at once and usually don't specialize in a particular product or market.

Licensing Arrangements Companies seeking more involvement may opt for **licensing arrangements**. Firms give foreign individuals or companies exclusive rights (called *licensing agreements*) to manufacture or market their products in that market. In return, the

Since Cold Stone Creamery first went international in 2001, the Arizona-based ice cream seller has awarded franchises to firms in 20 countries, including Mexico, China, and Japan.[18]

exporter receives a fee plus ongoing payments (royalties) that are calculated as a percentage of the license holder's sales. Franchising is an increasingly popular form of licensing. For example, McDonald's and Pizza Hut franchise around the world.

Branch Offices   Instead of developing relationships with foreign agents or licensing companies, a firm may send its own managers to overseas **branch offices**, where the firm has more direct control than it does over agents or license holders. Branch offices also furnish a more visible public presence in foreign countries, and foreign customers tend to feel more secure when there's a local branch office.

Strategic Alliances   In a **strategic alliance**, a company finds a partner in the country in which it wants to do business. Each party agrees to invest resources and capital into a new business or to cooperate in some mutually beneficial way. This new business—the alliance—is owned by the partners, who divide its profits. Such alliances are sometimes called *joint ventures*, but the term *strategic alliance* has arisen because such partnerships are playing increasingly important roles in the strategies of major companies. In many countries, such as Mexico, India, and China, laws make alliances virtually the only way to do international business. Mexico, for example, requires that all foreign firms investing there have local partners.

In addition to easing the way into new markets, alliances give firms greater control over foreign activities than agents and licensees. Alliances also allow firms to benefit from the knowledge and expertise of foreign partners. Microsoft, for example, relies heavily

Say What You Mean

When in Rome...

Venturing into the wide world of global business requires not only knowledge about local people and cultures, but also sensitivity to their ways of doing things. Despite the impact of globalization, local culture is extremely important when it comes to the way business is conducted in different places. Even the largest multinationals adapt their methods to the cultural conditions that prevail in host countries. The more readily you accept the need to adapt, the more likely you'll be able to thrive in the global business community. For example:

■ In Japan, the word *yes* is often used to mean *I understand*. If a U.S. businesswoman indicates that she wishes her Japanese supplier to lower prices and he responds by saying "Yes," he may mean, "I understand that you want me to lower prices," regardless of whether he intends to do so.

■ We've all been raised with certain cultural values that govern how we interact with other people. We must remember that people in other cultures do not necessarily share our values. Many Latin American cultures, for instance, do not place a high value on punctuality. Starting a meeting an hour or more "late" may actually be a common practice in such countries.

■ Cultural differences, though challenging, provide opportunities to improve interactions of all kinds, not just business transactions. Exchanging gifts among business partners is common practice in Japan, so Westerners who embrace this practice when doing business in Japan will build stronger relationships than those who do not.

Finally, language differences can also be a critical part of culture. KFC's classic blunder of not realizing that its famed "Finger-lickin' good" slogan translated to "Eat your fingers off" in Chinese led to serious setbacks when it opened its first restaurants in China.

on alliances as it expands into international markets. This approach has helped the firm learn the intricacies of doing business in China and India, two of the hardest emerging markets to crack.

Foreign Direct Investment **Foreign direct investment (FDI)** involves buying or establishing tangible assets in another country. Dell Computer, for example, has built assembly plants in Europe and China. Volkswagen has built a factory in Brazil. Each of these activities represents FDI by a firm in another country. Ford's purchase of Volvo, a Swedish company, is another kind of FDI, as is the acquisition of both Ben & Jerry's and SlimFast by the Dutch company Unilever.

Barriers to International Trade

Whether a business is truly multinational or sells to only a few foreign markets, several factors will affect its international operations. Success in foreign markets will depend largely on the ways it responds to *social*, *economic*, *legal*, and *political barriers* to international trade.

Social and Cultural Differences

Any firm planning to conduct business abroad must understand the social and cultural differences between host country and home country. Some differences are obvious. You must, for example, consider language factors when adjusting packaging, signs, and logos. Pepsi is the same product in Seattle and Moscow—except for the lettering on the bottle.

A wide range of subtle value differences can also affect operations. For example, many Europeans shop daily for groceries. To U.S. consumers accustomed to weekly supermarket trips, the European pattern may seem like a waste of time. For many Europeans, however, shopping is not just a matter of buying food; it's also an outlet for meeting friends and exchanging political views. Consider the implications of this difference for U.S. firms selling food and food-related products in European countries where gigantic American supermarkets are not the norm.

Economic Differences

Although cultural differences are often subtle, economic differences can be fairly pronounced. As we discussed in Chapter 1, in dealing with mixed market economies like those of France and Sweden, firms must know when—and to what extent—the government is involved in a given industry. The French government, for instance, is heavily involved in all aspects of airplane design and manufacturing. The impact of economic differences can be even greater in planned economies like those of China and Vietnam, where the government owns and operates many factors of production.

Legal and Political Differences

Governments can affect international business in many ways. They can set conditions for doing business within their borders and even prohibit doing business altogether. They can control the flow of capital and use tax legislation to discourage or encourage activity in a given industry. They can even confiscate the property of foreign-owned companies. In this section, we discuss some of the more common legal and political issues in international business: *quotas*, *tariffs*, and *subsidies*; *local content laws*; and *business practice laws*.

Quotas, Tariffs, and Subsidies Even free market economies, such as the United States, have some quotas and/or tariffs, both of which affect prices and quantities of foreign-made products. A **quota** restricts the number of products of a certain type that can be imported and, by reducing supply, raises the prices of those imports. Better terms are often given to friendly trading partners, and quotas are typically adjusted to protect domestic producers.

The ultimate quota is an **embargo**: a government order forbidding exportation and/or importation of a particular product—or even all products—from a specific country. Many nations control bacteria and disease by banning certain agricultural products. Because the United States has an embargo against Cuba, American firms can't invest in their Cuban counterparts, and Cuban products can't legally be sold on American markets.

Tariffs are taxes on imported products. They raise the prices of imports by making consumers pay not only for the products but also for tariff fees. Tariffs take two forms. *Revenue tariffs* are imposed to raise money for governments, but most tariffs, called *protectionist tariffs*, are meant to discourage particular imports.

Quotas and tariffs are imposed for numerous reasons. The U.S. government aids domestic automakers

FOREIGN DIRECT INVESTMENT (FDI) arrangement in which a firm buys or establishes tangible assets in another country

QUOTA restriction on the number of products of a certain type that can be imported into a country

EMBARGO government order banning exportation and/or importation of a particular product or all products from a particular country

TARIFF tax levied on imported products

by restricting the number of Japanese cars imported into this country. Because of national security concerns, we limit the export of technology (for example, computer and nuclear technology to China). The United States isn't the only country that uses tariffs and quotas. To protect domestic firms, Italy imposes high tariffs on electronic goods. As a result, CD players are prohibitively expensive.

A **subsidy** is a government payment to help a domestic business compete with foreign firms. They're actually indirect tariffs that lower the prices of domestic goods rather than raise the prices of foreign goods. For example, many European governments subsidize farmers to help them compete against U.S. grain imports.

The Protectionism Debate   In the United States, **protectionism**—the practice of protecting domestic business at the expense of free market competition—is controversial. Supporters argue that tariffs and quotas

protect domestic firms and jobs as well as shelter new industries until they're able to compete internationally. They contend that we need such measures to counter steps taken by other nations. Other advocates justify protectionism in the name of national security. A nation, they argue, must be able to produce efficiently the goods needed for survival in case of war. Thus, the U.S. government requires the Air Force to buy planes only from U.S. manufacturers.

Critics cite protectionism as a source of friction between nations. They also charge that it drives up prices by reducing competition. They maintain that although jobs in some industries would be lost as a result of free trade, jobs in other industries (for example, electronics and automobiles) would be created if all nations abandoned protectionist tactics.

Protectionism sometimes takes on almost comic proportions. Neither Europe nor the United States grows bananas, but both European and U.S. firms buy and sell bananas in foreign markets. Problems arose when the EU put a quota on bananas imported from Latin America—a market dominated by two U.S. firms, Chiquita and Dole—in order to help firms based in current and former European colonies in the Caribbean. To retaliate, the United States imposed a 100-percent tariff on certain luxury products imported from Europe, including Louis Vuitton handbags, Scottish cashmere sweaters, and Parma ham.

Local Content Laws   Many countries, including the United States, have **local content laws**—requirements that products sold in a country be at least partly made there. Firms seeking to do business in a country must either invest there directly or take on a domestic partner. In this way, some of the profits from doing business

These U.S. customs officials are examining a shipment of goods being imported into the country. Their job is to make sure that no banned items are being shipped and the shipper pays the appropriate tariff that has been levied on the goods.

in a foreign country stay there rather than flow to another nation.

Business Practice Laws   Many businesses entering new markets encounter problems in complying with stringent regulations and bureaucratic obstacles. Such practices are affected by the **business practice laws** by which host countries govern business practices within their jurisdictions. For example, German law required Wal-Mart to buy existing retailers rather than open brand-new stores and to stop refunding price differences on items sold for less by other stores. Of course, cooperating with foreign regulations does not guarantee global success—in 2006 Wal-Mart acknowledged its German stores were losing too much money to remain competitive and pulled out of Germany completely.[19]

Cartels and Dumping   Sometimes, a legal—even an accepted—practice in one country is illegal in another. In some South American countries, for example, it is legal to bribe business and government officials. The existence of **cartels**—associations of producers that control supply and prices—gives tremendous power to some nations, such as those belonging to the Organization of Petroleum Exporting Countries (OPEC). U.S. law forbids both bribery and cartels.

Finally, many (but not all) countries forbid **dumping**—selling a product abroad for less than the cost of production at home. U.S. antidumping legislation sets two conditions for determining whether dumping is being practiced:

1. Products are being priced at "less than fair value."
2. The result unfairly harms domestic industry.

For additional topics related to this material and end-of-chapter exercises and practices, please visit www.mybizlab.com.

Questions for Review

1. How does the balance of trade differ from the balance of payments?
2. What are the three possible levels of involvement in international business? Give examples of each.
3. How does a country's economic system affect the decisions of foreign firms interested in doing business there?
4. What aspects of the culture in your state or region would be of particular interest to a foreign firm thinking about locating there?

Questions for Analysis

5. List all the major items in your bedroom, including furnishings. Try to identify the country in which each item was made. Offer possible reasons why a nation might have a comparative advantage in producing a given good.
6. Suppose that you're the manager of a small firm seeking to enter the international arena. What basic information would you need concerning the market that you're thinking of entering?
7. Do you support protectionist tariffs for the United States? If so, in what instances and for what reasons? If not, why not?
8. Do you think that a firm operating internationally is better advised to adopt a single standard of ethical conduct or to adapt to local conditions? Under what kinds of conditions might each approach be preferable?

Application Exercises

9. Interview the manager of a local firm that does at least some business internationally. Why did the company decide to go international? Describe the level of the firm's international involvement and the organizational structure(s) it uses for international operations.
10. Select a product familiar to you. Using library reference works to gain some insight into the culture of India, identify the problems that might arise in trying to market this product to Indian consumers.

chapter 5

Business Management

After reading this chapter, you should be able to:

1 Describe the nature of management and identify the four basic functions that constitute the management process.

2 Identify different types of managers likely to be found in an organization by level and area.

3 Describe the basic skills required of managers.

4 Explain the importance of strategic management and effective goal setting in organizational success.

5 Discuss contingency planning and crisis management in today's business world.

6 Describe the development and explain the importance of corporate culture.

The Business of Bagging Customers

Fickle customers and rapid changes make planning difficult in the high-end fashion industry. Most fashion designers have adopted a design-driven business model in which the designer dictates style to the customers. Coach, however, has taken a different approach. The company asks customers what they want and then provides it.

Coach strives both to attract high-end fashion's elite customers and to remain an affordable luxury for customers who must save for a $300 handbag. But how to find and maintain that delicate balance? According to CEO Lew Frankfort, "To be successful you need to live your business. You have to understand it organically and thoroughly."

Coach's business model is centered on planning and forecasting. Frankfort has introduced many new analytical tools for tracking market trends, evaluating effectiveness, and managing risk. The firm's leaders look at sales data for each store and product type on a daily basis. But customer research remains the cornerstone of their planning. The company spends millions of dollars per year on surveys and other forms of market research, including one-on-one interviews with customers from locations around the world, to quiz them on everything from appearance and quality to the correct length for a shoulder strap.

The emphasis on research also extends to new products, which are first shown to selected buyers in 12 worldwide markets to gauge initial customer reaction. An initial demand forecast is then made, and 6 months before introduction the products are tested in another 12 markets. At launch time, sales are monitored closely and adjustments made quickly. For example, an unexpected spike in sales led managers to discover an increase in purchases made by Hispanic customers. Within a week, Coach had moved up the opening date of a South Miami store and begun advertising in Spanish for the first time.[1]

What's in It for Me?

Lew Frankfort is clearly an effective manager, and he understands how to carry out his responsibilities to help Coach continue to grow and prosper. In this chapter, we discuss these responsibilities and explore the relationship between effective management and organizational success. Along the way, we'll consider basic management skills and functions, including the need to establish and maintain a corporate culture. Understanding these things will help you better carry out various management responsibilities yourself and will allow you to assess and appreciate the quality of management in various companies.

Who Are Managers?

All corporations depend on effective management. Whether they run a multibillion-dollar business like Coach or a small local fashion boutique, managers perform many of the same functions and have many of the same responsibilities. These include analyzing their competitive environments and planning, organizing, directing, and controlling day-to-day operations. Ultimately, they are responsible for the performance and effectiveness of the teams, divisions, or companies that they head.

Although our focus is on managers in business settings, remember that the principles of management apply to all kinds of organizations. Managers work in charities, churches, social organizations, educational institutions, and government agencies. The prime minister of Canada, curators at the Museum of Modern Art, the dean of your college, and the chief administrator of your local hospital are all managers. Remember, too, that managers bring to small organizations much the same kinds of skills—the ability to make decisions and respond to a variety of challenges—that they bring to large ones. Regardless of the nature and size of an organization, managers are among its most important resources.

The Management Process

Management is the process of planning, organizing, leading, and controlling an organization's financial, physical, human, and information resources to achieve its goals. Managers oversee the use of all these resources in their respective firms. All aspects of a manager's job are interrelated. Any given manager is likely to be engaged in each of these activities during the course of any given day.

Planning

Determining what the organization needs to do and how best to get it done requires planning. **Planning** has three main components:

- Determine goals

- Develop a comprehensive *strategy* for achieving those goals

- Design *tactical and operational plans* for implementing the strategy

When Yahoo! was created, for example, its management set a strategic goal of becoming a top firm in the then-emerging market for Internet search engines. The company started by assessing the ways in which people actually use the Web and concluded that users wanted to be able to satisfy a wide array of needs by going to as few sites as possible to find what they were looking for. The goal of partnering with other

(b)

(a)

(c)

As top managers, (a) Marjorie Scardino (CEO of Pearson PLC), (b) Kenneth Chenault (CEO of American Express), and (c) James Sinegal (co-founder and CEO of Costco) are important resources for their companies. In particular, they set the strategic direction for their companies and provide leadership to others. They are also accountable to shareholders, employees, customers, and other key constituents for the performance and effectiveness of their businesses.

companies, whose resources could be accessed through Yahoo!'s comprehensive search engine, emerged as one set of *tactical plans* for moving forward.

Yahoo! managers then began fashioning alliances with such diverse partners as Reuters, Standard & Poor's, and the Associated Press (for news coverage), RE/MAX (for real estate information), and a wide array of information providers specializing in sports, weather, entertainment, shopping, and travel. The creation of individual partnership agreements with each of these partners represents a form of *operational planning*.

Organizing

Managers must also organize people and resources. Some businesses prepare charts that diagram the relationships among the various jobs within the company. These *organization charts* help everyone understand his or her role in the company. Some businesses go so far as to post their organization charts on an office wall. But in most larger businesses, roles and relationships, while important, may be too complex to draw as a simple box-and-line diagram.

Consider the example of Hewlett-Packard (HP). Once one of the leading high-tech firms in the world, HP began to lose some of its luster a few years ago. Ironically, one of the major reasons for its slide could be traced back to what had once been a major strength. Specifically, HP had long prided itself on being little more than a corporate confederation of individual businesses. Sometimes, these businesses even ended up competing among themselves. This approach had been beneficial for much of the firm's history: It was easier for each business to make its own decisions quickly and efficiently, and the competition kept each unit on its toes. By the late 1990s, however, problems had become apparent, and no one could quite figure out what was going on.

Enter Ann Livermore, then head of the firm's software and services business. Livermore realized that the decentralized structure of loosely affiliated businesses, though it had served well in the past, was now holding the firm back. To regain its competitive edge, HP needed an integrated, organization-wide strategy. Livermore led the charge to create one organization united behind one strategic plan. Eventually, a new team of top managers was handed control of the company, and every major component of the firm's structure was reorganized. As a result, the firm appears to be back on solid footing and recently passed chief rival IBM in total revenues.[2] The process that was used to revive HP—determining the best way to arrange a business's resources and activities into a coherent structure—is called **organizing**. We explore organizing in more detail in Chapter 6.

Leading

Managers have the power to give orders and demand results. Leading, however, involves more complex activities. When **leading**, a manager works to guide and motivate employees to meet the firm's objectives. Legendary management figures like Walt Disney, Sam Walton (of Wal-Mart), and Herb Kelleher (of Southwest Airlines) had the capacity to unite their employees in a clear and targeted manner and motivate them to work in the best interests of their employers. Their employees respected them, trusted them, and believed that by working together, both the firm and themselves as individuals would benefit.

Other managers have been noticeably lacking in their ability to lead others. One of the most glaring examples in recent years resulted from Hurricane Katrina, when many of the top managers at the Federal Emergency

Since 2000, Netflix CEO Reed Hastings has spent millions of dollars promoting charter schools and other educational reforms in an effort to break up what he calls "the last big government monopoly in America," the public school system. For Hastings, charter schools place the power to lead back in the hands of the teachers. With "more freedom to express their craft," he argues, "the innovators, the innovative teachers, are drawn to these schools."[3]

Management Agency (FEMA) came under fire for their poor leadership and decision making that contributed to the loss of over 1,800 lives and $80 billion in damages.[4] We discuss leadership and decision making more fully in Chapter 9.

Controlling

Controlling is the process of monitoring a firm's performance to make sure that it is meeting its goals. All CEOs must pay close attention to costs and performance. Managers at Continental Airlines, for example, focus almost relentlessly on numerous indicators of performance that they can constantly measure and adjust. As a result, no single element of the firm's performance can slip too far before it's noticed and fixed.

Figure 5.1 illustrates the control process that begins when management establishes standards, often for financial performance. If, for example, a company sets a goal of increasing its sales by 20 percent over the next 10 years, an appropriate standard to assess progress toward the 20-percent goal might be an increase of about 2 percent a year. Managers then measure actual performance each year against standards. If the two amounts agree, the organization continues along its present course. If they vary significantly, however, one or the other needs adjustment.

Control can also show where performance is running better than expected and can serve as a basis for providing rewards or reducing costs. For example, after the distributor of the surprise 2005 hit movie *March of the Penguins* saw how popular the movie was becoming, the firm was able to increase advertising and distribution even more, turning the niche movie into a major commercial success.

Types of Managers
• •

Although all managers plan, organize, lead, and control, not all managers have the same degree of responsibility for these activities. It is helpful to classify managers according to levels and areas of responsibility.

Levels of Management

As Table 5.1 illustrates, there are three basic levels of management: **top managers**, who are responsible for a firm's overall performance and effectiveness; **middle managers**, who implement the strategies and work toward the goals set by top managers; and **first-line managers**, who supervise the work of employees. Most firms have more middle managers than top managers and more first-line managers than middle managers. Both the power of managers and the complexity of their duties increase as they move up the ladder.

Areas of Management

In any large company, top, middle, and first-line managers work in a variety of areas, including human resources, operations, marketing, information, and finance.

Human Resource Managers   Most companies have *human resource managers* who hire and train employees, evaluate performance, and determine compensation. At large firms, separate departments deal with recruiting and hiring, wage and salary levels, and labor relations. A smaller firm may have a single department— or a single person—responsible for all human resource activities. (We discuss some key issues in human resource management in Chapter 10.)

Operations Managers   As we will see in Chapter 7, the term *operations* refers to the systems by which a firm produces goods and services. Among other duties, *operations managers* are responsible for production, inventory, and quality control. They may include *vice*

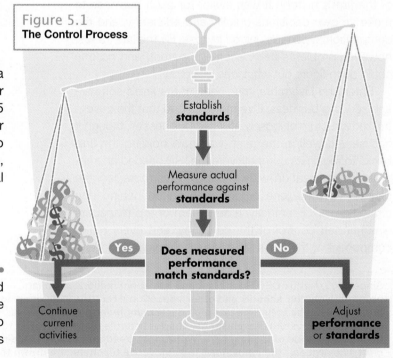

Figure 5.1
The Control Process

Establish **standards**

Measure actual performance against **standards**

Yes — **Does measured performance match standards?** — No

Continue current activities

Adjust **performance** or **standards**

Table 5.1 The Three Levels of Management

Levels	Examples	Responsibilities
Top Managers	president, vice president, treasurer, chief executive officer (CEO), chief financial officer (CFO)	• Responsible for the overall performance and effectiveness of the firm • Set general policies, formulate strategies, and approve all significant decisions • Represent the company in dealings with other firms and with government bodies
Middle Managers	plant manager, operations manager, division manager, regional sales manager	• Responsible for implementing the strategies and working toward the goals set by top managers
First-Line Managers	supervisor, office manager, project manager, group leader, sales manager	• Responsible for supervising the work of employees who report to them • Ensure employees understand and are properly trained in company policies and procedures

presidents for operations (top managers), *plant managers* (middle managers), and *production supervisors* (first-line managers).

Marketing Managers As we will see in Chapter 11, marketing encompasses the development, pricing, promotion, and distribution of goods and services. *Marketing managers* are responsible for getting products from producers to consumers. Firms that manufacture consumer products, such as Procter & Gamble, Coca-Cola, and Levi Strauss, often have large numbers of marketing managers at several levels, including a *vice president for marketing* (top manager), *regional marketing managers* (middle managers), and *district sales managers* (first-line managers).

Information Managers Occupying a fairly new managerial position in many firms, *information managers* design and implement systems to gather, organize, and distribute information. Some firms have a top-management position for a *chief information officer* (*CIO*). Middle managers help design information systems for divisions or plants. Computer systems managers within smaller businesses are usually first-line managers. We'll discuss information management in more detail in Chapter 13.

Financial Managers Nearly every company has *financial managers* to plan and oversee its accounting functions and

financial resources. Levels of financial management may include *CFO* or *vice president for finance* (top manager), a *division controller* (middle manager), and an *accounting supervisor* (first-line manager). We'll discuss financial management in more detail in Chapters 14 and 15.

Other Managers Some firms also employ other specialized managers. Many companies, for example, have public relations managers. Chemical and pharmaceutical companies such as Monsanto and Merck have research and development managers.

Basic Management Skills

Effective managers must develop *technical*, *human relations*, *conceptual*, *decision-making*, and *time management skills*.

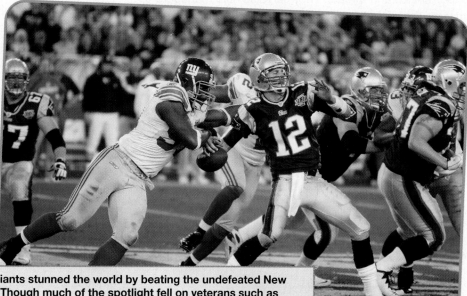

On February 3, 2008, the New York Giants stunned the world by beating the undefeated New England Patriots in Super Bowl XLII. Though much of the spotlight fell on veterans such as quarterback Eli Manning and defensive end Michael Strahan, a major reason for the Giants' victory was the stellar draft engineered the previous spring by first-year general manager Jerry Reese. All eight players drafted by Reese made the team and contributed during its playoff run.

Technical Skills

The skills needed to perform specialized tasks are called **technical skills**. Technical skills are especially important for first-line managers. Many of these managers spend considerable time helping employees solve work-related problems, training them in more efficient procedures, and monitoring performance.

Human Relations Skills

Human relations skills allow managers to understand and communicate with other people. A manager with poor human relations skills may have trouble getting along with subordinates, cause valuable employees to quit or transfer, and contribute to poor morale. Although human relations skills are important at all levels, they are probably most important for middle managers, who must often act as bridges between top managers, first-line managers, and managers from other areas of the organization.

Conceptual Skills

Conceptual skills refer to a person's ability to think in the abstract, to diagnose and analyze different situations, and to see beyond the present situation. Conceptual skills help managers recognize new market opportunities and threats. They can also help managers analyze the probable outcomes of their decisions. The need for conceptual skills differs at various management levels. Top managers depend most on conceptual skills, first-line managers least.

"I like to think of myself as a nice guy. Naturally, sometimes you have to step on a few faces."

Decision-Making Skills

Decision-making skills include the ability to define problems and to select the best course of action. These skills involve gathering facts, identifying solutions, evaluating alternatives, and implementing the chosen alternative. Periodically following up on and evaluating the effectiveness of the choice are also part of the decision-making process. We'll discuss decision making more fully in Chapter 9.

Time Management Skills

Time management skills refer to the productive use that managers make of their time. To manage time effectively, managers must address four leading causes of wasted time:

1. *Paperwork.* Some managers spend too much time deciding what to do with letters and reports. Most documents of this sort are routine and can be handled quickly. Managers must learn to recognize those documents that require more attention.

2. *Telephone calls.* Experts estimate that the telephone interrupts managers every five minutes. To manage this time more effectively, experts suggest having an assistant screen all calls and setting aside a certain block of time each day to return the important ones. Unfortunately, the explosive use of cell phones seems to be making this problem even worse for many managers.

3. *Meetings.* Many managers spend as much as four hours a day in meetings. To help keep this time productive, the person handling the meeting should specify a clear agenda, start on time, keep everyone focused on the agenda, and end on time.

4. *E-mail.* Increasingly, managers are relying heavily on e-mail and other forms of electronic communication. Time is wasted when managers have to sort through spam and a variety of electronic folders, in-boxes, and archives.

Management Skills for the Twenty-first Century

Although the skills discussed in this chapter have long been important parts of every successful manager's career, new skill requirements continue to emerge. Today, most experts point to the growing importance of skills involving *global management* and *technology*.

Global Management Skills Tomorrow's managers must equip themselves with the special tools, techniques, and skills needed to compete in a global environment. They will need to understand foreign markets, cultural differences, and the motives and practices of foreign rivals. They also need to understand how to collaborate with others around the world on a real-time basis. In the past, most U.S. businesses hired local managers to run their operations in the various countries in which they operated. More recently, however, the trend has been to transfer U.S. managers to foreign locations. This practice helps firms transfer their corporate cultures to foreign operations and better prepares managers for international competition as they advance within the organization. The top management teams of large corporations today are also likely to include directors from other countries.

Management and Technology Skills Another significant issue facing tomorrow's managers is technology, especially as it relates to communication. New forms of technology have added to a manager's ability to process information while simultaneously making it even more important to organize and interpret an ever-increasing wealth of input.

Technology has also begun to change the way the interaction of managers shapes corporate structures. Information now flows through elaborate computer networks to reach employees, clients, and customers simultaneously. As a result, decisions are made quicker, and more people are directly involved. E-mail, videoconferencing, and other forms of communication are breaking down bureaucracies, and the decision-making process is benefiting from group building and teamwork. We discuss the effects technology has on business in more detail in Chapter 13.

Strategic Management: Setting Goals and Formulating Strategy

• • • • • • • • • • • • • • • • • •

Strategic management is the process of helping an organization maintain an effective alignment with its environment. For instance, if a firm's business environment is heading toward fiercer competition, the business may need to start cutting its costs and developing more products and services before the competition really starts to heat up. Likewise, if an industry is globalizing, a firm's managers may need to start entering new markets and developing

international partnerships during the early stages of globalization rather than waiting for its full effects.

The starting point in effective strategic management is setting **goals**—objectives that a business hopes and plans to achieve. Setting goals is only the first step for an organization, however. Managers must also make decisions about which actions will and will not achieve company goals. Decisions cannot be made on a problem-by-problem basis or merely to meet needs as they arise. In most companies, decisions are guided by a **strategy**, or broad set of organizational plans for implementing the decisions made for achieving organizational goals.

Setting Business Goals

Goals are performance targets—the means by which organizations and their managers measure success or failure at every level.

Purposes of Goal Setting We can identify four main purposes of organizational goal setting:

1 *Goal setting provides direction and guidance for managers at all levels.* If managers know precisely where the company is headed, there is less potential for error in the different units of the company.

STRATEGIC MANAGEMENT process of helping an organization maintain an effective alignment with its environment

GOAL objective that a business hopes and plans to achieve

STRATEGY broad set of organizational plans for implementing the decisions made for achieving organizational goals

To run its operations in China, MTV needed someone who understood both conservative Chinese television regulators and China's young urban elite. The company chose Li Yifei, a former Baylor University student, UN intern, and tai chi champion. She brought the Chinese MTV awards to state-owned TV, receiving a 7.9 percent rating—a whopping 150 million viewers.

Starbucks, for example, has a goal of increasing capital spending by 15 percent, with all additional expenditures devoted to opening new stores. This goal clearly informs everyone in the firm that expansion into new territories is a high priority.

2 *Goal setting helps firms allocate resources.* Areas that are expected to grow will get first priority. The company allocates more resources to new projects with large sales potential than it allocates to mature products with established but stagnant sales potential.

3 *Goal setting helps to define corporate culture.* For years, the goal at General Electric has been to push each of its divisions to first or second in its industry. The result is a competitive (and often stressful) environment and a corporate culture that rewards success and has little tolerance for failure.

4 *Goal setting helps managers assess performance.* If a unit sets a goal of increasing sales by 10 percent in a given year, managers in that unit who attain or exceed the goal can be rewarded. Units failing to reach the goal will also be compensated accordingly.

Mission Statements Goals differ from company to company, depending on the firm's purpose and mission. Most companies articulate this in their **mission statements**—statements of how they will achieve their purposes in the environments in which they conduct their businesses.

A company's mission is usually easy to identify, at least at a basic level. Starbucks sums up its mission very succinctly: the firm intends to "establish Starbucks as the premier purveyor of the finest coffee in the world while maintaining [its] uncompromising principles as [it] grow[s]." But businesses sometimes have to rethink their strategies and missions as the competitive environment changes. A few years ago, for example, Starbucks announced that Internet marketing and sales were going to become core business initiatives. Managers subsequently realized, however, that this initiative did not fit the firm as well as they first thought. As a result, they scaled back this effort and made a clear recommitment to their existing retail business.

Entrepreneurship and New Ventures

Samuel Adams Makes Headway

In 1984 James Koch was a high-flying management consultant earning over $250,000 a year. To the surprise of his family and friends, however, he quit this job and invested his life's savings to start a business from scratch and go head-to-head with international competitors in a market that had not had a truly successful specialty product in decades. To everyone's even greater surprise, he succeeded.

Koch's company is Boston Beer, and its flagship product is a premium beer called Samuel Adams. James set up shop in an old warehouse in Boston, bought some surplus equipment from a large brewery, and started operations. Because he used only the highest-quality ingredients, Koch had to price his product at about $1 more per case than such premium imports as Heineken. Most distributors, doubting consumers would pay $6 per six-pack for an American beer, refused to carry it. So Koch began selling directly to retailers and bars.

Samuel Adams founder James Koch takes a personal interest in his company's product.

His big break came when Samuel Adams Lager won the consumer preference poll at the Great American Beer Festival. Koch quickly turned this victory into an advertising mantra, proclaiming Samuel Adams "The Best Beer in America." As sales took off, national distributors came calling; to meet surging demand, Koch contracted parts of his brewing operations to facilities in Pittsburgh and Cincinnati.

During the early 1990s, annual sales of Samuel Adams products grew at a rate of over 50 percent and today exceed $340 million. The 2008 purchase of a brewery outside Philadelphia increased the firm's brewing capacity by over 1.6 million barrels per year. Boston Beer even exports Samuel Adams to Germany, where it's become popular among finicky beer drinkers. Koch, who retains controlling interest in the business, still oversees day-to-day brewing operations. Indeed, he claims to have sampled at least one of the firm's products every day.[5]

Management and the Corporate Culture

Just as every individual has a unique personality, every company has a unique identity, a **corporate culture**: the shared experiences, stories, beliefs, and norms that characterize an organization. This culture helps define the work and business climate that exists in an organization.

A strong corporate culture directs employees' efforts and helps everyone work toward the same goals. It also helps newcomers learn accepted behaviors. If financial success is the key to a culture, newcomers quickly learn that they are expected to work long, hard hours and that the "winner" is the one who brings in the most revenue. But if quality of life is more fundamental, newcomers learn that balancing work and nonwork is encouraged.

A business's culture may emanate from the days of its founder. Firms such as Walt Disney, Wal-Mart, and J. C. Penney, for example, still bear the imprints of their founders. In other cases, an organization's culture is forged over a long period of time by a constant and focused business strategy. For example, Apple Computer has cultivated a sort of counterculture stemming from its self-styled image as the alternative to the staid IBM—and, more recently, Microsoft—corporate model for computer makers.

Communicating the Culture and Managing Change

Corporate culture influences management philosophy, style, and behavior. Managers, therefore, must carefully consider the kind of culture they want for their organizations and then work to nourish that culture by communicating with everyone who works there.

Communicating the Culture To use a firm's culture to its advantage, managers must transmit the culture to others in the organization. Thus, training and

---

In recent years, the pace of corporate change has been unprecedented: mergers, acquisitions, corporate failures, and the emergence of new names and brands have caused profound shifts in the business landscape. In addition, one of the biggest ongoing challenges to any company is effectively communicating what it does and where it stands on the major issues in the public mind, including social responsibility, the environment, human rights, and diversity, to name just a few.

The most successful companies control their communications activities by making clear mission statements, remaining open about both internal policies and external relationships, and convincing the public that they are ready to respond to environmental change. Many major companies now maintain corporate communications teams whose members are skilled in the art of public relations, though the specific process varies from firm to firm. In some instances, top managers become spokespeople, attracting media attention and providing the organization with a face. For example, just three months after his appointment as CEO of Sprint Nextel, Dan Hesse starred in a commercial advertising the company's new pricing plan and an improved customer service initiative. In other cases, groups of

people interact on a daily basis with the media, interest groups, politicians, and the general public.

One thing is certain: The ever-increasing pace of change means companies can't afford to be perceived as outdated and unresponsive. To succeed, they must project images of dynamic, up-to-date organizations that know how to engage with the larger community.

Just three months after his appointment as CEO of Sprint Nextel, Dan Hesse starred in a commercial advertising the company's new pricing plan and an improved customer service initiative.

Kinds of Goals In addition to its mission, every firm also has long-term, intermediate, and short-term goals.

- **Long-term goals** relate to extended periods of time, typically five years or more. For example, Visa might set a long-term goal of doubling the number of participating merchants during the next 10 years. Kodak might adopt a long-term goal of increasing its share of the digital picture processing market by 10 percent during the next eight years.

- **Intermediate goals** are set for a period of one to five years. Companies usually set intermediate goals in several areas. For example, the marketing department's goal might be to increase sales by 3 percent in two years, while the production department might want to reduce expenses by 6 percent in four years.

- **Short-term goals** are set for perhaps one year and are developed for several different areas. Increasing sales by 2 percent this year, cutting costs by 1 percent next quarter, and reducing employee turnover by 4 percent over the next 6 months are examples of short-term goals.

After a firm has set its goals, it then focuses attention on strategies to accomplish them.

Types of Strategies

There are three types of strategies that are usually considered by a company: *corporate stategy*, *business (or competitive) strategy*, and *functional strategy*.

Corporate Strategy The purpose of **corporate strategy** is to determine what business or businesses a company will own and operate. A company may decide to *grow* by increasing its activities or investments or to *retrench* by reducing them.

Sometimes a corporation buys and operates multiple businesses in compatible industries as part of its corporate strategy. For example, the restaurant chains operated by Yum! (KFC, Pizza Hut, Taco Bell, and Long John Silver's) are clearly related to one another. This strategy is called *related diversification*. However, if the businesses are not similar, the strategy is called *unrelated diversification*. When Pearson PLC, a British media company, ran such unrelated businesses as publishing and a wax museum, it was following this approach. Under CEO Kenneth Chenault, AmEx corporate strategy calls for strengthening operations through a principle of growth called *e-partnering*—buying shares of small companies that can provide technology that AmEx itself does not have.

Business (or Competitive) Strategy When a corporation owns and operates multiple businesses, it must develop strategies for each one. **Business (or competitive) strategy**, then, takes place at the level of the business unit or product line and focuses on

---

improving a company's competitive position. For example, Pepsi has one strategy for its soft-drink business as it competes with Coca-Cola, a different strategy for its sports-drink business, and yet another strategy for its bottled-water line.

Functional Strategy At the level of **functional strategy**, managers in specific areas such as marketing, finance, and operations decide how best to achieve corporate goals by performing their functional activities most effectively.

Formulating Strategy

Planning is often concerned with the nuts and bolts of setting goals, choosing tactics, and establishing schedules. In contrast, *strategy* is a broad concept that describes an organization's intentions, outlines how it intends to meet its goals, and includes its responsiveness to new challenges and new needs. Because a well-formulated strategy is so vital to a business's success, most top managers devote substantial attention and creativity to this process. **Strategy formulation** involves the three basic steps summarized in Figure 5.2.

Step 1: Setting Strategic Goals **Strategic goals** are derived directly from a firm's mission statement. For example, Chipotle Mexican Grill promotes itself as serving "Food with Integrity." In the words of founder and CEO Steve Ells, this means "we can always do better in terms of the food we buy." This strategy—serving food that is "better tasting, coming from better sources, better for the environment, better for the animals, and better for the farmers who raise the animals and grow the produce"—seems to be working: in 2007 Chipotle's revenues exceeded $1 billion.[6]

Step 2: Analyzing the Organization and the Environment: SWOT Analysis After strategic goals have been established, managers usually attempt to assess both their organization and its environment. A common

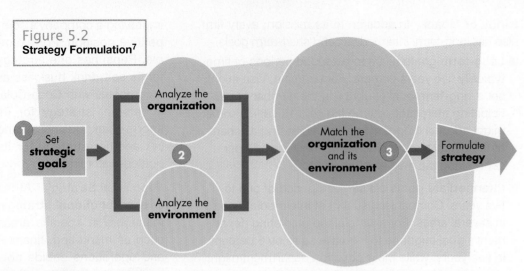

Figure 5.2
Strategy Formulation[7]

framework for this assessment is called a **SWOT analysis**. This process involves assessing organizational strengths and weaknesses (the **S** and **W**) and environmental opportunities and threats (the **O** and **T**).

Scanning the business environment for threats and opportunities is often called **environmental analysis**. Changing consumer tastes and hostile takeover offers are threats, as are new government regulations that will limit a firm's opportunities. Even more important threats come from new products and new competitors. For example, online music services like iTunes are a major threat to manufacturers of CDs and CD players. Opportunities, meanwhile, are areas in which a firm can potentially expand, grow, or take advantage of existing strengths.

In addition to analyzing external factors by performing an environmental analysis, managers must also examine internal factors. The purpose of such an **organizational analysis** is to better understand a company's strengths and weaknesses. Strengths might include surplus cash, a dedicated workforce, an ample supply of managerial talent, technical expertise, or little competition. A cash shortage, aging factories, a heavily unionized workforce, and a poor public image can all be important weaknesses.

Step 3: Matching the Organization and Its Environment The final step in strategy formulation is matching environmental threats and opportunities against corporate strengths and weaknesses. This matching

process is at the heart of strategy formulation. That is, a firm should attempt to leverage its strengths so as to capitalize on opportunities and counteract threats; it should also attempt to shield its weaknesses or at least not allow them to derail other activities.

Understanding strengths and weaknesses may determine whether a firm typically takes risks or behaves more conservatively. Either approach can be successful. Blue Bell, for example, is one of the most profitable ice-cream makers in the world, even though it sells its products in only a fifth of U.S. supermarkets.[8] Based in Brenham, Texas, the firm has resisted the temptation to expand too quickly. Its success is based on product freshness and frequent deliveries—strengths that may suffer if the company grows too large.

A Hierarchy of Plans

The final step in formulating strategy involves the creation of actual plans. Plans can be viewed on three levels: strategic, tactical, and operational. The levels constitute a hierarchy, because implementing plans is practical only when there is a logical flow from one level to the next.

- **Strategic plans** reflect decisions about resource allocations, company priorities, and the steps needed to meet strategic goals. They are usually created by the firm's top management team, but often rely on input from others in the organization.

- **Tactical plans** are shorter-term plans for implementing specific aspects of the company's strategic plans. They typically involve upper and middle management.

- **Operational plans,** which are developed by mid-level and lower-level managers, set short-term targets for daily, weekly, or monthly performance.

Contingency Planning and Crisis Management

Because business environments are often difficult to predict and because the unexpected can create major problems, even the best-laid plans sometimes do not work out. For instance, when Walt Disney announced plans to launch a cruise line replete with familiar Disney characters and themes, managers began aggressively marketing the new product. Three months before the first sailing, however, the shipyard constructing Disney's ship notified the company that it was behind schedule and that delivery would be several weeks late. When similar problems befall other cruise lines, they can offer to rebook passengers on alternative itineraries. But because Disney had no other ship, it had no choice but to refund the money it had collected as pre-booking deposits for its first 15 cruises.

Because managers know such things can happen, they often develop alternative plans in case things go awry. Two common methods of dealing with the unknown and unforeseen are *contingency planning* and *crisis management*.

Contingency Planning

Contingency planning seeks to identify in advance important aspects of a business or its market that might change. It also identifies the ways in which a company will respond to changes. Suppose, for example, that a company develops a plan to create a new division. It expects sales to increase at an annual rate of 10 percent for the next five years, and it develops a marketing strategy for maintaining that level. But suppose that sales have increased by only 5 percent by the end of the first year.

Does the firm (1) abandon the venture, (2) invest more in advertising, or (3) wait to see what happens in the second year? Whichever choice the firm makes, its efforts will be more efficient if managers decide in advance what to do in case sales fall below planned levels.

Contingency planning helps them do exactly Disney learned from its mistake with its first s when the second ship was launched a year later, agers allowed for an extra two weeks between the ship was supposed to be ready for sailing a first scheduled cruise.

Crisis Management

A crisis is an unexpected emergency requiring im ate response. **Crisis management** involves an c zation's methods for dealing with emergencies. S the consequences of poor crisis management aff terrorist attacks of September 11, 2001, and the canes that hit the Gulf Coast in 2005, many firms are working to create new and better crisis ma ment plans and procedures.

For example, both Reliant Energy and Duke E rely on computer trading centers where trading agers actively buy and sell energy-related commo If a terrorist attack or natural disaster were to strik trading centers, they would essentially be out of ness. Consequently, Reliant and Duke have create ondary trading centers at other locations. In the ev a shutdown at their main trading centers, these can quickly transfer virtually all their core tr activities to their seco centers within 30 mi or less.[9]

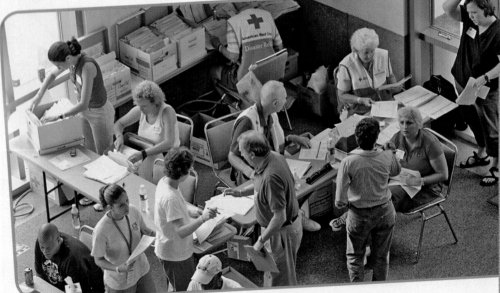

A business's founder or CEO plays a major role in shaping the company's culture. For example, Apple co-founder and CEO Steve Jobs helped establish an informal and laid-back culture at the company. Casual business attire and an open-door policy help him maintain that same culture today. And that culture, in turn, helps Apple continue to attract and retain talented people.

orientation for newcomers in an organization often includes information about the firm's culture. Managers then maintain that culture by rewarding and promoting those who understand it and work toward maintaining it.

Managing Change If an organization changes its culture, it must communicate the nature of the change to both employees and customers. According to the CEOs of several companies that have undergone radical change in the last decade or so, the process usually goes through three stages:

1 *At the highest level, analysis of the company's environment highlights extensive change as the most effective response to its problems.* Conflict and resistance typically characterize this period.

2 *Top management begins to formulate a vision of a new company.* Whatever that vision, it must include renewed focus on the activities of competitors and the needs of customers.

3 *The firm sets up new systems for appraising and compensating employees who enforce the firm's new values.* The purpose is to give the new culture solid shape from within the firm.

For additional topics related to this material and end-of-chapter exercises and practices, please visit www.mybizlab.com.

Questions for Review

1 Relate the five basic management skills (technical, human relations, conceptual, decision-making, and time management) to the four activities in the management process (planning, organizing, leading, and controlling). For example, which skills are most important in leading?

2 What are the four main purposes of setting goals in an organization?

3 Identify and explain the three basic steps in strategy formulation.

4 What is corporate culture? How is it formed? How is it sustained?

Questions for Analysis

5 Select any group of which you are a member (your company, your family, or a club or organization, for example). Explain how planning, organizing, leading, and controlling are practiced in that group.

6 Identify managers by level and area at your school, college, or university.

7 In what kind of company would the technical skills of top managers be more important than human relations or conceptual skills? Are there organizations in which conceptual skills are not important?

8 What differences might you expect to find in the corporate cultures of a 100-year-old manufacturing firm based in the Northeast and a 1-year-old e-commerce firm based in Silicon Valley?

Application Exercises

9 Interview the manager at any level of a local company. Identify that manager's job according to level and area. Show how planning, organizing, leading, and controlling are part of this person's job. Inquire about the manager's education and work experience. Which management skills are most important for this manager's job?

10 Compare and contrast the corporate cultures of two companies that do business in your community. Be sure to choose two companies in the same industry—for example, a Sears department store and a Wal-Mart discount store.

Organizing the Business

After reading this chapter, you should be able to:

1 Discuss the factors that influence a firm's organizational structure.

2 Explain specialization and departmentalization as two of the building blocks of organizational structure.

3 Describe centralization and decentralization, delegation, and authority as the key ingredients in establishing the decision-making hierarchy.

4 Explain the differences among functional, divisional, matrix, and international organizational structures and describe the most popular new forms of organizational design.

5 Describe the informal organization and discuss intrapreneuring.

PepsiCo's Performance with Purpose

PepsiCo's chairman and CEO, Indra Nooyi, has been leading company reorganizations since she joined PepsiCo in 1994. Since then, she has served as strategy chief, mergers and acquisitions head, and CFO. Fueled by her unique style, global perspective, and nutritional goals, Nooyi has led PepsiCo to an annual revenue increase of 72 percent since 2000.

In her first bold response to the market, Nooyi spun off PepsiCo's restaurant business in 1997, a move that shrank the company by a third. She has since built it up on a foundation of more nutritional foods with acquisitions such as Tropicana, Quaker Oats, and Naked Juice. To support the move in this direction, Nooyi appointed an endocrinologist as head of R&D and hired the company's first chief scientific officer. Nooyi has never shied away from change. In fact, she believes that "Companies today are bigger than many economies. We are little republics. We are engines of efficiency. If we don't do [responsible] things, who is going to? Why not start making change now?" This move away from being just another "ugly American company" has increased overseas sales, which grew 22 percent in 2007.

Since becoming CEO, Nooyi has reorganized the company to better reflect not only her management style but also the company's product share. She doubled the executive team to 29, which includes her former main challenger for the CEO job with whom she maintains a noncompetitive relationship. She also reorganized the company into three departmentalized units: Americas Foods, Americas Beverages, and International. Previously divided into North America and International departments, the new structure better reflects the company's focus on snack foods, which accounted for 45 percent of revenue in 2007.

These changes have all been in support of Nooyi's motto— Performance with Purpose—which guides how the organization, as well as the products, should function.[1]

What's in It for Me?

As PepsiCo illustrates, many factors that affect how a firm functions determine organizational structure. This chapter will further explore the factors that go into structuring an organization, the functions that must be determined, and the roles and responsibilities that must be defined. Elements that are increasingly relevant in today's business world, such as virtual and informal organizations and intrapreneuring, will also be discussed.

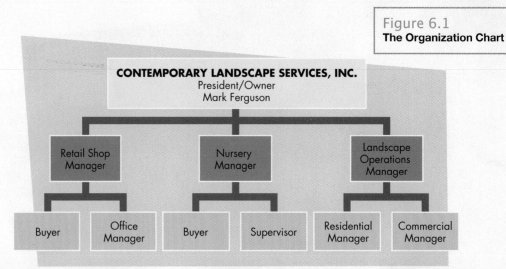

Figure 6.1
The Organization Chart

What Is Organizational Structure?

Organization Charts

Organizational structure is the specification of the jobs within an organization and the ways they relate to one another. Perhaps the easiest way to understand this structure is in terms of an *organization chart*.

Organization charts clarify structure and show employees where they fit into a firm's operations. Figure 6.1 is an organization chart for Contemporary Landscape Services, a small but thriving business in Bryan, Texas. Each box represents a job, and the lines represent how jobs relate to one another. The solid lines define the **chain of command**, or *reporting relationships*. For example, the retail shop, nursery, and landscape operations managers all report to the owner and president, Mark Ferguson. Within the landscape operation is one manager for residential accounts and another for commercial accounts. Similarly, there are other managers in the retail shop and the nursery.

Organization charts of large firms are often so complex that they may have one chart showing overall structure, separate charts for each division, and even more for individual departments or units. Virtually no two organizations will have the same structure: what works for one company may not work for another. For example, the American Red Cross will probably not have the same structure as Union Carbide or the University of Minnesota.

Determinants of Organizational Structure

Chief among the factors playing a part in determining an organization's optimal structure are *mission* and *strategy*. A dynamic and rapidly growing business, for example, needs an organizational structure that allows for flexibility and growth in response to environmental and strategic changes. A stable organization with only modest growth goals and a more conservative strategy will most likely function best with a different structure. A large corporation operating in a strongly competitive environment—for example, American Airlines or Hewlett-Packard—requires a different organizational structure than a local barbershop or video store. Even after an organizational structure has been created, it is rarely set in stone. Most organizations change their structures on an almost continuous basis.

Since it was first incorporated in 1903, Ford Motor Company has undergone dozens of major structural changes, hundreds of moderate changes, and thousands of minor changes. In the last decade alone, Ford has initiated several major structural changes. In 1994, the firm announced a major restructuring plan, Ford 2000, which was intended to integrate all of Ford's vast international operations into a single, unified structure by the year 2000.

By 1998, however, midway through implementation of the grand plan, top Ford executives announced major modifications, indicating that (1) additional changes would be made, (2) some previously planned changes would not be made, and (3) some recently realigned operations would be changed again. In early 1999, managers announced another set of changes intended to eliminate corporate bureaucracy, speed up decision making, and improve communication and working relationships among people at different levels of the organization. Early in 2001, Ford announced yet more sweeping changes intended to boost the firm's flagging bottom line and stem a decline in product quality. More significant changes followed in both 2003 and 2004, and in 2006, the firm announced several plant closings, resulting in even more changes.[2]

The Building Blocks of Organizational Structure

The first step in developing the structure of any business, large or small, involves three activities:

1 *Specialization:* Determining who will do what

2 *Departmentalization:* Determining how people performing certain tasks can best be grouped together

3 *Establishment of a decision-making hierarchy:* Deciding who will be empowered to make which decisions and who will have authority over others

Specialization

The process of identifying the specific jobs that need to be done and designating the people who will perform them leads to **job specialization**. In a sense, all organizations have only one major "job," such as making cars (Ford), selling finished goods to consumers (PepsiCo), or providing telecommunications services (Verizon). Usually, that job is extremely complex in nature. For example, the "job" of Chaparral Steel is converting scrap steel (often salvaged from wrecked automobiles) into finished steel products (such as beams and reinforcement bars).

Managers break down, or specialize, this one overall job into several smaller jobs. Thus, some workers transport the scrap steel to the company's mill. Others operate shredding equipment before turning raw materials over to the workers who then melt them into liquid. Other specialists oversee the flow of the liquid into molding equipment, where it is transformed into new products. Finally, others are responsible for moving finished products to a holding area before they are shipped to customers. When the overall job of the organization is broken down like this, workers can develop real expertise in their jobs, and employees can better coordinate their work with that done by others.

Specialization and Growth In a very small organization, the owner may perform every job. As the firm grows, however, so does the need to specialize jobs so that others can perform them. For example, when Walt Disney first opened his animation studio, he and his brother Roy did everything. When they created their very first animated feature, *Steamboat Willy*, they wrote the story, drew the pictures, transferred the pictures to film, provided the voices, and marketed the cartoon to theaters. Today, however, a Disney animated feature is made possible only through the efforts of hundreds of people. The job of one animator may be to create the face of a single character throughout an entire feature. Another artist may be charged with coloring background images in certain scenes. Others are responsible for the subsequent operations that turn individual computer-generated images into a moving picture or for the marketing of the finished product.

Job specialization is a natural part of organizational growth, and it has advantages and disadvantages. Specialized jobs can be learned and filled more easily and performed more efficiently than nonspecialized jobs. However, jobs at lower levels of the organization are especially susceptible to becoming too narrowly defined and overspecialized, which can cause employees to become bored and careless, to derive less satisfaction from their jobs, and to lose sight of their roles in the organization.[3]

When Walt Disney and his brother Roy made Mickey Mouse's debut animated film, *Steamboat Willy*, they handled every step of the creative process. Today, it takes hundreds of people to create an animated film like 2008's *WALL-E*.

Disney · PIXAR
WALL·E

Planning Departments

After jobs are specialized, they must be grouped into logical units, which is the process of **departmentalization**. With this division of activities, control and coordination are streamlined, and top managers can see easily how various units are performing.

Departmentalization allows the firm to treat each department as a **profit center**—a separate company unit responsible for its own costs and profits. Thus, Sears can calculate the profits it generates from men's clothing, appliances, home furnishings, and every other department within a given store separately. Managers can then use this information to make decisions about advertising and promotional events, space allocation, budgeting, and so forth.

In general, departmentalization may occur along *product*, *process*, *functional*, *customer*, or *geographic* lines (or any combination of these).

Product Departmentalization Manufacturers and service providers often opt for **product departmentalization**—dividing an organization according to the specific product or service being created. Kraft Foods uses this approach to divide departments: for example, the Oscar Mayer division focuses on hot dogs and lunch meats, the Kraft Cheese division focuses on cheese products, the Maxwell House and Post division focuses on coffee and breakfast cereal, and so on.[4] Because each division represents a defined group of products or services, managers at Kraft Foods are able—in theory—to focus on *specific* product lines in a clear and defined way.

Process Departmentalization Other manufacturers favor **process departmentalization**, in which the organization is divided according to production processes used to create a good or

service. This principle is logical for Vlasic, which has three separate departments to transform cucumbers into either fresh-packed pickles, pickles cured in brine, or relishes. Cucumbers destined to become fresh-packed pickles must be packed into jars immediately, covered with a solution of water and vinegar, and prepared for sale. Those slated to be brined pickles must be aged in brine solution before packing. Relish cucumbers must be minced and combined with a host of other ingredients. Each process requires different equipment and worker skills, and different departments were created for each.

Functional Departmentalization Many service and manufacturing companies, especially smaller ones, use **functional departmentalization** to develop departments according to a group's functions or activities. Such firms typically have production, marketing and sales, human resources, and accounting and finance departments. Departments may be further subdivided. For example, the marketing department might be divided into separate staffs for market research and advertising.

Customer Departmentalization Retail stores actually derive their generic name—department stores—from the manner in which they are structured—a men's department, a women's department, a luggage department, a lawn and garden department, and so on. Each department targets a specific customer category (men, women, people who want to buy luggage, people who want to buy a lawn mower) by using **customer departmentalization** to create departments that offer products and meet the needs of identifiable customer groups. Thus, a customer shopping for a baby's playpen at Sears can bypass lawn and garden supplies and head straight for children's furniture. In general, the store is more efficient, and customers get better service because salespeople tend to specialize

At plants like this one in Canton, Mississippi, Nissan has developed an assembly process so efficient that it can turn out a vehicle in up to 10 fewer hours than Ford. The key is the organization of the workstations. At this station, workers install just about everything that the driver touches inside the truck cab. Other stations take care of the whole vehicle frame, the entire electrical system, or completed doors.

and gain expertise in their departments. Another illustration of customer departmentalization is reflected in most banks. A customer wanting a consumer loan goes to the retail banking office, whereas a small business owner goes to the commercial banking office.

Geographic Departmentalization **Geographic departmentalization** divides firms according to the areas of the country or the world that they serve. Levi Strauss, for instance, has one division for North and South America; one for Europe, the Middle East, and North Africa; and one for the Asia Pacific region.[5] Within the United States, geographic departmentalization is common among utilities. For example, Southern Company organizes its power subsidiaries into four geographic departments—Alabama, Georgia, Gulf, and Mississippi Power.[6]

Multiple Forms of Departmentalization Because different forms of departmentalization have different advantages, larger companies tend to adopt different types of departmentalization for various levels. The company illustrated in Figure 6.2 uses functional departmentalization at the top level. At the middle level, production is divided along geographic lines. At a lower level, marketing is departmentalized by product group.

Establishing the Decision-Making Hierarchy

The third major building block of organizational structure is the establishment of a decision-making hierarchy. This is usually done by formalizing reporting relationships. When the focus is on the reporting relationships among individual managers and the people who report to them, it is most commonly referred to as *delegation*. However, when the focus is on the overall organization, it becomes a question of *decentralization* versus *centralization*.

Distributing Authority: Centralization and Decentralization

Some managers make the conscious decision to retain as much decision-making authority as possible at the higher levels of the organizational structure; others decide to push authority as far down the hierarchy as possible. While we can think of these two extremes as anchoring a continuum, most companies fall somewhere between the middle of such a continuum and one end point or the other.

Centralized Organizations In a **centralized organization**, most decision-making authority is held by upper-level managers.[7] McDonald's practices centralization as a way to maintain standardization. All restaurants must follow precise steps in buying products and making and packaging menu items. Most advertising is handled at the corporate level, and any local advertising must be approved by a regional manager. Restaurants even have to follow prescribed schedules for facilities' maintenance and upgrades like floor polishing and parking lot cleaning. Centralized authority is most commonly found in companies that face relatively stable and predictable environments and is also typical of small businesses.

Decentralized Organizations As a company gets larger, more decisions must be made; thus, the company tends to adopt **decentralized organization**, in which much decision-making authority is delegated to

GEOGRAPHIC DEPARTMENTALIZATION the dividing of an organization according to the areas of the country or the world served by a business

CENTRALIZED ORGANIZATION organization in which most decision-making authority is held by upper-level management

DECENTRALIZED ORGANIZATION organization in which a great deal of decision-making authority is delegated to levels of management at points below the top

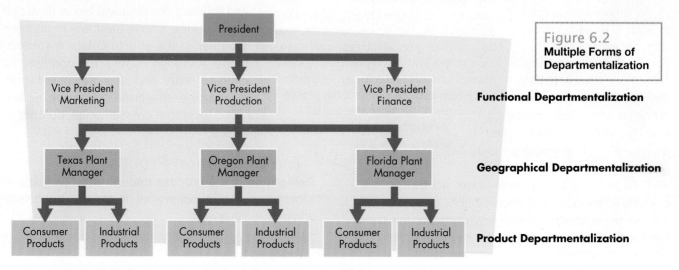

Figure 6.2
Multiple Forms of Departmentalization

President

Vice President Marketing / Vice President Production / Vice President Finance — **Functional Departmentalization**

Texas Plant Manager / Oregon Plant Manager / Florida Plant Manager — **Geographical Departmentalization**

Consumer Products / Industrial Products / Consumer Products / Industrial Products / Consumer Products / Industrial Products — **Product Departmentalization**

The oil-industry giant ExxonMobil owns vast reserves of natural gas, like this field in the former Soviet republic of Turkmenistan. In most respects, ExxonMobil is a highly centralized company, but in this less stable market, which tends to innovate rapidly, many experts are skeptical about the company's ability to decentralize the control that management exercises over corporate operations.

levels of management at various points below the top. Decentralization is typical in firms that have complex and dynamic environmental conditions. It makes a company more responsive by allowing managers more discretion to make quick decisions in their areas of responsibility. For example, Urban Outfitters practices relative decentralization in that it allows individual store managers considerable discretion over merchandising and product displays.

Tall and Flat Organizations Decentralized firms tend to have relatively fewer layers of management, resulting in a **flat organizational structure** like that of the hypothetical law firm shown in Figure 6.3(a). Centralized firms typically require multiple layers of management and thus **tall organizational structures**, as in the U.S. Army example in Figure 6.3(b). Because information, whether upward or downward bound, must pass through so many organizational layers, tall structures are prone to delays in information flow.

As organizations grow in size, it is both normal and necessary that they become at least somewhat taller. For instance, a small firm with only an owner-manager and a few employees is likely to have two layers—the owner-manager and the employees who report to that person. As the firm grows, more layers will be needed. A manager must ensure that he or she has only the number of layers his or her firm needs. Too few layers can create chaos and inefficiency, whereas too many layers can create rigidity and bureaucracy.

The Parts of Whole Foods

Whole Foods Market is an example of radical decentralization. Stores are broken up into small teams, which are responsible for making decisions on issues such as voting on which new staff members to hire and which products to carry based on local preferences. This practice taps into the idea that the people who will be most affected by decisions should be the ones making them.[8]

Span of Control As you can see in Figure 6.3, the distribution of authority in an organization also affects the number of people who work for any individual manager. In a flat organizational structure, the number of people directly managed by one supervisor—the manager's **span of control**—is usually wide. In tall organizations, span of control tends to be narrower. Employees' abilities and the supervisor's managerial skills influence how wide or narrow the span of control should be, as do the similarity and simplicity of tasks and the extent to which they are interrelated.

If lower-level managers are given more decision-making authority, their supervisors will have less work to do and may then be able to take on a widened span of control. Similarly, when several employees perform either the same simple task or a group of interrelated tasks, a wide span of control is possible and often desirable. For instance, because of the routine and interdependent nature of jobs on an assembly line, one supervisor may well control the entire line.

In contrast, when jobs are more diversified or prone to change, a narrow span of control is preferable. Consider how Electronic Arts develops video games. Design, art, audio, and software development teams have specialized jobs whose products must come together in the end to create a coherent game. Although related, the complexities involved with and the advanced skills required by each job mean that one supervisor can oversee only a small number of employees.[9]

The Delegation Process

Delegation is the process through which a manager allocates work to subordinates. In general, the delegation process involves:

1. Assigning **responsibility**, the duty to perform an assigned task

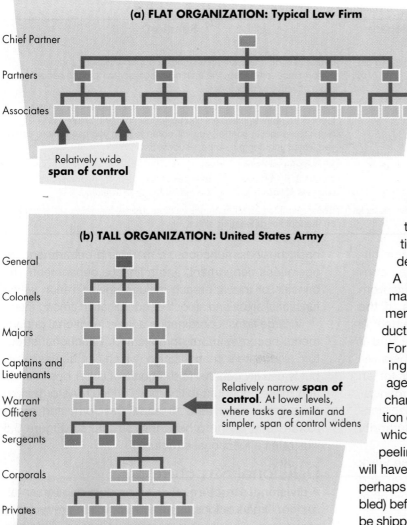

(a) FLAT ORGANIZATION: Typical Law Firm

Chief Partner

Partners

Associates

Relatively wide **span of control**

(b) TALL ORGANIZATION: United States Army

General

Colonels

Majors

Captains and Lieutenants

Warrant Officers

Sergeants

Corporals

Privates

Relatively narrow **span of control**. At lower levels, where tasks are similar and simpler, span of control widens

Figure 6.3
Organizational Structure and Span of Control

AUTHORITY power to make the decisions necessary to complete a task

ACCOUNTABILITY obligation employees have to their manager for the successful completion of an assigned task

LINE AUTHORITY organizational structure in which authority flows in a direct chain of command from the top of the company to the bottom

LINE DEPARTMENT department directly linked to the production and sales of a specific product

STAFF AUTHORITY authority based on expertise that usually involves counseling and advising line managers

STAFF MEMBERS advisers and counselors who help line departments in making decisions, but do not have the authority to make final decisions

COMMITTEE AND TEAM AUTHORITY authority granted to committees or teams involved in a firm's daily operations

along with sales and distribution (both of which are directly linked to sales).

As the doers and producers, each line department is essential to an organization's ability to sell and deliver finished goods. A bad decision by the manager in one department can hold up production for an entire plant. For example, the painting department manager at Clark Equipment changes a paint application on a batch of forklifts, which then show signs of peeling paint. The batch will have to be repainted (and perhaps partially reassembled) before the machines can be shipped.

2 Granting **authority**, or the power to make the decisions necessary to complete the task

3 Creating **accountability**, the obligation employees have for the successful completion of the task

For the delegation process to work smoothly, responsibility and authority must be equivalent. Table 6.1 lists some common obstacles that hinder the delegation process, along with strategies for overcoming them.

Three Forms of Authority

As individuals are delegated responsibility and authority, a complex web of interactions develops in the form of *line*, *staff*, and *committee and team* authorities.

Line Authority The type of authority that flows up and down the chain of command is **line authority**. Most companies rely heavily on **line departments** linked directly to the production and sales of specific products. For example, in the division of Clark Equipment that produces forklifts and small earthmovers, line departments include purchasing, materials handling, fabrication, painting, and assembly (all of which are directly linked to production)

Staff Authority Some companies also rely on **staff authority**, which is based on special expertise and usually involves advising line managers in areas such as law, accounting, and human resources. A corporate attorney, for example, may advise the marketing department as it prepares a new contract with the firm's advertising agency, but will not typically make decisions that affect how the marketing department does its job. **Staff members** help line departments make decisions, but do not usually have the authority to make final decisions.

Typically, the separation between line authority and staff responsibility is clearly delineated and is usually indicated in organization charts by solid lines (line authority) and dotted lines (staff responsibility), as shown in Figure 6.4. It may help to understand this separation by remembering that whereas *staff members* generally provide services to management, *line managers* are directly involved in producing the firm's products.

Committee and Team Authority Recently, more organizations have started to grant **committee and team authority** to groups that play central roles in

Table 6.1 **Learning to Delegate Effectively**

I'm afraid to delegate because ...	Solution
My team doesn't know how to get the job done.	If members of your team are exhibiting opportunities for improved performance, offer them the training necessary for them to become more effective at their jobs.
I like controlling as many things as possible.	Recognize that trying to accomplish everything yourself while your team does nothing only sets you up for burnout and failure. As you begin to relinquish control, you will come to trust your team more as you watch your team members succeed.
I don't want anyone on my team outperforming me.	High-performing team members are a reflection of your success as a manager. Encourage them to excel, praise them for it, and share the success of *your* team with the rest of the organization.
I don't know how to delegate tasks effectively.	Consider taking a management training course or reading some books on the topic of delegating effectively.

daily operations. A committee, for example, may consist of top managers from several major areas. If the work of the committee is especially important and if the committee members will be working together for an extended time, the organization may even grant it special authority as a decision-making body beyond the individual authority possessed by each of its members.

At the operating level, many firms today use **work teams** that are empowered to plan, organize, and perform their work with minimal supervision and often with special authority as well.

Basic Forms of Organizational Structure

Organizations can structure themselves in an almost infinite number of ways. However, four basic forms reflect the trends followed by most firms: *functional*, *divisional*, *matrix*, and *international*.

Functional Structure

Under a **functional structure**, relationships between group functions and activities determine authority. Functional structure is used by most small to medium-sized firms, which are usually structured around

basic business functions: a marketing department, an operations department, and a finance department. The benefits of this approach include specialization within functional areas and smoother coordination among them.

In large firms, coordination across functional departments becomes more complicated. Functional structure also fosters centralization (which can be desirable, but is usually counter to the goals of larger businesses) and makes accountability more difficult. As organizations grow, they tend to shed this form and move toward one of the other three structures. Figure 6.5 illustrates a functional structure.

Divisional Structure

A **divisional structure** relies on product departmentalization. Organizations using this approach are typically structured around several product-based **divisions** that resemble separate businesses in that they produce and market their own products. The head of each division may be a corporate vice president or, if the organization is large enough, a divisional president. In addition, each division usually has its own identity and operates as a relatively autonomous business under the larger corporate umbrella. Figure 6.6 illustrates a divisional structure.

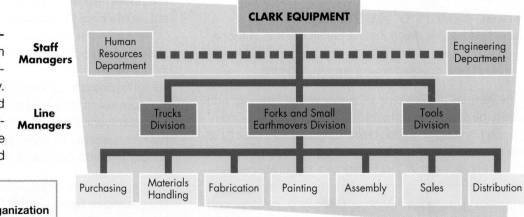

Figure 6.4
Line and Staff Organization

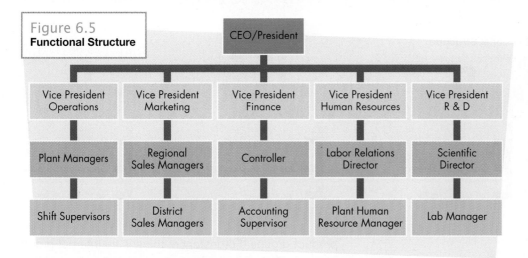

Figure 6.5
Functional Structure

CEO/President

- Vice President Operations
  - Plant Managers
    - Shift Supervisors
- Vice President Marketing
  - Regional Sales Managers
    - District Sales Managers
- Vice President Finance
  - Controller
    - Accounting Supervisor
- Vice President Human Resources
  - Labor Relations Director
    - Plant Human Resource Manager
- Vice President R & D
  - Scientific Director
    - Lab Manager

Johnson & Johnson, one of the most recognizable names in health care products, organizes its company into three major divisions: consumer health care products, medical devices and diagnostics, and pharmaceuticals. Each major division is then broken down further. The consumer health care products division relies on product departmentalization to separate baby care, skin and hair care, topical health care, oral health care, women's health, over-the-counter medicines, and nutritionals. These divisions reflect the diversity of the company, which can protect it during downturns, such as 2008, which showed the slowest pharmaceutical growth in four decades. Because they are divided, the other divisions are protected from this blight and can carry the company through it.

Consider that Johnson & Johnson's over-the-counter pain management medicines are competition for their pain management pharmaceuticals. Divisions can maintain healthy competition among themselves by sponsoring separate advertising campaigns, fostering different corporate identities, and so forth. They can also share certain corporate-level resources (such as market research data). However, if too much control is delegated to divisional managers, corporate managers may lose touch with daily operations. Also, competition between divisions can become disruptive, and efforts in one division may duplicate those of another.[10]

Entrepreneurship and New Ventures

Making the Grade

In 1965, undistinguished Yale undergrad Fred Smith wrote a paper describing how automated technology necessitated quicker, more reliable transportation. According to legend, the paper received a poor grade. But Smith himself debunks this myth. "It's become a well-known story because everybody likes to flout authority. But to be honest, I don't really remember what grade I got."

Whatever the grade, the idea was a winner. After serving in Vietnam, Smith invested his own money to start the air transport business Federal Express. FedEx was revolutionary in pioneering the hub-and-spoke system and using bar codes, handheld PDAs, and package tracking to compete with the monopolistic U.S. Postal Service.

When rival UPS entered the airfreight segment in 2000, FedEx acquired several key players in the ground transportation industry. "The economics of airplanes are such that we couldn't just keep taking prices down," Smith says. "We finally realized that if we wanted to grow, we had to get into surface transportation." FedEx's new fleet capitalized on the brand's reputation for speed and reliability: "People say 'FedEx this' when they mean 'Get it someplace fast,'" says investor Timothy M. Ghriskey. "No one says 'UPS this.'"

Although standardization is important, FedEx's commitment to decentralization breeds innovation. Managers are encouraged and rewarded for questioning, challenging, and developing new ideas, which are always given serious consideration. Developments have included teaming up with Motorola and Microsoft to create a proprietary pocket-size PC, sending package information to cell phones, and creating software products for small business logistics. "Engage in constant change," is a mantra for CEO Smith, and he adds, "Companies that don't take risks—some of which are going to work and some of which aren't—are going to end up getting punched up by the marketplace."[11]

MATRIX STRUCTURE organizational structure created by superimposing one form of structure onto another

INTERNATIONAL ORGANIZATIONAL STRUCTURES approaches to organizational structure developed in response to the need to manufacture, purchase, and sell in global markets

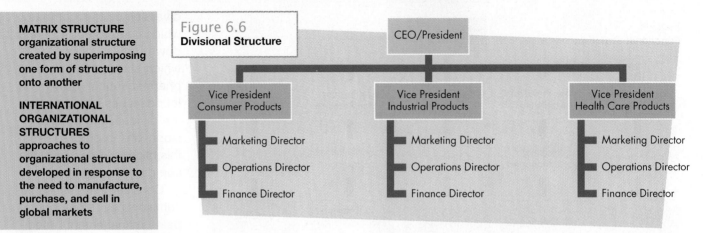

Figure 6.6
Divisional Structure

Matrix Structure

Sometimes a **matrix structure**—a combination of two separate structures—works better than either simpler structure alone. This structure gets its matrix-like appearance, when shown in a diagram, by using one underlying "permanent" organizational structure (say, the divisional structure flowing up-and-down in the diagram), and then superimposing a different organizing framework on top of it (e.g., the functional form flowing side-to-side in the diagram). This highly flexible and readily adaptable structure was pioneered by NASA for use in developing specific space programs.

Suppose a company using a functional structure wants to develop a new product as a one-time special project. A team might be created and given responsibility for that product. The project team may draw members from existing functional departments, such as finance and marketing, so that all viewpoints are represented as the new product is being developed; the marketing member may provide ongoing information about product packaging and pricing issues, for instance, and the finance member may have useful information about when funds will be available.

In some companies, the matrix organization is a temporary measure installed to complete a specific project and affecting only one part of the firm. In these firms, the end of the project usually means the end of the matrix—either a breakup of the team or a restructuring to fit it into the company's existing line-and-staff structure. Ford, for example, uses a matrix organization to design new models, such as the newest Mustang. A design team composed of people with engineering, marketing, operations, and finance expertise was created to design the new car. After its work was done, the team members moved back to their permanent functional jobs.

In other settings, the matrix organization is a semipermanent fixture. Figure 6.7 shows how Martha Stewart Living Omnimedia has created a permanent matrix organization for its lifestyle business. As you can see, the company is organized broadly into media and merchandising groups, each of which has specific product and product groups. For instance, there is an Internet group housed within the media group. Layered on top of this structure are teams of lifestyle experts led by area specialists organized into groups, such as cooking, entertainment, weddings, crafts, and so forth. Although each group targets specific customer needs, they all work, as necessary, across all product groups. An area specialist in weddings, for example, might contribute to an article on wedding planning for an Omnimedia magazine, contribute a story idea for an Omnimedia cable television program, and supply content for an Omnimedia site. This same individual might also help select fabrics suitable for wedding gowns that are to be retailed.

International Structure

Several different **international organizational structures** have emerged in response to the need to manufacture, purchase, and sell in global markets.

For example, when Wal-Mart opened its first store outside the United States in 1992, it set up a special projects team. In the mid-1990s, the firm created a small international department to handle overseas expansion. By 1999 international sales and expansion had become such a major part of operations that a separate international division headed up by a senior vice president was created. By 2002, international operations had become so important that the international division was further divided into geographic areas, such as Mexico and Europe. And as the firm expands into more foreign markets, such as Russia and India, new units are created to oversee those operations.[12]

Some companies adopt a truly global structure in which they acquire resources (including capital), produce goods and services, engage in research and development, and sell products in whatever local market is appropriate, without consideration of national boundaries. Until a few years ago, General Electric (GE) kept its international business operations as separate divisions, as illustrated in Figure 6.8. Now, however, the company functions as one integrated global organization. GE businesses around the world connect and interact with each

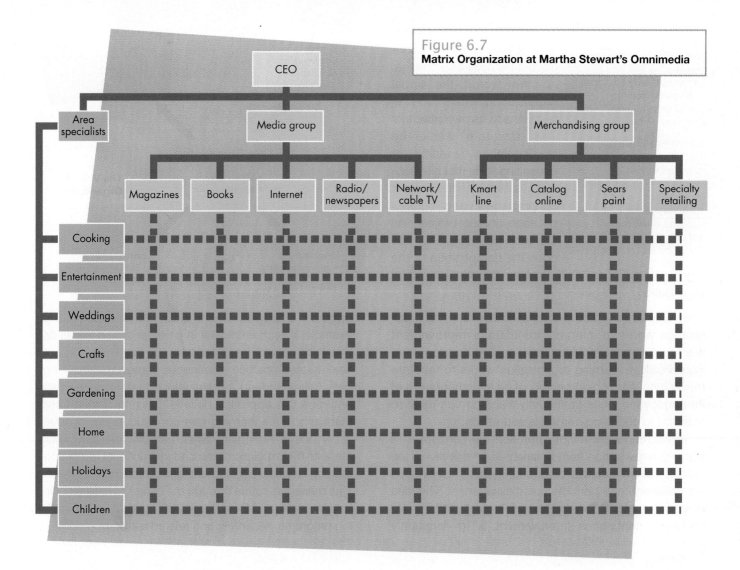

Figure 6.7
Matrix Organization at Martha Stewart's Omnimedia

other constantly, and managers freely move back and forth among them. This integration is also reflected in GE's executive team, which includes natives of Spain, Japan, Scotland, Ireland, and Italy.[13]

Organizational Design for the Twenty-first Century

As the world grows increasingly complex and fast-paced, organizations also continue to seek new forms of organization that permit them to compete effectively. Among the most popular of these new forms are the *team organization*, the *virtual organization*, and the *learning organization*.

Team Organization *Team organization* relies almost exclusively on project-type teams, with little or no underlying functional hierarchy. People float from project to project as dictated by their skills and the demands of those projects. As the term suggests, team authority is the underlying foundation of organizations that adopt this organizational structure.

Virtual Organization Closely related to the team organization is the *virtual organization*. A virtual organization has little or no formal structure. Typically, it has only a handful of permanent employees, a very small staff, and a modest administrative facility. As the needs of the organization change, its managers bring in temporary workers, lease facilities, and outsource basic support services to meet the demands of each unique situation. As the situation changes, the temporary workforce changes in parallel, with some people leaving the

Figure 6.8
International Division Structure

organization and others entering. Facilities and the subcontracted services also change. In other words, the virtual organization exists only in response to its own needs.[14] This structure would be applicable to research or consulting firms that hire consultants based on the specific content knowledge required by each unique project. As the projects change, so too does the composition of the organization. Figure 6.9 illustrates a hypothetical virtual organization.

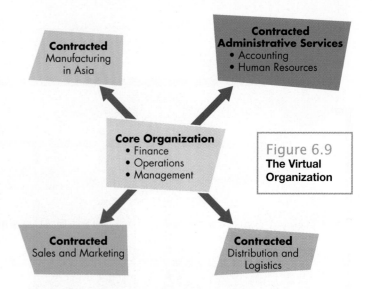

Figure 6.9
The Virtual Organization

Learning Organization The so-called *learning organization* works to integrate continuous improvement with continuous employee learning and development. Specifically, a learning organization works to facilitate the lifelong learning and personal development of all of its employees while continually transforming itself to respond to changing demands and needs.

While managers might approach the concept of a learning organization from a variety of perspectives, the most frequent goals are superior quality, continuous improvement, and performance measurement. The idea is that the most consistent and logical strategy for achieving continuous improvement is to constantly

upgrade employee talent, skill, and knowledge. For example, if each employee in an organization learns one new thing each day and can translate that knowledge into work-related practice, continuous improvement will logically follow. Indeed, organizations that wholeheartedly embrace this approach believe that only through constant employee learning can continuous improvement really occur. Shell Oil's Shell Learning Center boasts state-of-the-art classrooms and instructional technology, lodging facilities, a restaurant, and recreational amenities. Line managers rotate through the center to fulfill teaching assignments, and Shell employees routinely attend training programs, seminars, and related activities.

Say What You Mean

Boss, Buddy, or Both?

Bill? Billy-boy? Er, Mr. Gates, sir? Even in our own culture, we may sometimes face the anxiety of not knowing the best way to address a superior. When doing business internationally, things can get even more complicated, and it's important to consider how different cultures influence business communications across organizational levels.

German companies tend to have fairly rigid and formal organizational structures. Respect for status and titles means that using last names is the norm. Surprisingly, German companies like to keep everyone at all levels informed about what's going on in the decision-making process.

In contrast, U.S. companies tend to have formal organizational structures while fostering casual and easygoing communication. Even senior managers

and lower-level workers are often on a first-name basis. Bosses command respect, but people from different levels tend to interact quite easily.

In many Latin American and South American cultures, bosses have a great deal of power and authority, and workers give them a corresponding degree of respect. The Mexican boss, or *patrón,* is expected to provide employees with more than orders in the workplace, including moral and even material support and attendance at weddings, funerals, and christenings (where he's often called on to serve as godfather).

Sensitivity to culturally diverse workplace behaviors and attitudes is one of the most important qualities that a global company can bring to its relationships with foreign organizations.

Informal Organization

The structure of a company, however, is by no means limited to the *formal organization* as represented by the organization chart and the formal assignment of authority. Frequently, the **informal organization**—everyday social interactions among employees that transcend formal jobs and job interrelationships—effectively alters a company's formal structure.[15] This level of organization is sometimes just as powerful—if not more powerful—than the formal structure. In 2005, Hewlett-Packard fired its CEO, Carly Fiorina. Much of the discussion that led to her firing took place outside formal structural arrangements in the organization—members of the board of directors, for example, held secret meetings and reached confidential agreements among themselves before Fiorina's future with the company was addressed in a formal manner.[16]

On the negative side, the informal organization can reinforce office politics that put the interests of individuals ahead of those of the firm and can disseminate distorted or inaccurate information. For example, if the informal organization is highlighting false information about impending layoffs, valuable employees may act quickly (and unnecessarily) to seek other employment.

Intrapreneuring

Good managers recognize that the informal organization exists whether they want it or not and can use it not only to reinforce the formal organization, but also to harness its energy to improve productivity.

Many firms, including Rubbermaid, 3M, and Xerox, support **intrapreneuring**—creating and maintaining the innovation and flexibility of a small-business environment within a large, bureaucratic structure. Historically, most innovations have come from individuals in small businesses. As businesses increase in size, however, innovation and creativity tend to become casualties in the battle for more sales and profits. In some large companies, new ideas are even discouraged, and champions of innovation have been stalled in midcareer. At Lockheed Martin, the Advanced Development Programs (ADP) encourages intrapreneurship in the tradition of Skunk Works, a legendary team developed in 1943 engineer Kelly Johnson's response to Lockheed's need for a powerful jet fighter. Johnson's innovative organization approach broke all the rules, and not only did it work, but it also taught Lockheed the value of encouraging that kind of thinking.[17]

For additional topics related to this material and end-of-chapter exercises and practices, please visit www.mybizlab.com.

Questions for Review

1 What is an organization chart? What purpose does it serve?

2 Explain the significance of size as it relates to organizational structure. Describe the changes that are likely to occur as an organization grows.

3 What is the difference between responsibility and authority?

4 Why do some managers have difficulties delegating authority? What solutions are available for managers with difficulties delegating authority?

5 What are the basic forms of organizational structure?

6 Why is a company's informal organization important? What are some of the drawbacks and benefits of the informal organization?

Questions for Analysis

7 Draw up an organization chart for your college or university. How would you describe the organizational structure of your college or university?

8 Describe a hypothetical organizational structure for a small printing firm. Describe changes that might be necessary as the business grows.

9 Compare and contrast the matrix and divisional approaches to organizational structure. How would you feel personally about working in a matrix organization in which you were assigned simultaneously to multiple units or groups?

Application Exercises

10 Interview the manager of a local service business, such as a fast-food restaurant. What types of tasks does this manager typically delegate? Is the appropriate authority also delegated in each case? What problems occur when authority is not delegated appropriately?

11 Using books, magazines, or personal interviews, identify a person who has succeeded as an intrapreneur. In what ways did the structure of the intrapreneur's company help this individual succeed? In what ways did the structure pose problems?

7 chapter

Operations Management and Quality

After reading this chapter, you should be able to:

1 Explain the meaning of the term *production* or *operations*.

2 Describe the three kinds of utility that operations processes provide for adding customer value.

3 Explain how companies with different business strategies are best served by having different operations capabilities.

4 Identify the major factors that are considered in operations planning.

5 Discuss the information contained in four kinds of operations schedules—the master production schedule, detailed schedule, staff schedule, and project schedule.

6 Identify the activities involved in operations control.

7 Identify the activities and underlying objectives involved in total quality management.

8 Explain how a supply chain strategy differs from traditional strategies for coordinating operations among firms.

Troubled Times for Airlines

In September 2006, the Federal Aviation Administration (FAA) gave airlines until March 2008 to inspect a certain bundle of wires located near the main landing gear in all MD-80 airliners, and, if improperly secured, to repair the bundle. Eighteen months later, some 250,000 travelers found themselves stranded as American Airlines grounded its fleet of MD-80s and cancelled nearly 3,300 flights in a hurried effort to comply with the FAA directive.

How could the nation's largest carrier make such a costly and seemingly avoidable mistake? Shortly before the deadline to repair the wiring passed, the FAA was embarrassed by revelations that another carrier, Southwest Airlines, had violated federal regulations by flying planes that had missed their scheduled inspections. Suddenly, the FAA found itself under fire from Congress for failing to keep closer tabs on airlines. It is unsurprising, then, that the FAA would be extra vigilant in inspecting the MD-80s—more vigilant, it seems, than carriers such as American had come to expect.

None of this may be much consolation to frustrated travelers. According to Brent Bowen, co-author of the 2008 Airline Quality Rating (AQR), 2007 "was the worst year ever for the U.S. airlines." The AQR measures such performance indicators as the percentage of flights arriving on time, the amount of mishandled baggage, and the number of complaints ranging from high fares to misleading advertising to discriminatory practices. Such a varied list of concerns is a reminder that the fundamental service an airline provides—getting people from point A to point B—is only the beginning of operational performance and quality. As the American Airlines incident illustrates, however, even this fundamental service is impossible to provide in the absence of foresight and sound management practices.[1]

What's in It for Me?

If—like the thousands of American Airlines passengers disrupted by cancelled flights—you've ever been disappointed in a good or service that you bought, you'll find it easy to relate to the topics in this chapter. We'll explore the numerous ways companies align their operations processes with their business plans, and discuss how these decisions contribute to a firm's ability to create a high-quality product. Gaining an appreciation for the many steps it takes to bring high-quality goods and services to market will help make you a smarter consumer and more effective employee. And if you're a manager, understanding that production activities are pliable and should be reoriented to better support new business strategies will help you redefine your company and its marketplace over time.

SERVICE OPERATIONS (SERVICE PRODUCTION) activities producing intangible and tangible products, such as entertainment, transportation, and education

GOODS OPERATIONS (GOODS PRODUCTION) activities producing tangible products, such as radios, newspapers, buses, and textbooks

OPERATIONS (PRODUCTION) activities involved in making products—goods and services—for customers

UTILITY a product's ability to satisfy a human want or need

What Does *Operations* Mean Today?

Although you're not always aware of it, you're constantly involved in business activities that provide goods and services to customers. You wake up to the sound of your favorite radio station and pick up a newspaper on your way to the bus stop, where you catch your ride to work or school. Your instructors, the bus driver, the clerk at the 7-Eleven store, and the morning radio announcer all work in **service operations** (or service production). They provide intangible and tangible service products, such as entertainment, transportation, education, and food preparation. Firms that make only tangible products—radios, newspapers, buses, textbooks—are engaged in activities for **goods operations** (or goods production).

The term **operations** (or production) refers to all the activities involved in making products—goods and services—for customers. Although companies are typically classified as either goods producers or service providers, the distinction is often blurred. Consider General Electric. When you think of GE, you most likely think of appliances and jet engines. However, GE is not just a goods producer. According to its annual report,

GE's "growth engines"—its most vibrant business activities—are service operations, including media and entertainment (NBC Universal), consumer and commercial finance, investment, transportation services, and health care information, which account for over 80 percent of the company's revenues.[2]

Creating Value Through Operations

To understand a firm's production processes, we need to know what kinds of benefits its production provides, both for itself and for its customers. Production provides businesses with economic results: profits, wages, and goods purchased from other companies. At the same time, it adds customer value by providing **utility**—the ability of a product to satisfy a want or need—in terms of form, time, and place:

- Production makes products available: By converting raw materials and human skills into finished goods and services, production creates *form utility*, as when Regal Cinemas combines building materials, theater seats, projection equipment, and food concessions to create entertainment.

- When a theater offers mid-day, afternoon, and evening shows seven days a week, it creates *time utility*; that is, it adds customer value by making products available when consumers want them.

- When a theater offers a choice of 15 movies, all under one roof at a popular location, it creates *place utility*: It makes products available where they are convenient for consumers.

General Electric (GE) can be classified as both a goods producer (for example, of the Explosive Detection Trace Portal, shown here) and a service provider (for example, of media and entertainment shows such as *Saturday Night Live*).

Creating a product that customers value, then, is no accident, but instead results from organized effort. **Operations (production) management** is the systematic direction and control of the processes that transform resources into finished services and goods that create value for and provide benefits to customers. In overseeing production, **operations (production) managers** are responsible for ensuring that operations processes create what customers want and need.

Operations managers draw up plans to transform resources into products. First, they bring together basic resources: knowledge, physical materials, information, equipment, the customer, and human skills. Then they put them to effective use in a production facility. As demand for a product increases, they schedule and control work to produce the required amount. Finally, they control costs, quality levels, inventory, and facilities and equipment. In some businesses, the operations manager is one person. Typically, different employees work together to complete these different responsibilities.

Some operations managers work in factories; others work in offices and stores. Farmers are operations managers who create utility by transforming soil, seeds, fuel, and other inputs into soybeans, milk, and other outputs. They may hire crews of workers to plant and harvest, opt instead for automated machinery, or prefer some combination of workers and machinery. These decisions affect costs and determine the kinds of buildings and equipment in operations and the quality and quantity of goods produced.

Differences Between Service and Goods Manufacturing Operations

Both service and manufacturing operations transform raw materials into finished products. In service operations, however, the raw materials, or inputs, are not things like glass or steel. Rather, they are people who have either unsatisfied needs or possessions needing care or alteration. In service operations, finished products or outputs are people with needs met and possessions serviced.

Thus, there are several obvious differences between service and manufacturing operations. Four aspects of service operations can make them more complicated than simple goods production. These include (1) interacting with consumers, (2) the intangible and unstorable nature of some services, (3) the customer's presence in the process, and (4) service quality considerations.

Interacting with Consumers Manufacturing operations emphasize outcomes in terms of physical goods—for example, a new jacket. But the products of most

service operations are really combinations of goods and services—both making a pizza *and* delivering (serving) it. Service workers need different skills. For example, gas company employees may need interpersonal skills to calm frightened customers who have reported gas leaks. Thus, the job includes more than just repairing pipes. In contrast, factory workers who install gas pipes in manufactured homes without any customer contact don't need such skills.

Services Can Be Intangible and Unstorable Two prominent characteristics—*intangibility* and *unstorability*—set services apart from physical goods.

- **Intangibility.** Often, services can't be touched, tasted, smelled, or seen, but they're still there. An important satisfier for customers, therefore, is the *intangible* value they receive in the form of pleasure, gratification, or a feeling of safety. For example, when you hire an attorney, you purchase not only the intangible quality of legal expertise but also the equally intangible reassurance that help is at hand.

- **Unstorability.** Many services—such as trash collection, transportation, child care, and house cleaning—can't be produced ahead of time and then stored for high-demand periods. If a service isn't used when available, it's usually wasted. Services, then, are typically characterized by a high degree of *unstorability*.

Customer's Presence in the Operations Process Because service operations transform customers or their possessions, the customer is often present in the operations process. To get a haircut, for example, most of us have to go to the barbershop or hair salon. As physical participants in the operations process, consumers can affect it. As a customer, you expect the salon to be conveniently located (place utility), to be open for business at convenient times (time utility), to provide safe and comfortable facilities, and to offer high-quality grooming (form utility) at reasonable prices (value for money spent). Accordingly, the manager sets hours of operation, available services, and an appropriate number of employees to meet customer requirements. But what happens if a customer, scheduled to receive a haircut, also asks for additional services, such as highlights or a shave when he or she arrives? In this case, the service provider must balance customer satisfaction with a tight schedule. High customer contact has the potential to affect the process significantly.

Intangibles Count for Service Quality Consumers use different measures to judge services and goods because services include intangibles, not just physical objects. Most service managers know that quality of work and quality of service are not necessarily the same thing. Your car, for example, may have been flawlessly repaired (quality of work), but you'll probably be unhappy with the service if you're forced to pick it up a day later than promised (quality of service).

Operations Processes

To better understand the diverse kinds of production in various firms and industries, it is helpful to classify production according to general differences in operations processes. An **operations process** is a set of methods and technologies used to produce a good or a service. We can classify goods production, for example, by asking whether its operations process has a "make-to-order" or a "make-to-stock" emphasis. We can classify services according to the extent of customer contact required.

Goods Production Processes: Make-to-Order Versus Make-to-Stock Processes Clothing, such as evening gowns, is available either off-the-shelf in department stores or custom-made at a designer/tailor shop. The designer/tailor's **make-to-order operations** respond to one-of-a-kind gown requirements, including unique patterns, materials, sizes, and shapes, depending on customers' unique characteristics. **Make-to-stock operations**, in contrast, produce standard gowns in large quantities to be stocked on store shelves or in displays for mass consumption. The production processes are quite different for the two settings, including

procedures for designing gowns; planning for materials purchases; methods for cutting, sewing, and assembling gowns; and employee skills for production.

Service Production Processes: Extent of Customer Contact In classifying services, we may ask whether a service can be provided without the customer's being part of the production system. In answering this question, we classify services according to *extent of customer contact*.

Low-Contact Systems Consider the check-processing operations at your bank. Bank employees sort checks that have been cashed that day and send them to the banks on which they were drawn. This operation is a **low-contact system**: Customers are not in contact with the bank while the service is performed. They receive the service—funds are transferred to cover checks—without setting foot in the processing center. Gas and electric companies, auto repair shops, and lawn-care services are other examples of low-contact systems.

High-Contact Systems Think about your local public transit system. The service is transportation, and when you purchase transportation, you board a bus or train. For example, the Bay Area Rapid Transit (BART) system, which connects San Francisco with outlying suburbs and, like all public transit systems, is a **high-contact system**: To receive the service, the customer must be part of the system. Thus, managers must worry about the cleanliness of trains and the appearance of stations.

Because service operations transform customers or their possessions, the customer is often present in the operations process.

Business Strategy as the Driver of Operations

There is no one standard way for doing production. Rather, a company selects the kind of production that best achieves its larger business strategy.

The Many Faces of Production Operations

Consider the four firms listed in Table 7.1. Two are in goods production and two are in services. Each company has identified a business strategy that it can use for attracting customers in its industry. For Toyota, *quality* was

Table 7.1 **Business Strategies That Win Customers for Four Companies**

Company	Strategy for Attracting Customers	What the Company Does to Implement Its Strategy
Toyota	Quality	Cars perform reliably, have an appealing fit and finish, and consistently meet or exceed customer expectations at a competitive price
Save-A-Lot	Low price	Foods and everyday items offered at savings up to 40 percent less than conventional food chains
3M	Flexibility	Innovation, with more than 55,000 products in a constantly changing line of convenience items for home and office
FedEx	Dependability	Every delivery is fast and on time, as promised

OPERATIONS CAPABILITY (PRODUCTION CAPABILITY) an activity or process that production does especially well with high proficiency

chosen as the strategy for competing in selling autos. Save-A-Lot grocery stores, in contrast to others in the grocery industry, offer customers *lower prices*. The *flexibility* strategy at 3M emphasizes new product development in an ever-changing line of products for home and office. FedEx captures the overnight delivery market by emphasizing delivery *dependability*, first and foremost.

Business Strategy Determines Operations Capabilities Successful firms design their operations to support the company's business strategy.[3] In other words, production operations are adjusted to support the firms' target markets. Since our four firms use different business strategies, we should expect to see differences in their operations, too. The top-priority **operations**

capability (production capability)—the activity or process that production must do especially well, with high proficiency—is listed for each firm in Table 7.2, along with key operations characteristics for implementing that capability. Each company's operations capability matches up with its business strategy so that the firm's activities—from top to bottom—are focused in a particular direction.

For example, since Toyota's top priority focuses on quality, its operations—the resource inputs for production, the transformation activities, and the outputs from production—are devoted first and foremost to that characteristic. Its car designs and production processes emphasize appearance, reliable performance, and desirable features at a reasonable price. All production processes, equipment, and training are designed to build better cars. The entire culture supports a quality emphasis

Table 7.2 **Operations Capabilities and Characteristics for Four Companies**

Operations Capability	Key Operations Characteristics
Quality (Toyota)	• High-quality standards for materials suppliers • Just-in-time materials flow for lean manufacturing • Specialized, automated equipment for consistent product build-up • Operations personnel are experts on continuous improvement of product, work methods, and materials
Low Cost (Save-A-Lot)	• Avoids excessive overhead and costly inventory (no floral departments, sushi bars, or banks that drive up costs) • Limited assortment of products, staples, in one size only for low-cost restocking, lower inventories, and less paperwork • Many locations; small stores—less than half the size of conventional grocery stores—for low construction and maintenance costs • Reduces labor and shelving costs by receiving and selling merchandise out of custom shipping cartons
Flexibility (3M)	• Maintains some excess (expensive) production capacity available for fast start on new products • Adaptable equipment/facilities for production changeovers from old to new products • Hires operations personnel who thrive on change • Many medium- to small-sized facilities in diverse locations, which enhances creativity
Dependability (FedEx)	• Customer automation: uses electronic and online tools with customers to shorten shipping time • Wireless information system for package scanning by courier, updating of package movement, and package tracking by customer • Maintains a company air force, global weather forecasting center, and ground transportation for pickup and delivery, with backup vehicles for emergencies • Each of 30 automated regional distribution hubs processes up to 45,000 packages per hour for next-day deliveries

among employees, suppliers, and dealerships. Had Toyota instead chosen to compete as the low-price car in the industry, as some successful car companies do, then a cost-minimization focus would have been appropriate, giving Toyota's operations an altogether different form. Toyota's operations support its chosen business strategy, and do it successfully.

Expanding into Additional Capabilities Finally, it should be noted that excellent firms learn, over time, how to achieve more than just one competence. Our four example firms eventually became excellent in several capabilities. FedEx, for example, in addition to dependability, is noted for world-class service quality and cost containment, too. But in the earlier start-up years, its primary and distinguishing capability, which set it apart from the competition, was dependability, the foundation upon which future success was built.

Operations Planning

Let's turn now to a discussion of production activities and resources that are considered in every business organization. Like all good managers, we start with planning. Managers from many departments contribute to decisions about operations. As Figure 7.1 shows, however, no matter how many decision makers are involved, the process is a logical sequence of decisions.

The business plan and forecasts developed by top managers provide guidance for long-term operations plans. Covering a two- to five-year period, the operations plan anticipates the number of plants or service facilities and the amount of labor, equipment, transportation, and storage needed to meet future demand for new and existing products. The planning activities fall into five categories: *capacity*, *location*, *layout*, *quality*, and *methods planning*.

Capacity Planning

The amount of a product that a company can produce under normal conditions is its **capacity**. A firm's capacity depends on how many people it employs and the number and size of its facilities. A supermarket's capacity for customer checkouts, for instance, depends on its number of checkout stations. A typical store has excess capacity—more cash registers than it needs—on an average day, but on Saturday morning or during the three days before Thanksgiving, they'll all be running at full capacity.

Entrepreneurship and New Ventures

From a Missouri Garage to Hollywood

The upcoming feature films *The Red Canvas* and *Way of the Guardian* were not developed by your typical Hollywood production team. For starters, one of the films' co-creators lives and works in Missouri. Adam Boster and his partner, Ken Chamitoff, started Photo-Kicks—a marketing company specializing in action photography—in their garages in 2002. From their beginnings photographing students at local martial arts schools, Boster and Chamitoff built Photo-Kicks into a multi-million–dollar business employing photographers, graphic designers, and marketers throughout the United States and Canada. In 2007 Photo-Kicks came in at number 592 on *Inc.* magazine's list of the 5,000 fastest-growing private companies in America.

Just a quick glance at the many photographs on display at the Photo-Kicks Web site (http://photo-kicks.com) provides an eye-opening introduction to action photography. Athletes young and old punch, kick, and leap their way across the frames. But it's the countless other services that Photo-Kicks provides its customers that have allowed it to grow so rapidly. Photo-Kicks bills itself as "a fully equipped graphic design and marketing organization," creating such products as customized logos, brochures, Web sites, posters, and trading cards.

Then, of course, there are the movies. *Way of the Guardian* began as a card game and animated series also developed by Boster and Chamitoff. *The Red Canvas* is more personal. It tells the story of a struggling immigrant who finds success and redemption in the sport of mixed martial arts. Chamitoff acknowledges that the film could not have happened without the years he and Boster spent traveling the country photographing martial arts students. "I learned the stories of every person I encountered," said Chamitoff. Those stories shaped not only *The Red Canvas*, but Photo-Kicks as well.[4]

production decisions are being implemented—is a key and ongoing facet of operations.

Operations control includes *materials management* and *quality control*. Both activities ensure that schedules are met and products delivered, both in quantity and in quality.

Materials Management

Most of us have difficulty keeping track of personal items now and then—clothes, books, DVDs, and so on. Imagine keeping track of thousands or even millions of things at any one time. That's the challenge in **materials management**—the process by which managers plan, organize, and control the flow of materials from sources of supply through distribution of finished goods. For manufacturing firms, typical materials costs make up 50 to 75 percent of total product costs. For service firms, too, the materials stakes are high. UPS delivers 16 million packages every day and promises that all of them will arrive on schedule. It keeps this promise by tracking the locations, schedules, and on-time performance of 600 aircraft and 100,000 vehicles as they carry packages through the delivery system.

Materials Management Activities Once a product has been designed, successful materials flows depend on five activities. From selecting suppliers on through the distribution of finished goods, materials managers engage in the following areas that compose materials management:

- **Supplier selection** means finding and choosing suppliers of services and materials to buy from. It includes evaluating potential suppliers, negotiating terms of service, and maintaining positive buyer-seller relationships.

- **Purchasing** is the acquisition of all the raw materials and services that a company needs to produce its products. Most large firms have purchasing departments to buy proper materials in the amounts needed.

- **Transportation** includes the means of transporting resources to the producer and finished goods to buyers.

- **Warehousing** is the storage of both incoming materials for production and finished goods for distribution to customers.

- **Inventory control** includes the receiving, storing, handling, and counting of all raw materials, partly finished goods, and finished goods. It ensures that enough materials inventories are available to meet production schedules, while at the same time avoiding expensive excess inventories.

It's All In the Timing

Lean production systems, pioneered by Toyota, are designed for smooth production flows that avoid inefficiencies, eliminate unnecessary inventories, and continuously improve production processes. **Just-in-time (JIT) production**, a type of lean system, brings together all needed materials at the precise moment they are required for each production stage, not before, thus creating fast and efficient responses to customer orders. All resources flow continuously—from arrival as raw materials to final assembly and shipment of finished products.

JIT production reduces to practically nothing the number of goods in process (goods not yet finished). It minimizes inventory costs, reduces storage space requirements for inventories, and saves money by replacing stop-and-go production with smooth movement. Once smooth flow is the norm, disruptions are more visible and are resolved more quickly. Finding and eliminating disruptions by the continuous improvement of production is a major objective of JIT production.

Quality Control

Quality control means taking action to ensure that operations produce goods or services that meet specific quality standards. At a bank, for example, quality control for teller services might require supervisors to observe employees periodically and evaluate their work according to a checklist. The results would then be reviewed with employees and would either confirm proper performance or indicate changes for bringing performance up to standards.

The quality of customer-employee interactions is no accident in firms that monitor customer encounters and provide training for employee skills development. American Airlines employees faced the unpleasant task of calming thousands of irate customers face-to-face. Many managers realize that without employees trained in customer-relationship skills, quality suffers, and businesses, such as airlines and hotels, can lose customers to better-prepared competitors.

Quality control means taking action to ensure that operations produce products that meet specific quality standards.

Quality Improvement and Total Quality Management

It is not enough to *control* quality by inspecting products and monitoring service operations as they occur, like when a supervisor listens in on a catalog sales service representative's customer calls. Businesses must also consider *building* quality into products and services. In order to compete on a global scale, U.S. companies continue to emphasize a quality orientation. All employees, not just managers, participate in quality efforts, and firms have embraced new methods to measure progress and to identify areas for improvement. In many organizations, quality improvement has become a way of life.

Managing for Quality

Total quality management (TQM) includes all the activities necessary for getting high-quality goods and services into the marketplace. It must consider all aspects of a business, including customers, suppliers, and employees. To marshal the interests of all these stakeholders, TQM involves assigning and accepting responsibility for quality.

Quality Ownership: Taking Responsibility for Quality To assure high-quality goods and services, many firms assign responsibility for some aspects of TQM to specific departments or positions. These specialists and experts may be called in to assist with quality-related problems in any department, and they keep everyone informed about the latest developments in quality-related equipment and methods. They also monitor quality-control activities to identify areas for improvement.

The backbone of TQM, however, and its biggest challenge, is motivating all employees throughout the company and its suppliers to achieve quality goals. Leaders of the quality movement use various methods and resources to foster a quality focus—training, verbal encouragement, teamwork, and tying compensation to work quality. When those efforts succeed, employees and suppliers will ultimately accept **quality ownership**—the idea that quality belongs to each person who creates it while performing a job.

Tools for Total Quality Management

Hundreds of tools have proven useful for quality improvement, ranging from statistical analysis of product data, to satisfaction surveys of customers, to **competitive product analysis**—a process by which a company analyzes a competitor's products to identify desirable improvements. In this section, we survey five of the most commonly used tools for TQM: *value-added analysis*, *quality improvement teams*, *getting closer to the customer*, *the ISO series*, and *business process reengineering*.

Value-Added Analysis **Value-added analysis** refers to the evaluation of all work activities, materials flows, and paperwork to determine the value that they add for customers. It often reveals wasteful or unnecessary activities that can be eliminated without jeopardizing customer service.

Quality Improvement Teams Companies throughout the world have adopted **quality improvement teams** patterned after the successful Japanese concept of *quality circles*: collaborative groups of employees from various work areas who meet regularly to define, analyze, and solve common production problems. Their goal is to improve both their own work methods and the products they make. Quality improvement teams organize their own work, select leaders, and address problems in the workplace.

Getting Closer to the Customer Successful businesses take steps to know what their customers want in the products they consume. On the other hand, struggling companies have often lost sight of customers as the driving force behind all business activity. Such companies waste resources by designing products that customers do not want. Sometimes, they ignore customer reactions to existing products or fail to keep up with changing tastes.

Identifying Customers—Internal and External Improvement projects are undertaken for both external and internal customers. Internal suppliers and internal customers exist wherever one employee or activity relies on others. For example, marketing managers rely on internal accounting information—costs for materials, supplies, and wages—to plan marketing activities for coming months. The marketing manager is a customer of the firm's accountants—the information user relies on the information supplier. Accountants in a TQM environment recognize this supplier-customer connection and take steps to improve information for marketing.

The ISO Series Perhaps you've driven past companies proudly displaying large banners announcing, "This Facility Is ISO Certified." The ISO (pronounced ICE-oh) label is a mark of quality achievement that is respected throughout the world and, in some countries, it's a requirement for doing business.

ISO 9000 **ISO 9000** is a certification program attesting that a factory, a laboratory, or an office has met the rigorous quality management requirements set by the International Organization for Standardization. Today, more than 140 countries have adopted ISO 9000 as a national standard. To become certified, companies must document the procedures followed by workers during every stage of production. The purpose is to ensure that a company's processes can create products exactly the same today as it did yesterday and as it will tomorrow.

ISO 14000 The **ISO 14000** program certifies improvements in environmental performance by requiring a firm to develop an *environmental management system*: a plan documenting how the company has acted to improve its performance in using resources (such as raw materials) and in managing pollution. A company must not only identify hazardous wastes that it expects to create, but it must also stipulate plans for treatment and disposal.

Business Process Reengineering Every business consists of processes—activities that it performs regularly and routinely in conducting business, such as receiving and storing materials from suppliers, billing patients for medical treatment, and filing insurance claims for auto accidents.

Business process reengineering focuses on improving a business process—rethinking each of its steps by starting from scratch. *Reengineering* is the fundamental rethinking and radical redesign of business processes to achieve dramatic improvements as measured by cost, quality, service, and speed. As companies conduct an increasing amount of their business online, old processes must be reengineered to utilize the power of the Internet.

VALUE-ADDED ANALYSIS the process of evaluating all work activities, materials flows, and paperwork to determine the value that they add for customers

QUALITY IMPROVEMENT TEAM TQM tool in which collaborative groups of employees from various work areas work together to improve quality by solving common shared production problems

ISO 9000 program certifying that a factory, laboratory, or office has met the quality management standards set by the International Organization for Standardization

ISO 14000 certification program attesting to the fact that a factory, laboratory, or office has improved its environmental performance

BUSINESS PROCESS REENGINEERING the rethinking and radical redesign of business processes to improve performance, quality, and productivity

Adding Value Through Supply Chains

The term *supply chain* refers to the group of companies and stream of activities that work together to create a product. A **supply chain** (or **value chain**) for any product is the flow of information, materials, and services that starts with raw-materials suppliers and continues adding value through other stages in the network of firms until the product reaches the end customer.

Figure 7.5 shows the chain of activities for supplying baked goods to consumers. Each stage adds value for the final customer. This bakery example begins with raw materials (grain harvested from the farm). It also includes storage and transportation activities, factory operations for baking and wrapping, and distribution to retailers. Each stage depends on the others for success in getting freshly baked goods to consumers.

The Supply Chain Strategy

Traditional strategies assume that companies are managed as individual firms rather than as members of a coordinated supply system. Supply chain strategy is based on the idea that members of the chain will gain competitive advantage by working as a coordinated unit.

A traditionally managed bakery, for example, would focus simply on getting production inputs from flour millers and paper suppliers and supplying baked goods to distributors. Unfortunately, this approach limits the chain's performance and doesn't allow for possible improvements when activities are more carefully coordinated. Proper management and better coordination of the supply chain can provide fresher baked goods at lower prices.

Supply Chain Management **Supply chain management (SCM)** looks at the chain as a whole to improve the overall flow through a system composed of companies working together. Because customers ultimately get better value, supply chain management gains competitive advantage for each of the chain's members.

An innovative supply chain strategy was the heart of Michael Dell's vision when he established Dell Inc. Dell's concept improves performance by sharing information among chain members. Dell's long-term production plans and up-to-the-minute sales data are available to suppliers via the Internet. The process starts when customer orders are automatically translated into updated production schedules in the factory. These schedules are used not only by operations managers at Dell but also by such parts suppliers as Sony, which adjust their own production and shipping activities to better meet Dell's production needs. In turn, parts suppliers' updated schedules are transmitted to their materials suppliers, and so on up the chain. As Dell's requirements change, suppliers up and down the chain synchronize their schedules to produce only the right materials and parts. As a result,

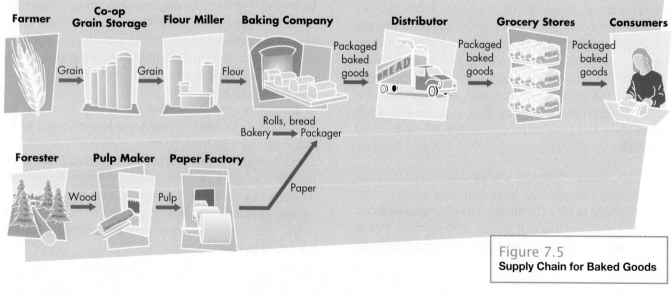

Figure 7.5
Supply Chain for Baked Goods

Dell's prices are low and turnaround time for shipping PCs to customers is reduced to a matter of hours instead of days.

Reengineering Supply Chains for Better Results
Process improvements and reengineering often are applied in supply chains to lower costs, speed up service, and coordinate flows of information and material. Because the smoother flow of accurate information along the chain reduces unwanted inventories and transportation, avoids delays, and cuts supply times, materials move faster to business customers and individual consumers. Faster deliveries result in lower costs than customers could get if each member acted only according to its own operations requirements.

Outsourcing and Global Supply Chains

Outsourcing is the strategy of paying suppliers and distributors to perform certain business processes or to provide needed materials or services. The decision to outsource expands supply chains and creates new operations jobs for supply chain management. Maytag, for example, had to develop its own internal global operations expertise before it could decide to open a new refrigerator factory in Mexico, import refrigerators from South Korea's Daewoo, and get laundry appliances from South Korea's Samsung Electronics. Global communications technologies are also essential. Although manufacturing operations are located remotely, they are closely integrated with the firm's home-base activities. That tightness of integration demands on-site operations expertise on both sides of the outsourcing equation.

For additional topics related to this material and end-of-chapter exercises and practices, please visit www.mybizlab.com.

Questions for Review

1 What are the major differences between goods-production operations and service operations?

2 What are the major differences between high-contact and low-contact service systems?

3 What are the five major categories of operations planning?

4 What are the major activities in materials management?

5 What activities are involved in total quality management?

Questions for Analysis

6 What are the input resources and finished products in the following services: a real estate firm, a child care facility, a bank, and a hotel?

7 Choose a consumer item and trace its supply chain. Identify at least four upstream stages in the chain. Based on your familiarity with the product and the supply chain stages you identified, what recommendations would you make to improve the supply chain?

8 Develop a list of internal customers and internal suppliers for some business that you use frequently (or where you work). Identify areas of potential quality improvement in these internal customer-supplier activity relationships.

Application Exercises

9 Think of an everyday activity, either personal or professional, that you would like to streamline for faster performance or more convenience. It could be something like gassing up your car, going to work or school, enrolling in classes at school, or any other activity that involves several stages with which you are familiar. Describe how you would use methods planning as described in the chapter to improve the activity. Draw a process flowchart that shows the stages in the activity you chose, then tell how you would use it.

10 Interview the manager of a local service business, or speak to a food service, bookstore, or other manager at your school. Identify the major decisions involved in planning that business's service operations.

chapter 8

Employee Behavior and Motivation

After reading this chapter, you should be able to:

1 Identify and discuss the basic forms of behaviors that employees exhibit in organizations.

2 Describe the nature and importance of individual differences among employees.

3 Explain the meaning and importance of psychological contracts and the person-job fit in the workplace.

4 Identify and summarize the most important models and concepts of employee motivation.

5 Describe some of the strategies and techniques used by organizations to improve employee motivation.

What's the Deal about Work?

The stereotypical overworked, underpaid, and unhappy worker is too often a reality caused by competitive environments, pressure to do more with less, economic uncertainty, and 24/7 connectivity.

Consequences for businesses include low retention, efficiency, and morale, or worse: employees have filed lawsuits against Electronic Arts for routinely making them work 65–85 hours a week without overtime pay. Consequences for workers are even direr. White-collar injuries, illnesses, and even suicides related to work reportedly continue to rise. One study found that 23 percent of male stockbrokers were clinically depressed, three times the national average for U.S. men. Other studies find that many workers feel overworked and constantly worry about both their job security and financial stability. In Japan, there is even a term for "death by overwork"—*karoshi*, which is a legally recognized cause of death.[1]

Yet many find happiness at work. One study finds that an overall average of 47 percent of U.S. workers are very satisfied with their jobs.[2] For college professors, nurses, and others, happiness often comes from satisfying intellectual curiosity or helping others. Others redefine their jobs to make them more satisfying. As publisher of *Forbes* magazine, Richard Karlgaard's job primarily involved the mundane task of assessing and managing the reporting of financial data. So, he gave himself a new set of responsibilities as an editor-at-large writing about technology and left the financial reporting to others.

For those without the power to change their responsibilities, looking elsewhere is often the best option. Sandor Zombori walked away from his engineering job and invested his savings into what would become his award-winning restaurant. Mary Lou Quinlan quit her job as CEO of a New York advertising agency to start a small consulting business. The pay is less, but she is happier: "Finally," she says, "I'm doing something I can picture doing for a long, long time."

What's in It for Me?

At the extremes, some people truly love their jobs, while others just as truly hate them. Most people, however, fall somewhere in between. This chapter will discuss the factors related to how people feel about their jobs, including different forms of behaviors that employees exhibit and different methods of employee motivation. By understanding the basic elements of this chapter, you will develop a better understanding of your own and others' feelings toward work from the perspective of employees and managers.

Forms of Employee Behavior

• • • • • • • • • • • • • • • • •

EMPLOYEE BEHAVIOR the pattern of actions by the members of an organization that directly or indirectly influences the organization's effectiveness

PERFORMANCE BEHAVIORS the total set of work-related behaviors that the organization expects employees to display

ORGANIZATIONAL CITIZENSHIP positive behaviors that do not directly contribute to the bottom line

COUNTERPRODUCTIVE BEHAVIORS behaviors that detract from organizational performance

ABSENTEEISM when an employee does not show up for work

Employee behavior is the pattern of actions by the members of an organization that directly or indirectly influences the organization's effectiveness. *Performance behaviors* directly contribute to productivity and performance. Other employee behaviors, referred to as *organizational citizenship*, provide positive benefits to the organization in more indirect ways. *Counterproductive behaviors* detract from performance and actually cost the organization. Let's look at each of these types of behavior in a bit more detail.

Performance Behaviors

Performance behaviors are the total set of work-related behaviors that the organization expects employees to display. Essentially, these are the behaviors directly targeted at performing a job. For some jobs, performance behaviors can be narrowly defined and easily measured. For example, an assembly-line worker who sits by a moving conveyor and attaches parts to a product as it passes by has relatively few performance behaviors. He or she is expected to remain at the workstation for a predetermined number of hours and correctly attach the parts. Such performance can often be assessed quantitatively by counting the percentage of parts correctly attached.

For many other jobs, however, performance behaviors are more diverse and difficult to assess. For example, a research-and-development scientist at Merck Pharmaceuticals works in a lab trying to discover breakthroughs with commercial potential. The scientist must apply knowledge and experience gained from previous research. Intuition and creativity are also important. But even with all the scientist's abilities and effort, a desired breakthrough may take months or even years to accomplish.

> For some jobs, performance behaviors can be narrowly defined and easily measured. For many other jobs, such as those held by scientists or doctors, however, performance behaviors are less objective, more diverse, and more difficult to assess.

Organizational Citizenship

Employees can also engage in **organizational citizenship**—positive behaviors and overall contributions that do not directly contribute to the bottom line.[3] Consider, for example, an employee who does work that is highly acceptable in terms of both quantity and quality. However, she refuses to work overtime, won't help newcomers learn the ropes, and is generally unwilling to make any contribution beyond the strict performance requirements of her job. This person may be seen as a good performer, but she is not likely to be seen as a good organizational citizen. Another employee may exhibit a comparable level of performance but may be seen as a better organizational citizen because she often works late when the boss asks her to, takes time to help newcomers learn their way around, and is perceived as helpful and committed to the organization's success.

A number of factors, including individual, social, and organizational variables, play roles in promoting or minimizing organizational citizenship behaviors. For example, the personality, attitudes, and needs of the individual may cause some to be more helpful than others. Similarly, the individual's work group may encourage or discourage such behaviors. And the organization itself, especially its corporate culture, may or may not promote, recognize, and reward these types of behaviors.

Counterproductive Behaviors

Counterproductive behaviors are those that detract from, rather than contribute to, organizational performance. **Absenteeism** occurs when an employee does not show up for work. Some absenteeism has a

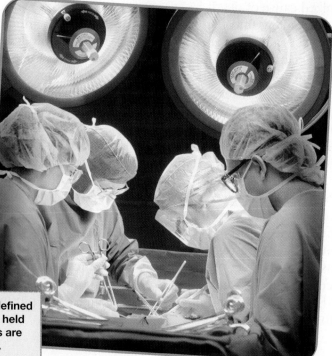

legitimate cause, such as illness, jury duty, or death or illness in the family. Other times, the employee may feign a legitimate cause as an excuse to stay home. When an employee is absent, legitimately or not, his or her work does not get done, a substitute must be hired to do it, or others in the organization must pick up the slack. In any event, absenteeism results in direct costs to a business.

Turnover occurs when people quit their jobs for various reasons, including aspects of the job, the organization, the individual, the labor market, and family influences. A poor person-job fit (which we'll discuss later in the chapter) is also a likely cause of turnover. An organization usually incurs costs as a result of turnover—lost productivity while seeking a replacement, training someone new, etc. There are some employees whose turnover doesn't hurt the business; however, when productive employees leave an organization, it does reflect counterproductive behavior.

Other forms of counterproductive behavior may be even more costly for an organization. *Theft and sabotage*, for example, result in direct financial costs. *Discriminatory harassment* also costs an organization, both indirectly (by lowering morale, producing fear, and driving off valuable employees) and directly (through financial liability if the organization responds inappropriately). *Workplace aggression and violence* are also of growing concern.

Individual Differences Among Employees

What causes some employees to be more productive, better citizens, or more counterproductive than others? As we already noted, every individual is unique. **Individual differences** are personal attributes that vary from one person to another and may be physical, psychological, and emotional. The individual differences that characterize a specific person make that person unique. As we see in the sections that follow, basic categories of individual differences include *personality* and *attitudes*.

Personality at Work

Personality is the relatively stable set of psychological attributes that distinguish one person from another. In recent years, researchers have identified the fundamental *"big five" personality traits* that are especially relevant to organizations. *Emotional intelligence*, while not part of the "big five," also plays a large role in employee personality.

The "Big Five" Personality Traits   The **"big five" personality traits** can be summarized as follows.

■ *Agreeableness* is a person's ability to get along with others. A person with a *high* level of agreeableness is gentle, cooperative, forgiving, understanding, and

good-natured in their dealings with others. A person with a *low* level of agreeableness is often irritable, short-tempered, uncooperative, stubborn, and generally antagonistic toward other people. Highly agreeable people are good at developing good working relationships with co-workers, whereas less agreeable people are not likely to have particularly good working relationships.

■ *Conscientiousness* in this context is a reflection of the number of things a person tries to accomplish. *Highly conscientious* people tend to focus on relatively few tasks at one time, as a result they're likely to be organized, responsible, and self-disciplined. *Less conscientious* people tend to pursue a wider array of tasks, so they are often more disorganized, irresponsible, and less self-disciplined. Highly conscientious people tend to be relatively higher performers in a variety of different jobs.

■ *Emotionality* refers to the degree to which people tend to be positive or negative in their outlook and behaviors toward others. People with *positive* emotionality are relatively poised, calm, and resilient; people with *negative* emotionality are more excitable, insecure, reactive, and moody. People with positive emotionality might be expected to better handle job stress. Their stability might also lead them to be seen as being more reliable than their less-stable counterparts.

■ *Extraversion* refers to a person's comfort level with relationships. *Extraverts* are sociable, assertive, and open to establishing new relationships. *Introverts* are much less sociable and assertive, and more reluctant to begin new relationships. Extraverts tend to be higher overall job performers than introverts and are more likely to be attracted to jobs based on personal relationships, such as sales and marketing positions.

■ *Openness* reflects how open or rigid a person's beliefs are. People with *high* levels of openness are curious and willing to consider and accept new ideas. People with *low* levels of openness tend to be less receptive to new ideas and less willing to change their minds. People with more openness are often more flexible and better accepted by others.

The "big five" framework continues to attract the attention of both researchers and managers. The potential value of this framework is that it encompasses an

TURNOVER annual percentage of an organization's workforce that leaves and must be replaced

INDIVIDUAL DIFFERENCES personal attributes that vary from one person to another

PERSONALITY the relatively stable set of psychological attributes that distinguish one person from another

"BIG FIVE" PERSONALITY TRAITS five fundamental personality traits especially relevant to organizations

EMOTIONAL INTELLIGENCE (EMOTIONAL QUOTIENT, EQ) the extent to which people are self-aware, can manage their emotions, can motivate themselves, express empathy for others, and possess social skills

ATTITUDES a person's beliefs and feelings about specific ideas, situations, or people

JOB SATISFACTION degree of enjoyment that people derive from performing their jobs

ORGANIZATIONAL COMMITMENT an individual's identification with the organization and its mission

PSYCHOLOGICAL CONTRACT set of expectations held by an employee concerning what he or she will contribute to an organization (referred to as contributions) and what the organization will in return provide the employee (referred to as inducements)

integrated set of traits that appear to be valid predictors of certain behaviors in certain situations. Thus, managers who can both understand the framework and assess these traits in their employees are in a good position to understand how and why they behave as they do.[4]

Emotional Intelligence The concept of emotional intelligence has also been identified in recent years and provides some interesting insights into personality. **Emotional intelligence**, or **emotional quotient (EQ)**, refers to the extent to which people are self-aware, manage their emotions, motivate themselves, express empathy for others, and possess social skills.[5] These various dimensions can be described as follows.

- *Self-awareness* refers to a person's capacity for understanding how she is feeling. In general, more self-awareness allows people to more effectively guide their own lives and behaviors.

- *Managing emotions* refers to a person's capacity to avoid letting anxiety, fear, anger, and other emotions interfere with getting things accomplished.

- *Motivating oneself* refers to a person's ability to remain optimistic and to continue striving toward goals in the face of obstacles and failure.

- *Empathy* refers to a person's ability to understand and have compassion for how others are feeling.

- *Social skills* refers to a person's ability to get along with others and to establish positive relationships.

Research suggests that people with high EQs may perform better than others, especially in jobs that require a high degree of interpersonal interaction and that involve influencing or directing the work of others. EQ appears to be something that people lacking these skills can work on and develop.[6]

Attitudes at Work

People's attitudes also affect their behavior in organizations. **Attitudes** are the mechanisms through which we express our beliefs and feelings about ideas, situations,

or people. An employee's comment that he feels underpaid by the organization reflects his feelings about his pay. Similarly, when a manager says that she likes the new advertising campaign, she is expressing her feelings about the organization's marketing efforts.

People in an organization form attitudes about many different things. Employees are likely to have attitudes about salary, promotion opportunities, bosses, benefits, and so on. Especially important attitudes are *job satisfaction* and *organizational commitment*.

- **Job satisfaction**, or *morale*, reflects the extent to which people have positive attitudes toward their jobs. A satisfied employee tends to have low absenteeism, to be a good organizational citizen, and to stay with the organization. Dissatisfied employees may be absent more often, may experience stress that disrupts co-workers, and may be continually looking for another job. While high job satisfaction does not guarantee high productivity, employees with low morale are unlikely to exhibit high productivity.

- **Organizational commitment**, sometimes called *job commitment*, reflects an individual's identification with the organization and its mission. A highly committed person will probably feel included in the organization and refer to it in personal terms, overlook minor sources of dissatisfaction, and see herself as a long-term member of the organization. A less committed person is more likely to see himself as an outsider and refer to the organization in impersonal terms, to express more dissatisfaction, and to see himself as a temporary member of the organization.

By treating employees fairly, providing fair rewards and job security, allowing employees a say in how things are done, and designing stimulating jobs, managers can foster satisfaction and commitment in employees. Another key element is understanding and respecting what experts call *psychological contracts*, which we will discuss in the next section.

Matching People and Jobs

Given the differences among individual employees and their behaviors within the organization, matching people to the jobs they perform is important. Two key methods for helping to understand how this match can be better understood are *psychological contracts* and the *person-job fit*.

Psychological Contracts

A **psychological contract** is the set of expectations held by employees and the organization regarding what employees will contribute and what the organization will provide in return. Unlike a business contract, a psychological contract is not written, nor are all of its terms explicitly negotiated.

Figure 8.1 illustrates the essential nature of a psychological contract. The individual makes a variety of *contributions* to the organization, such as effort, ability, loyalty, skills, and time. These contributions satisfy the employee's obligation under the contract. For example, Jill Henderson, a branch manager for Merrill Lynch, uses her knowledge of financial markets and investment opportunities to help her clients make profitable investments. Her MBA in finance, coupled with hard work and motivation, have led her to become one of the firm's most promising young managers. The firm believed she had these attributes when it hired her and expected that she would use them to contribute to the firm's success. In return for these contributions, the organization satisfies its contract obligation by providing *inducements* to the individual. Some inducements, such as pay and career opportunities, are tangible rewards. Others, such as job security and status, are more intangible. Jill Henderson started at Merrill Lynch at a very competitive salary and has received a salary increase each of the six years she has been with the firm. She has also been promoted twice and expects another promotion in the near future.

When employer and employee perceive that the psychological contract is equitable, both will be satisfied with the relationship and will do what they can to continue it. In other situations, however, either party may see an inequity in the contract and initiate a change. The employee might ask for a pay raise or promotion, put forth less effort, or look for a better job elsewhere. The organization can also initiate change by training the worker to improve his skills, transferring him to another job, or firing him.

All organizations face the basic challenge of managing psychological contracts. They want value from their employees, and they need to give employees the right inducements. For instance, underpaid employees may perform poorly, leave for better jobs elsewhere, or even steal from the company.

Recent trends in downsizing and cutbacks have complicated the process of managing psychological contracts. For example, many organizations used to offer at least reasonable assurances of job permanence as a fundamental inducement to employees. Now, however, job permanence is less likely, so alternative inducements, like training opportunities and flexible work schedules, may be used.

The Person-Job Fit

The **person-job fit** refers to the extent to which a person's contributions and the organization's inducements match one another. A good person-job fit is one in which the employee's contributions match the inducements the organization offers. In theory, each employee has a specific set of needs that she wants fulfilled and a set of job-related behaviors and abilities to contribute. If the organization can use those behaviors and abilities and fulfill her needs, it will have achieved a perfect person-job fit, which can result in higher performance and more positive attitudes. A poor person-job fit, though, can have the opposite effects.

Basic Motivation Concepts and Theories

Broadly defined, **motivation** is the set of forces that causes people to behave in certain ways.[7] One worker may be motivated to work hard to produce as much as possible, whereas another may be motivated to do just enough to get by. Managers must understand these differences in behavior and the reasons for them.

Over the years, a steady progression of theories and studies has attempted to address these issues. This section surveys the major studies and theories of employee motivation with particular focus on three approaches to human relations in the workplace that reflect a basic chronology of thinking in the area: (1) *classical theory* and *scientific management*, (2) *early behavioral theory*, and (3) *contemporary motivational theories*.

Classical Theory

According to the **classical theory of motivation**, workers are motivated solely by money. In his 1911 book, *The Principles of Scientific Management*, industrial engineer Frederick Taylor proposed a way for both companies and workers to benefit from this widely accepted

Contributions from the Individual
- effort
- ability
- loyalty
- skills
- time
- competency

Inducements from the Organization
- pay
- benefits
- job security
- status
- promotion opportunities
- career opportunities

Figure 8.1
The Psychological Contract

view of life in the workplace: If workers are motivated by money, paying them more should prompt them to produce more. Meanwhile, the firm that analyzed jobs and found better ways to perform them would be able to produce goods more cheaply, make higher profits, and pay and motivate workers better than its competitors.

Taylor's approach is known as *scientific management*. Many managers in the early twentieth century bought into his ideas, and manufacturing plants across the United States began hiring experts to perform time-and-motion studies. Industrial engineering techniques were applied to each facet of a job to determine how to perform it most efficiently. These studies were the first scientific attempts to break down jobs into easily repeated components and to devise more efficient tools and machines for performing them.[8]

Early Behavioral Theory

In 1925, a group of Harvard researchers began a study at the Hawthorne Works of Western Electric outside Chicago. With an eye to increasing productivity, they wanted to examine the relationship between changes in the physical environment and worker output.

The results of the experiment were unexpected, even confusing. For example, increased lighting levels improved productivity. For some reason, however, so did lower lighting levels. Moreover, against all expectations, increased pay failed to increase productivity. Gradually, the researchers pieced together the puzzle. The explanation lay in the workers' response to the attention they were receiving. The researchers concluded that productivity rose in response to almost any management action that workers interpreted as special attention. This finding—known today as the **Hawthorne effect**—had a major influence on human relations theory, although in many cases it amounted simply to convincing managers that they should pay more attention to employees.

Following the Hawthorne studies, managers and researchers alike focused more attention on the importance of good human relations in motivating employee performance. Stressing the factors that cause, focus, and sustain workers' behavior, most motivation theorists became concerned with the ways in which management thinks about and treats employees. The major motivation theories include the *human resources model*, the *hierarchy of needs model*, and the *two-factor theory*.[9]

Human Resources Model: Theories X and Y Behavioral scientist Douglas McGregor concluded that managers had radically different beliefs about how best to use the human resources employed by a firm. He classified these beliefs into sets of assumptions that he labeled "Theory X" and "Theory Y." The basic differences between these two theories are shown in Table 8.1.

Say What You Mean

Securing Satisfaction

Customer satisfaction is a well-established value in most companies, but what about employee satisfaction? One of the best ways for a company to engage its employees, gain their commitment, and improve their job satisfaction is to give them a voice. BBVA, Spain's second-largest bank, accomplishes this by including employees in the performance evaluation process. Not only is one's own self-evaluation considered, but co-workers also answer 35–64 questions about each employee's performance. Infosys Technologies in Bangalore, India, started a Voice of Youth program, which gives top-performing twenty-somethings a seat on its management council.[10] At Ritz-Carlton hotels across the world, after every employee hears a daily "wow story" of someone in the company who went to customer

service extremes, managers then open the floor for employees to discuss issues from what cleaner the housekeeping staff prefers to their own stories about guest experiences.[11] By approaching employees as internal customers who deserve the same level of service, these companies are likely to create a level of commitment and devotion in their employees that will keep them—and the customers they serve—satisfied.

> **Many companies solicit direct feedback from employees through surveys, performace evaluations, or company meetings in which employees have the opportunity to voice their problems and opinions on a regular basis.**

Table 8.1 Theory X and Theory Y

Theory X	Theory Y
People are lazy.	People are energetic.
People lack ambition and dislike responsibility.	People are ambitious and seek responsibility.
People are self-centered.	People can be selfless.
People resist change.	People want to contribute to business growth and change.
People are gullible and not very bright.	People are intelligent.

Managers who subscribe to **Theory X** tend to believe that people are naturally lazy and uncooperative and must be either punished or rewarded to be made productive. Managers who accept **Theory Y** tend to believe that people are naturally energetic, growth-oriented, self-motivated, and interested in being productive.

McGregor argued that Theory Y managers are more likely to have satisfied and motivated employees. Theory X and Y distinctions are somewhat simplistic and offer little concrete basis for action. Their value lies primarily in their ability to highlight and classify the behavior of managers in light of their attitudes toward employees.

Maslow's Hierarchy of Needs Model Psychologist Abraham Maslow's **hierarchy of human needs model** proposes that people have several different needs that they attempt to satisfy in their work. Maslow classified these needs into five basic types and suggested that they be arranged in the hierarchy of importance shown in Figure 8.2. According to Maslow, needs are hierarchical because lower-level needs must be met before a person will try to satisfy higher-level needs.

Once a set of needs has been satisfied, it ceases to motivate behavior. For example, if you feel secure in your job, your security needs have been met, so additional opportunities to achieve even more security, such as being assigned to a long-term project, will probably be less important to you than the chance to fulfill social or esteem needs, such as working with a mentor or becoming the member of an advisory board.

If, however, a lower-level need suddenly becomes unfulfilled, most people immediately refocus on that lower level. Suppose, for example, you are seeking to meet your self-esteem needs by working as a divisional manager at a major company. If you learn that your division and, consequently, your job may be eliminated, you might very well find the promise of job security at a new firm as motivating as a promotion once would have been at your old company.

Two-Factor Theory After studying a group of accountants and engineers, psychologist Frederick Herzberg concluded that job satisfaction and dissatisfaction depend on two factors: *hygiene factors*, such as working conditions, and *motivation factors*, such as recognition for a job well done.

According to Herzberg's **two-factor theory**, hygiene factors affect motivation and satisfaction only if they are absent or fail to meet expectations. For example, workers will be dissatisfied if they believe they have poor working conditions. If working conditions are improved, however, they will not necessarily become satisfied; they will simply not be dissatisfied. On the other hand, if workers receive no recognition for successful work, they may be neither dissatisfied nor satisfied. If recognition is provided, they will likely become more satisfied.

THEORY X theory of motivation holding that people are naturally lazy and uncooperative

THEORY Y theory of motivation holding that people are naturally energetic, growth-oriented, self-motivated, and interested in being productive

HIERARCHY OF HUMAN NEEDS MODEL theory of motivation describing five levels of human needs and arguing that basic needs must be fulfilled before people work to satisfy higher-level needs

TWO-FACTOR THEORY theory of motivation holding that job satisfaction depends on two factors, hygiene and motivation

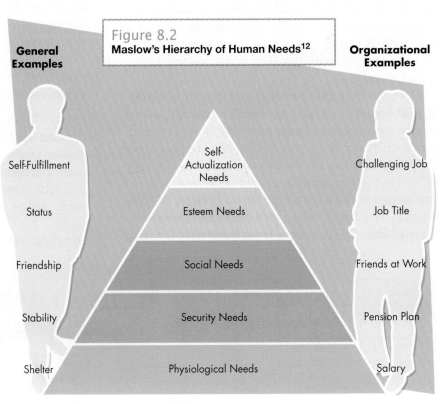

Figure 8.2
Maslow's Hierarchy of Human Needs[12]

General Examples | Organizational Examples

General Examples		Organizational Examples
Self-Fulfillment	Self-Actualization Needs	Challenging Job
Status	Esteem Needs	Job Title
Friendship	Social Needs	Friends at Work
Stability	Security Needs	Pension Plan
Shelter	Physiological Needs	Salary

Figure 8.3 illustrates the two-factor theory. Note that motivation factors lie along a continuum from satisfaction to no satisfaction. Hygiene factors, in contrast, are likely to produce feelings that lie on a continuum from dissatisfaction to no dissatisfaction. Whereas motivation factors are directly related to the work that employees actually perform, hygiene factors refer to the environment in which they work.

This theory suggests that managers should follow a two-step approach to enhancing motivation. First, they must ensure that hygiene factors—working conditions, for example, or clearly stated policies—are acceptable. This practice will result in an absence of dissatisfaction. Then they must offer motivation factors—recognition or added responsibility—as a way to improve satisfaction and motivation.

Contemporary Motivation Theory

Recently, other more complex models of employee behavior and motivation have been developed.[13] Two of the more interesting and useful ones are *expectancy theory* and *equity theory*.

Expectancy Theory
Expectancy theory suggests that people are motivated to work toward rewards that they want and that they believe they have a reasonable chance—or expectancy—of obtaining. A reward that seems out of reach is likely to be undesirable even if it is intrinsically positive. Figure 8.4 illustrates expectancy theory in terms of issues that are likely to be considered by an individual employee.

Consider the case of an assistant department manager who learns that her firm needs to replace a retiring division manager three levels above her in the organization. Even though she wants the job, she does not apply because she doubts she will be selected. In this case, she considers the performance-reward issue: she believes that her performance will not get her the position. She also learns that the firm is looking for a production manager on the night shift. She thinks she could get this job but does

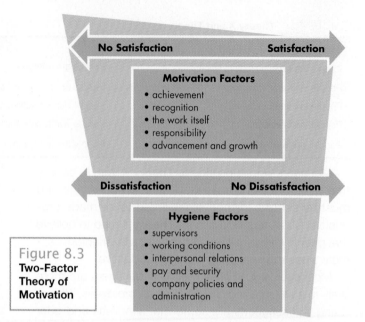

Figure 8.3
Two-Factor Theory of Motivation

not apply because she does not want to work nights (the rewards-personal goals issue). Finally, she learns of an opening one level higher—department manager—in her own division. She may well apply for this job because she both wants it and thinks that she has a good chance of getting it. In this case, her consideration of all the issues has led to an expectancy that she can reach a goal.

Expectancy theory helps explain why people whose salaries are based purely on seniority may not work as hard as they can. Paying employees the same whether they work very hard or just hard enough to get by removes the financial incentive for them to work harder. In other words, they ask themselves, "If I work harder, will I get a pay raise?" (the performance-reward issue) and conclude that the answer is no. Similarly, if hard work will result in one or more undesirable outcomes—for example, a transfer to another location or a promotion to a job that requires unpleasant travel (the rewards-personal goal issue)—employees will not be motivated to work hard.

Equity Theory
Equity theory focuses on social comparisons—people evaluating their treatment by the organization relative to the treatment of others. This approach holds that people analyze inputs (what they contribute to their jobs in terms of time, effort, education, and experience) relative to outputs (what they receive in return—salary, benefits, recognition, and security). This comparison is very similar to the psychological contract. As viewed by equity theory, the result is a ratio of contribution to return. Then they compare their own ratios

Effort–Performance Issue   Performance–Reward Issue   Rewards–Personal Goals Issue

Figure 8.4
Expectancy Theory Model

with those of other employees and ask whether their ratios are equal to, greater than, or less than those of others. Depending on their assessments, they experience feelings of equity or inequity. Figure 8.5 illustrates the three possible results of such an assessment.

For example, suppose a new college graduate gets a starting job at a large manufacturing firm. His starting salary is $45,000 a year, he gets an inexpensive company car, and he shares an assistant with another new employee. If he later learns that another new employee has received the same salary, car, and staff arrangement, he will feel equitably treated (result 1 in Figure 8.5). If the other newcomer, however, has received $70,000, a more expensive company car, and a personal assistant, he may feel inequitably treated (result 2 in Figure 8.5).

Note, however, that for an individual to feel equitably treated, the two ratios do not have to be identical, only equitable. Assume, for instance, that our new employee has a bachelor's degree and two years of work experience. Perhaps he learns subsequently that the

other new employee has an advanced degree and ten years of experience. After first feeling inequity, the new employee may conclude that the person with whom he compared himself is actually contributing more to the organization. That employee is equitably entitled, therefore, to receive more in return (result 3 in Figure 8.5).

When people feel they are being inequitably treated, they may do various constructive and some not-so-constructive things to restore fairness. For example, they may speak to their boss about the perceived inequity. Or (less constructively) they may demand a raise, reduce their efforts, work shorter hours, or just complain to co-workers. They may also rationalize ("Management succumbed to pressure to promote a minority"), find different people with whom to compare themselves, or leave their jobs.

Strategies and Techniques for Enhancing Motivation

Understanding what motivates workers is only one part of the manager's job. The other part is applying that knowledge. Experts have suggested—and many companies have implemented—a range of programs designed to make jobs more interesting and rewarding, to make the work environment more pleasant, and to motivate employees to work harder.

Reinforcement/Behavior Modification

Some companies try to control workers' behavior through systematic rewards and punishments for specific behaviors. Such companies first try to define the specific behaviors that they want their employees to exhibit (working hard, being courteous to customers, and stressing quality) and the specific behaviors they want to eliminate (wasting time, being rude to customers, and ignoring quality). Then they try to shape employee behavior by linking positive reinforcement with desired behaviors and punishment with undesired behaviors.

Positive reinforcement is used when a company or manager provides a reward when employees exhibit desired behaviors. When rewards are tied directly to performance, they serve as positive reinforcement. For example, paying large cash bonuses to salespeople who exceed quotas prompts them to work even harder during the next

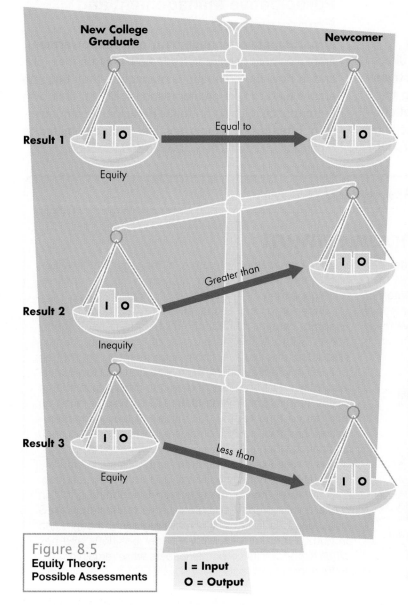

Figure 8.5
Equity Theory: Possible Assessments

New College Graduate   Newcomer

Result 1   I O   Equal to   I O
Equity

Result 2   I O   Greater than   I O
Inequity

Result 3   I O   Less than   I O
Equity

I = Input
O = Output

selling period. John Deere has adopted a reward system based on positive reinforcement. The firm gives pay increases when its workers complete college courses and demonstrate mastery of new job skills.

Punishment is designed to change behavior by presenting people with unpleasant consequences if they exhibit undesired behaviors. Employees who are repeatedly late for work, for example, may be suspended or have their pay docked. Similarly, when the National Football League or Major League Baseball fines or suspends players found guilty of substance abuse, the organization is seeking to change players' behaviors.

Using Goals to Motivate Behavior

Performance goals are also commonly used to direct and motivate behavior. **Management by objectives (MBO)** is a system of collaborative goal setting that extends from the top of an organization to the bottom. MBO involves managers and subordinates in setting goals and evaluating progress. After the organization specifies its overall goals and plans, managers collaborate with each of their subordinates to set individual goals accordingly. Managers meet periodically to review progress toward individual goals, and then, usually on an annual basis, goal achievement is evaluated and used as a basis for starting the cycle over again.

According to many experts, motivational impact is the biggest advantage of MBO. When employees sit down with managers to set upcoming goals, they learn more about companywide objectives, feel that they are an important part of a team, and see how they can improve companywide performance by reaching their own goals. If an MBO system is used properly, employees should leave meetings not only with an understanding of the value of their contributions but also with fair rewards for their performances. They should also accept and be committed to the moderately difficult and specific goals they have helped set for themselves.[14]

Participative Management and Empowerment

In **participative management and empowerment**, employees are given a voice in how they do their jobs and in how the company is managed—they become empowered to take greater responsibility for their own performance. Not surprisingly, participative empowerment often makes employees feel more committed to organizational goals they have helped to shape.

Entrepreneurship and New Ventures

Extreme Employee Empowerment

In the mid-1980s, Roger Sant and Dennis Bakke decided to take advantage of the Public Utility Regulatory Policy Act and establish what would become a huge international energy company built on the values of social responsibility, integrity, fairness, and fun. To achieve these ideals, Sant and Bakke established AES Corporation under a management structure, or more accurately a lack of one, that has been called "adhocracy" and "empowerment gone mad."

Under an organizational structure AES dubs a "honeycomb," small, multifunctional teams manage themselves without the assistance of any legal, human resources, or other functional department or any written policies or procedures. AES strives to have as few supervisory layers as possible, and no one person is in charge of the teams. Employees make HR decisions, such as how much time to take for maternity leave, for themselves, and they consult outside experts on matters such as finance when necessary.

Dennis Bakke, co-founder of AES Corporation, speaks worldwide about the advantages of the Public Utility Regulatory Policy Act.

As a result of this structure, employees are empowered, flexible, multidimensional, and constantly learning. Furthermore, the company is high-functioning and can make decisions and complete projects efficiently. AES continues to adapt to its increasing growth, though, and in 2002 added five executive officer positions and has since expanded its corporate leaders while remaining true to its honeycomb roots.[15]

"O.K., I messed up. He didn't have to rub my nose in it."

Participation and empowerment can be used in large or small firms with managers and operating employees. For example, sports gear company And1 allows its designers considerable latitude in testing new ideas—a designer can make a few prototypes of a new product, distribute them to kids on a neighborhood basketball court, and then get their feedback.

Although some employees thrive in participative programs, such programs are not for everyone. People may be frustrated by responsibilities they are not equipped to handle by a symbolic rather than substantive invitation to participate. One key, say most experts, is to invite participation only to the extent that employees want to have input and only if participation will have real value for an organization.

Team Management

We have already noted the increased use of teams in organizations. Yet another benefit that some companies get from using teams is increased motivation and enhanced job satisfaction. Although teams are often less effective in traditional and rigidly structured bureaucratic organizations, they often help smaller, more flexible organizations make decisions more quickly and effectively, enhance companywide communication, and encourage members to feel more like a part of an organization. In turn, these attitudes usually lead to higher levels of both employee motivation and job satisfaction.[16]

But managers should remember that teams are not for everyone. Levi Strauss, for example,

> This team of workers at Germany's Apollo car production plant work together to design and manufacture the Apollo sports car. Such teams often help firms make decisions more effectively, enhance communication, and lead to increased employee motivation and satisfaction.

encountered major problems when it tried to use teams. Individual workers previously performed repetitive, highly specialized tasks, such as sewing zippers into jeans, and were paid according to the number of jobs they completed each day. In an attempt to boost productivity, company management reorganized everyone into teams of 10 to 35 workers and assigned tasks to the entire group. Each team member's pay was determined by the team's level of productivity. In practice, however, faster workers became resentful of slower workers because they reduced the group's total output. Slower workers, meanwhile, resented the pressure put on them by faster-working co-workers. As a result, motivation, satisfaction, and morale all dropped, and Levi Strauss eventually abandoned the teamwork plan altogether.

Job Enrichment and Job Redesign

Whereas goal setting and MBO programs and empowerment can work in a variety of settings, *job enrichment* and *job redesign* programs are generally used to increase satisfaction in jobs significantly lacking in motivating factors.[17]

Job Enrichment Programs **Job enrichment** is designed to add one or more motivating factors to job activities. For example, *job rotation* programs expand growth opportunities by rotating employees through various positions in the same firm. Workers gain not only new skills but also broader overviews of their work and their organization. Other programs focus on increasing responsibility or recognition. At Continental Airlines, for example, flight attendants now have more control over their own scheduling. The jobs of flight service managers were enriched when they were given more responsibility and

> **JOB ENRICHMENT** method of increasing job satisfaction by adding one or more motivating factors to job activities

JOB REDESIGN method of increasing job satisfaction by designing a more satisfactory fit between workers and their jobs

WORK SHARING (JOB SHARING) method of increasing job satisfaction by allowing two or more people to share a single full-time job

FLEXTIME PROGRAMS method of increasing job satisfaction by allowing workers to adjust work schedules on a daily or weekly basis

TELECOMMUTING form of flextime that allows people to perform some or all of a job away from standard office settings

authority for assigning tasks to flight crew members.

Job Redesign Programs

Job redesign acknowledges that different people want different things from their jobs. By restructuring work to achieve a more satisfactory fit between workers and their jobs, job redesign can motivate individuals with strong needs for career growth or achievement. Job redesign is usually implemented through one of three ways:

■ *Combining tasks* involves enlarging jobs and increasing their variety to make employees feel that their work is meaningful and, in turn, become more motivated. For example, the job done by a programmer who maintains computer systems might be redesigned to include some system design and system development work. While developing additional skills, the programmer also gets involved in the overall system development.

■ *Forming natural work groups* allows people who do different jobs on the same projects to help employees see their place and importance in the total structure of the firm. They are valuable to management because the people working on a project are usually the most knowledgeable about it and the most capable problem solvers.

■ *Establishing client relationships* means letting employees interact with customers to increase job variety and give workers both a greater sense of control and more performance feedback. For example, software writers at Microsoft watch test users work with programs and discuss problems with them directly rather than receive feedback from third-party researchers.

Modified Work Schedules

As another way of increasing job satisfaction, many companies are experimenting with *modified work schedules*—different approaches to working hours.[18]

Work-Share Programs   At Steelcase, the country's largest maker of office furnishings, two very talented women in the marketing division both wanted to work only part-time. The solution: they now share a single full-time job and each work 2.5 days a week to get the job done well. The practice, known as **work sharing** (or **job sharing**), has "brought sanity back to our lives," according to at least one Steelcase employee.

Job sharing usually benefits both employees and employers. Employees tend to appreciate the organization's attention to their personal needs, while the company can reduce turnover and save on the cost of benefits. On the negative side, job-share employees generally receive fewer benefits than their full-time counterparts and may be the first to be laid off when cutbacks are necessary.

Flextime Programs and Alternative Workplace Strategies   **Flextime programs** allow people to choose their working hours by adjusting a standard work schedule on a daily or weekly basis. Often, there are limits to flextime: Steelcase, for instance, requires all employees to work certain core hours during which everyone works and can communicate. Employees can then decide whether to make up the rest of the standard eight-hour day by coming in and leaving early or late. Companies may also allow employees to choose the number of days during which to work each week, provided they still complete 40 hours of work.

Telecommuting   A rapidly growing number of U.S. workers do a significant portion of their work via **telecommuting**—performing some or all of a job away from standard office settings. Working from a home office outfitted with a PC, high-speed Internet, and a company intranet connection, telecommuters can keep abreast of everything going on at the office. In 2004, at least 14 million U.S. workers spent at least part of their

Best Buy is taking the modified schedules and alternative workplaces to new extremes with its corporate "results-only work environment" or ROWE. Under ROWE, Best Buy employees can work anytime, anywhere, as long as they achieve results. The program has been so successful that Best Buy has begun introducing the program into its retail stores in 2007.

working hours telecommuting. This trend is on the rise: in 2005, 44 percent of U.S. companies offered some telecommuting options, up from 32 percent in 2001.[19]

Advantages and Disadvantages of Modified Work Schedules and Alternative Workplaces Flextime gives employees more freedom in their professional and personal lives by allowing them to plan around family schedules. Studies show that the increased sense of freedom and control reduces stress and improves individual productivity. Companies also benefit in other ways. In urban areas, for example, such programs can reduce traffic congestion and similar problems that contribute to stress and lost work time, and employers benefit from higher levels of commitment and job satisfaction. John Hancock Insurance, Atlantic Richfield, and Metropolitan Life are among the major U.S. corporations that have successfully adopted some form of flextime.

Conversely, flextime sometimes complicates coordination because people are working different schedules. In addition, if workers are paid by the hour, flextime may make it difficult for employers to keep accurate records of when employees are actually working.

As for telecommuting, it may not be for everyone. For example, consultant Gil Gordon points out that telecommuters are attracted to the ideas of "not having to shave and put on makeup or go through traffic, and sitting in their blue jeans all day." However, he suggests that would-be telecommuters ask themselves several other questions: "Can I manage deadlines? What will it be like to be away from the social context of the office five days a week?" One study has shown that even though telecommuters may be producing results, those with strong advancement ambitions may miss out on day-to-day networking opportunities.

Another obstacle to establishing a telecommuting program is convincing management of its benefits. Telecommuters may have to fight the perception from both bosses and co-workers that if they are not being supervised, they are not working. Managers, admits one experienced consultant, "usually have to be dragged kicking and screaming into this. They always ask 'How can I tell if someone is working when I can't see them?'" But, he adds, "that's based on the erroneous assumption that if you can see them, they are working." Most experts agree that clear expectations, reeducation, and constant communication are requirements of a successful telecommuting arrangement. Both managers and employees must determine expectations in advance.

> **For additional topics related to this material and end-of-chapter exercises and practices, please visit www.mybizlab.com.**

Questions for Review

1. Describe the psychological contract you currently have or have had in the past with an employer. If you have never worked, describe the psychological contract that you have with the instructor in this class.

2. Do you think that most people are relatively satisfied or dissatisfied with their work? What factors do you think most contribute to satisfaction or dissatisfaction?

3. Compare and contrast the hierarchy of human needs with the two-factor theory of motivation.

4. How can participative management programs enhance employee satisfaction and motivation?

Questions for Analysis

5. Some evidence suggests that recent college graduates show high levels of job satisfaction. Levels then drop dramatically as they reach their late twenties, only to increase gradually once they get older. What might account for this pattern?

6. Under what sort of circumstances might you, as a manager, apply each of the theories of motivation discussed in this chapter? Which would be easiest to use? Which would be hardest? Why?

7. Suppose you realize one day that you are dissatisfied with your job. Short of quitting, what might you do to improve your situation?

8. Describe what you would tell a low-skill worker performing a simple and routine job who wants more challenge and enjoyment from work.

Application Exercises

9. Assume you are about to start your own business. What might you do from the very beginning to ensure that your employees will be satisfied and motivated?

10. Interview the manager of a local manufacturing company. Identify as many different strategies for enhancing job satisfaction at that company as you can. Are the strategies effective at enhancing employee job satisfaction? Why or why not?

chapter 9

Leadership and Decision Making

After reading this chapter, you should be able to:

1 Define *leadership* and distinguish it from management.

2 Summarize early approaches to the study of leadership.

3 Discuss the concept of situational approaches to leadership.

4 Describe transformational and charismatic perspectives on leadership.

5 Identify and discuss leadership substitutes and neutralizers.

6 Discuss leaders as coaches and examine gender and cross-cultural issues in leadership.

7 Describe strategic leadership, ethical leadership, and virtual leadership.

8 Relate leadership to decision making and discuss both rational and behavioral perspectives on decision making.

A Bid for Improvement

When John Donahoe took the reins from Meg Whitman, who stepped down as CEO of eBay in March 2008, he knew he'd be in for a bumpy ride. Although Whitman's leadership had been instrumental in guiding the online auction pioneer to a billion-dollar firm servicing hundreds of millions of users around the world, she'd left eBay at a critical moment in its development. Google and Amazon had launched auction venues that cut into eBay's market share, and eBay's notoriously vocal community of buyers and sellers had been growing increasingly frustrated by high fees and inefficient search technology.

Donahoe had already demonstrated a willingness to make sweeping institutional changes. Prior to becoming CEO he'd spent three years as president of eBay Marketplaces, during which time he reorganized corporate headquarters to facilitate closer relationships between the engineers who design products and the businesspeople who market them, and pushed to expand eBay's array of services by acquiring such online marketplaces as Shopping.com and StubHub. One of his first moves as CEO was to announce a decrease in the fees paid upfront by sellers, and he announced plans to streamline eBay's search engine so that buyers would have a more focused shopping experience.

At the office, Donahoe is known for his enthusiasm and accessibility (not to mention his 70-hour workweeks). His actions since taking over suggest he is well aware of the criticisms leveled at his company by investors and customers alike and is committed to addressing them. "I think when we are really objective with ourselves," he said recently, "we have to admit our user experience has not kept up with other e-commerce sites all around us." It will require a recommitment to user experience to lead eBay back to the vanguard of online businesses.[1]

What's in It for Me?

It is time to examine in detail how leaders—who may or may not also be managers such as John Donahoe—actually go about affecting employee behavior and motivating their performance. We shall place these strategies and tactics in the context of various approaches to leadership throughout the years, including the situational perspective accepted today. Understanding these concepts will help you function more effectively as a leader and give you more insight into how your manager or boss strives to motivate you through his or her own leadership.

The Nature of Leadership

Because *leadership* is a term that is often used in everyday conversation, you might assume that it has a common and accepted meaning. It is a word that is often misused. We define **leadership** as the processes and behaviors used by someone, such as a manager, to motivate, inspire, and influence the behaviors of others. One of the biggest errors people make is assuming that leadership and management mean the same thing when they are really different concepts. A person can be a manager, a leader, both, or neither.[2] Some of the basic distinctions between the two are summarized in Table 9.1. The first column lists four dimensions that differentiate leadership from management. The second and third columns show how each dimension differs when considered from the perspectives of managers versus leaders. For example, when they are executing plans, managers focus on monitoring results and identifying deviations. In contrast, leaders focus on energizing people to overcome bureaucratic hurdles to reach goals.

Consider the various roles of managers and leaders in a hospital setting. The chief of staff (chief physician) of a large hospital, though clearly a manager by virtue of his position, may not be respected or trusted by others and may have to rely solely on the authority vested in the position to get people to do things. On the other hand, an emergency-room nurse with no formal authority may be quite effective at taking charge of a chaotic situation and directing others in dealing with specific patient problems. The chief of staff is a manager but not a leader, while the nurse is a leader but not a manager.

Finally, the head of pediatrics, supervising a staff of 20 other doctors, nurses, and attendants, may also enjoy the staff's complete respect, confidence, and trust. They readily take her advice and follow directives without question, and often go far beyond what is necessary to help carry out the unit's mission. Thus, the head of pediatrics is both a manager and a leader.

Organizations need both management and leadership if they are to be effective. Management in conjunction with leadership can help achieve planned orderly change, and leadership in conjunction with management can keep the organization properly aligned with its environment.

Early Approaches to Leadership

Although leaders and leadership have profoundly influenced history, careful scientific study of them began only about a century ago. Early studies focused on the *traits*, or personal characteristics, of leaders. Later research shifted to examine actual leader *behaviors*.

Trait Approaches to Leadership

Early researchers believed that notable leaders had some unique set of qualities or traits that distinguished them from their peers and endured throughout history.

Table 9.1   **Kotter's Distinctions Between Management and Leadership[3]**

Activity	Management	Leadership
Creating an Agenda	**Planning and budgeting.** Establishing detailed steps and timetables for achieving needed results; allocating the resources necessary to make those needed results happen.	**Establishing direction.** Developing a vision of the future, often the distant future, and strategies for producing the changes needed to achieve that vision.
Developing a Human Network for Achieving the Agenda	**Organizing and staffing.** Establishing some structure for accomplishing plan requirements, staffing that structure with individuals, delegating responsibility and authority for carrying out the plan, providing policies and procedures to help guide people, and creating methods or systems to monitor implementation.	**Aligning people.** Communicating the direction by words and deeds to all those whose cooperation may be needed to influence the creation of teams and coalitions that understand the vision and strategies and accept their validity.
Executing Plans	**Controlling and problem solving.** Monitoring results vs. plan in some detail, identifying deviations, and then planning and organizing to solve these problems.	**Motivating and inspiring.** Energizing people to overcome major political, bureaucratic, and resource barriers to change by satisfying very basic, but often unfulfilled, human needs.
Outcomes	Produces a degree of predictability and order and has the potential to consistently produce major results expected by various shareholders (e.g., for customers, always being on time; for stockholders, being on budget).	Produces change, often to a dramatic degree, and has the potential to produce extremely useful change (e.g., new products that customers want, new approaches to labor relations that help make a firm more competitive).

Leaders have always played important roles in society. For instance, even though Abraham Lincoln, Mohandas Gandhi, and Eleanor Roosevelt lived at different times and worked in different areas, each is recognized as an exemplary leader. Early approaches to leadership attempted to identify the key traits or behaviors that characterized these and other leaders.

This **trait approach to leadership** led researchers to focus on identifying the essential leadership traits, including intelligence, dominance, self-confidence, energy, activity (versus passivity), and knowledge about the job. Unfortunately, the list quickly became so long that it lost any practical value. In addition, the results of many studies were inconsistent. For example, one arugment stated that the most effective leaders were tall, like Abraham Lincoln. But critics were quick to point out that neither Napoleon Bonaparte nor Adolf Hitler was tall, but both were effective leaders in their own way.

Although the trait approach was all but abandoned several decades ago, in recent years, it has resurfaced. For example, some researchers have again started to focus on a limited set of traits. These traits include emotional intelligence, mental intelligence, drive, motivation, honesty and integrity, self-confidence, knowledge of the business, and charisma. Some people even believe that biological factors, such as appearance or height, may play a role in leadership. However, it is too early to know whether these traits really do relate to leadership.

Behavioral Approaches to Leadership

In the late 1940s, most researchers began to shift away from the trait approach and to look at leadership as a set of actual behaviors. The goal of the **behavioral approach to leadership** was to determine what *behaviors* were employed by effective leaders. These researchers assumed that the behaviors of effective leaders differed somehow from the behaviors of less effective leaders, and that the behaviors of effective leaders would be the same across all situations.

This research led to the identification of two basic forms of leader behavior. While different researchers applied different names, the basic leader behaviors identified during this period were

■ **Task-focused leader behavior**: Task-focused leader behavior occurs when a leader focuses on how tasks should be performed in order to meet certain goals and to achieve certain performance standards.

■ **Employee-focused leader behavior**: Employee-focused leader behavior occurs when a leader focuses on the satisfaction, motivation, and well-being of his or her employees.

During this period, people believed that leaders should always try to engage in a healthy dose of both behaviors, one to increase performance and the other to increase job satisfaction and motivation. Experts also began to realize that they could train managers to engage in these behaviors in a systematic manner. But they also discovered that there were other leader behaviors that needed to be considered, and that there were circumstances in which different combinations of leader behavior might be more effective than other combinations.

For instance, suppose a new manager takes over a work site that is plagued by low productivity and whose workers, while perhaps satisfied, are not motivated to work hard. The leader should most likely focus on task-focused behaviors in order to improve lagging productivity. But now suppose the situation is different—productivity is very high, but workers are stressed out about their jobs and have low levels of job satisfaction. In this instance, the manager should most likely concentrate on employee-focused behaviors to help improve job satisfaction. This line of thinking led to the creation of *situational theories*.

The Situational Approach to Leadership

The **situational approach to leadership** assumes that appropriate leader behavior varies from one situation to another. This approach was first proposed as a continuum of leadership behavior, which is shown in Figure 9.1. This continuum ranges from the one extreme of having the leader make decisions alone to the other extreme of having employees make decisions with only minimal guidance from the leader. Each point on the continuum is influenced by *characteristics of the leader*, *his or her subordinates*, and the *situation*.

Leadership characteristics include the manager's value system, confidence in subordinates, personal inclinations, and feelings of security. Subordinate characteristics include the subordinates' need for independence, readiness to assume responsibility, tolerance for ambiguity, interest in the problem, understanding of goals, knowledge, experience, and expectations. Situational characteristics that affect decision making include the type of organization, group effectiveness, the problem itself, and time pressures.

Leadership through the Eyes of Followers

Another recent perspective that has been adopted by some leadership experts focuses on how leaders are seen through the eyes of their followers. The two primary approaches to leadership through the eyes of followers are *transformational leadership* and *charismatic leadership*.

Transformational Leadership

Transformational leadership focuses on the importance of leading for change (as opposed to leading during a period of stability). According to this view, much of what a leader does involves carrying out what might be thought of as basic management "transactions"—assigning work, evaluating performance, making decisions, and so forth. Occasionally, however, the leader has to engage in transformational leadership to initiate and manage major change, such as managing a merger, creating a new work team, or redefining the organization's culture.

Thus, **transformational leadership** is the set of abilities that allows a leader to recognize the need for change, to create a vision to guide that change, and to execute

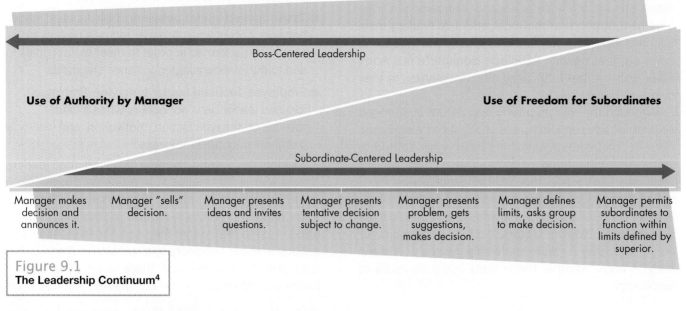

Boss-Centered Leadership

Use of Authority by Manager

Use of Freedom for Subordinates

Subordinate-Centered Leadership

| Manager makes decision and announces it. | Manager "sells" decision. | Manager presents ideas and invites questions. | Manager presents tentative decision subject to change. | Manager presents problem, gets suggestions, makes decision. | Manager defines limits, asks group to make decision. | Manager permits subordinates to function within limits defined by superior. |

Figure 9.1
The Leadership Continuum[4]

Rupert Murdoch, CEO of News Corp., has used transformational leadership to expand and consolidate his media empire of newspapers, film, and television. He will need to strike a balance between transformational and transactional leadership as he manages his newest acquisition, the *Wall Street Journal*.

and acceptance. Charismatic leaders are likely to have a lot of confidence in their beliefs and ideals and a strong need to influence people. They also tend to communicate high expectations about follower performance and to express confidence in their followers. Many of the most influential leaders in history have been extremely charismatic, including entrepreneurs Mary Kay Ash, Steve Jobs, and Ted Turner; civil rights leader Martin Luther King, Jr.; and Pope John Paul II. Unfortunately, charisma can also empower leaders in other directions. Adolf Hitler, for instance, had strong charismatic qualities.

Most experts today acknowledge three crucial elements of charismatic leadership:[6]

1 Charismatic leaders *envision* likely future trends and patterns, set high expectations for themselves and for others, and behave in ways that meet or exceed those expectations.

2 Charismatic leaders *energize* others by demonstrating personal excitement, personal confidence, and consistent patterns of success.

3 Charismatic leaders *enable* others by supporting them, empathizing with them, and expressing confidence in them.

Charismatic leadership ideas are quite popular among managers today and are the subject of numerous books and articles.[7] Unfortunately, few studies have specifically attempted to test the meaning and impact of charismatic leadership. Lingering ethical concerns about charismatic leadership also trouble some people. They stem from the fact that some charismatic leaders inspire such blind faith in their followers that they may engage in inappropriate, unethical, or even illegal behaviors just because the leader instructed them to do so. This tendency likely played a role in the unwinding of both Enron and Arthur Andersen, as people followed orders from their charismatic bosses to hide information, shred documents, and mislead investigators.

Taking over a leadership role from someone with substantial personal charisma is also a challenge. For instance, the immediate successors to very successful and

the change effectively. Some experts believe that change is such a vital organizational function that even successful firms need to change regularly to avoid becoming complacent and stagnant. In contrast, **transactional leadership** is essentially the same as management in that it involves routine, regimented activities. Only a leader with tremendous influence can hope to perform both functions successfully. Some experts believe that change is such a vital organizational function that even successful firms need to change regularly to avoid becoming complacent and stagnant; accordingly, leadership for change is extremely important.

Charismatic Leadership

Charismatic leadership is a type of influence based on the leader's charisma, a form of interpersonal attraction that inspires support

Under New Ownership

Some leaders are able to adopt either transformational or transactional perspectives, depending on their circumstances. For instance, Rupert Murdoch, CEO of News Corp., has a long history of transforming the media properties he acquires in order to expand their reach and turn a profit. Early in his career Murdoch relaunched *The Sun*, a British daily newspaper, as a tabloid notorious for its sensationalistic focus on sex. On the other hand, he has generally avoided retooling another of his British acquisitions, the well-regarded *Times*. When he purchased the struggling *Wall Street Journal* in 2007, he pledged to remain a hands-off manager. In the months since, the paper's signature coverage of U.S. business news has decreased to make room for increased coverage of politics and foreign events, and it remains to be seen how Murdoch will balance transformational and transactional leadership at the *Journal*.[5]

charismatic athletic coaches like Vince Lombardi (Green Bay Packers) and Phil Jackson (Chicago Bulls) each failed to measure up to their predecessors' legacies and were subsequently fired.

Highly charismatic leaders often achieve great success. Vince Lombardi's charisma helped lead the Green Bay Packers to win five league championships and two Super Bowls. Succeeding a charismatic leader can be difficult, however—Lombardi's successor Phil Bengtson was fired after following up Lombardi's successes with two losing seasons.

Special Issues in Leadership

Another interesting perspective on leadership focuses on *alternatives* to leadership. In some cases, certain factors may actually *substitute* for leadership, making actual leadership unnecessary or irrelevant. In other cases, factors may exist that *neutralize* or negate the influence of a leader even when that individual is attempting to exercise leadership.

Leadership Substitutes

Leadership substitutes are individual, task, and organizational characteristics that tend to outweigh the need for a leader to initiate or direct employee performance. In other words, if certain factors are present, the employee will perform his or her job capably, without the direction of a leader. Table 9.2 identifies several basic leadership substitutes.

Consider, for example, what happens when an ambulance with a critically injured victim screeches to the door of a hospital emergency room. Do the ER employees stand around waiting for someone to take control and instruct them on what to do? The answer is no—they are highly trained and well-prepared professionals who know how to respond and work together as a team without someone playing the role of leader.

Leadership Neutralizers

In other situations, even if a leader is present and attempts to engage in various leadership behaviors, those behaviors may be rendered ineffective—or neutralized—by various factors that can be called **leadership neutralizers**. Suppose, for example, that a relatively new and inexperienced leader is assigned to a work group composed of very experienced employees with long-standing performance norms and a high level of group cohesiveness. The norms and cohesiveness of the group may be so strong that there is nothing the new leader can do to change things.

In addition to group factors, elements of the job itself may also limit a leader's ability to "make a difference." Consider, for example, employees working on a moving assembly line. Employees may only be able to work at the pace of the moving line, so performance quantity and quality are constrained by the speed of the line and simplicity of each individual task.

Finally, organizational factors can also neutralize at least some forms of leader behavior. Suppose a new leader is accustomed to using merit pay increases as a way to motivate people. But in his or her new job, pay increases are dictated by union contracts and are based primarily on employee seniority and cost of living. The leader's previous approach to motivating people would be neutralized, and new approaches would have to be identified.

Table 9.2 Leadership Substitutes and Neutralizers

Individual Factors	• Individual professionalism
	• Individual ability, knowledge, and motivation
	• Individual experience and training
	• Indifference to rewards
Job Factors	• Structured/automated
	• Highly controlled
	• Intrinsically satisfying
	• Embedded feedback
Organization Factors	• Explicit plans and goals
	• Rigid rules and procedures
	• Rigid reward system not tied to performance
	• Physical distance between supervisor and subordinate
Group Factors	• Group performance norms
	• High level of group cohesiveness
	• Group interdependence

The Changing Nature of Leadership

Various alternatives to leadership aside, many settings still call for at least some degree of leadership, although the nature of that leadership continues to evolve. Among the recent changes in leadership that managers should recognize are the increasing role of *leaders as coaches* as well as *gender and cross-cultural patterns* of leader behavior.

Leaders as Coaches

We noted in Chapter 6 that many organizations today are using teams. Many other organizations are attempting to become less hierarchical—that is, to eliminate the old-fashioned command-and-control mentality often inherent in bureaucratic organizations and to motivate and empower individuals to work independently. In each case, the role of leaders is also changing. Whereas leaders were once expected to control situations, direct work, supervise people, closely monitor performance, make decisions, and structure activities, many leaders today are being asked to change how they manage people. Perhaps the best description of this new role is for the leader to become a *coach* instead of an *overseer*.[8]

From the standpoint of a business leader, a coaching perspective would call for the leader to help select and train team members and other new employees, to provide some general direction, and to help the team get the information and other resources it needs. Coaches from different teams may play important roles in linking the activities and functions of their respective teams. Some leaders may function as *mentors*, helping less experienced employees learn the ropes and better preparing them to advance within the organization; they may also help resolve conflicts among team members and mediate other disputes that arise. But beyond these activities, the leader keeps a low profile and lets the group get its work done with little or no direct oversight, just as during a game an athletic coach trusts his or her players to execute the plays successfully.

Gender and Leadership

Another factor that is clearly altering the face of leadership is the growing number of women advancing to higher levels in organizations. Given that most leadership theories and research studies have focused on male leaders, developing a better understanding of how women lead is

---

Say What You Mean

No More Secrets?

As the public faces of their companies, CEOs are subject to intense scrutiny and take the heat from critics and consumer advocates for any company fault or misdeed. As a result, many CEOs take a very cautious and calculated approach to communicating with consumers. Many companies have strict guidelines regarding employees' blogging and reporting on internal issues. This kind of closed-doors approach keeps competitors in the dark and presumably minimizes public scrutiny.

However, a realistic evaluation of today's limitless capacity for information dissemination might lead a CEO to doubt the effectiveness of this policy. Some CEOs have embraced a philosophy of accessibility. In lieu of a carefully worded press release, they are using blogs and Web sites like YouTube to personally deliver messages to the public. In a YouTube video, the CEO of Jet Blue apologized to passengers who had been trapped for hours in planes grounded by bad weather, and Microsoft now allows its engineers to write about current projects in

blogs. Glenn Kelman, CEO of the real estate brokerage firm Redfin, started a blog to air his frustrations regarding real estate sales practices that he judged unfair to the consumer. His blog elicited angry responses in the comments section, to which he posted his own rebuttals. Redfin's customer base expanded, suggesting that Kelman's personal approach made his sympathy for the consumer more believable.

A strategy of transparency may have a humanizing effect on a company, making it more sympathetic to consumers who feel alienated by the trend toward an increasingly automated customer service experience. All firms have flaws and commit errors, and an admission of culpability, frustration, or weakness can make a company more relatable. Responsive, accessible CEOs may not be able to prevent criticism or scrutiny, but they may take a little air out of free-swinging critics used to hammering faceless offenders. Occasionally, the CEO may even beat the critics to the punch.[9]

clearly an important next step. Some early observers, for instance, predicted that (consistent with prevailing stereotypes) female leaders would be relatively warm, supportive, and nurturing as compared to their male counterparts. But research suggests that female leaders are not necessarily more nurturing or supportive than male leaders. Likewise, male leaders are not systematically harsher, more controlling, or more task focused than female leaders.

The one difference that has arisen in some cases is that women may be slightly more democratic in making decisions, whereas men have a tendency to be more autocratic.[10] However, much more work needs to be done in order to better understand the dynamics of gender and leadership. In the meantime, high-profile and successful female leaders, such as Andrea Jung (CEO of Avon Products) and Angela Merkel (chancellor of Germany), continue to demonstrate the effectiveness with which women can be exceptional leaders.

Cross-Cultural Leadership

Another changing perspective on leadership relates to cross-cultural issues. In this context, *culture* is used as a broad concept to encompass both international differences and diversity-based differences within one culture. For instance, Japan is generally characterized by *collectivism* (group before individual), whereas the United States is based more on *individualism* (individual before group). So when a Japanese firm sends an executive to head up the firm's operation in the United States, that person will likely find it necessary to recognize the importance of individual contributions and rewards and the differences in individual and group roles that exist in Japanese and U.S. businesses.

Similarly, cross-cultural factors also play a growing role in organizations as their workforces become more diverse. As African Americans, Asian Americans, Hispanics, and members of other ethnic groups achieve leadership positions, it may be necessary to reassess how applicable current theories and models of leadership are when applied to an increasingly diverse pool of leaders.

Emerging Issues in Leadership

Finally, there are also three emerging issues in leadership that warrant discussion. These issues are *strategic leadership*, *ethical leadership*, and *virtual leadership*.

Strategic Leadership

Strategic leadership is a new concept that explicitly relates leadership to the role of top management. **Strategic leadership** is a leader's ability to understand the complexities of both the organization and its environment and to lead change in the organization so as to enhance its competitiveness.

To be effective as a strategic leader, a manager needs to have a thorough and complete understanding of the organization—its history, its culture, its strengths, and its weaknesses. In addition, the leader needs a firm grasp of the organization's external environment. This needs to include current business and economic conditions and circumstances as well as significant trends and issues on the horizon. The strategic leader also needs to recognize the firm's current strategic advantages and shortcomings.

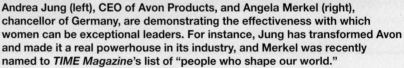

Andrea Jung (left), CEO of Avon Products, and Angela Merkel (right), chancellor of Germany, are demonstrating the effectiveness with which women can be exceptional leaders. For instance, Jung has transformed Avon and made it a real powerhouse in its industry, and Merkel was recently named to *TIME Magazine*'s list of "people who shape our world."

Ethical Leadership

Most people have long assumed that business leaders are ethical people. But in the wake of recent corporate scandals at firms like Enron, Boeing, and AIG, faith in business leaders has been shaken. Perhaps now more than ever, high standards of ethical conduct are being held up as a prerequisite for effective leadership. More specifically, business leaders are being called on to maintain high ethical standards for their own conduct, to unfailingly exhibit ethical behavior, and to hold others in their organizations to the same standards—in short, to practice **ethical leadership**.

The behaviors of top leaders are being scrutinized more than ever, and those responsible for hiring new leaders for a business are looking more closely at the backgrounds of those being considered. And the emerging pressures for stronger corporate governance models are likely to further increase the commitment to select only those individuals with high ethical standards for leadership positions in business and to hold them more accountable than in the past for both their actions and the consequences of those actions.

Virtual Leadership

Finally, **virtual leadership** is also emerging as an important issue for organizations. In earlier times, leaders and their employees worked together in the same physical location and engaged in face-to-face interactions on a regular basis. But in today's world, both leaders and their employees may work in locations that are far from one another. Such arrangements might include people telecommuting from a home office one or two days a week to people actually living and working far from company headquarters.

Increasingly, then, communication between leaders and their subordinates happens largely by telephone and e-mail. One implication may be that leaders in these situations must work harder at creating and maintaining relationships with their employees that go beyond words on a computer screen. While nonverbal communication, such as smiles and handshakes, may not be possible online, managers can instead make a point of adding

> **ETHICAL LEADERSHIP** leader behaviors that reflect high ethical standards
>
> **VIRTUAL LEADERSHIP** leadership in settings where leaders and followers interact electronically rather than in face-to-face settings

Entrepreneurship and New Ventures

An Apple a Day

As CEO of Apple Computer, Steve Jobs has developed a reputation for brilliance, originality, and charm. His leadership style has been criticized as well. One industry observer portrayed Jobs as intimidating and power hungry, while others said he commanded "a cult-like following from employees and consumers." Yet Jobs is clearly a leader who can deliver success in businesses that are evolving, highly technical, and demanding. Writer Steven Berglas says, "Jobs, the *enfant terrible* widely reputed to be one of the most aggressive egotists in Silicon Valley, has an unrivaled track record when it comes to pulling development teams through start-ups."

But how do Jobs's charisma, confidence, and vision shape his leadership style during times of prosperity and success? In a recent interview, Jobs discussed how his passion and focus enable the company to succeed in any type of situation or environment. "Lots of companies have tons of great engineers and smart people," said Jobs. "But ultimately, there needs to be some gravitational force that pulls it all together. . . . That's what was missing at Apple for a while. There were bits and pieces of interesting things floating around, but not that gravitational pull."

Today, Jobs is riding high, as he focuses on bringing Apple's unique blend of hi-tech gadgetry and cool design to applications reaching far beyond the computers that first made his fortune. The company has released several versions of the iPod, its hugely popular digital music player, supported by Apple's online music store, iTunes. The iPhone, a mobile phone that connects to the Internet, was named 2007's Invention of the Year by *TIME Magazine*. And Jobs's confidence and excitement for the future are only growing. "Apple is doing the best work in its history," he says, "and there's a lot more coming."[11]

a few personal words in an e-mail (whenever appropriate) to convey appreciation, reinforcement, or constructive feedback.

Leadership, Management, and Decision Making

We noted earlier the differences and similarities between managing and leading. **Decision making** is another important related concept, and both managers and leaders must frequently make decisions.

Rational Decision Making

Managers and leaders should strive to be rational in making decisions. Figure 9.2 shows the steps in the rational decision-making process.

Recognizing and Defining the Decision Situation

The first step in rational decision making is recognizing that a decision is necessary—that is, there must be some stimulus or spark to initiate the process. The stimulus for a decision may be either positive or negative. Managers who must decide how to invest surplus funds, for example, face a positive decision situation. A negative financial stimulus could involve having to trim budgets because of cost overruns.

Inherent in making such a decision is the need to define precisely what the problem is. Consider the situation currently being faced in the international air travel industry. Because of the growth of international travel related to business, education, and tourism, global carriers need to increase their capacity. Because most major international airports are already operating at or near capacity, adding a significant number of new flights to existing schedules is not feasible. As a result, the most logical alternative is to increase capacity on existing flights. Thus, Boeing and Airbus, the world's only manufacturers of large commercial aircraft, have recognized an important opportunity and have defined their decision situation as how best to respond to the need for increased global travel capacity.[13]

Identifying Alternatives

Once the decision situation has been recognized and defined, the second step is to identify alternative courses of effective action. Developing both obvious, standard alternatives and creative, innovative alternatives is useful. In general, the more important the decision, the more attention is directed to developing alternatives. Although managers should seek creative solutions, they must also

Step	Detail	Example
1. Recognizing and defining the decision situation	Some stimulus indicates that a decision must be made. The stimulus may be positive or negative.	The plant manager sees that employee turnover has increased by 5 percent.
2. Identifying alternatives	Both obvious and creative alternatives are desired. In general, the more important the decision, the more alternatives should be generated.	The plant manager can increase wages, increase benefits, or change hiring standards.
3. Evaluating alternatives	Each alternative is evaluated to determine its feasibility, its satisfactoriness, and its consequences.	Increasing benefits may not be feasible. Increasing wages and changing hiring standards may satisfy all conditions.
4. Selecting the best alternative	Consider all situational factors and choose the alternative that best fits the manager's situation.	Changing hiring standards will take an extended period of time to cut turnover, so increase wages.
5. Implementing the chosen alternative	The chosen alternative is implemented into the organizational system.	The plant manager may need permission from corporate headquarters. The human resource department establishes a new wage structure.
6. Following up and evaluating the results	At some time in the future, the manager should ascertain the extent to which the alternative chosen in step 4 and implemented in step 5 has worked.	The plant manager notes that six months later, turnover dropped to its previous level.

Figure 9.2
Steps in the Rational Decision-Making Process[12]

recognize that various constraints often limit their alternatives. Common constraints include legal restrictions, moral and ethical norms, and constraints imposed by the power and authority of the manager, available technology, economic considerations, and unofficial social norms. After assessing the question of how to increase international airline capacity, Boeing and Airbus identified three different alternatives: they could independently develop new large planes, they could collaborate in a joint venture to create a single new large plane, or they could modify their largest existing planes to increase their capacity.

Evaluating Alternatives   The third step in the decision-making process is evaluating each of the alternatives. Some alternatives may not be feasible because of legal or financial barriers. Limited human, material, and information resources may make other alternatives impractical. Managers must thoroughly evaluate all the alternatives in order to increase the chances that the alternative finally chosen will be successful. For example, Airbus felt it would be at a disadvantage if it tried simply to enlarge its existing planes because the Boeing 747 is already the largest aircraft being made and could readily be expanded to remain the largest. Boeing, meanwhile, was seriously concerned about the risk inherent in building a new and even larger plane, even if it shared the risk with Airbus as a joint venture.

Selecting the Best Alternative
Choosing the best available alternative is the real crux of decision making. Even though many situations do not lend themselves to objective, mathematical analysis, managers and leaders can often develop subjective estimates and weights for choosing an alternative. Decision makers should also remember that finding multiple acceptable alternatives may be possible; selecting just one alternative and rejecting all the others might not be necessary. For example, Airbus proposed a joint venture with Boeing. Boeing, meanwhile, decided that its best course of action was to modify its existing 747 to increase its capacity. As a result, Airbus decided to proceed on its own to develop and manufacture a new jumbo jet. Boeing then decided that in addition to modifying its 747, it would develop a new plane to offer as an alternative, albeit one not as large as the 747 or the proposed Airbus plane.

Implementing the Chosen Alternative   After an alternative has been selected, managers and leaders must put it into effect. Boeing set its engineers to work expanding the capacity of its 747 by adding 30 feet to the plane's body; the firm also began developing another plane intended for international travel, the 787. Airbus engineers, meanwhile, developed design concepts for a new jumbo jet equipped with escalators and elevators and capable of carrying 655 passengers. Airbus's development costs alone were estimated to exceed $12 billion.

Managers must also consider people's resistance to change when implementing decisions. The reasons for such resistance include insecurity, inconvenience, and fear of the unknown. Managers should anticipate potential resistance at various stages of the implementation process. However, even when all alternatives have been evaluated as precisely as possible and the consequences of each alternative have been weighed, unanticipated consequences are still likely. Employees may resist or protest change; they may even quit rather than agree to it. Other factors, such as unexpected cost increases, a less-than-perfect fit with existing organizational subsystems, or unpredicted effects on cash flow or operating expenses, could develop after implementation has begun. Both Boeing and Airbus have been plagued by production delays that have pushed back delivery of their respective aircrafts by years and could end up costing each company billions of dollars.

After a long decision-making process, Airbus decided to design its own jumbo jet. The Airbus A380's design allows seating for up to 850 people, and major airports around the world have been building new runways and terminal areas to accommodate the behemoth. Boeing, meanwhile, went through a similar decision-making process but concluded that the risks were too great to gamble on such an enormous project. Instead, the firm decided to modify its existing 747 design and develop a new fuel-efficient aircraft, the 787.

Following Up and Evaluating the Results The final step in the decision-making process requires that managers and leaders evaluate the effectiveness of their decision—that is, they should make sure that the chosen alternative has served its original purpose. If an implemented alternative appears not to be working, they can respond in several ways. Another previously identified alternative (the original second or third choice, for instance) could be adopted. Or they might recognize that the situation was not correctly defined to begin with and start the process all over again. Finally, managers and leaders might decide that the original alternative is in fact appropriate but either has not yet had time to work or should be implemented in a different way.

At this point, both Boeing and Airbus are nearing the crucial period when they will learn whether they made good decisions. Airbus's A380 made its first commercial flight in 2007, though delays continue to push back its production schedule, and the firm may be forced to compensate airlines for late deliveries of A380s. Meanwhile, Boeing's 787 is facing an 18-month delay that will keep it grounded until 2009, though the expanded 747 is on schedule and should be in service by 2010. Most airlines seem willing to wait patiently for the 787s, which are designed to be much more fuel efficient than other international airplanes. Given the dramatic surge in fuel costs in recent years, a fuel-efficient option like the 787 could be an enormous success. Indeed, Airbus has begun developing its own fuel-efficient jet, the A350.[14]

Behavioral Aspects of Decision Making

If all decision situations were approached as logically as described in the previous section, more decisions would prove successful. Yet decisions are often made with little consideration for logic and rationality. Some experts have estimated that U.S. companies use rational decision-making techniques less than 20 percent of the time. Of course, even when organizations try to be logical, they sometimes fail. For example, when Starbucks opened its first coffee shops in New York, it relied on scientific marketing research, taste tests, and rational deliberation in making a decision to emphasize drip over espresso coffee. However, that decision proved wrong, as it became clear that New Yorkers strongly preferred the same espresso-style coffees that were Starbucks mainstays in the West. Hence, the firm had to reconfigure its stores hastily to meet customer preferences.

On the other hand, sometimes a decision made with little regard for logic can still turn out to be correct.[15] Important ingredients in how these forces work are behavioral aspects of decision making. These include *political forces*, *intuition*, *escalation of commitment*, and *risk propensity*.

Political Forces in Decision Making Political forces contribute to the behavioral nature of decision making. One major element of politics, *coalitions*, is especially relevant to decision making. A **coalition** is an informal alliance of individuals or groups formed to achieve a common goal. This common goal is often a preferred decision alternative. For example, coalitions of stockholders frequently band together to force a board of directors to make a certain decision.

When these coalitions enter the political arena and attempt to persuade lawmakers to make decisions favorable to their interests, they are called *lobbyists*. Lobbyists may also donate money to help elect a candidate who is more likely to pursue their agendas. A recurring theme in U.S. politics is the damaging influence these special interest groups have on politicians, who may feel unduly obligated to favor campaign donors when making decisions.

Intuition **Intuition** is an innate belief about something, often without conscious consideration. Managers sometimes decide to do something because it "feels right" or they have a hunch. This feeling is usually not arbitrary, however. Rather, it is based on years of experience and practice in making decisions in similar situations. Such an inner sense may help managers make an occasional decision without going through a full-blown rational sequence of steps.

That said, all managers, but most especially inexperienced ones, should be careful not to rely too heavily on intuition. If rationality and logic are continually flouted for "what feels right," the odds are that disaster will strike one day.

Escalation of Commitment Another important behavioral process that influences decision making is **escalation of commitment** to a

Major League Deal

The New York Yankees once contacted three major sneaker manufacturers—Nike, Reebok, and Adidas—and informed them that they were looking to make a sponsorship deal. While Nike and Reebok were carefully and rationally assessing the possibilities, managers at Adidas quickly realized that a partnership with the Yankees made a lot of sense for them. They responded very quickly to the idea and ended up hammering out a contract while the competitors were still analyzing details.[16]

chosen course of action. In particular, decision makers sometimes make decisions and then become so committed to the course of action suggested by that decision that they stay with it, even when it appears to have been wrong.[17] For example, when people buy stock in a company, they sometimes refuse to sell it even after repeated drops in price. They choose a course of action—buying the stock in anticipation of making a profit—and then stay with it even in the face of increasing losses. Moreover, after the value drops they may rationalize that they can't sell at such a low price because they will lose money.

Risk Propensity and Decision Making   The behavioral element of **risk propensity** is the extent to which a decision maker is willing to gamble when making a decision. Some managers are cautious about every decision they make. They try to adhere to the rational model and are extremely conservative in what they do. Such managers are more likely to avoid mistakes, and they infrequently make decisions that lead to big losses. Others are extremely aggressive in making decisions and willing to take risks.[18] They rely heavily on intuition, reach decisions quickly, and often risk big investments on their decisions. As in gambling, these managers are more likely than their conservative counterparts to achieve big successes with their decisions; they are also more likely to incur greater losses.[19] The organization's culture is a prime ingredient in fostering different levels of risk propensity.

For additional topics related to this material and end-of-chapter exercises and practices, please visit www.mybizlab.com.

Questions for Review

1 What are the basic differences between management and leadership?

2 Summarize the basic premises underlying the trait, behavioral, and situational approaches to leadership.

3 What are leadership substitutes and neutralizers?

4 List and briefly explain the steps in rational decision making.

Questions for Analysis

5 Identify five people you would consider to be excellent leaders. Explain why you feel that way about each person.

6 What factors are present in your job that motivate you to perform without the direction of a leader? Are there factors that neutralize the efforts of your leader?

7 The impact of virtual leadership is likely to grow in the future. As a potential "follower" in a virtual leadership situation, what issues would be of most concern to you? What would the issues be from the perspective of the "leader" role in such a situation?

8 Identify and discuss examples of how your decision making has been affected by at least two of the behavioral processes noted in the chapter.

Application Exercises

9 Interview a senior manager at a local company. Ask that manager if he or she believes that leadership can be taught. What are the key implications of his or her position?

10 Review the running example in the textbook regarding the decisions made by Airbus and Boeing regarding new long-haul aircraft. Research the most current information available about the status of both planes. Based on the information you have available, which firm seems to have made the better decision?

chapter 10

Human Resource Management and Labor Relations

After reading this chapter, you should be able to:

1 Define *human resource management* and explain how managers plan for their organization's human resource needs.

2 Identify the tasks in staffing a company and discuss ways in which organizations select, develop, and appraise employee performance.

3 Describe the main components of a compensation system and describe some of the key legal issues involved in hiring, compensating, and managing workers in today's workplace.

4 Discuss workforce diversity, the management of knowledge workers, and the use of a contingent workforce as important changes in the contemporary workplace.

5 Explain why workers organize into labor unions and describe the collective bargaining process.

Las Vegas Gambles Online

The task facing the human resource (HR) managers at the new Bellagio hotel and casino in Las Vegas was daunting: Hire 9,600 workers in 24 weeks and have everyone trained and on payroll when the first customer walked through the door. To meet the challenge, the Bellagio team designed and implemented one of the most sophisticated HR selection systems ever devised—and all without using a single sheet of paper!

To apply for a position, applicants called and requested an appointment. They were then scheduled to arrive at the resort's hiring center in batches where they filled out applications at computer terminals. One hundred terminals were kept busy 12 hours a day, 6 days a week. Meanwhile, employees at the checkout desk conducted unobtrusive assessments of the applicants' communication skills and overall demeanor, eliminating about 20 percent of the applicants immediately.

Next came 27,000 interviews. The database system ranked the candidates according to predetermined criteria. Managers might then call in three applicants for each open position for face-to-face interviews. During an interview, the manager discreetly evaluated the applicant's response to each question on a hidden keypad. These data were then fed back into the database.

If a manager wanted to hire a particular applicant, a team of online investigators would verify employment and education history; for some jobs, a drug test was mandatory. About 8 percent of the applicants were rejected at this stage because of falsified information on their applications. Those who were offered and accepted jobs completed various required documents—again, in electronic form—for benefits and income tax purposes. They were also scheduled for relevant training sessions. And when the Bellagio officially threw open its doors, 9,600 new employees were in place and ready to work.[1]

What's in It for Me?

Effectively managing human resources is the lifeblood of an organization. Successful firms develop clear, consistent approaches to staffing, training, evaluating, and compensating employee performance, whether those employees number in the tens or the tens of thousands. In this chapter we'll explore these various approaches. We'll also look at some key legal issues involved in human resources management, and consider why workers organize into labor unions. Whether employee or employer, your company's HR policies will shape your working experience greatly. This chapter will help you understand the rationale behind those policies.

HUMAN RESOURCE MANAGEMENT (HRM) set of organizational activities directed at attracting, developing, and maintaining an effective workforce

JOB ANALYSIS systematic analysis of jobs within an organization

JOB DESCRIPTION description of the duties and responsibilities of a job, its working conditions, and the tools, materials, equipment, and information used to perform it

JOB SPECIFICATION description of the skills, abilities, and other credentials and qualifications required by a job

REPLACEMENT CHART list of each management position, who occupies it, how long that person will likely stay in the job, and who is qualified as a replacement

EMPLOYEE INFORMATION SYSTEM (SKILLS INVENTORY) computerized system containing information on each employee's education, skills, work experiences, and career aspirations

The Foundations of Human Resource Management

Human resource management (HRM) is the set of organizational activities directed at attracting, developing, and maintaining an effective workforce.

The Strategic Importance of HRM

Human resources (or *personnel*, as the department is sometimes called) has a substantial impact on a firm's bottom-line performance. Consequently, the chief HR executive of most large businesses is a vice president directly accountable to the CEO, and many firms are developing strategic HR plans that are integrated with other strategic planning activities.

HR Planning

As you can see in Figure 10.1, the starting point in attracting qualified human resources is planning. Specifically, HR planning involves job analysis and forecasting the demand for, and supply of, labor.

Job Analysis **Job analysis** is a systematic analysis of jobs within an organization. A job analysis results in two things:

■ The **job description** lists the duties and responsibilities of a job; its working conditions; and the tools, materials, equipment, and information used to perform it.

■ The **job specification** lists the skills, abilities, and other credentials and qualifications needed to perform the job effectively.

Job analysis information is used in many HR activities. For instance, knowing about job content and job requirements is necessary to develop appropriate selection methods, to create job-relevant performance appraisal systems, and to set equitable compensation rates.

Forecasting HR Demand and Supply After managers comprehend the jobs to be performed within an organization, they can start planning for the organization's future HR needs. The manager starts by assessing trends in past HR usage, future organizational plans, and general economic trends.

Forecasting the supply of labor is really two tasks:

1 Forecasting *internal supply*—the number and type of employees who will be in the firm at some future date.

2 Forecasting *external supply*—the number and type of people who will be available for hiring from the labor market at large.

Replacement Charts At higher levels of an organization, managers plan for specific people and positions. The technique most commonly used is the **replacement chart**, which lists each important managerial position, who occupies it, how long that person will probably stay in it before moving on, and who is now qualified or soon will be qualified to move into it. This technique allows ample time to plan developmental experiences for people identified as potential successors for critical managerial jobs.

Skills Inventories To facilitate both planning and identifying people for transfer or promotion, some organizations also have **employee information systems (skills inventories)** that contain information on each employee's education, skills, work experience, and career aspirations. Such a system can quickly locate every employee who is qualified to fill a position.

Forecasting the external supply of labor is a different problem altogether. Planners must rely on information from outside sources, such as state employment commissions, government reports, and figures

Figure 10.1
The HR Planning Process

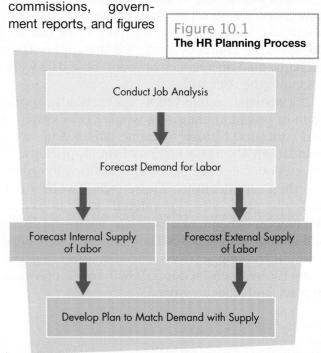

Conduct Job Analysis

Forecast Demand for Labor

Forecast Internal Supply of Labor

Forecast External Supply of Labor

Develop Plan to Match Demand with Supply

supplied by colleges on the numbers of students in major fields.

Matching HR Supply and Demand After comparing future demand and internal supply, managers can make plans to manage predicted shortfalls or overstaffing. If a shortfall is predicted, new employees can be hired, present employees can be retrained and transferred into understaffed areas, individuals approaching retirement can be convinced to stay on, or labor-saving or productivity-enhancing systems can be installed. If over-staffing is expected to be a problem, the main options are transferring the extra employees, not replacing individuals who quit, encouraging early retirement, and laying off workers.

Staffing the Organization

When managers have determined that new employees are needed, they must then turn their attention to recruiting and hiring the right mix of people. This involves two processes: acquiring staff from outside the company and promoting staff from within. Both external and internal staffing, however, start with effective *recruiting*.

Recruiting Human Resources

Recruiting is the process of attracting qualified persons to apply for the jobs that are open.

Internal Recruiting **Internal recruiting** means considering present employees as candidates for openings. Promotion from within can help build morale and keep high-quality employees from leaving. For higher-level positions, a skills inventory system may be used to identify internal candidates, or managers may be asked to recommend individuals to be considered.

External Recruiting **External recruiting** involves attracting people outside the organization to apply for jobs. External recruiting methods include posting jobs on the company Web site or other job sites, such as Monster.com; holding campus interviews for potential college recruits; using employment agencies or executive search firms to scout out potential talent; seeking referrals by present employees; advertising in print publications; and hiring "walk-ins" (unsolicited applicants).

Selecting Human Resources

Once the recruiting process has attracted a pool of applicants, the next step is to select someone to hire. The intent of the selection process is to gather from

> **RECRUITING** process of attracting qualified persons to apply for jobs an organization is seeking to fill
>
> **INTERNAL RECRUITING** process of considering present employees as candidates for openings
>
> **EXTERNAL RECRUITING** process of attracting persons outside the organization to apply for jobs

---

Entrepreneurship and New Ventures

Be Your Own Boss . . . and Someone Else's, Too

No matter how satisfied they are with their jobs, from time to time it seems most people who work daydream about being self-employed. Between 600,000 and 700,000 small businesses open every year, and though each has its own mission and history, chances are good that each one is being run by somebody who not long before was working for somebody else.

Often an insight gained or a skill learned at a previous job provides the inspiration for the new start-up. Jay Hagan and Scott Gaidano learned how to recover data from damaged hard drives while working for a company that manufactured them; when that company went bankrupt, they started their own business, DriveSavers, that serviced many of the same customers whose hard drives they once built. Likewise, Gina Bianchini met software engineer and online entrepreneur Mark Andreessen working for a company that later foundered; they discovered a shared interest in the fast-growing world of social networking and together created Ning, a platform that gives users the freedom to design their own online networks.

If a successful startup is to grow, however, it needs employees, which means at some point the entrepreneur must become a boss. Jerome Boykin started JB Sweeping

Service when the manager of a local Wal-Mart expressed dissatisfaction with the man paid to clean the parking lot. Boykin bought a sweeper truck, taught himself how to operate it, and saw his business grow so rapidly he bought two more trucks and hired eight people to drive them. "It's a challenge," he confesses. "I have a routine, and it's hard to get those guys to understand the way that I want it done." In meeting that challenge, Boykin has seen himself become an HR director as well.[2]

applicants the information that will predict job success and then to hire the candidates likely to be most successful.

Application Forms The first step in selection is usually asking the candidate to fill out an application. An application form is an efficient method of gathering information about the applicant's previous work history, educational background, and other job-related demographic data. Application forms are seldom used for upper-level jobs; candidates for such positions usually provide the same information on their résumé.

Tests Employers sometimes ask candidates to take tests during the selection process. Tests of ability, skill, aptitude, or knowledge relevant to a particular job are usually the best predictors of job success, although tests of general intelligence or personality are occasionally useful as well. Some companies use a test of the "big five" personality dimensions discussed in Chapter 8 to predict success.

Interviews *Interviews* are a very popular selection device, although they are sometimes a poor predictor of job success. For example, biases inherent in the way people perceive and judge others on first meeting affect subsequent evaluations. Interview validity can be improved by training interviewers to be aware of potential biases and by tightening the structure of the interview. In a structured interview, questions are written in advance, and all interviewers follow the same question list with each candidate. For interviewing managerial or professional candidates, a somewhat less structured approach can be used. Although question areas and information-gathering objectives are still planned in advance, specific questions vary with the candidates' backgrounds. Sometimes, companies are looking for especially creative employees and may try to learn more about the individual's creativity during an interview.

Interviews are a very popular selection device. In a structured interview, such as the kind that typically takes place during a job fair, questions are written in advance, and all interviewers follow the same question list with each candidate.

Other Techniques Organizations also use other selection techniques that vary with circumstances. Polygraph tests, once popular, are declining in popularity. On the other hand, organizations occasionally require applicants to take physical exams (being careful that their practices are consistent with the Americans with Disabilities Act). More organizations are using drug tests, especially in situations in which drug-related performance problems could create serious safety hazards. Some organizations also run credit checks on prospective employees. Reference checks with previous employers are also used, but have been shown to have limited value because individuals are likely to only provide the names of references that will give them positive recommendations.

A Simulating Experience

A variation of off-site training is **vestibule training**, which takes place in simulated work environments that make the off-the-job training more realistic; increasingly, these simulations are computerized or Web-based. American Airlines, for example, trains flight attendants at a vestibule training site that resembles the interior cabin of an airplane; it also uses simulation software to help acquaint its pilots with new instrumentation that is added to its aircraft.[3]

Developing the Workforce

After a company has hired new employees, it must acquaint them with the firm and their new jobs. Managers also take steps to train employees and to further develop necessary job skills. In addition, every firm has some system for performance appraisal and feedback.

Training

As its name suggests, **on-the-job training** occurs while an employee is at work. **Off-the-job training** takes place at locations away from a work site. This approach offers a controlled environment and allows focused study without interruptions.

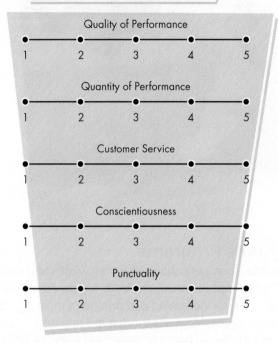

Supervisor: _____

Employee: _____

Rate the employee on each of the following scales:

1 = Outstanding
2 = Very Good
3 = Acceptable
4 = Needs Some Improvement
5 = Needs Substantial Improvement

Quality of Performance

1 2 3 4 5

Quantity of Performance

1 2 3 4 5

Customer Service

1 2 3 4 5

Conscientiousness

1 2 3 4 5

Punctuality

1 2 3 4 5

Figure 10.2
Sample Performance Evaluation Form

Performance Appraisal

Performance appraisals are designed to show workers precisely how well they are doing their jobs. Typically, the appraisal process involves a written assessment issued on a regular basis. As a rule, however, the written evaluation is only one part of a multistep process.

The appraisal process begins when a manager defines performance standards for an employee. The manager then observes the employee's performance. For some jobs, a rating scale like the abbreviated one in Figure 10.2 is useful in providing a basis for comparison. Comparisons drawn from such scales form the basis for written appraisals and for decisions about raises, promotions, demotions, and firings. The process is completed when the manager and employee meet to discuss the appraisal.

Compensation and Benefits

People who work for a business expect to be paid, and most workers today also expect certain benefits from their employers. Indeed, a major factor in retaining skilled workers is a company's **compensation system**—the total package of rewards that it offers employees in return for their labor. Finding the right combination of compensation elements is always complicated by the need to make employees feel valued, while holding down company costs.

Wages and Salaries

Wages and salaries are the dollar amounts paid to employees for their labor. **Wages** are paid for time worked. A **salary** is paid for performing a job. A salaried executive earning $100,000 per year is paid to achieve results even if that means working 5 hours one day and 15 the next. Salaries are usually expressed as an amount paid per year.

In setting wage and salary levels, a company may start by looking at its competitors' levels. Firms must also decide how their internal wage and salary levels will compare for different jobs. Although two employees may do exactly the same job, the employee with more experience may earn more.

Incentive Programs

As we discussed in Chapter 8, studies have shown that beyond a certain point, more money will not produce better performance. Money motivates employees only if it is tied directly to performance. The most common method of establishing this link is the use of **incentive programs**—special pay programs designed to motivate high performance. Some programs are available to individuals, whereas others are distributed on a companywide basis.

Individual Incentives   A sales bonus is a typical incentive. Employees receive a **bonus**—special payments above their salaries—when they sell a certain number or certain dollar amount of goods for the year. Employees who fail to reach this goal earn no bonuses. **Merit salary systems** link pay raises to performance levels in non-sales jobs.

PAY FOR PERFORMANCE (VARIABLE PAY) individual incentive that rewards a manager for especially productive output

PROFIT-SHARING PLAN incentive plan for distributing bonuses to employees when company profits rise above a certain level

GAINSHARING PLAN incentive plan that rewards groups for productivity improvements

PAY-FOR-KNOWLEDGE PLAN incentive plan to encourage employees to learn new skills or become proficient at different jobs

BENEFITS compensation other than wages and salaries

WORKERS' COMPENSATION INSURANCE legally required insurance for compensating workers injured on the job

Many professional athletes have "incentive clauses" in their contracts that award them bonuses for their on-the-field accomplishments. Colorado Rockies first baseman Todd Helton, for example, would earn $25,000 for being voted to the All-Star team and $150,000 for winning the league's Most Valuable Player Award.

Executives commonly receive stock options as incentives. Halliburton CEO David Lesar, for example, can buy several thousand shares of company stock each year at a predetermined price. If his managerial talent leads to higher profits and stock prices, he can buy the stock at a price lower than the market value for which, in theory, he is largely responsible. He is then free to sell the stock at market price, keeping the profits for himself.

A newer incentive plan is called **pay for performance** (or **variable pay**). In essence, middle managers are rewarded for especially productive output—for producing earnings that significantly exceed the cost of bonuses. The number of variable pay programs in the United States has been growing consistently for the last decade, and most experts predict that they will continue to grow in popularity. Many firms say that variable pay is a better motivator than merit raises because the range between generous and mediocre merit raises is usually quite small.

Companywide Incentives Some incentive programs apply to all the employees in a firm. Under **profit-sharing plans**, for example, profits earned above a certain level are distributed to employees. Also, **gainsharing plans** distribute bonuses to employees when a company's costs are reduced through greater work efficiency. **Pay-for-knowledge plans** pay workers to learn new skills and to become proficient at different jobs.

Benefits Programs

Benefits—compensation other than wages and salaries and other incentives offered by a firm to its workers—account for an increasing percentage of most compensation budgets. Most companies are required by law to pay tax for Social Security retirement benefits and provide **workers' compensation insurance** (insurance for compensating workers injured on the job). Most businesses also provide health, life, and disability insurance for their workers, as well as paid time off for vacations and holidays. Many also allow employees to use payroll deductions to buy stock at discounted prices. Counseling services for employees with alcohol, drug, or emotional problems are also becoming more common, as are on-site child-care centers. Some companies even provide reduced membership fees at gyms and health clubs, as well as insurance or other protection for identity theft.[4]

Retirement Plans Retirement plans (or pension plans) constitute another important—and sometimes controversial—benefit that is available to many employees. Most company-sponsored retirement plans are set up to pay pensions to workers when they retire. In some cases, the company contributes all the money to the pension fund. In others, contributions are made by both the company and employees. In recent years, some companies have run into problems because they have not set aside enough money to cover the retirement funds they have agreed to provide. Both FedEx and Goodyear, for instance, recently announced that they were freezing their pension programs in order to transition workers to riskier 401(k)s, in which payroll deductions are invested in stocks and other non-guaranteed funds.[5]

Containing the Costs of Benefits   As the range of benefits has increased, so has concern about containing the costs of these benefits. Many companies are experimenting with cost-cutting plans while still attracting and retaining valuable employees. One approach is the **cafeteria benefits plan**. A certain dollar amount of benefits per employee is set aside so that each employee can choose from a variety of alternatives.

Another area of increasing concern is health care costs. Medical expenses have increased insurance premiums, which have increased the cost to employers of maintaining benefits plans. Many employers are looking for new ways to cut those costs. One increasingly popular approach is for organizations to create their own networks of health care providers. These providers agree to charge lower fees for services rendered to employees of member organizations. In return, they enjoy established relationships with large employers and, thus, more clients and patients. Insurers also charge less to cover the employees of network members because they make lower reimbursement payments.

The Legal Context of HRM

Federal law and judicial review heavily influence HRM as much or more than any area of business. In this section, we summarize some of the most important and far-reaching areas of HR regulation.

Equal Employment Opportunity

The basic goal of all **equal employment opportunity** regulation is to protect people from unfair or inappropriate discrimination in the workplace.[6] Let's begin by noting that discrimination in itself is not illegal. Whenever one person is given a pay raise and another is not, for example, the organization has made a decision to distinguish one person from another. As long as the basis for this discrimination is purely job related (made, for example, on the basis of performance or seniority) and is applied objectively and consistently, the action is legal and appropriate. Problems arise when distinctions among people are not job related. In such cases, the resulting discrimination is illegal.

Protected Classes in the Workplace   To combat illegal discrimination, laws have been passed to protect various classes of individuals. A **protected class** consists of all individuals who share one or more common characteristics as indicated by a given law. The most common criteria for defining protected classes include race, color, religion, gender, age, national origin, disability status, and status as a military veteran.[7] One recent illustration of this protection is the Americans with Disabilities Act of 1990. This law requires employers to not discriminate on the basis of physical limitations and to provide reasonable work-related modifications to help disabled individuals do their jobs.

Enforcing Equal Employment Opportunity
The enforcement of equal opportunity legislation is handled by two agencies. The **Equal Employment Opportunity Commission (EEOC)** is a division of the Department of Justice. It was created by Title VII of the 1964 Civil Rights Act and has specific responsibility for enforcing Title VII, the Equal Pay Act, and the Americans with Disabilities Act.

The other agency charged with monitoring equal employment opportunity legislation is the *Office of Federal Contract Compliance Programs* (*OFCCP*). The OFCCP is responsible for enforcing executive orders that apply to companies doing business with the federal government. A business with government contracts must have on file a written **affirmative action plan**—that is, a written statement of how the organization intends to actively recruit, hire, and develop members of relevant protected classes.

CAFETERIA BENEFITS PLAN benefit plan that sets limits on benefits per employee, each of whom may choose from a variety of alternative benefits

EQUAL EMPLOYMENT OPPORTUNITY legally mandated nondiscrimination in employment on the basis of race, creed, sex, or national origin

PROTECTED CLASS set of individuals who by nature of one or more common characteristics is protected under the law from discrimination on the basis of that characteristic

EQUAL EMPLOYMENT OPPORTUNITY COMMISSION (EEOC) federal agency enforcing several discrimination-related laws

AFFIRMATIVE ACTION PLAN written statement of how the organization intends to actively recruit, hire, and develop members of relevant protected classes

"I see by your résumé that you're a woman."

OCCUPATIONAL SAFETY AND HEALTH ACT OF 1970 (OSHA) federal law setting and enforcing guidelines for protecting workers from unsafe conditions and potential health hazards in the workplace

Legal Issues in Compensation As noted earlier, most employment regulations are designed to provide equal employment opportunity. Some legislation, however, deals with other issues such as compensation. For example, the Fair Labor Standards Act (passed in 1938) established a minimum hourly wage, whereas the Employee Retirement Income Security Act of 1974 sets standards by which companies must manage pension funds.

Contemporary Legal Issues in HRM

In addition to these established areas of HR legal regulation, several emerging legal issues will likely become more important in the future. These include employee safety and health, various emerging areas of discrimination law, employee rights, and employment at will.

Employee Safety and Health The **Occupational Safety and Health Act of 1970 (OSHA)** is the single most comprehensive piece of legislation ever passed regarding worker safety and health. OSHA holds that every employer has an obligation to furnish each employee with a place of employment that is free from hazards that cause or are likely to cause death or physical harm. It is generally enforced through inspections of the workplace by OSHA inspectors. Serious or willful and repeated violations may incur fines up to $10,000 per incident.

Emerging Areas of Discrimination Law Managers must also be familiar with several emerging areas of discrimination law.

AIDS in the Workplace Although AIDS is considered a disability under the Americans with Disabilities Act of 1990, the AIDS situation itself is severe enough that it warrants special attention. Employers cannot legally require an HIV test or any other medical examination as a condition for making an offer of employment. Organizations must accommodate or make a good-faith effort to accommodate individuals with HIV, maintain the confidentiality of all medical records, and try to educate coworkers about AIDS.

Say What You Mean

Top-Down Sensitivity

By definition, global companies must communicate with employees in many different countries and cultures, and a firm's success in communicating with local workers can mean success or failure in an overseas operation. The most successful global companies know how to talk to the people who work for them.

In some countries, the gap between managers and workers is quite wide, and managers are used to bridging it with nonnegotiable orders. In many Asian cultures, for example, you simply don't question the boss's decisions or the policies of the company. In the United States, on the other hand, people are often encouraged to provide feedback and to say what they think. The gap between workers and management is relatively narrow, and communication channels tend to be informal and wide open.

Similar consideration must be given to resolving workplace disputes. In some countries, such as Germany and Sweden, there's a formal system for ensuring that everyone involved is heard. In these countries, although communication channels are always open, they're also highly structured.

But being culturally sensitive to local employees means much more than just knowing how to settle workplace disputes. As a rule, companies also need to convey a sense of good "citizenship" in the host country. This means respecting the social and cultural values of employees and communicating to them the fact that the organization cares about these things.

Sexual Harassment   **Sexual harassment** is defined by the EEOC as unwelcome sexual advances in the work environment. If the conduct is indeed unwelcome and occurs with sufficient frequency to create an abusive work environment, the employer is responsible for changing the environment by warning, reprimanding, or perhaps firing the harasser.[8]

The courts have defined two types of sexual harassment:

1 In cases of **quid pro quo harassment**, the harasser offers to exchange something of value for sexual favors. A male supervisor, for example, might tell or suggest to a female subordinate that he will recommend her for promotion or give her a raise in exchange for sexual favors.

2 The creation of a **hostile work environment** is a subtler form of sexual harassment. A group of male employees who continually make off-color jokes and lewd comments and perhaps decorate the work environment with inappropriate photographs may create a hostile work environment for a female colleague, who may become uncomfortable working in that environment.

In recent years, the concept of harassment has been expanded to encompass unwelcome or inappropriate behaviors regarding ethnicity, religion, and age.

Employment at Will   The concept of **employment at will** holds that both employer and employee have the mutual right to terminate an employment relationship at any time for any reason, with or without advance notice to the other. Over the last two decades, however, terminated employees have challenged the employment-at-will doctrine by filing lawsuits against former employers on the grounds of wrongful discharge.

In the last several years, such suits have put limits on employment-at-will provisions in certain circumstances. In the past, for example, organizations were guilty of firing employees who filed workers' compensation claims or took "excessive" time off to serve on jury duty. More recently, however, the courts have ruled that employees may not be fired for exercising rights protected by law.

The Patriot Act   In response to the terrorist attacks of September 11, 2001, the U.S. government passed legislation that increases its powers to investigate and prosecute suspected terrorists. This legislation, known as the Patriot Act, has several key implications for HRM. For instance, certain "restricted" individuals (including ex-convicts and aliens from countries deemed by the State Department to have "repeatedly provided support for acts of international terrorism") are ineligible to work with potentially dangerous biological agents. More controversial are sections granting government investigators access to previously confidential personal and financial records.[9]

New Challenges in the Changing Workplace

● ● ● ● ● ● ● ● ● ● ● ● ● ● ● ● ●

In addition to the challenges we have already considered, HR managers face several new challenges reflecting the changing economic and social environments of business.

SEXUAL HARASSMENT unwelcome sexual advances in the workplace

QUID PRO QUO HARASSMENT form of sexual harassment in which sexual favors are requested in return for job-related benefits

HOSTILE WORK ENVIRONMENT form of sexual harassment deriving from off-color jokes, lewd comments, and so forth

EMPLOYMENT AT WILL principle, increasingly modified by legislation and judicial decision, that organizations should be able to retain or dismiss employees at their discretion

WORKFORCE DIVERSITY the range of workers' attitudes, values, beliefs, and behaviors that differ by gender, race, age, ethnicity, physical ability, and other relevant characteristics

Managing Workforce Diversity

One extremely important set of HR challenges centers on **workforce diversity**—the range of workers' attitudes, values, beliefs, and behaviors that differ by gender, race, age, ethnicity, physical ability, and other relevant characteristics. In the past, organizations tended to work toward homogenizing their workforces, getting everyone to think and behave in similar ways. Partly as a result of affirmative action efforts, however, many U.S. organizations are now creating more diverse workforces than ever before.

Figure 10.3 projects the racial and ethnic composition of the U.S. workforce through 2050. The picture is clearly one of increasing diversity. The number of white Americans as a percentage of the total workforce is declining steadily, offset by increases in every other racial group. Most striking are the growing numbers of people of Hispanic origin (who may be members of any racial group). By 2050 the U.S. Department of Labor estimates that nearly a quarter of the workforce will be Hispanic.

Today, organizations are recognizing that diversity can be a competitive advantage. For example, by hiring the best people available from every single group rather

KNOWLEDGE WORKERS employees who are of value because of the knowledge they possess

CONTINGENT WORKER employee hired on something other than a full-time basis to supplement an organization's permanent workforce

than hiring from just one or a few groups, a firm can develop a higher-quality labor force. Similarly, a diverse workforce can bring a wider array of information to bear on problems and can provide insights on marketing products to a wider range of consumers.

Managing Knowledge Workers

Traditionally, employees added value to organizations because of what they did or because of their experience. In the information age, however, many employees add value because of what they *know*.

The Nature of Knowledge Work Employees who add value because of what they know are usually called **knowledge workers**. Knowledge workers—including computer scientists, engineers, physical scientists, and game developers—typically require extensive and highly specialized training; once they are on the job, retraining and training updates are critical to prevent their skills from becoming obsolete. It has been suggested, for example, that the half-life of a technical education in engineering is about three years.

A firm's failure to update the skills of its knowledge workers will not only result in the loss of competitive advantage, it will also increase the likelihood that those workers will go to other firms that are more committed to updating their skills. Hence, HR managers must ensure that the proper training is prepared to enable knowledge workers to stay current while also making sure they are compensated at market rates.

Contingent and Temporary Workers

A final contemporary HR issue of note involves the use of contingent and temporary workers. In recent years there has been an explosion in the use of such workers by organizations.

Trends in Contingent and Temporary Employment A **contingent worker** is a person who works for an organization on something other than a permanent or full-time basis. Categories of contingent workers include independent contractors, on-call workers, temporary employees (usually hired through outside agencies), and contract and leased employees. Another category is part-time workers.

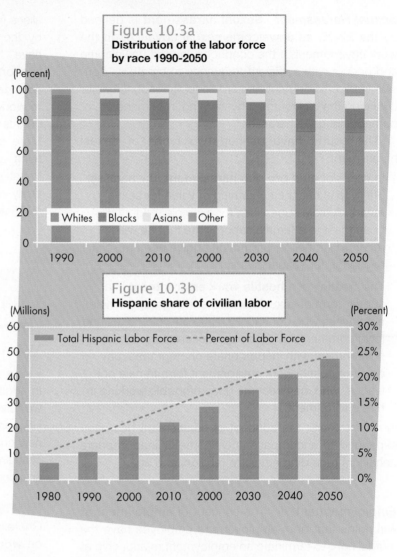

Figure 10.3a
Distribution of the labor force by race 1990-2050

Figure 10.3b
Hispanic share of civilian labor

Managing Contingent and Temporary Workers One key to managing contingent workers effectively is careful planning and analysis. Rather than having to call in workers sporadically, and with no prior notice, organizations try to bring in specified numbers of workers for well-defined periods of time. Firms should also be able to document the labor-cost savings of using contingent workers.

A second key is recognizing what can and cannot be achieved by using contingent and temporary workers. For instance, these workers may lack the firm-specific knowledge to perform as effectively as a permanent employee would perform. They are also less committed to the organization and less likely to engage in organizational citizenship behaviors.

Finally, managers must make decisions about how to integrate contingent workers into the organization. These decisions may be as simple as whether to invite contingent workers to the holiday party, or they may be more complicated, such as whether to grant contingent workers access to such employee benefits as counseling services and child care.

Dealing with Organized Labor

A **labor union** is a group of individuals working together to achieve shared job-related goals, such as higher pay, shorter working hours, more job security, greater benefits, or better working conditions. **Labor relations** refers to the process of dealing with employees who are represented by a union.

Unionism Today

In the years immediately following World War II and continuing through the mid-1960s, most unions routinely won certification elections. In recent years, however, labor unions have been winning certification less than 50 percent of the times that workers are called upon to vote. As a result, although millions of workers still belong to unions, union membership as a percentage of the total workforce has steadily declined. In 2007, only 12.1 percent of U.S. workers belonged to a labor union, down from 20.1 percent in 1983, when the U.S. Department of Labor first began compiling data.[10]

The Future of Unions Even though several of its members withdrew from the parent organization in 2005, the American Federation of Labor and Congress of Industrial Organizations (AFL-CIO), as well as independent major unions such as the Teamsters and the National Education Association (NEA), still play a major role in U.S. business. Unions in the traditional strongholds of goods-producing industries continue to wield considerable power as well. The United Auto Workers (UAW), for example, remains one of the largest unions in the United States.

Collective Bargaining

The power of unions comes from collective action—forcing management to listen to the demands of all workers rather than to just the few who speak out. **Collective bargaining** is the process by which labor and management negotiate conditions of employment for union-represented workers and draft a labor contract.

Reaching Agreement on Contract Terms

The collective bargaining process begins when the union is recognized as the exclusive negotiator for its members and union leaders meet with management representatives to agree on a contract. By law, both parties must sit down at the bargaining table and negotiate in good faith.

Sometimes, this process goes quite smoothly. At other times, the two sides cannot agree. Resolving the impasse depends in part on the nature of the contract issues, the willingness of each side to use certain tactics, such as strikes, and the prospects for mediation or arbitration.

Contract Issues

The labor contract itself can address an array of different issues. Issues that are typically most important to union negotiators include *compensation*, *benefits*, and *job security*. Certain management rights, such as

LABOR UNION group of individuals working together to achieve shared job-related goals, such as higher pay, shorter working hours, more job security, greater benefits, or better working conditions

LABOR RELATIONS process of dealing with employees who are represented by a union

COLLECTIVE BARGAINING the process by which labor and management negotiate conditions of employment and draft a labor contract for union-represented workers

Knowledge workers such as Ann Quinn, a self-employed marketing consultant, often prefer to work independently. However, this arrangement may make it difficult for them to secure adequate health care coverage. Consequently, nonprofit organizations have stepped forward to assist. Quinn insures herself, her daughter, and her husband through Freelancers Union, a nonprofit that furnishes portable, affordable health insurance to freelance workers in New York and many other states.

COST-OF-LIVING ADJUSTMENT (COLA) labor contract clause tying future raises to changes in consumer purchasing power

WAGE REOPENER CLAUSE clause allowing wage rates to be renegotiated during the life of a labor contract

STRIKE labor action in which employees temporarily walk off the job and refuse to work

PICKETING labor action in which workers publicize their grievances at the entrance to an employer's facility

BOYCOTT labor action in which workers refuse to buy the products of a targeted employer

WORK SLOWDOWN labor action in which workers perform jobs at a slower than normal pace

LOCKOUT management tactic whereby workers are denied access to the employer's workplace

STRIKEBREAKER worker hired as a permanent or temporary replacement for a striking employee

MEDIATION method of resolving a labor dispute in which a third party suggests, but does not impose, a settlement

ARBITRATION method of resolving a labor dispute in which both parties agree to submit to the judgment of a neutral party

control over hiring policies and work assignments, are also negotiated in most bargaining agreements. Other possible issues might include such specific details as working hours, overtime policies, rest period arrangements, differential pay plans for shift employees, the use of temporary workers, grievance procedures, and allowable union activities (dues collection, union bulletin boards, and so forth).

Compensation Compensation includes both current and future wages. One common tool for securing wage increases is a **cost-of-living adjustment (COLA)**. Most COLA clauses tie future raises to the *Consumer Price Index (CPI)*, a government statistic that reflects changes in consumer purchasing power. Almost half of all labor contracts today include COLA clauses.

A union might be uncomfortable with a long-term contract based solely on COLA wage increases. One solution is a **wage reopener clause**, which allows wage rates to be renegotiated at preset times during the life of the contract.

Benefits Employee benefits are also an important component in most labor contracts. Unions typically want employers to pay all or most of the costs of insurance for employees. Other benefits commonly addressed during negotiations include retirement benefits, paid holidays, and working conditions. Due to surging health care costs, employee health insurance premiums have become a major point of contention in recent years.

Job Security Job security also remains an important agenda item in many bargaining sessions today. In some cases, a contract may dictate that if the workforce is reduced, seniority will be used to determine which employees keep their jobs. Unions are setting their sights on preserving jobs for workers in the United States in the face of business efforts to outsource production in some sectors to countries where labor costs are cheaper. For example, the AFL-CIO has been an outspoken opponent of efforts to normalize trade relations with China, fearing that more businesses might be tempted to move jobs there.

When Bargaining Fails

An impasse occurs when, after a series of bargaining sessions, management and labor have failed to agree on a new contract or a contract to replace an agreement that is about to expire. Although it is generally agreed that both parties suffer when an impasse is reached and some action by one part against the other is taken, each side can use several tactics to support its cause until the impasse is resolved.

Union Tactics Historically, one of the most common union tactics has been the **strike**, which occurs when employees temporarily walk off the job and refuse to work. Far fewer strikes occur today than in previous years. From 1960 to 1980, for example, an average of 281 strikes occurred per year. Since 1990, however, the annual number of strikes has ranged from a high of 45 (in 1994) to a low of 14 (in 2003).[11]

To support a strike, a union faced with an impasse has recourse to additional legal activities:

■ In **picketing**, workers march at the entrance to the employer's facility with signs explaining their reasons for striking.

■ A **boycott** occurs when union members agree not to buy the products of a targeted employer. Workers may also urge consumers to boycott the firm's products.

■ Another alternative to striking is a **work slowdown**. Instead of striking, workers perform their jobs at a much slower pace than normal. A variation is the *sickout*, during which large numbers of workers call in sick.

Management Tactics Like workers, management can respond forcefully to an impasse with the following:

■ **Lockouts** occur when employers deny employees access to the workplace. Lockouts are illegal if they are used as offensive weapons to give management a bargaining advantage. However, they are legal if management has a legitimate business need (for instance, avoiding a buildup of perishable inventory).

■ A firm can also hire temporary or permanent replacements called **strikebreakers**. However, the law forbids the permanent replacement of workers who strike because of unfair practices. In some cases, an employer can obtain legal injunctions that either prohibit workers from striking or prohibit a union from interfering with its efforts to use replacement workers.

Mediation and Arbitration Rather than wield these often unpleasant weapons against one another, labor and management can agree to call in a third party to help resolve the dispute:

- In **mediation**, the neutral third party (the mediator) can suggest, but cannot impose, a settlement on the other parties.

- In **arbitration**, the neutral third party (the arbitrator) dictates a settlement between the two sides, which have agreed to submit to outside judgment. In some disputes, such as those between the government and public employees, arbitration is compulsory, or required by law.

Managing an organization's human resources is both a complex and an important undertaking. Most businesses can buy the same equipment and use the same technology as their competitors. But differences in employee talent and motivation are not easily copied. Consequently, most well-managed companies today recognize the value provided by their employees and strive to insure that the HR function is managed as efficiently and effectively as possible.

For additional topics related to this material and end-of-chapter exercises and practices, please visit www.mybizlab.com.

Questions for Review

1. What are the advantages and disadvantages of internal and external recruiting? Under what circumstances is each more appropriate?

2. Why is the formal training of workers so important to most employers? Why don't employers simply let people learn about their jobs as they perform them?

3. What different forms of compensation do firms typically use to attract and keep productive workers?

4. What tactics do unions use to overcome an impasse at the bargaining table? What tactics does management use?

Questions for Analysis

5. What are your views on drug testing in the workplace? What would you do if your employer asked you to submit to a drug test?

6. Workers at Ford, GM, and DaimlerChrysler are represented by the UAW. However, the UAW has been unsuccessful in its attempts to unionize U.S. workers employed at Toyota, Nissan, and Honda plants in the United States. Why do you think this is so?

7. What training do you think you are most likely to need when you finish school and start your career?

8. How much will benefit considerations affect your choice of an employer after graduation?

Application Exercises

9. Interview an HR manager at a local company. Focus on a position for which the firm is currently recruiting applicants and identify the steps in the selection process.

10. Interview the managers of two local companies, one unionized and one nonunionized. Compare the wage and salary levels, benefits, and working conditions of employees at the two firms.

Marketing Processes and Consumer Behavior

After reading this chapter, you should be able to:

1 Explain the concept of marketing and identify the five forces that constitute the external marketing environment.

2 Explain the purpose of a marketing plan and identify the four components of the marketing mix.

3 Explain market segmentation and how it is used in target marketing.

4 Describe the key factors that influence the consumer buying process.

5 Discuss the three categories of organizational markets.

6 Explain the definition of a product as a value package and classify goods and services.

7 Describe the key considerations in the new product development process.

8 Explain the importance of branding and packaging.

9 Discuss the challenges that arise in adopting an international marketing mix.

10 Identify the ways that small businesses can benefit from an understanding of the marketing mix.

Why So Serious?

The five Batman movies that have been released since 1989 have grossed more than $1.6 billion worldwide. It would be understandable, then, if the producers decided to skimp on the marketing budget for film number 6—if ever a movie could be expected to "market itself," it would be *The Dark Knight*.

Instead, they teamed with 42 Entertainment, a California-based creator of alternate reality games, to immerse fans in one of the most elaborate viral marketing campaigns ever conceived. The fun began over a year before the movie opened, with the appearance of posters and a Web site "supporting" one of the film's characters, Harvey Dent, in his campaign for district attorney of Gotham City. Visitors to the Web site quickly discovered a link to a similar site, whysoserious.com, that appeared to have been vandalized by the movie's main villain, the Joker.

The emergence of the Joker set in motion a series of games in which fans vied with one another to solve puzzles. The fastest fans received cell phones that let them access information that led them deeper into the puzzle. Meanwhile, the Web sites multiplied: fake newspapers with articles like "Batman Stops Mob Melee"; safety tips from the Gotham Police Department; even a link to Betty's House of Pies, a restaurant that plays a small but crucial role in the movie's plot.

The appeal of viral marketing, according to Jonathan Waite, owner of the Alternate Reality Gaming Network, is that "you're not a passive onlooker, you're taking an active role. And any time you take an active role, you're emotionally connecting." Or, as one blogger put it, "I've never been a fan of the Batman series, but this sort of thing makes me want to go see it."[1]

The Dark Knight's innovative marketing campaign helped catapult the movie to a record-breaking box office debut, earning over $158 million in its opening weekend. Domestically and internationally, the film was a great success, earning more than $873 million worldwide—over half that of the previous five Batman movies combined.

What's in It for Me?

Viral marketing is an example of how a company can apply marketing basics in an innovative way to appeal to the forces of the external marketing environment. This chapter discusses these basics along with the marketing plan and components of the marketing mix, as well as target marketing and market segmentation. It also explores key factors that influence consumer and organizational buying processes, as well as how new products are developed and how they are defined by branding and packaging. By grasping the marketing methods and ideas in this chapter, you will not only be better prepared as a marketing professional, but also as an informed consumer.

MARKETING the activity, set of institutions, and processes for creating, communicating, delivering, and enhancing offerings that have value for customers, clients, partners, and society at large

VALUE relative comparison of a product's benefits versus its costs

UTILITY ability of a product to satisfy a human want or need

CONSUMER GOODS physical products purchased by consumers for personal use

INDUSTRIAL GOODS physical products purchased by companies to produce other products

SERVICES products having nonphysical features, such as information, expertise, or an activity that can be purchased

What Is Marketing?

What comes to mind when you think of marketing? Most of us think of marketing as advertisements for detergents and soft drinks. Marketing, however, encompasses a much wider range of activities. The American Marketing Association defines **marketing** as "the activity, set of institutions, and processes for creating, communicating, delivering, and exchanging offerings that have value for customers, clients, partners, and society at large."[2] Let's see this definition in action.

Providing Value and Satisfaction

Although our desires for the many goods and services available to us may be unbounded, limited financial resources force most of us to be selective. Accordingly, consumers buy products that offer the best value when it comes to meeting their needs and wants.

Value and Benefits The **value** of a product compares its benefits with its costs. Benefits include not only the functions of the product, but also the emotional satisfaction associated with owning, experiencing, or possessing it. But every product has costs, including sales price, the expenditure of the buyer's time, and even the emotional costs of making a purchase decision. A satisfied buyer perceives the benefits derived from the purchase to be greater than its costs. Thus, the simple but important ratio for value is derived as follows:

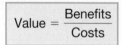

$$\text{Value} = \frac{\text{Benefits}}{\text{Costs}}$$

The marketing strategies of leading firms focus on increasing value for customers. Marketing resources are deployed to add benefits and decrease costs of products to provide greater value. To satisfy customers, a company may:

- Develop an entirely new product that performs better (provides greater performance benefits) than existing products;

- Keep a store open longer hours during a busy season (adding the benefit of greater shopping convenience);

- Offer price reductions (the benefit of lower costs).

Value and Utility To understand how marketing creates value for customers, we need to know the kind of benefits that buyers get from a firm's goods or services. Those benefits provide consumers with **utility**—the ability of a product to satisfy a human want or need. Marketing strives to provide utility in the following ways:

- **Form utility.** Marketing has a voice in designing products with features that customers want.

- **Time utility.** Marketing creates sales agreements that stipulate when products will be delivered to customers.

- **Place utility.** Marketing creates sales agreements that stipulate where products will be delivered to customers.

- **Ownership utility.** Marketing arranges for transferring product ownership to customers by setting selling prices, setting terms for customer credit payments, and providing ownership documents.

Because they determine product features, and the timing, place, and terms of sale that provide utility and add value for customers, marketers must understand customers' wants and needs. Their methods for creating utility are described in this and the following chapter.

Goods, Services, and Ideas

The marketing of tangible goods is obvious in everyday life. Think of the products that you bought the last time you went to the mall or the grocery store. These products are all **consumer goods**: tangible goods that you, the consumer, may buy for personal use. Firms that sell goods to consumers for personal consumption are engaged in consumer marketing.

Marketing also applies to **industrial goods**: physical items used by companies to produce other products. Firms that sell goods to other companies are engaged in industrial marketing.

But marketing techniques are also applied to **services**—products with intangible (nonphysical) features. Service marketing—the application of marketing for services—continues to be a major growth area in the United States. Insurance companies, airlines, and health clinics all engage in service marketing, both to individuals (consumer markets) and to other companies (industrial markets). Thus, the terms consumer marketing and industrial marketing include services as well as goods.

Finally, marketers also promote ideas. Ads in theaters, for example, warn us against copyright infringement and piracy. Other ads stress the advantages of avoiding fast foods, wearing our seat belts, or quitting smoking.

Relationship Marketing Although marketing often focuses on single transactions for products, services, or ideas, marketers also take a longer-term perspective. Thus, **relationship marketing** emphasizes building lasting relationships with customers and suppliers. Stronger relationships—including stronger economic and social ties—can result in greater long-term satisfaction, customer loyalty, and customer retention.[3]

The Marketing Environment

Marketing strategies are not determined unilaterally by any business—rather, they are strongly influenced by powerful outside forces. Every marketing program must recognize the factors in a company's external environment, which is everything outside an organization's boundaries that might affect it.

Political-Legal Environment Political activities, both global and domestic, have profound effects on marketing. For example, environmental legislation has determined the destinies of entire industries. Marketing managers try to maintain favorable political and legal environments in several ways. To gain public support for products and activities, marketers use ad campaigns to raise public awareness of important issues. Companies contribute to political candidates and frequently support the activities of political action committees (PACs) maintained by their respective industries.

Sociocultural Environment Changing social values force companies to develop and promote new products for both individual consumers and industrial customers. Just a few years ago, organic foods were available only in specialty food stores like Whole Foods. Today, in response to a growing demand for healthy foods, Target's Archer Farms product line brings affordable organic food to a much larger audience. This and other trends reflect the values, beliefs, and ideas that shape society.

Technological Environment New technologies create new goods and services. New products make existing products obsolete, and many products change our values and lifestyles. In turn, lifestyle changes often stimulate new products not directly related to the new

technologies themselves. Cell phones, for example, not only facilitate business communication but free up time for recreation and leisure.

Managing the Information Overload

Marketers rely on technology to build better relationships with customers and to predict what customers will want and buy. The compiling and storage of consumer data, known as data warehousing, provides the raw materials from which marketers can extract information that enables them to better know their customers and supply more of what they need. Data mining automates the massive analysis of data by using computers to sift, sort, and search for previously undiscovered clues about what customers look at, react to, and how they might be influenced. The hoped-for result is a clearer picture of how marketing can use resources more effectively to build closer relationships with customers.

Economic Environment Because they determine spending patterns by consumers, businesses, and governments, economic conditions influence marketing plans for product offerings, pricing, and promotional strategies. Marketers are concerned with such economic variables as inflation, interest rates, and recession. Thus, they monitor the general business cycle to anticipate trends in consumer and business spending.

The interconnected global economy has become an increasingly important concern for marketers worldwide—for example, in 2008, rising oil prices broke records on an almost daily basis. Surging oil prices reflected a variety of circumstances in the global economic environment: fears of terrorism, skyrocketing demand, and a weak U.S. dollar. The possible repercussions include reduced consumer

Marketing strategies are strongly influenced by powerful outside forces. For example, new technologies create new products, such as the Chinese cell phone "gas station" kiosk shown here. Called *shouji jiayouzhan* in Chinese, these kiosks enable customers to recharge their cell phones just as they would refuel their cars. The screens on the kiosks also provide marketers with a new way to display ads to waiting customers.

spending on other products, lower corporate profits, and inflation.

Competitive Environment

In a competitive environment, marketers must convince buyers that they should purchase one company's products rather than those of some other seller. Because both consumers and commercial buyers have limited resources, every dollar spent on one product is no longer available for other purchases. Each marketing program, therefore, seeks to make its product the most attractive. Expressed in business terms, a failed program loses the buyer's dollar forever (or at least until it is time for the next purchase decision).

To promote products effectively, marketers must first understand which of three types of competition they face:

■ **Substitute products** may not look alike or they may seem very different from one another, but they can fulfill the same need. For example,

your cholesterol level may be controlled with either of two competing products: a physical fitness program or a drug regimen. The fitness program and the drugs compete as substitute products.

■ **Brand competition** occurs between similar products and is based on buyers' perceptions of the benefits of products offered by particular companies.

■ **International competition** matches the products of domestic marketers against those of foreign competitors. The intensity of international competition has been heightened by the formation of alliances, such as the European Union and NAFTA.

Having identified the kind of competition, marketers can then develop a strategy for attracting more customers.

Strategy: The Marketing Mix

A company's **marketing managers** are responsible for planning and implementing all the activities that result in the transfer of goods or services to its customers. These activities culminate in the **marketing plan**—a detailed strategy for focusing marketing efforts on consumers' needs and wants. Therefore, marketing strategy begins when a company identifies a consumer need and develops a product to meet it.

In planning and implementing strategies, marketing managers develop the four basic components (often called the "Four Ps") of the **marketing mix**: product, pricing, place, and promotion.

Product Marketing begins with a **product**—a good, a service, or an idea designed to fill a consumer's need or want. Conceiving and developing new products is a constant challenge for marketers, who must always consider the factor of change—changing technology, changing wants and needs of consumers, and changing economic conditions. Meeting consumers' needs often means changing existing products to keep pace with emerging markets and competitors.

Wenner Media Chair and CEO Jann Wenner (right) is hoping that his strategy for greater differentiation between his *Us Weekly* magazine and rival *People* will continue to pay off. *People* is news driven, reporting on ordinary people as well as celebrities, whereas *Us Weekly* features more coverage of celebrity sex and glitter.

American Eagle is one chain that specializes in clothes and accessories designed to appeal to Generation Y and Millennials—a demographic consisting of American consumers between 13 and 17. In 2006, the brand expanded its line with aerie, a stand-alone store that sells intimates, workout wear and Dormwear, a collection of leggings, hoodies and fashionable sweats appropriate for lounging in the dorm or wearing to a morning class.

Product Differentiation Producers often promote particular features of products in order to distinguish them in the marketplace. **Product differentiation** is the creation of a feature or image that makes a product differ enough from existing products to attract consumers.

Pricing The **pricing** of a product—selecting the best price at which to sell it—is often a balancing act. On the one hand, prices must support a variety of costs—operating, administrative, research costs, and marketing costs. On the other hand, prices can't be so high that consumers turn to competitors. Successful pricing means finding a profitable middle ground between these two requirements.

Place (Distribution) In the marketing mix, *place* refers to **distribution**. Placing a product in the proper outlet—for example, a retail store—requires decisions about several activities, all of which are concerned with getting the product from the producer to the consumer. Decisions about warehousing and inventory control are distribution decisions, as are decisions about transportation options.

Promotion The most visible component of the marketing mix is no doubt **promotion**, which refers to techniques for communicating information about products. The most important promotional tools include advertising, personal selling, sales promotions, publicity, and public relations.

Target Marketing and Market Segmentation

Marketers have long known that products cannot be all things to all people. The emergence of the marketing concept and the recognition of consumers' needs and wants led marketers to think in terms of **target markets**—groups of people with similar wants and needs and who can be expected to show interest in the same products. Selecting target markets is usually the first step in the marketing strategy.

Target marketing requires **market segmentation**—dividing a market into categories of customer types or "segments." Once they have identified segments, companies may adopt a variety of strategies. Some firms market products to more than one segment. General Motors, for example, offers automobiles with various features and at various price levels. GM's strategy is to provide an automobile for nearly every segment of the market.

In contrast, some businesses offer a narrower range of products, such as Ferrari's high-priced sports cars, aiming at just one segment. Note that segmentation is a strategy for analyzing consumers, not products. Once a target segment is identified, the marketing of products for that segment begins. The process of fixing, adapting, and communicating the nature of the product itself is called product positioning.

Identifying Market Segments
By definition, members of a market segment must share some common traits that affect their purchasing decisions. In identifying segments, researchers look at several different influences on consumer behavior. Here are three of the most important variables:

Geographic Segmentation Many buying decisions are affected by the places people call home. Urban residents don't need agricultural equipment, and sailboats sell better along the coasts than on the Great Plains.

PRODUCT DIFFERENTIATION creation of a product feature or product image that differs enough from existing products to attract consumers

PRICING process of determining the best price at which to sell a product

DISTRIBUTION (PLACE) part of the marketing mix concerned with getting products from producers to consumers

PROMOTION aspect of the marketing mix concerned with the most effective techniques for communicating information about products

TARGET MARKET group of people that have similar wants and needs and can be expected to show interest in the same products

MARKET SEGMENTATION process of dividing a market into categories of customer types, or "segments"

GEOGRAPHIC VARIABLES geographical units that may be considered in developing a segmentation strategy

DEMOGRAPHIC VARIABLES characteristics of populations that may be considered in developing a segmentation strategy

PSYCHOGRAPHIC VARIABLES consumer characteristics, such as lifestyles, opinions, interests, and attitudes that may be considered in developing a segmentation strategy

CONSUMER BEHAVIOR study of the decision process by which people buy and consume products

Table 11.1　**Demographic Variables**

Age	Under 5, 5–11, 12–19, 20–34, 35–49, 50–64, 65+
Education	Grade school or less, some high school, graduated high school, some college, college degree, advanced degree
Family Life Cycle	Young single, young married without children, young married with children, older married with children under 18, older married without children under 18, older single, other
Family Size	1, 2–3, 4–5, 6+
Income	Under $9,000, $9,000–$14,999, $15,000–$24,999, $25,000–$34,999, $35,000–$45,000, over $45,000
Nationality	African, American, Asian, British, Eastern European, French, German, Irish, Italian, Latin American, Middle Eastern, Scandinavian
Race	Native American, Asian, African American, Caucasian
Religion	Buddhist, Catholic, Hindu, Jewish, Muslim, Protestant
Sex	Male, female

Geographic variables are the geographical units, from countries to neighborhoods, that may be considered in a segmentation strategy.

Demographic Segmentation Demographic variables describe populations by identifying traits, such as age, income, gender, ethnic background, marital status, race, religion, and social class, as detailed in Table 11.1. Depending on the marketer's purpose, a demographic segment can be a single classification (ages 20–34) or a combination of categories (ages 20–34, married without children, earning $25,000–$44,999 a year).

Psychographic Variables Markets can also be segmented according to such **psychographic variables** as lifestyles, interests, and attitudes. Psychographics are particularly important to marketers because, unlike demographics and geographics, they can be changed by marketing efforts. For example, Polish companies have overcome consumer resistance by promoting the safety and desirability of using credit cards rather than depending solely on cash.[4]

Understanding Consumer Behavior

Although marketing managers can tell us what features people want in a new refrigerator, they cannot tell us why they buy particular refrigerators. What desire are consumers fulfilling? Is there a psychological or sociological explanation for why they purchase one product and not another? These questions and many others are addressed in the study of **consumer behavior**—the study of the decision process by which people buy and consume products.

"I'd get out of children and into older people."

Influences on Consumer Behavior

To understand consumer behavior, marketers draw heavily on such fields as psychology and sociology. By identifying which influences are most active in certain circumstances, marketers try to explain consumer choices and predict future buying behavior.

1. Psychological influences include an individual's motivations, perceptions, ability to learn, and attitudes.

2. Personal influences include lifestyle, personality, and economic status.

3. Social influences include family, opinion leaders (people whose opinions are sought by others), and such reference groups as friends, co-workers, and professional associates.

4. Cultural influences include culture (the way of living that distinguishes one large group from another), subculture (smaller groups with shared values), and social class (the cultural ranking of groups according to such criteria as background, occupation, and income).

Although these factors can have a strong impact on a consumer's choices, their effect on actual purchases is sometimes weak or negligible. Some consumers, for example, exhibit high **brand loyalty**—they regularly purchase products because they are satisfied with their performance. Such people are less subject to influence and stick with preferred brands.[5] On the other hand, the clothes you wear and the food you eat often reflect social and psychological influences on your consumer behavior.

The Consumer Buying Process

Students of consumer behavior have constructed various models to help show how consumers decide to buy products. Figure 11.1 presents one such model. At the core of this and similar models is an awareness of the many influences that lead to consumption. Ultimately, marketers use this information to develop marketing plans.

Problem/Need Recognition This process begins when the consumer recognizes a problem or need. Need recognition also occurs when you have a chance to change your buying habits. When you obtain your first job after graduation, your new income may let you buy things that were once too expensive for you. You may find that you need professional clothing, apartment furnishings, and a car. American Express and Citi cater to such shifts in needs when they market credit cards to college seniors.

Information Seeking Having recognized a need, consumers often seek information. The search is not always extensive, but before making major purchases, most people seek information from personal sources, public sources, and experience.

Evaluation of Alternatives By analyzing product attributes (price, prestige, quality), consumers compare products before deciding which one best meets their needs.

Purchase Decision Ultimately, consumers make purchase decisions. "Buy" decisions are based on rational motives, emotional motives, or both. **Rational motives** involve the logical evaluation of product attributes: cost, quality, and usefulness. **Emotional motives** involve nonobjective factors and include sociability, imitation of others, and aesthetics.

Postpurchase Evaluation Marketing does not stop with the sale of a product. What happens after the sale is important. Marketers want consumers to be happy after buying products so that they are more likely to buy them again. Because consumers do not want to go through a complex decision process for every purchase, they often repurchase products they have used and liked. Not all consumers are satisfied with their purchases. These buyers are not likely to purchase the same product(s) again and are much more apt to broadcast their experiences than are satisfied customers.

Organizational Marketing and Buying Behavior

In the consumer market, buying and selling transactions are visible to the public. Equally important, though far less visible, are organizational (or commercial) markets.

BRAND LOYALTY pattern of regular consumer purchasing based on satisfaction with a product's performance	

RATIONAL MOTIVES reasons for purchasing a product that are based on a logical evaluation of product attributes

EMOTIONAL MOTIVES reasons for purchasing a product that are based on nonobjective factors

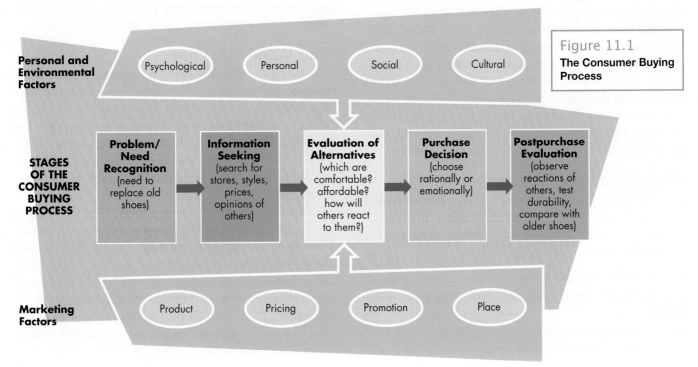

Figure 11.1
The Consumer Buying Process

INDUSTRIAL MARKET organizational market consisting of firms that buy goods that are either converted into products or used during production

RESELLER MARKET organizational market consisting of intermediaries that buy and resell finished goods

INSTITUTIONAL MARKET organizational market consisting of such nongovernmental buyers of goods and services as hospitals, churches, museums, and charitable organizations

PRODUCT FEATURES tangible and intangible qualities that a company builds into its products

VALUE PACKAGE product marketed as a bundle of value-adding attributes, including reasonable cost

Marketing to organizations that buy goods and services used in creating and delivering consumer products involves various kinds of markets and buying behaviors different from those in consumer markets.

Organizational Markets

Organizational or commercial markets fall into three categories: industrial, reseller, and government/institutional markets. Taken together, these markets do over $25 trillion in business annually—more than two times the amount done in the U.S. consumer market.[6]

Industrial Market The **industrial market** includes businesses that buy goods to be converted into other products or that are used up during production. It includes farmers, manufacturers, and some retailers.

Reseller Market Before products reach consumers, they pass through a **reseller market** consisting of intermediaries, including wholesalers and retailers, that buy and resell finished goods.

Government and Institutional Market In addition to federal and state governments, there are some 87,000 local governments in the United States. State and local governments annually spend nearly $5 trillion for durable goods, nondurables, services, and construction.[7] The **institutional market** consists of nongovernmental organizations, such as hospitals, churches, museums, and charities, that also use supplies and equipment as well as legal, accounting, and transportation services.

Organizational Buying Behavior

In some respects, organizational buying behavior bears little resemblance to consumer buying practices. Differences include the buyers' purchasing skills and an emphasis on buyer-seller relationships.

Differences in Buyers Unlike most consumers, organizational buyers are professional, specialized, and well informed.

■ As professionals, organizational buyers are trained in methods for negotiating purchase terms. Once

buyer-seller agreements have been reached, they also arrange formal contracts.

■ As a rule, industrial buyers are company specialists in a line of items. As one of several buyers for a large bakery, for example, you may specialize in food ingredients. Another buyer may specialize in baking equipment (industrial ovens and mixers), whereas a third may buy office equipment and supplies.

■ Industrial buyers are often experts about the products they buy. On a regular basis, organizational buyers study competing products and alternative suppliers by attending trade shows, reading trade magazines, and conducting technical discussions with sellers' representatives.

Differences in the Buyer-Seller Relationship Consumer-seller relationships are often impersonal, short-lived, one-time interactions. In contrast, industrial situations often involve frequent and enduring buyer-seller relationships. The development of a long-term relationship provides each party with access to the technical strengths of the other as well as the security of knowing what future business to expect. Thus, a buyer and a supplier may form a design team to create products to benefit both parties. Accordingly, industrial sellers emphasize personal selling by trained representatives who understand the needs of each customer.

What is a Product?

In developing the marketing mix for any product, whether goods or services, marketers must consider what consumers really buy when they purchase products. Only then can these marketers plan strategies effectively.

The Value Package

Whether it is a physical good, a service, or some combination of the two, customers get value from the various benefits, features, and even intangible rewards associated with a product. **Product features** are the qualities, tangible and intangible, that a company builds into its products. However, as we discussed earlier, to attract buyers, features must also provide benefits, or intangible rewards.

Today's consumer regards a product as a bundle of attributes—benefits and features—that, taken together, marketers call the **value package**. Increasingly, buyers expect to receive products with greater value—with more benefits and features at reasonable costs—so firms must compete on the basis of enhanced value packages. They find that the addition of a new service often pleases customers far beyond the cost of providing it. Just making the purchase transaction faster and

Table 11.2 Categories of Consumer Products

CATEGORY	DESCRIPTION	EXAMPLES
Convenience goods and services	• Consumed rapidly and regularly • Inexpensive • Purchased often and with little input of time and effort	• Milk • Newspaper • Fast food
Shopping goods and services	• Purchased less often • More expensive • Consumers may shop around and compare products based on style, performance, color, price, and other criteria.	• Television set • Tires • Car insurance
Specialty goods and services	• Purchased infrequently • Expensive • Consumer decides on a precise product and will not accept substitutions and spends a good deal of time choosing the "perfect" item.	• Jewelry • Wedding gown • Catering

more convenient, for example, adds value by sparing customers long waits and cumbersome paperwork.

Classifying Goods and Services

We can classify products according to expected buyers, who fall into two groups: buyers of consumer products and buyers of industrial products. Marketing products to consumers is vastly different from marketing products to other companies.

Classifying Consumer Products Consumer products are commonly divided into three categories that reflect buyer behavior: **convenience goods and services**, **shopping goods and services**, and **specialty goods and services**. These are outlined in Table 11.2.

Classifying Industrial Products Depending on how much they cost and how they will be used, industrial products can be divided into two categories: **expense items** and **capital items**. These are explained in Table 11.3.

The Product Mix

The group of products that a company makes available for sale, whether consumer, industrial, or both, is its **product mix**. Black & Decker, for example, makes toasters, vacuum cleaners, electric drills, and a variety of other appliances and tools.

Product Lines Many companies begin with a single product. Over time, they find that the initial product fails to suit every consumer shopping for the product type. To meet market demand, they introduce similar products designed to reach more consumers. A group of products that are closely related because they function in a similar manner or are sold to the same customer group who will use them in similar ways is a **product line**.

Companies may extend their horizons and identify opportunities outside existing product lines. The result—multiple (or diversified) product lines—is evident at Starbucks. Beyond just serving beverages to customers at coffee bars, Starbucks has lines of home-brewing equipment, supermarket products, music products, and industry services. Multiple product lines allow a company to grow rapidly and can help offset the consequences of slow sales in any one product line.

Developing New Products

To expand or diversify product lines—in fact, just to survive—firms must develop and introduce streams of new products. Faced with competition and shifting consumer preferences, no firm can count on a single successful product to carry it forever. Even products that have been popular for decades need ongoing renewal. Product development is a long and expensive process, and many firms have research and development (R&D) departments for exploring new product possibilities. Why do they devote so many resources to exploring product possibilities, rejecting many seemingly good ideas along the way?

Product Mortality Rates

It is estimated that it takes 50 new product ideas to generate one product that finally reaches the market. Even then, only a few of these survivors become successful products. Many seemingly great ideas have failed as products. Creating a successful new product has become increasingly difficult—even for the most experienced marketers. Why? The number of new products

CONVENIENCE GOOD/CONVENIENCE SERVICE inexpensive good or service purchased and consumed rapidly and regularly

SHOPPING GOOD/SHOPPING SERVICE moderately expensive, infrequently purchased good or service

SPECIALTY GOOD/SPECIALTY SERVICE expensive, rarely purchased good or service

EXPENSE ITEM industrial product purchased and consumed rapidly and regularly for daily operations

CAPITAL ITEM expensive, long-lasting, infrequently purchased industrial good, such as a building, or industrial service, such as building maintenance

PRODUCT MIX group of products that a firm makes available for sale

PRODUCT LINE group of products that are closely related because they function in a similar manner or are sold to the same customer group who will use them in similar ways

SPEED TO MARKET
strategy of introducing
new products to respond
quickly to customer or
market changes

**PRODUCT LIFE CYCLE
(PLC)** series of stages
in a product's
commercial life

Table 11.3 **Industrial Products**

CATEGORY	DESCRIPTION	EXAMPLES
Expense items	• Goods or services that are consumed within a year by firms producing other goods or supplying other services • Industrial goods used directly in the production process	• Loads of tea processed into tea bags • Oil and electricity for machines
Capital items	• Permanent (expensive and long-lasting) goods and services • Life expectancy of more than a year • Purchased infrequently so transactions often involve decisions by high-level managers	• Buildings (offices, factories) • Fixed equipment (water towers, baking ovens) • Accessory equipment (computers, airplanes) • Building maintenance • Legal services

hitting the market each year has increased dramatically; more than 180,000 new household, grocery, and drugstore items are introduced annually. In 2006 the beverage industry alone launched 100,000 new products and packaging variations.[8] At any given time, however, the average supermarket carries a total of only 20,000 to 40,000 different items. Because of lack of space and customer demand, about 9 out of 10 new products will fail. Those with the best chances are innovative and deliver unique benefits.

Speed to Market The more rapidly a product moves from the laboratory to the marketplace, the more likely it is to survive. By introducing new products ahead of competitors, companies establish market leadership. They become entrenched in the market before being challenged by newer competitors. How important is **speed to market**—that is, a firm's success in responding to customer demand or market changes? One study reports that a product that is only three months late to market (three months behind the leader) loses 12 percent of its lifetime profit potential. At six months, it will lose 33 percent.

Product Life Cycle

When a product reaches the market, it enters the **product life cycle (PLC)**: a series of stages through which it passes during its commercial life. Depending on the product's ability to attract and keep customers, its PLC may be a matter of months, years, or decades.

Stages in the PLC The life cycle for both goods and services is a natural process in which products are born, grow

At Equity Marketing, engineers like Mark Barbato and Frank Kautzman used to design toys by sculpting models out of clay. Now they use "rapid prototyping," a technology that allows several employees to work simultaneously on 3D "models" that can then be e-mailed to clients for instant review. It now takes five days instead of three weeks to make an initial sculpture.

in stature, mature, and finally decline and die. Look at the two graphics in Figure 11.2. In Figure 11.2(a), the four phases of the PLC are applied to several products with which you are familiar:

1 **Introduction.** This stage begins when the product reaches the marketplace. Marketers focus on making potential consumers aware of the product and its benefits. Extensive promotional and development costs erase all profits.

2 **Growth.** If the new product attracts enough consumers, sales start to climb rapidly. Marketers lower price slightly and continue promotional expenditures to increase sales. The product starts to show a profit, and other firms move rapidly to introduce their own versions.

3 **Maturity.** Sales growth starts to slow. Although the product earns its highest profit level early in this stage, increased competition eventually forces price-cutting, increasing advertising and promotional expenditures, and lower profits. Toward the end of the stage, sales start to fall.

4 **Decline.** Sales and profits continue to fall, as new products in the introduction stage take away sales. Firms end or reduce promotional support (ads and salespeople), but may let the product linger to provide some profits.

Figure 11.2(b) plots the relationship of the PLC to a product's typical sales, costs, and profits or losses. Although the early stages of the PLC often show financial losses, increased sales for successful products recover earlier losses and continue to generate profits until the decline stage. For most products, profitable life spans are short—thus, the importance placed by so many firms on the constant replenishment of product lines.

Identifying Products

Marketers must also identify products so that consumers recognize them. Two important tools for this task are branding and packaging.

Branding Products

Branding is a process of using names and symbols, like Coca-Cola or McDonald's golden arches, to communicate the qualities of a particular product made by a particular producer. Brands are designed to signal uniform quality; customers who try and like a product can return to it by remembering its name or its logo.

Several benefits result from successful branding, including brand loyalty and **brand awareness**—the brand name that first comes to mind when you consider a particular product category. What company, for example, comes to mind when you need to ship a document a long way on short notice? For many people, FedEx has the necessary brand awareness.

Gaining Brand Awareness

The expensive, sometimes fierce struggle for brand recognition is perhaps nowhere more evident than in branding battles among dot-com firms. Collectively, the top Internet brands—Google, Yahoo!, eBay, and Amazon.com—spend billions a year, even though only Google (ranked twentieth) has cracked the ranks of the top 50 global brands.[10] Moreover, the mounting costs of establishing a brand identity mean that many more would-be e-businesses do and will probably fail.

With its growing importance in nearly every industry, marketers are finding more effective, less expensive ways to gain brand awareness. Recent successes have been found with several methods: product placements, buzz marketing, and viral marketing.

Product Placements

Television commercials can be a real turnoff for many viewers, but entertainment programming gets our full attention. And that's when marketers are turning up the promotional juice with **product placement**—a promotional tactic for brand exposure in which characters in television, film, music, magazines, or video games use a real product with a brand visible to viewers.

Product placements are effective because the message is delivered in an attractive setting that holds the consumer's interest. When used in successful films and TV shows, the brand's

> **BRANDING** process of using symbols to communicate the qualities of a product made by a particular producer
>
> **BRAND AWARENESS** extent to which a brand name comes to mind when a consumer considers a particular product category
>
> **PRODUCT PLACEMENT** a promotional tactic for brand exposure in which characters in television, film, music, magazines, or video games use a real product with its brand visible to viewers

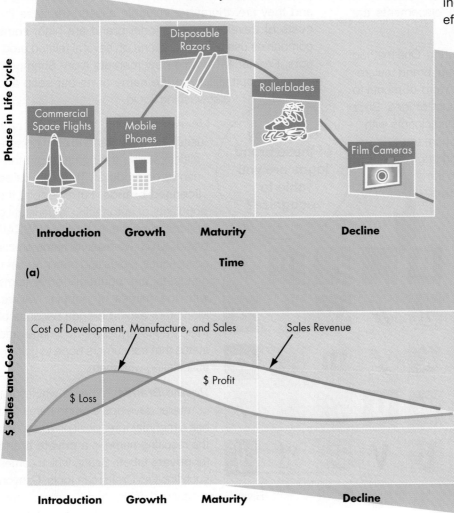

(a) Phase in Life Cycle / Time: Commercial Space Flights, Mobile Phones (Introduction); Disposable Razors (Growth); Rollerblades (Maturity); Film Cameras (Decline)

(b) $ Sales and Cost: Cost of Development, Manufacture, and Sales; Sales Revenue; $ Loss; $ Profit — Introduction, Growth, Maturity, Decline

Figure 11.2

Products in the Life Cycle: Stage, Sales, Cost, and Profit[9]

association with famous performers is an implied celebrity endorsement. The idea is to legitimize the brand in the mind of the consumer. In all, nearly $5 billion is spent annually on product placements, especially in television, and major marketers are putting more into product placements instead of television advertisements. The video game Guitar Hero is the focus of an episode of the TV show *Gossip Girl*. In print placements, Hewlett-Packard computers appear in the photo layouts in the IKEA catalog. Television placements are widespread, especially as digital video recorders (DVRs) gain popularity. Viewers can use their DVRs to skip commercials in recorded shows, but product placements are unavoidable.

Buzz Marketing One method for increasing brand awareness is **buzz marketing** which relies on word-of-mouth to spread "buzz" about a particular product or idea. Buzz marketing agencies provide volunteer participants with new products to try and ask them to share the buzz with their friends, family, co-workers, and others in their social network. Here's the key—most companies running word-of-mouth campaigns require full disclosure, which means the participants should let people know they are participating in a campaign. This is essential so that those on the receiving end of the "buzz" don't feel tricked or taken advantage of.

Viral Marketing **Viral marketing** is a form of buzz marketing that relies on the Internet to spread information like a "virus" from person to person. Messages about new cars, sports events, and numerous other goods and services flow via the Internet among potential customers who pass the information on to others. Using various formats—games, contests, chat rooms, and bulletin boards—marketers

encourage potential customers to try out products and tell other people about them.[11]

How effective can it be? Viral marketing can lead to consumer awareness faster and with wider reach than traditional media messages—and at a lower cost. It works for two reasons. First, people rely on the Internet for information that they used to get from newspapers, magazines, and television. Equally important, however, is the interactive element: The customer becomes a participant in the process of spreading the word by forwarding information to other Internet users, as with the viral marketing campaign for the latest Batman movie.

Types of Brand Names Just about every product has a brand name. Generally, different types of brand names—national, licensed, or private—increase buyers' awareness of the nature and quality of competing products. When consumers are satisfied with a product, marketers try to build brand loyalty among the largest possible segment of repeat buyers.

National Brands **National brands** are produced by, widely distributed by, and carry the name of the manufacturer. These brands are often widely recognized by consumers because of national advertising campaigns, and they are, therefore, valuable assets. Because the costs of developing a national brand are high, some companies use a national brand on several related products. Procter & Gamble now markets Ivory Shampoo, capitalizing on the name of its bar soap and dishwashing liquid.

Licensed Brands We have become used to companies (and even personalities) selling the rights to put their names on products. These are called **licensed brands**. For example, the popularity of auto racing is generating millions in revenues for the NASCAR brand, which licenses its name on car accessories, ladies and men's apparel, headsets, and countless other items with the names of popular drivers. Marketers exploit brands because of their public appeal—the image and status that consumers hope to gain by associating with them.

Private Brands When a wholesaler or retailer develops a brand name and has a manufacturer put it on a product, the resulting name is a **private brand** (or **private label**). Sears, which carries such lines as Craftsman tools, Canyon River Blues denim clothing, and Kenmore appliances, is a well-known seller of private brands.

How many of these brand logos are you able to recognize?

Say What You Mean

Cyber Consumers Strike Back

Online marketing can be a marketing boom for many companies, but what happens when it's turned against a company? With so many individuals participating in social networking sites like Facebook or MySpace and keeping personal blogs, it's increasingly common for a single disgruntled customer to wage war against a company for poor service or faulty products. Unhappy customers have taken to the Web to complain about broken computers or poor customer service. Individuals may post negative reviews of products on blogs, upload angry videos outlining complaints on YouTube, or join public discussion forums where they can voice their

opinion about the good and the bad. In the same way that companies celebrate the viral spread of good news, they must also be on guard for online backlash that can damage a reputation.

and consumer behavior. If they go global, marketers must reconsider each element of the marketing mix—product, pricing, place, and promotion.

International Products

Some products can be sold abroad with virtually no changes. Budweiser, Coca-Cola, and Marlboros are the same in Peoria, Illinois, and Paris, France. In other cases, U.S. firms have had to create products with built-in flexibility— for example, an electric shaver that is adaptable to either 115- or 230-volt outlets, so travelers can use it in both U.S. and European electrical outlets. Frequently, however, domestic products require a major redesign for buyers in foreign markets. To sell computers in Japan, for example, Apple had to develop a Japanese-language operating system.

Packaging Products

With a few exceptions, products need some form of **packaging** to reduce the risk of damage, breakage, or spoilage, and to increase the difficulty of stealing small products. A package also serves as an in-store advertisement that makes the product attractive, displays the brand name, and identifies features and benefits. Also, packaging features, such as no-drip bottles of Clorox bleach, add utility for consumers.

The International Marketing Mix

Marketing internationally means mounting a strategy to support global business operations. Foreign customers, for example, differ from domestic buyers in language, customs, business practices,

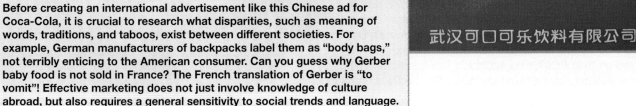

Before creating an international advertisement like this Chinese ad for Coca-Cola, it is crucial to research what disparities, such as meaning of words, traditions, and taboos, exist between different societies. For example, German manufacturers of backpacks label them as "body bags," not terribly enticing to the American consumer. Can you guess why Gerber baby food is not sold in France? The French translation of Gerber is "to vomit"! Effective marketing does not just involve knowledge of culture abroad, but also requires a general sensitivity to social trends and language.

International Pricing

When pricing for international markets, marketers must consider the higher costs of transporting and selling products abroad. For example, because of the higher costs of buildings, rent, equipment, and imported meat, a McDonald's Big Mac costs more in Switzerland than in the United States.

International Distribution

In some industries, delays in starting new international distribution networks can be costly. Therefore, companies with existing distribution systems often enjoy an advantage. Many companies have avoided time delays by buying existing businesses with already-established distribution and marketing networks.

International Promotion

Occasionally, a good ad campaign is a good campaign just about anywhere. Quite often, however, U.S. promotional tactics do not succeed in other countries. Many Europeans believe that a product must be inherently shoddy if a company resorts to any advertising, particularly the American hard-sell variety.

International marketers are ever more aware of cultural differences that can cause negative reactions to improperly advertised products. Some Europeans, for example, are offended by TV commercials that show weapons or violence. Meanwhile, cigarette commercials that are banned from U.S. television thrive in many Asian and European markets. Product promotions must be carefully matched to local customs and cultural values.

Because of the need to adjust the marketing mix, success in international markets is hard won. But whether a firm markets in domestic or international markets, the basic principles of marketing still apply; only their implementation changes.

Small Business and the Marketing Mix

Many of today's largest firms were yesterday's small businesses. Behind the success of many small firms lie a skillful application of the marketing concept and an understanding of each element in the marketing mix.

Entrepreneurship and New Ventures

DVDs as Easy as Netflix.com

What happens when you're a week late in returning a rented copy of a movie, and you get hit with a $39 late fee? If you're Reed Hastings, you think, "There's got to be a better way." That's how Hastings came up with the idea for online DVD subscription services. When the online store was launched, back in 1999, VCRs were all the rage, but Hastings believed consumer tastes would change and DVDs would soon sweep the market. Those projections were prophetic: Today, more than 8 million Netflix subscribers choose from a library of over 90,0000 titles and get their choice of service level for a monthly fee.

How well does Netflix stack up against the competition? Apparently, customers appreciate the value package they receive, including fast front-door delivery service and no late fees. Rental giant Blockbuster holds 25 percent of the online market, while online innovator Netflix, with its larger selection of films, nationwide reach, and faster delivery speed, enjoys a whopping 70 percent.

What's Hastings' next move? DVD-less movie watching. A first step toward eliminating DVDs altogether came in 2007, with the Netflix Internet viewing option. DVD subscribers have unlimited streaming of movies and TV shows on their PCs for no additional fee. For viewers who prefer watching on their high-definition TVs, Netflix is teaming with Korea's LG Electronics in developing a set-top box that can deliver movies and other streaming content directly from the Web. Little wonder, then, that Hastings is betting on a high-flying future for his company and its chances for transforming the movie business.[12]

Small-Business Products Some new products and firms are doomed at the start because few consumers want or need what they have to offer. Many fail to estimate realistic market potential, and some offer new products before they have clear pictures of their target segments. In contrast, a thorough understanding of what customers want has paid off for many small firms. Take, for example, the case of Little Earth Productions, a company that makes fashion accessories, such as handbags. Originally, the company merely considered how consumers would use its handbags. But after examining shopping habits, Little Earth Productions redesigned for better in-store display. Because stores can give handbags better visibility by hanging them instead of placing them on floors or low countertops, Little Earth Productions added small handles specifically for that purpose.

Small-Business Pricing Haphazard pricing can sink a firm with a good product. Small-business pricing errors usually result from a failure to estimate operating expenses accurately. But when small businesses set prices by carefully assessing costs, many earn satisfactory profits.

Small-Business Distribution The ability of many small businesses to attract and retain customers depends partly on the choice of location, especially for new service businesses.

In distribution as in other aspects of the marketing mix, however, smaller companies may have advantages over larger competitors. A smaller company may be able to address customer's needs more quickly and efficiently with an added personal touch. Everex Systems of Fremont, California, sells personal computers to wholesalers and dealers through a system that the company calls *zero response time*. Because Everex Systems is small and flexible, phone orders can be reviewed every two hours and factory assembly adjusted to match demand.

Small-Business Promotion Successful small businesses plan for promotional expenses as part of start-up costs. Some hold down costs by using less expensive promotional methods, like publicity in local newspapers. Other small businesses identify themselves and their products with associated groups, organizations, and events. Thus, a crafts gallery might join with a local art league to organize public showings of their combined products.

> **For additional topics related to this material and end-of-chapter exercises and practices, please visit www.mybizlab.com.**

Questions for Review

1 What are the key similarities and differences between consumer buying behavior and organizational buying behavior?

2 Why and how is market segmentation used in target marketing?

3 What are the various classifications of consumer and industrial products? Give an example of a good and a service for each category other than those discussed in the text.

Questions for Analysis

4 Select an everyday product (personal fitness training, CDs, dog food, cell phones, or shoes, for example). Show how different versions of your product are aimed toward different market segments. Explain how the marketing mix differs for each segment.

5 Select a second everyday product and describe the consumer buying process that typically goes into its purchase.

6 Consider a service product, such as transportation, entertainment, or health care. What are some ways that more customer value might be added to this product? Why would your improvements add value for the buyer?

7 How would you expect the branding and packaging of convenience, shopping, and specialty goods to differ? Why? Give examples to illustrate your answers.

Application Exercises

8 Interview the marketing manager of a local business. Identify the degree to which this person's job is focused on each element in the marketing mix.

9 Select a product made by a foreign company and sold in the United States. What is the product's target market? What is the basis on which the target market is segmented? Do you think that this basis is appropriate? How might another approach, if any, be beneficial? Why?

10 Choose a product that could benefit from word-of-mouth buzz marketing. Then create a marketing campaign kit for participants to spread the word about this product.

chapter 12

Pricing, Distributing, and Promoting Products

After reading this chapter, you should be able to:

1 Identify the various pricing objectives that govern pricing decisions, and describe the price-setting tools used in making these decisions.

2 Discuss pricing strategies that can be used for different competitive situations and identify the pricing tactics that can be used for setting prices.

3 Explain the meaning of *distribution mix* and identify the different channels of distribution.

4 Describe the role of wholesalers and explain the different types of retailing.

5 Describe the role of e-intermediaries and explain how they add value for advertisers and consumers on the Internet.

6 Define *physical distribution* and describe the major activities in the physical distribution process.

7 Identify the important objectives of promotion, discuss the considerations in selecting a promotional mix, and discuss advertising promotions.

8 Outline the tasks involved in personal selling, describe the various types of sales promotions, and distinguish between publicity and public relations.

iTunes Is It

iTunes allows you to download multiple albums to your Apple iPod in minutes.

In 2008, iTunes took the top spot as the number one music retailer in the United States with a 19 percent market share. Launched just 5 years earlier, iTunes has sold over 4 billion songs to over 50 million customers and holds 70 percent of the market share for global digital downloads.

Apple has perfected the art of creating a buzz by coupling iTunes's massive music library with stylish, must-have gadgets like the iPod and iPhone. TV ads feature products showing off their groundbreaking functionality to the soundtrack of songs so infectious you can hardly resist shelling out $.99 each for them at the iTunes music store. And that pricing policy is part of Apple CEO Steve Jobs's plan to keep a customer base of loyal purchasers from resorting to piracy. He has criticized the "greedy" music industry for its push to raise digital download prices. But don't assume that Jobs is all generosity—his contentment with a relatively meager profit from the iTunes music store is more than made up for by the $5.8 billion Apple raked in last quarter from sales of its own iTunes-compatible MP3 players.[1]

iTunes has also capitalized on the fastest method of product delivery—high-speed Internet—and the tech savvy of its target teen market. The result has been that 48 percent of U.S. teens didn't purchase a single CD in 2007 and brick-and-mortar retailers like Wal-Mart have reduced the amount of physical store space devoted to CDs.[2] As gadgets and software become increasingly affordable and user-friendly, teens aren't the only demographic flooding the market. Baby Boomers can tap into iTunes's increasing supply of classic music titles to replace their worn-out vinyl. Even older generations can download books and informational podcasts through iTunes and its latest venture iTunes U, which offers downloadable lectures and other educational programs.

What's in It for Me?

To become the number-one retailer in any market takes a solid understanding of how best to set prices to achieve profit and market share objectives, and how to promote and distribute products to customers. This chapter also describes different types of wholesalers, retailers, and intermediaries, as well as how the online marketplace has changed the nature of how companies do business. By understanding this chapter's methods for pricing, distributing, and promoting products, you'll have a clearer picture of how to sort out and identify the different kinds of people that are targeted by various companies, products, and advertising campaigns. You'll also be prepared to evaluate a company's marketing programs, distribution methods, and competitive potential.

Determining Prices

After deciding what *products* a company will offer to customers, the second major component of the marketing mix is **pricing**—determining what the customer pays and the seller receives in exchange for a product. Setting prices involves understanding how they contribute to achieving the firm's sales objectives.

Pricing to Meet Business Objectives

Pricing objectives are the goals that sellers hope to achieve in pricing products for sale. Some companies have *profit-maximizing pricing objectives*, while others have *market share pricing objectives*. Pricing decisions are also influenced by the need to compete in the marketplace, by social and ethical concerns, and even by corporate image.

Profit-Maximizing Objectives   The seller's pricing decision is critical for determining the firm's revenue, which is the selling price times the number of units sold.

$$\text{Revenue} = \text{Selling price} \times \text{Units sold}$$

Companies that set prices to maximize profits want to set the selling price to sell the number of units that will generate the highest possible total profits. If a company sets prices too low, it will probably sell many units but may miss out on additional profits on each unit (and may even lose money on each exchange). If a company sets prices too high, it will make a large profit on each item but will sell fewer units. Again, the firm loses money, and it may also be left with excess inventory.

In calculating profits, managers weigh sales revenues against costs for materials and labor, as well as capital resources (plant and equipment) and marketing costs (such as maintaining a large sales staff). To use these resources efficiently, many firms set prices to cover costs and achieve a targeted level of return for owners.

Market Share (Market Penetration) Objectives   In the long run, a business must make a profit to survive. Because they are willing to accept minimal profits, even losses, to get buyers to try products, companies may initially set low prices for new products to establish **market share** (or **market penetration**)—a company's percentage of the total industry sales for a specific product type.

Price-Setting Tools

Before deciding on final prices, managers can use *cost-oriented pricing* and *breakeven analysis* to measure potential impact.

Cost-Oriented Pricing   **Cost-oriented pricing** considers a firm's desire to make a profit and its need to cover production costs.

$$\text{Selling price} = \text{Seller's costs} + \text{Profit}$$

A music-store manager would price CDs by calculating the cost of making them available to shoppers. Thus, price would include the costs of store rent, employee wages, utilities, product displays, insurance, and the CD-manufacturer's price.

If the manufacturer's price is $8 per CD and the store sells CDs for $8, the store won't make any profit. Nor will it make a profit if it sells CDs for $8.50 each—or even $10 or $11. To be profitable, the company must charge enough to cover product and other costs. Together, these factors determine the **markup**—the amount added to an item's purchase cost to sell it at a profit. In this case, a reasonable markup of $7 over the purchase cost means a $15 selling price. The following equation calculates

Using low-cost, direct-to-consumer selling and market share pricing, Dell profitably dominated the personal computer market, while its competitors—Apple, IBM, Compaq, and Hewlett-Packard—sold through retailers, adding extra costs that prevented them from matching Dell's low prices. Competitors have switched to direct-to-consumer sales, but Dell is strongly anchored as the industry's number-two PC maker (after Hewlett-Packard).[3]

Figure 12.1
Breakeven Analysis

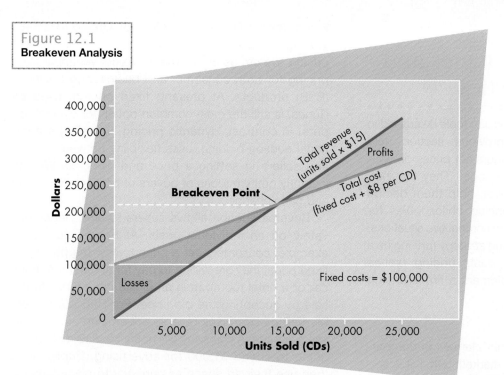

VARIABLE COST cost that changes with the quantity of a product produced and sold

FIXED COST cost that is incurred regardless of the quantity of a product produced and sold

BREAKEVEN ANALYSIS for a particular selling price, an assessment of the seller's costs versus revenues at various sales volumes

BREAKEVEN POINT sales volume at which the seller's total revenue from sales equals total costs (variable and fixed) with neither profit nor loss

the markup percentage and determines what percent of every dollar of revenue is gross profit:

$$\text{Markup percentage} = \frac{\text{Markup}}{\text{Sales price}} \times 100\%$$

For our CD retailer, the markup percentage is 46.7:

$$\text{Markup percentage} = \frac{\$7}{\$15} \times 100\% = 46.7\%$$

For experienced price setters, an even simpler method uses a standard cost-of-goods percentage to determine the markup amount. Many retailers, for example, use 100 percent of cost-of-goods as the standard markup. If the manufacturer's price is $8 per CD, the markup (100 percent) is also $8, so the selling price is $16.

Breakeven Analysis: Cost-Volume-Profit Relationships Using cost-oriented pricing, a firm will cover **variable costs**—costs that change with the number of units of a product produced and sold, such as raw materials, sales commissions, and shipping. Firms also need to pay **fixed costs**—costs, such as rent, insurance, and utilities, that must be paid *regardless of the number of units produced and sold*.

Costs, selling price, and the number of units sold determine how many units a company must sell before all costs, both variable and fixed, are covered, and it begins to make a profit. **Breakeven analyses** assess costs versus revenues for various sales volumes and show, at any particular selling price, the amount of loss or profit for each possible volume of sales.

If you were the manager of a music store, how would you determine how many CDs you needed to sell to break even? We know that the *variable cost* of buying each CD from the manufacturer is $8. This means that the store's annual variable costs depend on how many CDs are sold—the number of CDs sold times the $8 cost for each CD. Say that *fixed costs* for keeping the store open for 1 year are $100,000 (no matter how many CDs are sold). At a selling price of $15 each, how many CDs must be sold *so that total revenues exactly cover both* fixed and variable costs? The answer is the **breakeven point**, which is 14,286 CDs:

$$\text{Breakeven point (in units)} = \frac{\text{Total Fixed Cost}}{\text{Price} - \text{Variable Cost}}$$
$$= \frac{\$100,000}{\$15 - \$8} = 14,286 \text{ CDs}$$

Look at Figure 12.1. If the store sells fewer than 14,286 CDs, it loses money for the year. If sales go over 14,286, profits grow by $7 for each additional CD. If the store sells exactly 14,286 CDs, it will cover all its costs but earn zero profit.

Zero profitability at the breakeven point can also be seen by using the profit equation:

$$\text{Profit} = \frac{\text{Total}}{\text{Revenue}} - \begin{pmatrix} \text{Total} & \text{Total} \\ \text{Fixed} + \text{Variable} \\ \text{Cost} & \text{Cost} \end{pmatrix}$$
$$= (14,286 \text{ CDs} \times \$15) - (\$100,000 \text{ Fixed Cost}$$
$$+ [14,286 \text{ CDs} \times \$8 \text{ Variable Cost}])$$

$$\$0 = (\$214,290) - (\$100,00 + \$114,288)$$
$$(\text{rounded to the nearest whole CD})$$

Pricing Strategies and Tactics

The pricing tools discussed in the previous section help managers set prices on specific goods. They do not, however, help them decide on pricing philosophies for diverse competitive situations. In this section, we discuss pricing *strategy* (pricing as a planning activity) and some basic pricing *tactics* (ways in which managers implement a firm's pricing strategies).

Pricing Strategies

Pricing is an extremely important element in the marketing mix, as well as a flexible marketing tool: it is certainly easier to change prices than to change products or distribution channels. This section will look at how pricing strategies can result in widely differing prices for very similar products.

Pricing Existing Products
A firm has three options for pricing existing products:

1. Pricing above prevailing market prices for similar products to take advantage of the common assumption that higher price means higher quality

2. Pricing below market prices while offering a product of comparable quality to higher-priced competitors

3. Pricing at or near market prices

Pricing New Products
When introducing new products, companies must often choose between very high prices or very low prices. **Price skimming**—setting an initial high price to cover development and introduction costs and generate a large profit on each item sold—works only if marketers can convince consumers that a new product is truly different from existing products. In contrast, **penetration pricing**—setting an initial low price to establish a new product in the market—seeks to create consumer interest and stimulate trial purchases.

Fixed Versus Dynamic Pricing for Online Business
The digital marketplace has introduced a highly variable pricing system as an alternative to conventional fixed pricing for both consumer and business-to-business (B2B) products. At present, fixed pricing, used by iTunes, is still the most common option for cybershoppers. In contrast, dynamic pricing, like eBay's traditional auction bidding, uses flexibility between buyers and sellers in setting a price and uses the Web to instantly notify millions of buyers of product availability and price changes.

Reverse auction allows sellers to alter prices privately on an individual basis. At Priceline.com, for example, consumers set a price (below the published fixed price) they are willing to pay for airfare (or a rental car or a hotel room); then an airline can complete the sale by accepting the bid price. For B2B purchases, MediaBids.com uses reverse advertising auctions to sell ad space. A company will notify MediaBids that it is going to spend $1,000 for advertising. Publications then use their ad space as currency to place bids for the advertising dollars. The company can then accept the bid that offers the most ad exposure in the best publication.[4]

Pricing Tactics

Regardless of its pricing strategy, a company may adopt one or more *pricing tactics*. Companies selling multiple items in a product category often use **price lining**—offering all items in certain categories at a limited number of prices. A department store, for example, might predetermine $175, $250, and $400 as the *price*

Roy Cooper scours the markets of Quito, Ecuador, for tapestries, baskets, and religious relics. He then sells them on the Internet, usually at substantial markups, by privately negotiating prices with buyers.

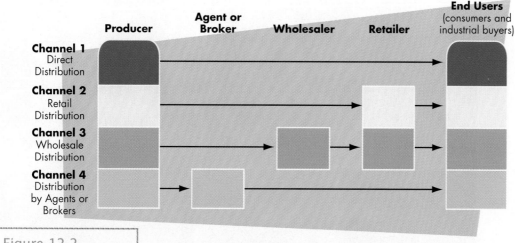

Figure 12.2
Channels of Distribution

points for men's suits, so all men's suits would be set at one of these three prices.

Psychological pricing takes advantage of the fact that customers are not completely rational when making buying decisions. One type, **odd-even pricing**, is based on the theory that customers prefer prices that are not stated in even dollar amounts. Thus, customers regard prices of $1,000, $100, $50, and $10 as significantly higher than $999.95, $99.95, $49.95, and $9.95, respectively. Finally, sellers must often resort to price reductions—**discounts**—to stimulate sales.

The Distribution Mix

In addition to a good product mix and effective pricing, the success of any product also depends on its **distribution mix**—the combination of distribution channels by which a firm gets products to end users.

Intermediaries and Distribution Channels

Once called *middlemen*, **intermediaries** help to distribute goods, either by moving them or by providing information that stimulates their movement from sellers to customers. **Wholesalers** are intermediaries who sell products to other businesses for resale to final consumers. **Retailers** sell products directly to consumers.

Distribution of Goods and Services A **distribution channel** is the path a product follows from producer to end user. Figure 12.2 shows how four popular distribution channels can be identified according to the channel members involved in getting products to buyers.

Channel 1: Direct Distribution In a **direct channel**, the product travels from the producer to the consumer or industrial buyer without intermediaries. Avon, Dell,

GEICO, and Tupperware, as well as many companies on the Internet, use this channel. Most business goods, especially those bought in large quantities, are sold directly by the manufacturer to the industrial buyer.

Channel 2: Retail Distribution In Channel 2, producers distribute consumer products through retailers. Goodyear, for example, maintains its own system of retail outlets. Levi's has its own outlets but also produces jeans for other retailers. Large outlets, such as Wal-Mart, buy merchandise directly from producers. Many industrial buyers, such as businesses buying office supplies at Staples, rely on this channel.

Channel 3: Wholesale Distribution Once the most widely used method of nondirect distribution, Channel 2 requires a large and costly amount of floor space for storing and displaying merchandise. Wholesalers relieve the space problem by storing merchandise and restocking store displays frequently. With approximately 90 percent of its space used to display merchandise and only 10 percent left for storage and office facilities, the combination convenience store/gas station's use of wholesalers is an example of Channel 3.

Channel 4: Distribution by Agents or Brokers Sales agents or brokers represent producers and receive commissions on the goods they sell to consumers or

At the plant of the world's largest auto parts supplier, Delphi Automotive Systems, Jessica V. Prince assembles fuel pumps according to a process that she helped engineers and consultants design. The auto parts are shipped from the plant to an auto manufacturer, illustrating a direct (producer to consumer) channel of distribution.

industrial users. **Sales agents**, including many travel agents, generally deal in the related product lines of a few producers to meet the needs of many customers. **Brokers**, in such industries as real estate and stock exchanges, match numerous sellers and buyers as needed, often without knowing in advance who they will be.

The Pros and Cons of Nondirect Distribution One downfall of nondirect distribution is higher prices: The more members in the channel—the more intermediaries making a profit by charging a markup or commission—the higher the final price. Intermediaries, however, can provide *added value* by providing time-saving information and making the right quantities of products available where and when consumers need them. Figure 12.3 illustrates the problem of making chili without the benefit of a common intermediary—the supermarket. As a consumer, you would obviously spend a lot more time, money, and energy if you tried to gather all the ingredients from separate producers.

Wholesaling

Most wholesalers are independent operations that buy products from manufacturers and sell them to various consumers or other businesses. They usually provide storage, delivery, and additional value-adding services, including credit, marketing advice, and merchandising services, such as marking prices and setting up displays.

Unlike wholesalers, agents and brokers do not own their merchandise. Rather, they serve as sales and merchandising arms for producers or sellers who do not have their own sales forces. The value of agents and brokers lies in their knowledge of markets and their merchandising expertise. They show sale items to potential buyers and, for retail stores, they provide such services as shelf and display merchandising and advertising layout. They remove open, torn, or dirty packages; arrange products neatly; and generally keep goods attractively displayed.

Figure 12.3
The Value-Adding Intermediary

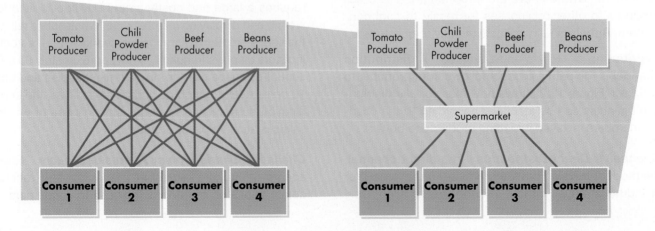

Retailing

There are more than 3 million brick-and mortar retail establishments in the United States. Many consist only of owners and part-time help. Indeed, over one-half of the nation's retailers account for less than 10 percent of all retail sales. Retailers also include huge operations, such as Wal-Mart, the world's largest corporate employer, and Home Depot. Although there are large retailers in many other countries—Metro in Germany, Carrefour in France, and Daiei in Japan—most of the world's largest retailers are U.S. businesses.

Types of Retail Outlets

U.S. retail operations vary widely by type as well as size. They can be classified by their pricing strategies, location, range of services, or range of product lines. Choosing the right types of retail outlets is a crucial aspect of distribution strategy. This section describes U.S. retail stores by using three classifications: *product-line retailers*, *bargain retailers*, and *convenience stores*.

Product Line Retailers

Retailers featuring broad product lines include **department stores**, which are organized into specialized departments: shoes, furniture, women's petite sizes, and so on. Stores are usually large, handle a wide range of goods, and offer a variety of services, such as credit plans and delivery. Similarly, **supermarkets** are divided into departments of related products: food products, household products, and so forth. They stress low prices, self-service, and wide selection.

In contrast, **specialty stores**, like Sunglass Hut International, are small, serve specific market segments with full product lines in narrow product fields, and often feature knowledgeable sales personnel.

> **DEPARTMENT STORE** large product-line retailer characterized by organization into specialized departments
>
> **SUPERMARKET** large product-line retailer offering a variety of food and food-related items in specialized departments
>
> **SPECIALTY STORE** retail store carrying one product line or category of related products

---

Entrepreneurship and New Ventures

Lifestyle Centers: No Finer Place For Sure

The suburban shopping mall may have had its heyday in the 1980s, but the "fastest growing retail format today," according to Terry McEwan, is the lifestyle center. McEwan is president of Poag & McEwan, the company credited with developing the lifestyle center retail format. Typically smaller, cheaper to operate, and quicker to construct than malls, lifestyle centers offer upscale retail shopping with open-air, downtown ambience. They have capitalized on the booming luxury industry—springing up near affluent neighborhoods and featuring higher-priced boutique-style stores alongside sidewalk cafés and day spas.

Historic downtowns that may have once offered a similar retail format tend to have cramped setups, small storefronts, and little space for growth. The lifestyle center's "new downtown" offers a highly attractive middle ground between the cramped old downtown and the expansive shopping mall. While national retailers like Talbots and Banana Republic fit right in, merchants in original downtowns aren't exactly thrilled with the competition.

W/S Development built Massachusetts's first lifstyle center in Hingham with the hope of having a "symbiotic" relationship with the old downtown. But downtown merchants say they have suffered. As developers seize this highly profitable and popular retail format, there may be little that downtowns and shopping malls can do to turn the tide.[5]

Typical lifestyle centers have convenient parking and restaurants built into a high-end group of shops for a one-stop shopping experience.

Bargain Retailers **Bargain retailers** carry wide ranges of products at low prices. **Discount houses** began by selling large numbers of items at substantial price reductions to cash-only customers. As name-brand items became more common, they offered better product assortments while still transacting cash-only sales in low-rent facilities. As they became firmly entrenched, they began moving to better locations, improving decor, selling better-quality merchandise at higher prices, and offering services such as credit plans and non-cash sales.

Catalog showrooms mail catalogs to attract customers into showrooms to view display samples, place orders, and wait briefly while clerks retrieve orders from attached warehouses. **Factory outlets** are manufacturer-owned stores that avoid wholesalers and retailers by selling merchandise directly from factory to consumer. **Wholesale clubs**, like Costco, offer large discounts on a wide range of brand-name merchandise to customers who pay annual membership fees.

Convenience Stores **Convenience store** chains, such as 7-Eleven and Circle K stores, stress easily accessible locations, extended store hours, and speedy service. They differ from most bargain retailers in that they do not feature low prices.

Nonstore Retailing

Some of the largest retailers sell all or most of their products without brick-and-mortar stores. Certain types of products—snack foods, pinball, jukeboxes, pool, and cigarettes—sell well from coin-operated machines. But even at $110 billion per year, vending machine sales still make up less than 3 percent of all U.S. retail sales.[6]

Nonstore retailing also includes **direct-response retailing**, in which firms contact customers directly to inform them about products and to receive sales orders. **Mail order** (or **catalog marketing**) is a popular form of direct-response retailing practiced by Crate & Barrel and Sharper Image. Less popular in recent years due to do-not-call registries, **telemarketing** uses phone calls to sell directly to consumers. Finally, more than 600 U.S. companies, including Mary Kay cosmetics, use **direct selling** to sell door-to-door or through home-selling parties. Avon Products, the world's largest direct seller, has about four million door-to-door sales representatives in over 100 countries.[7]

Online Distribution with E-Intermediaries

The ability of e-commerce to bring together millions of widely dispersed consumers and businesses has changed the types and roles of intermediaries. **E-intermediaries** are Internet-based channel members who collect information about sellers and present it to consumers and/or help deliver Internet products to buyers. Two types of e-intermediaries are *shopping agents* and *e-retailers*.

Shopping Agents

Shopping agents (e-agents), like PriceSCAN.com, rapidly gather, sort, and present accurate information to help Internet consumers compare Web sites, stores, prices, and product features.

Electronic Retailing

Over 85 percent of the world's online population—nearly 1 billion consumers—have made purchases on the Internet. iTunes has outsold brick-and-mortar music retailers, and Amazon.com is the world's largest online retailer, with annual sales of $11 billion.[8] **Electronic retailing (online retailing)** allows sellers to inform, sell to, and distribute to consumers via the Web. The largest U.S. "e-tailers" are shown in Table 12.1. In addition to large companies, millions of small businesses around the globe have their own Web sites.

Electronic Catalogs **E-catalogs** use online displays of products to give millions of retail and business customers instant access to product information. The seller avoids mail distribution and printing costs, and once an online catalog is in place, there is little cost in

Table 12.1 Top 10 Online Retailers

Source: Nielsen Online, December 2007

Rank	Online Retailer	Dec. 07 Unique Audience	Dec. 07 Active Reach
1	eBay	124,132,042	36.1%
2	Amazon	99,863,339	29.1%
3	Target	37,717,553	11.0%
4	Wal-Mart Stores	36,994,959	10.8%
5	Best Buy	24,089,267	7.0%
6	Circuit City	19,725,537	5.7%
7	Sears	17,651,868	5.1%
8	ToysRUs	17,610,395	5.1%
9	Overstock.com	17,192,765	5.0%
10	JCPenney	16,331,132	4.8%

maintaining and accessing it. About 90 percent of all catalogers are now on the Internet, with sales via Web sites accounting for nearly 50 percent of all catalog sales.[9]

Electronic Storefronts and Cybermalls Each seller's Web site is an **electronic storefront** (or *virtual storefront*) from which consumers collect information about products and buying opportunities, place orders, and pay for purchases. Producers of large product lines, such as Dell, dedicate storefronts to their own product lines. Other sites, such as Newegg.com, which offers computer and other electronics equipment, are category sellers whose storefronts feature products from many manufacturers.

Search engines like Yahoo! serve as **cybermalls**—collections of virtual storefronts representing diverse products and offering speed, convenience, 24-hour access, and efficient searching. After entering a cybermall, shoppers can navigate by choosing from a list of stores (L.L. Bean or Macy's), product listings (computers or MP3 players), or departments (apparel or bath/beauty).

Interactive and Video Marketing Today, both retail and B2B customers interact with multimedia sites using voice, graphics, animation, film clips, and access to live human advice. As an example of **interactive marketing**, LivePerson.com is a leading provider of real-time sales and customer service that allows customers to enter a live chat room with a service operator who can answer their specific product questions.

Video marketing, a long-established form of interactive marketing, lets viewers shop

QVC host Bob Bowersox is getting ready to offer bedding made by Northern Lights, which distributes regularly through the TV home-shopping channel. Northern Lights markets through such electronic-retailing outlets as eBay and Shopping.com as well as QVC, which also sells online through its Web site and through six outlet stores.

Specializing in long-haul shipping, U.S. Xpress Enterprises employs nearly 6,000 drivers to operate 5,300 trucks and 12,000 trailers. Trucks have satellite capabilities, anticollision radar, vehicle-detection sensors, computers for shifting through 10 speeds, and roomy cabs with sleepers, refrigerators, and microwaves.

at home from channels on their TVs. QVC, for example, displays and demonstrates products and allows viewers to phone in or e-mail orders.

Physical Distribution

Physical distribution refers to the activities needed to move products from manufacturer to consumer and includes *warehousing* and *transportation operations*. Its purpose is to make goods available when and where consumers want them, keep costs low, and provide services to satisfy customers. Because of its importance for customer satisfaction, some firms have adopted distribution as their marketing strategy of choice.

Warehousing Operations

Storing, or **warehousing**, is a major part of distribution management. In selecting a strategy, managers must keep in mind both the different characteristics and costs of warehousing operations. **Private warehouses** are owned by a single manufacturer, wholesaler, or retailer that deals in mass quantities and needs regular storage.

Independently owned and operated **public warehouses**, which rent to companies only the space they need, are popular with firms needing storage only during peak periods and with manufacturers who need multiple storage locations to get products to multiple markets.

Transportation Operations

Physically moving a product creates the highest cost many companies face. In addition to transportation methods, firms must also consider the nature of the product, the distance it must travel, the speed with which it must be received, and customer wants and needs.

Transportation Modes   Differences in cost among the major transportation modes—trucks, railroads, planes, digital transmission, water carriers, and pipelines—are usually most directly related to delivery speed.

Trucks   With more than 3 million drivers, trucks haul more than two-thirds of all tonnage carried by all modes of U.S. freight transportation. The advantages of trucks include flexibility for any-distance distribution, fast service, and dependability. Increasing truck traffic, however, is raising safety and courtesy concerns.

Planes   Air is the fastest and most expensive mode of transportation for physical goods. Airfreight customers benefit from lower inventory costs by eliminating the need to store items that might deteriorate. Shipments of fresh fish, for example, can be picked up by restaurants each day, avoiding the risk of spoilage from packaging and storing.

High-Speed Digital Transmission   iTunes's transportation mode of choice, online transmission is newer, faster, and less expensive than all other modes. It is also restricted to products—such as music, images, movies, and software—that exist as digital bits that can be transmitted over communication channels.

Water Carriers   Aside from high-speed digital transmission, water is the least expensive mode but, unfortunately, also the slowest. Networks of waterways—oceans, rivers, and lakes—let water carriers reach many areas throughout the world. Boats and barges are used mostly for moving bulky products (such as oil, grain, and gravel).

Railroads   Railroads can economically transport high-volume, heavy, bulky items, such as cars, steel, and coal. However, their delivery routes are limited by fixed, immovable rail tracks.

Pipelines   Pipelines are slow and lack flexibility and adaptability, but for specialized products, like liquids and gases, they provide economical and reliable delivery.

Distribution as a Marketing Strategy

Instead of just offering advantages in product features, quality, price, and promotion, many firms have turned to distribution as a cornerstone of business strategy.

This approach means assessing and improving the entire stream of activities—wholesaling, warehousing, and transportation—involved in getting products to customers.

Consider, for example, the distribution system of National Semiconductor, one of the world's largest microchip makers. Finished microchips are produced in plants around the world and shipped to 1,700 customers, such as IBM, Toshiba, and Hewlett-Packard, which also run factories around the globe. Chips originally traveled 20,000 different routes on as many as 12 airlines and sat waiting at one location after another—on factory floors, at customs, in distributors' facilities, and in warehouses—before reaching customers. National has streamlined the system and now airfreights ship worldwide from a single center in

Say What You Mean

What's in a Label?

Sales of organic foods have increased every year for the past decade, with a 21 percent increase in 2006. But what are the chances that enthusiastic consumers willing to pay extra for the "organic" label are getting what they expect, if they don't even know what they're expecting? Organic foods are highly sought after because consumers have an often vague notion that they are in some way healthier than nonorganic foods, but even equally reputable sources can't agree on a definition. Pesticide-free? Hormone-free? Chemical-free? Free-range? Natural? Even the various terms used to define organic have myriad meanings.

In 2002, the USDA established standards required for products to carry the "USDA Certified Organic" label, but these standards still leave room for interpretation. Even informed consumers seeking out the organic label may be paying for just that—a label. While some companies may have the best of intentions to offer food that meets their own standards for organic, others may be more than willing to use this confusion as a marketing tool for their own profit.

Rather than try to parse out the true definition of organic, let's focus instead on how the inconsistent meanings of this label stand to hurt the companies who use it—even in good faith. Based on sales increases, consumers still seem to be increasingly willing to pay higher prices for food purported to be organic. But if the market becomes saturated with "organic" products, the label will cease to have any meaning or distinguish products in any way. If faced with a bevy of seemingly equal organic products, consumers may focus more on getting the best price, which may mean that the farmer with the most stringent standards and therefore higher-priced products loses out on the sale.[10]

As an increasing number of products are labeled "organic," it is likely that consumers are not always getting what they think they are paying for.

PROMOTION aspect of the marketing mix concerned with the most effective techniques for communicating information about and selling a product

POSITIONING process of establishing an identifiable product image in the minds of consumers

PROMOTIONAL MIX combination of tools used to promote a product

ADVERTISING promotional tool consisting of paid, nonpersonal communication used by an identified sponsor to inform an audience about a product

Singapore. Every activity—storage, sorting, and shipping—is run by FedEx. By outsourcing the activities, National's distribution costs have fallen, delivery times have been reduced by half, and sales have increased.

The Importance of Promotion

Promotion refers to techniques for communicating information about products and is part of the *communication mix*—the total message any company sends to consumers about its product. Promotional techniques, especially advertising, must communicate the uses, features, and benefits of products, and marketers use an array of tools for this purpose.

Promotional Objectives

The ultimate objective of any promotion is to increase sales. In addition, marketers may use promotion to *communicate information*, *position products*, *add value*, and *control sales volume*.

Positioning is the process of establishing an easily identifiable product image in the minds of consumers by fixing, adapting, and communicating the nature of the product itself. First, a firm must identify which market segments are likely to purchase its product and how its product measures up against competitors. Then, it can focus on promotional choices for differentiating its product and positioning it in the minds of the target audience.

Promotional mixes are often designed to communicate a product's *value-added benefits* to distinguish it from the competition. Mercedes automobiles and Ritz-Carlton Hotels, for example, promote their products as upscale goods and services featuring high quality, style, and performance, all at a higher price.

The Promotional Mix

Four of marketing's most powerful promotional tools are *advertising*, *personal selling*, *sales promotions*, and *publicity and public relations*. The best combination of these tools—the best **promotional mix**—depends on many factors. The most important is the target audience. As an example, two generations from now, 25 percent of the U.S. workforce will be Hispanic. The rise in Latinos' disposable income has made them a potent economic force, and marketers are scrambling to redesign and promote products to appeal to them. Spanish-language media is one obvious outlet: the audience for programming from Univision, the biggest Spanish-language media company in the United States—with television, radio, music, and Internet—has ballooned by 44 percent since 2001 to become the number five network in the United States.[11]

The Target Audience: Promotion and the Buyer Decision Process In establishing a promotional mix, marketers match promotional tools with the five stages in the buyer decision process:

1. When buyers first recognize the need to make a purchase, marketers use advertising and publicity to make sure buyers are aware of their products.

2. As buyers search for information about available products, advertising and personal selling are important methods to educate consumers.

3. Personal selling can become vital as buyers compare competing products. Sales representatives can demonstrate product quality, features, and performance in comparison with competitors' products.

4. When buyers are ready to purchase products, sales promotion can give consumers an incentive to buy. Personal selling can help by bringing products to convenient purchase locations.

5. After making purchases, buyers evaluate products and note (and remember) their strengths and deficiencies. Advertising and personal selling can remind consumers that they made wise purchases.

Advertising Promotions

Advertising is paid, nonpersonal communication by which an identified sponsor informs an audience about a product. In 2006, U.S. firms spent $285 billion on advertising— $105 billion of it by just 100 companies.[12] Figure 12.4 shows U.S. advertising expenditures for the top-spending firms. Let's take a look at the different types of advertising media, noting some of the advantages and limitations of each.

Advertising Media Consumers tend to ignore the bulk of advertising messages that bombard them; they pay attention to what interests them. Marketers must find out who their customers are which media they pay

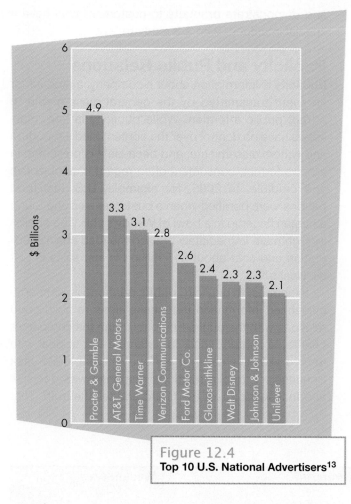

Figure 12.4
Top 10 U.S. National Advertisers[13]

attention to, what messages appeal to them, and how to get their attention. Thus, marketers use several different **advertising media**—specific communication devices for carrying a seller's message to potential customers. The combination of media through which a company advertises is called its **media mix**. Table 12.2 shows the relative sizes of media usage and their strengths and weaknesses.

Personal Selling

In the oldest and most expensive form of sales, **personal selling**, a salesperson communicates one-on-one with potential customers to identify their needs and align them with the product. Salespeople gain credibility by investing a lot of time getting acquainted with potential customers and answering their questions.

Salespeople must be adept at performing three basic tasks of personal selling. In **order processing**, a salesperson receives an order and sees to its handling and delivery. When potential customers are not aware that they need or want a product, **creative selling** involves providing information and demonstrating

product benefits to persuade buyers to complete a purchase. Finally, a salesperson may use **missionary selling** to promote a company and its products rather than simply to close a sale. Pharmaceutical companies often use this method to make doctors aware of the company and its products so they will recommend the company's products to others.

Sales Promotions

Sales promotions are short-term promotional activities designed to encourage consumer buying, industrial sales, or cooperation from distributors. They can increase the likelihood that buyers will try products, enhance product recognition, and increase purchase size and sales revenues.

Types of Sales Promotions

Most consumers have taken part in a variety of sales promotions such as free *samples* (giveaways), which let customers try products without risk, and **coupon** promotions, which use certificates entitling buyers to discounts in order to encourage customers to try new products, lure them away from competitors, or induce them to buy more of a product. **Premiums** are free or reduced-price items, such as pencils, coffee mugs, and six-month low-interest credit cards, given to

consumers in return for buying a specified product. *Contests* can boost sales by rewarding high-producing distributors and sales representatives with vacation trips to Hawaii or Paris. Consumers, too, may win prizes by entering their cats in the Purina Cat Chow calendar contest, for example, by submitting entry blanks from the backs of cat-food packages.

ADVERTISING MEDIA variety of communication devices for carrying a seller's message to potential customers

MEDIA MIX combination of advertising media chosen to carry a message about a product

PERSONAL SELLING promotional tool in which a salesperson communicates one-on-one with potential customers

ORDER PROCESSING personal-selling task in which salespeople receive orders and see to their handling and delivery

CREATIVE SELLING personal-selling task in which salespeople try to persuade buyers to purchase products by providing information about their benefits

MISSIONARY SELLING personal-selling task in which salespeople promote their firms and products rather than try to close sales

SALES PROMOTION short-term promotional activity designed to encourage consumer buying, industrial sales, or cooperation from distributors

COUPON sales-promotion technique in which a certificate is issued entitling the buyer to a reduced price

PREMIUM sales-promotion technique in which offers of free or reduced-price items are used to stimulate purchases

To grab customers' attention in stores, companies use **point-of-sale (POS) displays** at the ends of aisles or near checkout counters to ease finding products and to eliminate competitors from consideration. In addition to physical goods, POS pedestals also provide services, namely information for consumers. Bank lobbies and physicians' waiting rooms, for example, have computer-interactive kiosks inviting clients to learn more about bank products and educational information about available treatments on consumer-friendly touch-screen displays. For B2B promotions, industries sponsor **trade shows** where companies rent booths to display and demonstrate products to customers who have a special interest or who are ready to buy.

Publicity and Public Relations

Publicity is information about a company, a product, or an event transmitted by the general mass media to attract public attention. While publicity is free, marketers have no control over the content media reporters and writers disseminate, and because it is presented in a news format, consumers often regard it as objective and credible. In 2005, for example, U.S. fast-food patrons were horrified when a customer said she found a human fingertip in a bowl of Wendy's chili. The publicity nightmare immediately bruised the food chain's reputation and cost about $15 million in lost sales in just six weeks.[15]

In contrast to publicity, **public relations** is company-influenced information that seeks either to build good relations with the public—by publicizing the company's charitable contributions, for example—or to deal with unfavorable events. In the Wendy's case, CEO Jack Schuessler's public relations response was decisive and focused: protect the brand and tell the truth. That

Table 12.2   **Media Usage, Strengths, and Weaknesses**[14]

Advertising Medium	Percentage of Advertising Outlays	Strengths	Weaknesses
Television	25%	Program demographics allow for customized ads Large audience	Most expensive
Direct mail	18%	Targeted audience Personal messages Predictable results	Easily discarded Environmentally irresponsible
Newspapers	15%	Broad coverage Ads can be changed daily	Quickly discarded Broad readership limits ability to target specific audience
Magazines	11%	Often reread and shared Variety of ready market segmentation	Require advanced planning Little control over ad placement
Radio	7%	Inexpensive Large audience Variety of ready market segmentation	Easy to ignore
Internet	4%	Targeted audience Measurable success	Nuisance to consumers Easy to ignore
Outdoor	2%	Inexpensive Difficult to ignore Repeat exposure	Presents limited information Little control over audience

A combination of other media, including catalogs, sidewalk handouts, skywriting, telephone calls, special events, movies, and door-to-door communication, make up the remaining 18 percent of all U.S. advertising.

meant there would be no payoff or settlement to keep it out of the news. Instead, Wendy's enlisted cooperation with the health department and police, did visual inspections, polygraphed employees, publicly announced a hotline for tips, and offered a reward for information, all leading to the conclusion that the reported episode was a hoax. Energetic public relations was an effective promotional tool for clearing the Wendy's name and preserving the company's reputation.[16]

For additional topics related to this material and end-of-chapter exercises and practices, please visit www.mybizlab.com.

Questions for Review

1 How does breakeven analysis help managers measure the potential impact of prices?

2 Discuss the goal of price skimming and penetration pricing.

3 Identify the channels of distribution. In what key ways do they differ from one another?

4 Explain how e-agents or e-brokers differ from traditional agents or brokers.

5 Select four advertising media and compare the advantages and disadvantages of each.

Questions for Analysis

6 Suppose that a small publisher selling to book distributors has fixed operating costs of $600,000 each year and variable costs of $3.00 per book. How many books must the firm sell to break even if the selling price is $6.00?

7 Choose two advertising campaigns: one that you think is effective and one that you think is ineffective. What makes one campaign better than the other?

8 Give examples of two products that typify the products sold to shoppers through each form of nonstore retailing. Explain why different products are best suited to each form of nonstore retailing.

Application Exercises

9 Select a product and analyze pricing objectives for it. What information would you want if you were to adopt a profit-maximizing objective or a market share objective?

10 Select a product and identify the media used in its promotion. On the whole, do you think the campaign is effective? Why or why not? If the campaign is not effective, what changes would you suggest to improve it?

Information Technology for Business

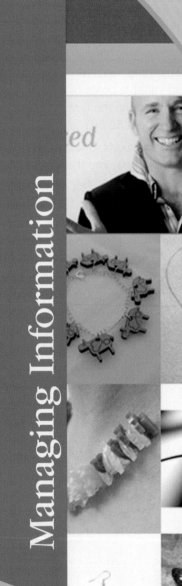

After reading this chapter, you should be able to:

1 Discuss the impacts information technology has had on the business world.

2 Identify the IT resources businesses have at their disposal and how these resources are used.

3 Describe the role of information systems, the different types of information systems, and how businesses use such systems.

4 Identify the threats and risks information technology poses on businesses.

5 Describe the ways in which businesses protect themselves from the threats and risks information technology poses.

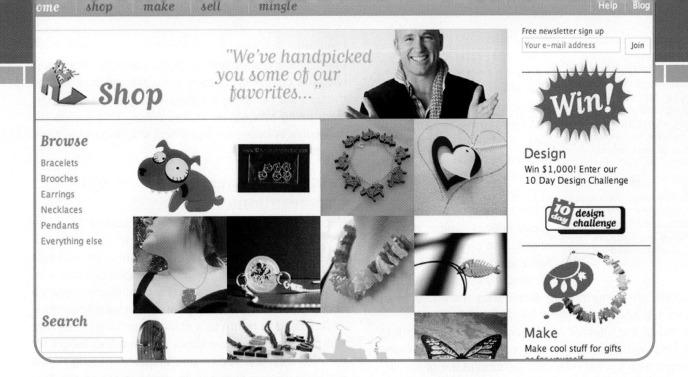

The Instapreneur

Have you ever had an idea for a great new product, but lacked the resources and specialized knowledge necessary to make it a reality? Did you ever wish that your ideas and designs could be magically transformed into finished products without having to manufacture them on your own? Well, a web-based production company called Ponoko is helping to make this fantasy a reality for customers worldwide.

Launched in 2007, Ponoko is a personal manufacturing service based in San Francisco that allows users to upload designs for anything from jewelry to furniture. The designer needs only to upload a blueprint of their idea to the Ponoko Web site. The design information is then transferred to a computer-directed laser cutter, which cuts each product exactly as the designer specified. Ponoko also maintains an online storefront so that users can sell their designs directly on the Web site. The Web site administrators pick featured products, free of charge to the designer, and display them on the main page of Ponoko.com. Designers can also mingle on the site's forums, where they can share their designs and receive valuable feedback and advice.

The Ponoko service is uniquely tailored to each customer's demands, and there are no minimum orders or warehousing fees. Since users only pay for materials and cutting fees on an as-needed basis, there is very little risk involved for entrepreneurs interested in selling their designs. Designers can set the price for their products, whether they sell them on the Ponoko Web site or independently. Ponoko, and other services like it, is enabling anyone with an idea and an Internet connection to instantly start their own business, and become what *Wired* magazine has dubbed an *instapreneur*.[1]

What's in It for Me?

Services such as Ponoko are extreme examples of the way the Internet and related technologies are reshaping the business landscape. But even the most traditional businesses must change with the times, whether those times are defined by paper and pencil, telephone and fax machine, or smartphone and Wi-Fi. Indeed, it may seem like the times are changing more rapidly with each passing year, and it is in this context that our discussion of the various kinds of information technology, their functions, and the benefits and risks associated with each assumes particular importance. By understanding the material in this chapter, you'll have a clearer picture of how technology is used by and affects business, and how you can use it to your best advantage.

IT Impacts

The effect of **information technology (IT)** on business has been immeasurable. In fact, IT—the various appliances and devices for creating, storing, exchanging, and using information in diverse modes, including visual images, voice, multimedia, and business data— has altered the very structure of business organizations, radically changing the way employees and customers interact. **E-commerce** (short for *electronic commerce*)— the use of the Internet and other electronic means for retailing and business-to-business transactions—has created new market relationships around the globe. In this section, we'll look at how businesses are using IT to bolster productivity, improve operations and processes, create new opportunities, and communicate and work in ways not possible before.

Creating Portable Offices: Providing Remote Access to Instant Information

IT devices such as the BlackBerry, a smartphone that features wireless Internet access and PC-style office applications, save businesses time and travel expenses by enabling employees, customers, and suppliers to communicate from any location. Employees no longer work only at the office or the factory, nor are all of a company's operations performed at one place. When using such devices, off-site employees have continuous access to information, instead of being forced to be at a desk to access their files and the Internet. Such benefits have attracted 14 million enthusiastic subscribers to BlackBerry, making it the leader in the handheld wireless industry.[2]

Enabling Better Service by Coordinating Remote Deliveries

Meanwhile, with access to the Internet, company activities may be geographically scattered but remain coordinated through a networked system that provides better service for customers. Many businesses, for example, coordinate activities from one centralized location, but their deliveries flow from several remote locations, often at lower cost. When you order furniture—for example, a chair, a sofa, a table, and two lamps—from an Internet storefront, the chair may come from a warehouse in Philadelphia and the lamps from a manufacturer in California; the sofa and table may be shipped direct from different suppliers in North Carolina. Beginning with the customer's order, activities are coordinated through the company's network, as if the whole order were being processed at one place. This avoids the expensive in-between step of first shipping all the items to a central location.

Creating Leaner, More Efficient Organizations

Networks and technology are also leading to leaner companies with fewer employees and simpler structures. Because networks enable firms to maintain information linkages among both employees and customers, more work and customer satisfaction can be accomplished with fewer people. For example, truck drivers used to return to a shipping terminal to receive instructions from supervisors on reloading freight for the next delivery. Today, one dispatcher using IT has replaced several supervisors. Instructions to the fleet arrive on electronic screens in trucks on the road so drivers know in advance the next delivery schedule, while satellite navigation services, such as the XM NavTraffic, alert drivers of traffic incidents ahead so they can reroute to avoid delivery delays.[3]

Enabling Increased Collaboration

Collaboration among internal units and with outside firms is greater when firms use collaboration software and other IT communications devices, which we'll discuss later in this chapter. Companies are learning that complex problems can be better solved through IT-supported collaboration, either with formal teams or spontaneous interaction among people and

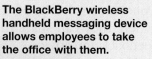

The BlackBerry wireless handheld messaging device allows employees to take the office with them.

departments. The design of new products, for example, was once an engineering responsibility. Now it is a shared activity using information from people in marketing, finance, production, engineering, and purchasing who, collectively, determine the best design. For example, the design of Boeing's 787 Dreamliner aircraft is the result of collaboration, not just among engineers, but also from passengers (who wanted electric outlets to recharge personal electronic devices), cabin crews (who wanted more bathrooms and wider aisles), and air-traffic controllers (who wanted larger, safer air brakes).

Enabling Global Exchange

The global reach of IT is enabling business collaboration on a scale that was unheard of before. Consider Lockheed Martin's contract for designing and supplying thousands of Joint Strike Fighters in different versions for the United States, Britain, Italy, Denmark, Canada, and Norway. Lockheed can't do the job alone—over the project's 20-year life, more than 1,500 firms will supply everything from radar systems to engines to bolts. Web collaboration on a massive scale is essential for coordinating design, testing, and construction while avoiding delays, holding down costs, and maintaining quality.[4]

Improving Management Processes

IT has also changed the nature of the management process. The activities and methods of today's manager differ significantly from those that were common just a few years ago. At one time, upper-level managers didn't concern themselves with all of the detailed information filtering upward from the workplace because it was expensive to gather, slow in coming, and quickly became out of date. Workplace management was delegated to middle and first-line managers.

With databases, specialized software, and networks, however, instantaneous information is accessible and useful to all levels of management. For example, consider *enterprise resource planning (ERP)*: an information system for organizing and managing a firm's activities across product lines, departments, and geographic locations. The ERP stores real-time information on work status and upcoming transactions and notifies employees when action is required if certain schedules are to be met. It coordinates internal operations with activities of outside suppliers and notifies customers of upcoming deliveries and billings. Consequently, more managers use it routinely for planning and controlling company-wide operations. Today, a manager at Hershey Foods, for example, uses ERP to check on the current status of any customer order for Kisses or Jolly Ranchers, inspect productivity statistics for each workstation, and analyze the delivery performance on any shipment. Managers can better coordinate company-wide performance. They can identify departments that are working well together and those that are lagging behind schedule and creating bottlenecks.

Providing Flexibility for Customization

IT networks and other IT advances also create new manufacturing capabilities that enable businesses to offer customers greater variety, customizable options, and faster delivery cycles. Many designs at Ponoko.com can be altered to suit each buyer's tastes. Similarly, at San Francisco–based Timbuk2's Web site, you can "build your own" custom messenger bag at different price levels with your choice of size, fabric, color combination, accessories, liner material, strap, and even left- or right-hand access.[5] This principle is called **mass-customization**: Although companies produce in large volumes, IT allows each unit to feature the unique options the customer prefers. With IT, the old standardized assembly line has become quickly adaptable because workers have instantaneous access to assembly instructions for all the product options, and equipment can be changed quickly for each customer's order.

As shown in Figure 13.1, flexible production and speedy delivery depend on an integrated network of information to coordinate all the activities among customers, manufacturers, suppliers, and shippers.

Providing New Business Opportunities

Not only is IT improving existing businesses, it is creating entirely new businesses where none existed before. For big businesses, this means developing new products, offering new services, and reaching new clients. Only a few years ago, the multibillion-dollar behemoth known as Google was a fledgling search engine. Today, that company boasts not just a search engine but instant messaging, e-mail, and online software services including photo editing and document creation.

The IT landscape has also presented small-business owners with new e-business opportunities. Services like eBay, an online marketplace, allow entrepreneurs to sell directly to consumers, bypassing conventional retail outlets and business models and giving them access to a

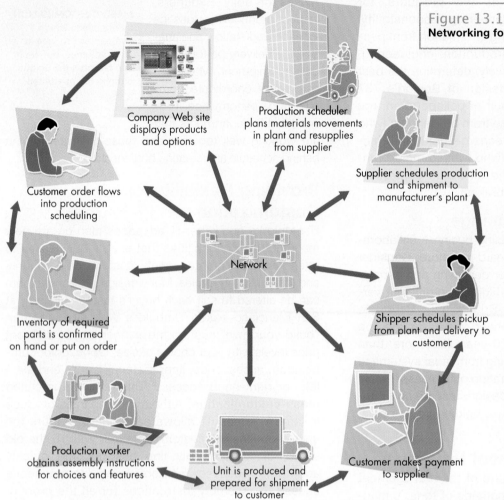

Figure 13.1
Networking for Mass Customization

Company Web site displays products and options

Production scheduler plans materials movements in plant and resupplies from supplier

Supplier schedules production and shipment to manufacturer's plant

Customer order flows into production scheduling

Network

Inventory of required parts is confirmed on hand or put on order

Shipper schedules pickup from plant and delivery to customer

Production worker obtains assembly instructions for choices and features

Unit is produced and prepared for shipment to customer

Customer makes payment to supplier

companies certainly think so. For example, when treating combat injuries, surgeons at Walter Reed Army Medical Center now rely on high-tech imaging systems that convert two-dimensional photographs of their patients' anatomies into three-dimensional physical models for presurgical planning. These 3-D mockups of shoulders, femurs, and facial bones give doctors the opportunity to see and feel the anatomy as it will be seen in the operating room, before they even use their scalpels. Meanwhile, pill-sized cameras that patients swallow are providing doctors with images of the insides of the human body, helping them to make better diagnoses for such ailments as ulcers and cancer.[7]

worldwide customer base. To assist start-up businesses, eBay's services network is a ready-made online business model, not just an auction market. Services range from credit financing to protection from fraud and misrepresentation, information security, international currency exchanges, and post-sales management. These features enable users to complete sales transactions, deliver merchandise, and get new merchandise for future resale, all from the comfort of their own homes.

Improving the World and Our Lives

Can advancements in IT really make the world a better place? Hospitals and medical equipment

Software as a Service

Google's efforts at developing software as an online service, rather than a physical good, are changing the way consumers and businesses work. For example, Google Docs offers much of the same functionality as Microsoft's pricey Office suite for free, and is usable from any computer that has Internet access without software discs. Services like this are driving traditionally offline firms online in order to compete—in late 2007, Microsoft introduced Office Live Workspace, a companion service to its Office 2007 suite that allows users to store documents online and work on them with other users. Analysts predict that by 2010, software as a service (SaaS) will make up over 40 percent of the software market.[6]

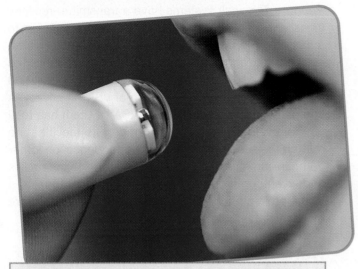

After this capsule is swallowed, the camera inside it can transmit almost 50,000 images during its eight-hour journey through the digestive tract.

IT Building Blocks: Business Resources

Businesses today have a wide variety of IT resources at their disposal. In addition to the Internet and e-mail, these include communications technologies, networks, hardware devices, and software.

The Internet and Other Communication Resources

The **Internet** is a gigantic system of interconnected computers—more than 100 million computers in over 100 countries make up the Internet we know today.[8] These computers are connected by numerous applications utilizing different communications protocols. The most familiar Internet protocols are **hypertext transfer protocol (HTTP)**—which is used for the **World Wide Web**, a branch of the Internet consisting of interlinked hypertext documents, or Web pages—and **simple message transfer protocol (SMTP)** and **post office protocol (POP)**, which are used to send and receive e-mail. For thousands of businesses, the Internet has replaced the telephone, fax machine, and standard mail as the primary communications tool.

The Internet has spawned a number of other business communications technologies, including *intranets*, *extranets*, *electronic conferencing*, and *VSAT satellite communications*.

Intranets   Many companies have extended Internet technology by maintaining internal Web sites linked throughout the firm. These private networks, or **intranets**, are accessible only to employees and may contain confidential information on benefits programs, production management tools, or product design resources. For firms such as Ford Motor Company, whose intranet is accessed by 200,000 people daily, sharing information on engineering, distribution, and marketing has reduced the lead time for getting new models into production and has

INTERNET a gigantic system of interconnected computers—more than 100 million computers in over 100 countries

HYPERTEXT TRANSFER PROTOCOL (HTTP) the communications protocol used for the World Wide Web, in which related pieces of information on separate Web pages are connected using hyperlinks

WORLD WIDE WEB a branch of the Internet consisting of interlinked hypertext documents, or Web pages

SIMPLE MESSAGE TRANSFER PROTOCOL (SMTP) the basic communications protocol used to send e-mail

POST OFFICE PROTOCOL (POP) one of the basic communications protocols used to receive e-mail

INTRANET an organization's private network of internally linked Web sites accessible only to employees

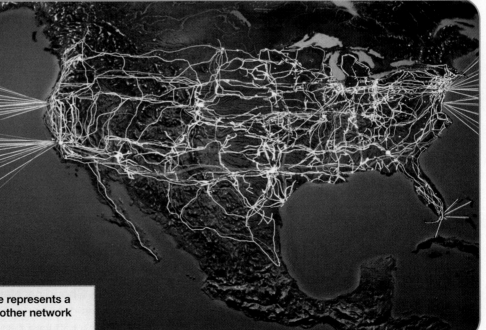

In this map of the Internet, each line represents a connection between computers or other network devices.[9]

shortened customer delivery times.[10]

Extranets

Extranets allow outsiders limited access to a firm's internal information network. The most common application allows buyers to enter a system to see which products are available for sale and delivery, thus providing convenient product-availability information. Industrial suppliers are often linked into customers' information networks so that they can see planned production schedules and prepare supplies for customers' upcoming operations. The extranet at Chaparral Steel, for example, lets customers shop electronically through its storage yards and gives them electronic access to Chaparral's planned inventory of industrial steel products.

Electronic Conferencing

Electronic conferencing allows groups of people to communicate simultaneously from various locations via e-mail, phone, or video, thereby eliminating travel time and saving money. One form, called *dataconferencing*, allows people in remote locations to work simultaneously on one document. *Videoconferencing* allows participants to see one another on video screens while the conference is in progress. For example, Lockheed Martin's Joint Strike Fighter project, discussed earlier, uses Internet collaboration systems with both voice and video capabilities. Although separated by oceans, partners can communicate as if they were in the same room for redesigning components and production schedules. Electronic conferencing is attractive to many businesses because it eliminates travel and saves money.

VSAT Satellite Communications

Another Internet technology businesses use to communicate is **VSAT satellite communications**. VSAT (short for *Very Small Aperture Terminal*) systems have a transmitter-receiver (*transceiver*) that sits outdoors with a direct line of sight to a satellite. The hub—a ground-station computer at the company's headquarters—sends signals to and receives signals from the satellite, exchanging voice, video, and data transmissions. An advantage of VSAT is privacy. A company that operates its own VSAT system has total control over communications among its facilities, no matter their location, without dependence on other companies. A firm might use VSAT to exchange sales and inventory information, advertising messages, and visual presentations between headquarters and store managers at remote sites.

Networks: System Architecture

A **computer network** is a group of two or more computers linked together, either hardwired or wirelessly, to share data or resources, such as a printer. The most common type of network used in businesses is a **client-server network**. In client-server networks, *clients* are usually the laptop or desktop computers through which users make requests for information or resources. *Servers* are the computers that provide the services shared by users. In big organizations, servers are usually assigned a specific task. For example, in a local university or college network, an *application server* stores the word-processing, spreadsheet, and other programs used by all computers connected to the network. A *print server* controls the printers, stores printing requests from client computers, and routes jobs as the printers become available. An *e-mail server* handles all incoming and outgoing e-mail. With a client-server system, users can share resources and Internet connections—and avoid costly duplication.

Networks can be classified according to geographic scope and means of connection (either wired or wireless).

Wide Area Networks (WANs)

Computers that are linked over long distances—statewide or even nationwide—through telephone lines, microwave signals, or satellite communications make up what are called **wide area networks (WANs)**. Firms can lease lines from communications vendors or maintain private WANs. Wal-Mart, for example, depends heavily on a private satellite network that links thousands of U.S. and international retail stores to its Bentonville, Arkansas, headquarters.

Local Area Networks (LANs)

In **local area networks (LANs)**, computers are linked in a smaller area such as an office or a building. For example, a LAN unites hundreds of operators who enter call-in orders at TV's Home Shopping Network facility. The arrangement requires only one computer system with one database and one software system.

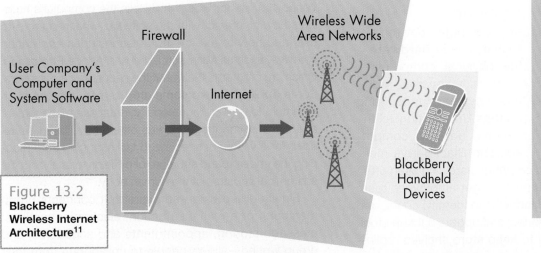

Firewall

User Company's Computer and System Software

Internet

Wireless Wide Area Networks

BlackBerry Handheld Devices

Figure 13.2
BlackBerry Wireless Internet Architecture[11]

Wireless Networks Wireless networks use airborne electronic signals to link network computers and devices. Like wired networks, wireless networks can reach across long distances or exist within a single building or small area. For example, the BlackBerry system shown in Figure 13.2 consists of devices that send and receive transmissions on the **wireless wide area networks (WWANs)** of more than 100 service providers—such as Cellular One (United States), T-Mobile (United Kingdom and United States), and Vodafone (Italy)—in over 40 countries. The wireless format that the system relies on to control wireless messaging is supplied by Research in Motion (RIM), the company that makes the BlackBerry, and is installed on the user-company's computer. A *firewall* provides privacy protection. We'll discuss firewalls in more detail later in the chapter.

Wi-Fi You've no doubt heard of "hotspots"—specific locations such as coffee shops, hotels, and airport terminals that provide wireless Internet connections for people on the go. Each hotspot, or **Wi-Fi** (a play on audio recording term Hi-Fi) access point, uses its own small network, called a **wireless local area network (wireless LAN or WLAN)**. Although wireless service is free at some hotspots, others charge a fee—a daily or hourly rate—for the convenience of Wi-Fi service.

The benefit of Wi-Fi is that you're not tethered to a wire for accessing the Internet. Employees can wait for a delayed plane in the airport and still be connected to the Internet through their wireless-enabled laptops. However, as with every technology, Wi-Fi has limitations, including a short range of distance. This means that your laptop's Internet connection can be severed if you move farther than about 300 feet from the hotspot. In addition, thick walls, construction beams, and other obstacles can interfere with the signals sent out by the network. So, while a city may have hundreds of hotspots, your laptop must remain near one to stay connected. *WiMAX (Worldwide Interoperability for Microwave Access)*, the next step in wireless advancements, will improve this distance limitation with its wireless range of 30 miles.

Apple's latest iPhone features an application that allows travelers to wirelessly map an entire city layout.

Hardware and Software

Any computer network or system needs **hardware**—the physical components, such as keyboards, monitors, system units, and printers. In addition to the laptops, desktop computers, and BlackBerrys mentioned earlier, *handheld computers* are also used often in businesses. For example, Target employees roam the store aisles using handhelds to identify, count, and order items; track deliveries; and update backup stock at distribution centers to keep store shelves replenished with merchandise.

The other essential in any computer system is **software**: programs that tell the computer how to function.

Software includes *system software*, such as Microsoft Windows Vista for PCs, which tells the computer's hardware how to interact with the software, what resources to use, and how to use them. It also includes *application software*, such as Microsoft Excel and Adobe Photoshop, which are programs that meet the needs of specific users. Some application programs are used to address such common, long-standing needs as database management and inventory control, whereas others have been developed for a variety of specialized tasks ranging from mapping the underground structure of oil fields to analyzing the anatomical structure of the human body.

Finally *groupware*—software that connects group members for e-mail distribution, electronic meetings, message storing, appointments and schedules, and group writing—allows people to collaborate from their own desktop PCs, even if they're remotely located. It is especially useful when people work together regularly and rely heavily on information sharing. Groupware

---

Say What You Mean

The Illusion of Online Anonymity

When registering for online services under a screen name, it can be tempting to think your identity is a secret to other users. Many people will say or do things on the Internet that they would never do in real life because they believe that they are acting anonymously. However, most blogs, e-mail and instant messenger services, and social networking sites are tied to your real identity in some way. While your identity may be superficially concealed by a screen name, it often takes little more than a quick Google search to uncover your name, address, and other personal and possibly sensitive information. Even if you take precautions and limit the amount of personal information you place on the Internet, a determined investigator can still use your computer's unique IP address to track you down.

Take the example of Jessica Zenner, a contract employee for the electronic entertainment company Nintendo. In 2007, she was fired for comments she made on her personal blog about her job and her co-workers. Though Zenner used an alias and never mentioned Nintendo or her co-workers by name, the company was still able to link her to her inflammatory comments. Zenner's is not an isolated case—an increasing number of

bloggers have been fired for comments they have published online. The free-speech protections afforded by the First Amendment generally do not extend to complaining about your employer or your co-workers. When speaking online, it is a good idea to ask yourself whether you would voice the same sentiments publicly and in person. If not, it may be wise to keep your comments to yourself lest you face serious repercussions in the real world.[12]

systems include IBM Lotus Domino, Microsoft Exchange Server, and Novell GroupWise.

Information Systems: Harnessing the Competitive Power of IT

● ●

Business today relies on information management in ways that no one could foresee a decade ago. Managers now treat IT as a basic organizational resource for conducting daily business. At major firms, every activity—designing services, ensuring product delivery and cash flow, and evaluating personnel—is linked to *information systems*. An **information system (IS)** is a system that uses IT resources and enables managers to take **data**—raw facts and figures that, by themselves, may not have much meaning—and turn that data into **information**—the meaningful, useful interpretation of data. Information systems also enable managers to collect, process, and transmit that information for use in decision making.

One company well-known for its strategic use of information systems is Wal-Mart. The nerve center for company operations is a centralized IS in Bentonville, Arkansas. The IS drives costs down and raises efficiency because the same methods and systems are applied for all 5,000-plus stores in Europe, Asia, and the Americas. Data on the billions of sales transactions—time, date, and place—flows to Bentonville. The information system tracks nearly 700 million stock-keeping units (SKUs) weekly, enforces uniform reordering and

delivery procedures for more than 30,000 suppliers, and regulates the flow of merchandise through its distribution centers and stores.

Beyond the firm's daily operations, information systems are also crucial in planning. Managers routinely use the IS to decide on products and markets for the next 5 to 10 years. The company's vast database enables marketing managers to analyze demographics, and it is also used for financial planning, materials handling, and electronic funds transfers with suppliers and customers.

Wal-Mart, like most businesses, regards its information as a private resource—an asset that's planned, developed, and protected. Therefore, it's not surprising that they have **information systems managers** who operate the systems used for gathering, organizing, and distributing information, just as they have production, marketing, and finance managers. These managers use many of the IT resources we discussed earlier—the Internet, communications technologies, networks, hardware, and software—to sift through information and apply it to their jobs.

Leveraging Information Resources: Data Warehousing and Data Mining

Almost everything you do leaves a trail of information about you. Your preferences in movie rentals, television viewing, Internet sites, and groceries; the destinations of your phone calls, your credit card charges, your financial status; personal information about age, gender, marital status, and even your health are just a few of the items about each of us that are stored in scattered databases. The behavior patterns of millions of users can be traced by analyzing files of information gathered over time from their Internet usage and in-store purchases.

The collection, storage, and retrieval of such data in electronic files is called

Retailers such as Wal-Mart and Sam's Club rely on data warehousing and mining to keep shelves stocked with in-demand merchandise.

data warehousing. For managers, the data warehouse is a goldmine of information about their business. Indeed, Ohio-based IT firm Teradata creates databases that, for its biggest clients (which include Coca-Cola and Verizon), have storage capacities that exceed 500 terabytes (a thousand billion bytes) of data.[13]

Data Mining After collecting information, managers use **data mining**—the application of electronic technologies for searching, sifting, and reorganizing pools of data to uncover useful information. Data mining helps managers plan for new products, set prices, and identify trends and shopping patterns. By analyzing what consumers actually do, businesses can determine what subsequent purchases they are likely to make and then send them tailor-made ads. The *Washington Post*, for example,

uses data-mining software to analyze census data and target households likely to respond to sales efforts.[14]

Information Linkages with Suppliers The top priority for Wal-Mart's IS—improving in-stock reliability—requires integration of Wal-Mart's and suppliers' activities with store sales. That's why P&G, Johnson & Johnson, and other suppliers connect into Wal-Mart's information system to observe up-to-the-minute sales data on individual items, by store. They can use the system's computer-based tools—spreadsheets, sales forecasting, and weather information—to forecast sales demand and plan delivery schedules. Coordinated planning avoids excessive inventories, speeds up deliveries, and holds down costs throughout the supply chain while keeping shelves stocked for retail customers.

Types of Information Systems

Employees have a variety of responsibilities and decision-making needs, and a firm's *information system* may actually be a set of several systems that share information

---

Entrepreneurship and New Ventures

Living the Virtual Life

The virtual worlds of online games like *Second Life* and *World of Warcraft* have created many new opportunities for virtual entrepreneurs to make real-world profits. For example, *Second Life* has its own currency, the Linden (L$), which can be bought and sold for U.S. dollars on the game's online currency exchange, the LindeX. The Linden averages about L$265 per US$, and in 2006 *Second Life's* virtual world was estimated to have a gross domestic product of US$150 million. Entrepreneurs can also earn real money in *Second Life* from the sale of a wide variety of goods and services. In 2006, Ailin Graef was the first person to become a millionaire from business conducted in *Second Life*, buying and selling virtual real estate.

Unfortunately, not all entrepreneurs take advantage of the potential of virtual worlds in ethical ways. *World of Warcraft* requires a substantial time investment to make the richest and most powerful characters, but there are many players who are

willing to pay to enjoy the benefits of high-level play instead of earning them. This demand has created a huge business in developing countries like China, where gamers work in sweatshop-like conditions for low wages to slay monsters and earn virtual gold. Though this practice, known as *gold farming*, is a violation of the game's terms of service, there were an estimated 100,000 gold farmers operating in 2005 in China alone.[15]

---

while serving different levels of the organization, different departments, or different operations. Because they work on different kinds of problems, managers and their employees have access to the specialized information systems that satisfy their different information needs.

In addition to different types of users, each business *function*—marketing, human resources, accounting, production, or finance—has its own information needs, as do groups working on major projects. Each user group and department, therefore, may need a special IS.

Information Systems for Knowledge Workers

As we discussed in Chapter 10, *knowledge workers* are employees for whom information and knowledge are the raw materials of their work, such as engineers, scientists, and IT specialists who rely on IT to design new products or create new processes. These workers require **knowledge information systems**, which provide resources to create, store, use, and transmit new knowledge for useful applications—for instance, databases to organize and retrieve information, and computational power for data analysis.

Specialized support systems have also increased the productivity of knowledge workers. **Computer-aided design (CAD)** helps knowledge workers—and now ordinary people too, as we saw at the beginning of this chapter—design products ranging from cell phones to jewelry to auto parts by simulating them and displaying them in 3-D graphics. The older method—making handcrafted prototypes from wood, plastic, or clay—is replaced with faster, cheaper prototyping: the CAD system electronically transfers instructions to a computer-controlled machine that builds the prototypes.

In archaeology, CAD is helping scientists uncover secrets hidden in fossils using 3-D computer models of skeletons, organs, and tissues constructed with digital data from CT (computed tomography) scans of dinosaur fossils. From these models, scientists have learned, for example, that the giant apatosaurus's neck curved downward, instead of high in the air as once thought. By seeing how the animals' bones fit together with cartilage, ligaments, and vertebrae, scientists are discovering more about how these prehistoric creatures interacted with their environment.[16]

Information Systems for Managers

Each manager's information activities and IS needs vary according to his or her functional area (accounting or marketing and so forth) and management level. The following are some popular information systems used by managers for different purposes.

Management Information Systems Management information systems (MIS) support managers by providing reports, schedules, plans, and budgets that can then be used for making decisions, both short- and long-term. For example, at Walsworth Publishing Company, managers rely on detailed information—current customer orders, staffing schedules, employee attendance, production schedules, equipment status, and materials availability—for moment-to-moment decisions during the day. They require similar information to plan such mid-range activities as personnel training, materials movements, and cash flows. They also need to anticipate the status of the jobs and projects assigned to their departments. Many MIS—cash flow, sales, production scheduling, and shipping—are indispensable for helping managers complete these tasks.

For longer-range decisions involving business strategy, Walsworth managers need information to analyze trends in the publishing industry and overall company performance. They need both external and internal information, current and future, to compare current performance data to data from previous years and to analyze consumer trends and economic forecasts.

The 3-D computer model of this dinosaur is constructed from digital scans of fossilized tissue.

DECISION SUPPORT SYSTEM (DSS) interactive system that creates virtual business models for a particular kind of decision and tests them with different data to see how they respond

HACKER cybercriminal who gains unauthorized access to a computer or network, either to steal information, money, or property or to tamper with data

IDENTITY THEFT unauthorized use of personal information (such as Social Security number and address) to get loans, credit cards, or other monetary benefits by impersonating the victim

Decision Support Systems

Managers who face a particular kind of decision repeatedly can get assistance from **decision support systems (DSS)**—interactive systems that create virtual business models and test them with different data to see how they respond. When faced with decisions on plant capacity, for example, Walsworth managers can use a capacity DSS. The manager inputs data on anticipated sales, working capital, and customer-delivery requirements. The data flow into the DSS processor, which then simulates the plant's performance under the proposed data conditions. After experimenting with various data conditions, the DSS makes recommendations on the best levels of plant capacity for each future time period.

IT Risks and Threats

• • • • • • • • • • • • •

As with other technologies throughout history, IT has attracted abusers set on doing mischief, with severity ranging from mere nuisance to outright destruction. Hackers break into computers, stealing personal information and company secrets, and launching attacks on other computers. Meanwhile, the ease of information sharing on the Internet has proven costly for companies who are having an increasingly difficult time protecting their intellectual property, and viruses that crash computers have cost companies millions. In this section, we'll look at these and other IT risks. In the next section, we'll discuss ways in which businesses are protecting themselves from these risks.

Hackers

Breaking and entering no longer refers merely to physical intrusion. Today, it applies to IT intrusions as well. **Hackers** are cybercriminals who gain unauthorized access to a computer or network, either to steal information, money, or property or to tamper with data. Another common hacker activity is to launch *denial of service (DoS) attacks*. DoS attacks flood networks or Web sites with bogus requests for information and resources, thereby shutting the networks or Web sites down and preventing legitimate users from accessing them.

Wireless mooching is a growing industry for cybercriminals. In just five minutes, a *St. Petersburg Times* (Florida) reporter using a laptop found six unprotected wireless networks that were wide open to outside users.[17] Once inside an unsecured wireless network, hackers use it to commit identity theft and to steal credit card numbers, among other things. When police officers try to track down these criminals, they're long gone, leaving you, the network host, exposed to criminal prosecution.

Identity Theft

Once inside a computer network, hackers are able to commit **identity theft**, the unauthorized stealing of personal information (such as

Of Pirates and Profits

Hackers often break into company networks to steal company or trade secrets. But it's not just hackers who are doing the stealing. Because the chances of getting caught seem slim, home users continue, illegally, to download unpaid-for movies, music, and other resources from file-swapping networks. A recent study shows that sound piracy costs the United States $12.5 billion and 71,060 jobs annually. However, these losses also showcase what can happen to businesses who fail to adapt to changes in technology. The recording industry has been reluctant to embrace the Internet as a path for distribution, preferring to prosecute pirates rather than offer them legal online alternatives. On the other hand, Apple has benefitted immensely from its online distribution models—some analysts predict that by 2012 Apple's iTunes music store will account for 28% of all music sold throughout the world.[18]

Social Security number and address) to get loans, credit cards, or other monetary benefits by impersonating the victim.

Not all identity theft is committed by hackers, though. Clever crooks get information on unsuspecting victims by digging in trash, stealing mail, or using *phishing* or *pharming* schemes to lure Internet users to bogus Web sites. For instance, a cybercriminal might send an American Online subscriber an e-mail notifying him or her of a billing problem with his or her account. When the customer clicks on the AOL Billing Center link, he or she is transferred to a spoofed (falsified) Web page, modeled after AOL's. The customer then submits the requested information—credit card number, Social Security number, and PIN—into the hands of the thief.

Intellectual Property Theft

Nearly every company faces the dilemma of protecting product plans, new inventions, industrial processes, and other **intellectual property**: something produced by the intellect or mind that has commercial value. Its ownership and right to its use may be protected by patent, copyright, trademark, and other means.

Computer Viruses, Worms, and Trojan Horses

Another IT risk facing businesses is rogue programmers who disrupt IT operations by contaminating and destroying software, hardware, or data files. Viruses, worms, and Trojan horses are three kinds of malicious programs that, once installed, can shut down any computer system. A *computer virus* exists in a file that attaches itself to a program and migrates from computer to computer as a shared program or as an e-mail attachment. It does not infect the system unless the user opens the contaminated file, and users typically are unaware they are spreading the virus by file sharing. It can, for example, quickly copy itself over and over again, using up all available memory and effectively shutting down the computer.

Worms are a particular kind of virus that travel from computer to computer within networked computer systems, without your needing to open any software to spread the contaminated file. In a matter of days, the notorious Blaster worm infected some 400,000 computer networks, destroying files and even allowing outsiders to take over computers remotely. The worm replicates itself rapidly, sending out thousands of copies to other computers in the network. Traveling

through Internet connections and e-mail address books in the network's computers, it absorbs system memory and shuts down network servers, Web servers, and individual computers.

Unlike viruses, a *Trojan horse* does not replicate itself. Instead, it most often comes into the computer, at your request, masquerading as a harmless, legitimate software product or data file. Once installed, the damage begins. For instance, it may simply redesign desktop icons or, more maliciously, delete files and destroy information.

Spyware

As if forced intrusion isn't bad enough, Internet users unwittingly invite spies—masquerading as a friendly file available as a giveaway or shared among individual users on their PCs. This so-called **spyware** is downloaded by users that are lured by "free" software. Once installed, it crawls around to monitor the host's computer activities, gathering e-mail addresses, credit card numbers, passwords, and other inside information that it transmits back to someone outside the host system. Spyware authors assemble incoming stolen information to create their own "intellectual property" that they then sell to other parties to use for marketing and advertising purposes or for identity theft.[19]

Spam

Spam—junk e-mail sent to a mailing list or a newsgroup (an online discussion group)—is a greater nuisance than postal junk mail because the Internet is open to the public, e-mail costs are negligible, and massive mailing lists are accessible through file sharing or by theft. Spam operators send unwanted messages ranging from explicit pornography to hate mail to advertisements, and even destructive computer viruses. In addition to wasting users' time, spam also consumes a network's bandwidth, thereby reducing the amount of data that can be transmitted in a fixed amount of time for useful purposes. U.S. industry experts estimate spam's damage in lost time and productivity at more than

$100 billion worldwide annually, a figure that has doubled since 2005.[20]

IT Protection Measures

Security measures against intrusion and viruses are a constant challenge. Most systems guard against unauthorized access by requiring users to have protected passwords. Other measures include firewalls, special software, and encryption.

Preventing Unauthorized Access: Firewalls

Firewalls are security systems with special software or hardware devices designed to keep computers safe from hackers. A firewall is located where two networks—for example, the Internet and a company's internal network—meet. It contains two components for filtering each incoming data:

- The company's *security policy*—Access rules that identify every type of data that the company doesn't want to pass through the firewall.

- A *router*—A table of available routes or paths; a "traffic switch" that determines which route or path on the network to send each piece of data after it is tested against the security policy.

Only that information that meet the conditions of the user's security policy is routed through the firewall and permitted to flow between the two networks. Data that fail the access test are blocked and cannot flow between the two networks.

Preventing Identity Theft

While foolproof prevention is impossible, steps can be taken to avoid being victimized. A visit to the Identity Theft Resource Center (**http://www.idtheftcenter.org**) is a valuable first step to get information on everything from scam alerts to victim issues to legislation such as the Fair and Accurate Credit Transactions Act (FACTA). FACTA, which took effect in 2005, strengthens identity-theft protections by specifying how organizations must destroy information instead of dropping it in a dumpster. When a

company disposes of documents that contain credit or Social Security information, they must be shredded, pulverized, or burned, and all electronic records (in computers and databases) must be permanently removed to keep them out of the hands of intruders.[21]

Preventing Viruses: Anti-Virus Software

Combating viruses, worms, and Trojan horses has become a major industry for systems designers and software developers. Installation of any of hundreds of **anti-virus software** products protects systems by searching incoming e-mail and data files for "signatures" of known viruses and virus-like characteristics. Contaminated files are discarded or placed in quarantine for safekeeping.

Many viruses take advantage of weaknesses in operating systems, such as Microsoft Windows, in order to spread and propagate. Network administrators must make sure that the computers on their systems are using the most up-to-date operating system that includes the latest security protection.

Protecting Electronic Communications: Encryption Software

Security for electronic communications is another concern for businesses. Unprotected e-mail can be intercepted, diverted to unintended computers, and opened, revealing the contents to intruders. Protective software is available to guard against those intrusions, adding a layer of security by encoding e-mails so that only intended recipients can open them. An **encryption system** works by scrambling an e-mail message so that it looks like garbled nonsense to anyone who doesn't possess the key.

Avoiding Spam and Spyware

To help their employees avoid privacy invasion and to improve productivity, businesses often install anti-spyware and spam-filtering software on their systems. While dozens of anti-spyware products provide protection—software such as Webroot Spy Sweeper and Microsoft Windows Defender—they must be continually updated to keep pace with new spyware techniques.

The federal CAN-SPAM Act of 2003 requires the Federal Trade Commission to shield the public from falsified header information, sexually explicit e-mails that are not so labeled, Internet spoofing (using trickery to make a message appear as if it came from a trusted source), and hijacking of computers through worms or Trojan horses. While it cannot be prevented entirely, spam is abated by many Internet service providers (ISPs) that ban the spamming of ISP subscribers. In a now-classic punishment, an ISP in Iowa was awarded $1 billion in a lawsuit against 300 spammers that jammed the ISP system with an astounding 10 million e-mails a day. Anti-spam groups, too, promote the public's awareness of known spammers. The Spamhaus Project (http://www.spamhaus.org), for example, maintains a list—the Register of Known Spam Operators (ROKSO)—of over 100 professional spammers that are responsible for over 80 percent of spam traffic in North America and Europe.

Questions for Review

1 Why must a business manage information as a resource?

2 How can electronic conferencing increase a company's productivity and efficiency?

3 Why do different users in an organization need different kinds of information from the information system?

4 Why has the BlackBerry become a popular tool among business people?

5 What is the definition of *intellectual property*? List three examples of intellectual property.

Questions for Analysis

6 Describe how a company might use data warehousing and data mining in its information system to better plan for new products.

7 Aside from the eBay example in this chapter, describe one or more ways that IT presents new business opportunities for small businesses.

8 Give three examples (other than those in this chapter) of how a company can become leaner and more efficient by adopting IT.

Application Exercises

9 Consider your daily activities—as a consumer, student, parent, friend, homeowner or renter, car driver, employee, etc.—and think about the ways that you are involved in transactions with IT systems. Make a list of your recent IT encounters and then recall instances in those encounters that you revealed personal information that could be used to steal your identity. Are some encounters on your list riskier than others? Why or why not?

10 Describe the computer network at your school. Identify its components and system architecture. What features either promote or inhibit intrusions from hackers? What features either promote or inhibit intellectual property theft? What features either promote or inhibit computer viruses and spam?

For additional topics related to this material and end-of-chapter exercises and practices, please visit www.mybizlab.com.

14 chapter

The Role of Accountants and Accounting Information

After reading this chapter, you should be able to:

1 Explain the role of accountants and distinguish between the kinds of work done by public accountants, private accountants, management accountants, and forensic accountants.

2 Explain how the accounting equation is used.

3 Describe the three basic financial statements and show how they reflect the activity and financial condition of a business.

4 Explain the key standards and principles for reporting financial statements.

5 Describe how computing financial ratios can help users get more information from financial statements to determine the financial strengths of a business.

6 Discuss the role of ethics in accounting.

CSI: Wall Street

In the aftermath of major accounting scandals such as the Enron case of 2001, many companies are showing an increased interest in the field of forensic accounting: the use of accounting for legal purposes. The expansion of the forensic accounting field—the Association of Certified Fraud Examiners has experienced a 50 percent increase in membership since 2003—is due to increased vigilance as a result of recent scandals, as well as a strong desire on the part of companies to protect themselves from accounting fraud.

Fraud examiners typically begin an investigation of a company by interviewing high-level executives. Team members then comb through e-mails, searching for suspicious words and phrases. The combination of interviews and e-mails may lead investigators to specific accounting files or ledger entries. According to Al Vondra, a Certified Fraud Examiner at PricewaterhouseCoopers, some of the most common fraudulent practices involve hiding revenues and expenses under phony categories such as "Total Noncurrent Assets" or "Other Current Liabilities."

Although major accounting scandals have declined since the early 2000s, recently approved, laxer standards of accounting may soon lead investigators such as Vondra in new directions. Regulations passed by the Financial Accounting Standards Board (FASB) in 2006 allow companies to classify certain stock earnings as Level 3 gains. Under the new FASB standards, Level 3 assets, which are traded infrequently and have no reliable market price, may be counted as earnings according to the judgment of the company based on "unobservable inputs"—or, as journalist Jonathan Weil of Bloomberg News characterizes it, these earnings are "pretty much whatever the companies want them to be." In 2007, Level 3 earnings comprised 35 percent of Wells Fargo Bank's record-breaking third-quarter pretax income of $3.44 billion. Without the Level 3 earnings, Wells Fargo would have posted a loss.[1]

What's in It for Me?

For most of us, the words and ideas in accounting can seem like a foreign language. As we have seen, the specialized terminology can be used to mask fraud and corruption. However, it's also a necessary tool that allows professionals in every industry to analyze growth, understand risk, and communicate complex ideas about a firm's financial health. This chapter will cover the fundamental concepts of accounting and apply them to familiar business situations. By grasping the basic accounting vocabulary you will be able to participate when the conversation turns to the financial matters that constitute so great a part of a firm's daily operations.

What Is Accounting and Who Uses Accounting Information?

Accounting is a comprehensive system for collecting, analyzing, and communicating financial information to a firm's owners and employees, to the public, and to various regulatory agencies. To perform these functions, accountants keep records of taxes paid, income received, and expenses incurred—a process called **bookkeeping**—and they assess the effects of these transactions on business activities.

Because businesses engage in thousands of transactions, ensuring consistent, dependable financial information is mandatory. This is the job of the **accounting information system (AIS)**—an organized procedure for identifying, measuring, recording, and retaining financial information so that it can be used in accounting statements and management reports. The system includes all of the people, reports, computers, procedures, and resources that are needed to compile financial transactions.[2]

Users of accounting information are numerous:

- *Business managers* use it to develop goals and plans, set budgets, and evaluate future prospects.

- *Employees and unions* use it to plan for and receive compensation and such benefits as health care, vacation time, and retirement pay.

- *Investors and creditors* use it to estimate returns to stockholders, determine growth prospects, and decide whether a firm is a good credit risk.

- *Tax authorities* use it to plan for tax inflows, determine the tax liabilities of individuals and businesses, and ensure that correct amounts are paid on time.

- *Government regulatory agencies* rely on it to fulfill their duties toward the public. The Securities and Exchange Commission (SEC), for example, requires firms to file financial disclosures so that potential investors have valid information about their financial status.

Who Are Accountants and What Do They Do?

The **controller**, or chief accounting officer, manages a firm's accounting activities by ensuring that the AIS provides the reports and statements needed for planning, decision making, and other management activities. This range of activities requires different types of accounting specialists. In this section, we begin by distinguishing between the two main fields of accounting: *financial* and *managerial*. Then, we discuss the different functions and activities of *certified public accountants*, *private accountants*, *management accountants*, and *forensic accountants*.

Financial Versus Managerial Accounting

In any company, the two fields of accounting—financial and managerial—can be distinguished by the users they serve: those outside the company and those within.[3]

Financial Accounting   A firm's **financial accounting** system is concerned with external information users: consumer groups, unions, stockholders, suppliers, creditors, and government agencies. It prepares reports such as income statements and balance sheets that focus on the activities of the company as a whole rather than on individual departments or divisions.[4]

Managerial Accounting   **Managerial (management) accounting** serves internal users. Managers at all levels need information to make departmental decisions, monitor projects, and plan future activities. Other employees also need accounting information. To set performance goals, for example, salespeople need past sales data organized by geographic region.

Certified Public Accountants

Certified public accountants (CPAs) offer accounting services to the public. They are licensed by a state after passing an exam prepared by the American Institute of Certified Public Accountants (AICPA), which also provides technical support and discipline in matters of ethics. Whereas some CPAs work as individual

Sometimes, companies ignore GAAP and accountants fail to disclose violations. Jamie Olis (left) was a mid-level executive at Texas-based energy producer Dynegy. To cover up the company's financial difficulties and dodge $79 million in federal taxes, Olis helped devise an accounting scheme to disguise a $300 million loan as cash flow. He was sentenced to 24 years in jail, though the judge later reduced it to six years.

practitioners, many form or join existing partnerships or professional corporations.

CPA Services   Virtually all CPA firms, whether large or small, provide auditing, tax, and management services. Larger firms such as Deloitte Touche Tohmatsu and Ernst & Young earn much of their revenue from auditing services, though consulting (management advisory) services constitute a major growth area. Smaller firms earn most of their income from tax and management services.

Auditing   An **audit** examines a company's AIS to determine whether financial reports reliably represent its operations.[5] Organizations must provide audit reports when applying for loans, selling stock, or when going through a major restructuring. Independent auditors who do not work for the company must ensure that clients' accounting systems follow **generally accepted accounting principles (GAAP)**, which are formulated by the Financial Accounting Standards Board (FASB) of the AICPA and govern the content and form of financial reports.[6] The Securities and Exchange Commission (SEC) is the U.S. government agency that legally enforces accounting and auditing rules and procedures.

Tax Services   **Tax services** include assistance not only with tax-return preparation but also with tax planning. A CPA's advice can help a business structure (or

restructure) operations and investments and perhaps save millions of dollars in taxes. Staying abreast of tax-law changes is no simple matter. Some critics charge that tax changes have become a full-time vocation among some state and federal legislators who add increasingly complicated laws and technical corrections on taxation each year.

Management Advisory Services   As consultants, accounting firms provide **management advisory services** ranging from personal financial planning to planning corporate mergers. Other services include production scheduling, computer-feasibility studies, AIS design, and even executive recruitment. The staffs of the largest CPA firms include engineers, architects, mathematicians, and psychologists, all of whom are available for consulting.

Noncertified Public Accountants   Many accountants don't take the CPA exam; others work in the field while getting ready for it or while meeting requirements for state certification. Many small businesses, individuals, and even larger firms rely on these noncertified public accountants for income-tax preparation, payroll accounting, and financial-planning services.

The CPA Vision Project   The recent talent shortage in accounting has led the profession to rethink its culture and lifestyle.[7] With grassroots participation from CPAs, educators, and industry leaders, the AICPA, through its

Table 14.1   **Core Competencies for Accounting[8]**

Strategic and Critical Thinking Skills	The accountant can provide competent advice for strategic action by combining data, knowledge, and insight.
Communications and Leadership Skills	The accountant can exchange information meaningfully in a variety of business situations with effective delivery and interpersonal skills.
Focus on the Customer, Client, and Market	The accountant can meet the changing needs of clients, customers, and employers better than the competition and can anticipate those needs better than competitors.
Skills in Interpreting Converging Information	The accountant can interpret new meaning by combining financial and nonfinancial information into a broader understanding that adds more business value.
Technology Skills	The accountant can use technology to add value to activities performed for employers, customers, and clients.

CPA Vision Project, is redefining the role of the accountant for today's world economy. The Vision Project identifies a unique combination of skills, technology, and knowledge—called **core competencies for accounting**—that will be necessary for the future CPA. As Table 14.1 shows, those skills—which include communication, critical thinking, and leadership—go far beyond the ability to "crunch numbers." They include certain communications skills, along with skills in critical thinking and leadership. Indeed, the CPA Vision Project foresees CPAs who combine specialty skills with a broad-based orientation in order to communicate more effectively with people in a wide range of business activities.

Private Accountants and Management Accountants

To ensure integrity in reporting, CPAs are always independent of the firms they audit. However, many businesses also hire their own salaried employees—**private accountants**—to perform day-to-day activities.

Private accountants perform numerous jobs. An internal auditor at ConocoPhillips might fly to the North Sea to confirm the accuracy of oil-flow meters on offshore petroleum drilling platforms. A supervisor responsible for $2 billion in monthly payouts to vendors and employees may never leave the executive suite, with duties such as hiring and training, assigning projects, and evaluating performance of accounting personnel. Large businesses employ specialized accountants in such areas as budgeting, financial planning, internal auditing, payroll, and taxation. In small businesses, a single person may handle all accounting tasks.

Most private accountants are **management accountants** who provide services to support managers in various activities (marketing, production, engineering, and so forth). Many hold the **certified management accountant (CMA)** designation, awarded by the Institute of Management Accountants (IMA), recognizing qualifications of professionals who have passed IMA's experience and examination requirements.

Forensic Accountants

The fastest growing area in accounting is **forensic accounting**—the use of accounting for legal purposes.[9] Forensic accountants may be called upon—by law enforcement agencies, insurance companies, law firms, and business firms—for both investigative accounting and litigation support in crimes against companies, crimes by companies, and civil disagreements. Civil cases often require investigating and quantifying claims of personal injury loss due to negligence and analyzing financial issues in matrimonial disputes. Forensic accountants also assist business firms in tracing and recovering lost assets from employee business fraud or theft.

Investigative Accounting   A forensic accountant may be asked to investigate a trail of financial transactions behind a suspected crime, as in a money-laundering scheme or an investment swindle. Try your hand, for example, at "Catch Me If You Can," the popular interactive forensic accounting game sponsored by the AICPA (at **www.startheregoplaces.com**). The forensic accountant, being familiar with the legal concepts and procedures of the case, identifies and analyzes pertinent financial evidence—documents, bank accounts, phone calls, computer records, and people—and presents accounting conclusions and their legal implications.

Litigation Support   Forensic accountants assist in the application of accounting evidence for judicial proceedings by preparing and preserving evidence for these proceedings. They also assist by presenting visual aids

Table 14.2   Selected Provisions of the Sarbanes-Oxley Act[10]

- Creates a national Accounting Oversight Board that, among other activities, must establish the ethics standards used by CPA firms in preparing audits.
- Requires that auditors retain audit working papers for specified periods of time.
- Requires auditor rotation by prohibiting the same person from being the lead auditor for more than five consecutive years.
- Requires that the CEO and CFO certify that the company's financial statements are true, fair, and accurate.
- Prohibits corporations from extending personal loans to executives and directors.
- Requires that the audited company disclose whether it has adopted a code of ethics for its senior financial officers.
- Requires that the SEC regularly review each corporation's financial statements.
- Prevents employers from retaliating against research analysts that write negative reports.
- Imposes criminal penalties on auditors and clients for falsifying, destroying, altering, or concealing records (10 years in prison).
- Imposes a fine or imprisonment (up to 25 years) on any person that defrauds shareholders.
- Increases penalties for mail and wire fraud from 5 to 20 years in prison.
- Establishes criminal liability for failure of corporate officers to certify financial reports.

CERTIFIED FRAUD EXAMINER (CFE) professional designation administered by the Association of Certified Fraud Examiners in recognition of qualifications for a specialty area within forensic accounting

SARBANES-OXLEY ACT OF 2002 (SARBOX) enactment of federal regulations to restore public trust in accounting practices by imposing new requirements on financial activities in publicly traded corporations

ACCOUNTING EQUATION Assets = Liabilities + Owners' Equity; used by accountants to balance data for the firm's financial transactions at various points in the year

to support trial evidence, by testifying as expert witnesses, and, especially, in determining economic damages in any case before the court.

Certified Fraud Examiners The **Certified Fraud Examiner (CFE)** designation, administered by the Association of Certified Fraud Examiners, is awarded to those with expertise in fraud-related issues and investigations. Many CFEs, like Al Vondra from our opening story, find employment in corporations seeking to prevent fraud from within. The CFE examination covers four areas:

1 *Criminology and ethics.* Includes theories of fraud prevention and ethical situations

2 *Financial transactions.* Examines types of fraudulent financial transactions incurred in accounting records

3 *Fraud investigation.* Pertains to tracing illicit transactions, evaluating deception, and interviewing and taking statements

4 *Legal elements of fraud.* Includes rules of evidence, criminal and civil law, and rights of the accused and accuser

Federal Restrictions on CPA Services and Financial Reporting: Sarbox

The financial wrongdoings associated with firms such as ImClone Systems, Tyco, WorldCom, Enron, Arthur Andersen, and others have not gone unnoticed in legislative circles. Federal regulations, in particular the **Sarbanes-Oxley Act of 2002 (Sarbox** or **SOX)**, have been enacted to restore public trust in corporate accounting practices.

Sarbox restricts the kinds of nonaudit services that CPAs can provide. Under the new law, for example, a CPA firm cannot help design a client's financial information system if it also does the client's auditing. By prohibiting CPAs from providing auditing and nonauditing services to the same client, Sarbox encourages audits that are independent and unbiased.

Sarbox Compliance Requirements   Sarbox imposes new requirements on virtually every financial activity in publicly traded corporations, as well as severe criminal penalties for persons committing or concealing fraud or destroying financial records. Table 14.2 provides brief descriptions of several of Sarbox's many provisions.

The Accounting Equation

All accountants rely on record keeping to enter and track transactions. Underlying all record-keeping procedures is the most basic tool of accounting—the **accounting equation**:

$$\text{Assets} = \text{Liabilities} + \text{Owners' Equity}$$

After each financial transaction (e.g., payments to suppliers, sales to customers, wages to employees), the accounting equation must be in balance. If it isn't, then an accounting error has occurred. To better understand the importance of this equation, we must understand the terms *assets*, *liabilities*, and *owners' equity*.

Assets and Liabilities An **asset** is any economic resource that is expected to benefit a firm or an individual who owns it. Assets include land, buildings, equipment, inventories, and payments due the company (accounts receivable). Google, the Internet search and information provider, for example, held assets amounting to $25.336 billion at year-end 2007.[11]

A **liability** is a debt that a firm owes to an outside party. The total of Google's liabilities—all the debt owed to others—was $2.646 billion at the end of 2007.

Owners' Equity **Owners' equity** is the amount of money that owners would receive if they sold all of a company's assets and paid all of its liabilities. Google's financial reports for 2007 declared shareholders' equity of $22.690 billion. For the Google example, we see that the accounting equation is in balance, as it should be.

> Assets = Liabilities + Owners' Equity
> $25.336 = $2.646 + $22.690 billion

We can rewrite the equation to highlight how owners' equity relates to assets and liabilities.

> Assets − Liabilities = Owners' Equity

Another term for this is *net worth*: the difference between what a firm owns (assets) minus what it owes (liabilities) is its net worth, or owners' equity. If a company's assets exceed its liabilities, owners' equity is *positive*. If the company goes out of business, the owners will receive some cash (a gain) after selling assets and paying off liabilities. If liabilities outweigh assets, owners' equity is *negative*; assets are insufficient to pay off all debts, and the firm is bankrupt. If the company goes out of business, the owners will get no cash, and some creditors won't be paid.

Owners' equity is meaningful for both investors and lenders. Before lending money to owners, for example,

The inventory at this Toyota dealership is among the company's assets: The cars constitute an economic resource because the firm will benefit financially as it sells them.

lenders want to know the amount of owners' equity in a business. A larger owners' equity indicates greater security for lenders. Owners' equity consists of two sources of capital:

1 The amount that the owners originally invested

2 Profits (also owned by the owners) earned by and reinvested in the company

Financial Statements

As noted previously, accountants summarize the results of a firm's transactions and issue reports to help managers make informed decisions. Among the most important reports are **financial statements**, which fall into three broad categories: *balance sheets*, *income statements*, and *statements of cash flows*.

Balance Sheets

Balance sheets supply detailed information about the accounting equation factors: *assets*, *liabilities*, and *owners' equity*. Because they also show a firm's financial condition at one point in time, they are sometimes called *statements of financial position*. Figure 14.1 is a simplified presentation of the balance sheet for Google, Inc.

Assets   From an accounting standpoint, most companies have three types of assets: *current*, *fixed*, and *intangible*.

Current Assets   Current assets include cash and assets that can be converted into cash within a year. The act of converting something into cash is called *liquidating*. Assets are normally listed in order of **liquidity**—the ease of converting them into cash. Debts, for example, are usually paid in cash. A company that needs but cannot generate cash—a company that's not "liquid"—may be forced to sell assets at reduced prices or even to go out of business.

By definition, cash is completely liquid. *Marketable securities* purchased as short-term investments are slightly less liquid but can be sold quickly. These include stocks or bonds of other companies, government securities, and money market certificates. Many companies hold other nonliquid assets such as *merchandise inventory*—the cost of merchandise that's been acquired for sale to customers and is still on hand.

Fixed Assets   Fixed assets (such as land, buildings, and equipment) have long-term use or value, but as buildings and equipment wear out or become obsolete, their value decreases. Accountants use **depreciation** to spread the cost of an asset over the years of its useful life. To reflect decreasing value, accountants calculate an asset's useful life in years, divide its worth by that many years, and subtract the resulting amount each year. Every year, therefore, the remaining value (or net value) decreases on the books.

Intangible Assets   Although their worth is hard to set, **intangible assets** have monetary value in the form of expected benefits, which may include fees paid by others for obtaining rights or privileges—including patents, trademarks, copyrights,

---

BALANCE SHEET financial statement that supplies detailed information about a firm's assets, liabilities, and owners' equity

CURRENT ASSET asset that can or will be converted into cash within a year

LIQUIDITY ease with which an asset can be converted into cash

FIXED ASSET asset with long-term use or value, such as land, buildings, and equipment

DEPRECIATION accounting method for distributing the cost of an asset over its useful life

INTANGIBLE ASSET nonphysical asset, such as a patent or trademark, that has economic value in the form of expected benefit

---

Figure 14.1
Google's Balance Sheet[12]

Google, Inc.
Summary of Balance Sheet (condensed)
as of December 31, 2007
(in millions)

Assets		Liabilities and Shareholders' Equity	
Current assets:		Current liabilities:	
Cash	$6,081.59	Accounts payable	$282.11
Marketable securities	8,137.02	Other	1,753.49
Other	3,070.52	**Total current liabilities**	**$2,035.60**
Total current assets	**$17,289.13**		
		Long-term liabilities:	
Fixed assets:		All long-term debts	0.00
Property and equipment, net	$4,039.26	Other	610.52
Other	1,261.44	**Total long-term liabilities**	**$610.52**
Total fixed assets	**$5,300.70**		
		Total liabilities	**$2,646.12**
Intangible assets:			
Intangible assets	446.60	Shareholders' equity:	
Goodwill	2,299.37	Paid-in capital	$13,241.22
Total intangible assets	**$2,745.97**	Retained earnings	9,448.46
		Total shareholders' equity	**$22,689.68**
Total assets	**$25,335.80**		
		Total liabilities and shareholders' equity	**$25,335.80**

Google's balance sheet for year ended December 31, 2007. The balance sheet shows clearly that the firm's total assets are equal to its total liabilities and owners' equity.

GOODWILL amount paid for an existing business above the value of its other assets

CURRENT LIABILITY debt that must be paid within one year

ACCOUNTS PAYABLE (PAYABLES) current liability consisting of bills owed to suppliers, plus wages and taxes due within the coming year

LONG-TERM LIABILITY debt that is not due for at least one year

PAID-IN CAPITAL money that is invested in a company by its owners

RETAINED EARNINGS earnings retained by a firm for its use rather than paid out as dividends

INCOME STATEMENT (PROFIT-AND-LOSS STATEMENT) financial statement listing a firm's annual revenues and expenses so that a bottom line shows annual profit or loss

REVENUES funds that flow into a business from the sale of goods or services

Figure 14.2 **Google's Income Statement**[13]

Google, Inc.
Summary of Income Statement (condensed)
as of December 31, 2007
(in millions)

Revenues (gross sales)		**$16,593.99**
Cost of revenues	**6,649.09**	
Gross profit		**9,944.90**
Operating expenses:		
Sales and marketing	2,740.51	
Administrative and general	2,119.99	
Total operating expenses		**$4,860.50**
Operating income (before taxes)		5,084.40
Income taxes*		880.68
Net income		**$4,203.72**

*approximated

Google's income statement for year ended December 31, 2007. The final entry on the income statement, the bottom line, reports the firm's profit or loss.

and franchises—to your products. **Goodwill** is the amount paid for an existing business beyond the value of its other assets. A purchased firm, for example, may have a particularly good reputation or location.

Liabilities Like assets, liabilities are often separated into different categories. **Current liabilities** are debts that must be paid within one year. These include **accounts payable (payables)**—unpaid bills to suppliers for materials as well as wages and taxes that must be paid in the coming year. **Long-term liabilities** are debts that are not due for at least a year. These normally represent borrowed funds on which the company must pay interest.

Owners' Equity The final section of the balance sheet in Figure 14.1 shows owners' equity broken down into *paid-in capital* and *retained earnings*. **Paid-in capital** is money invested by owners, such as purchases of Google's initial public offering of stock in 2004. **Retained earnings** are net profits kept by a firm rather than paid out as dividend payments to stockholders.

The balance sheet for any company, then, is a barometer for its financial condition at one point in time. By comparing the current balance sheet with those of previous years, creditors and owners can better interpret the firm's financial progress and future prospects in terms of changes in its assets, liabilities, and owners' equity.

Income Statements

The **income statement** is sometimes called a **profit-and-loss statement** because its description of revenues and expenses results in a figure showing the firm's annual profit or loss. In other words,

Revenues − Expenses = Profit (or Loss)

Popularly known as the *bottom line*, profit or loss is probably the most important figure in any business enterprise. Figure 14.2 shows the 2007 income statement for Google, whose bottom line was $4.20 (rounded) billion. The income statement is divided into four major categories: *revenues*, *cost of revenues*, *operating expenses*, and *net income*. Unlike a balance sheet, which shows the financial condition at a specific *point in time*, an income statement shows the financial results that occurred during a *period of time*, such as a month, quarter, or year.

Revenues When a law firm receives $250 for preparing a will or a supermarket collects $65 from a grocery shopper, both are receiving **revenues**—the funds that flow into a business from the sale of goods or services. In 2007, Google reported revenues of $16.59 (rounded) billion from the sale of advertising and Web-search services to Google Network members, such as AOL.

Cost of Revenues (Cost of Goods Sold) In the Google income statement, the **cost of revenues** section shows the costs of obtaining the revenues from other companies during the year. These are fees Google must pay its network members—revenue sharing from advertising income—and also include expenses arising from the operation of Google's data centers, including labor, energy, and costs of processing customer transactions.

While cost of revenues is a relevant income statement category for service providers like Google, goods producers do not use it. Instead, income statements for manufacturing firms such as Procter & Gamble use the corresponding category, **cost of goods sold**: costs of obtaining materials to make products sold during the year.

Gross Profit Managers are often interested in **gross profit**, a preliminary, quick-to-calculate profit figure that considers just two pieces of data—revenues and cost of revenues (the direct costs of getting those revenues)—from the income statement. To calculate gross profit, subtract cost of revenues from revenues obtained by selling the firm's products.

Operating Expenses In addition to costs directly related to generating revenues, every company has general expenses ranging from erasers to the CEO's salary. Like cost of revenues and cost of goods sold, **operating expenses** are resources that must flow out of a company if it is to earn revenues.

Sales and marketing expenses result from activities related to selling goods or services, such as sales-force salaries and advertising expenses. *Administrative and general expenses*, such as management salaries and maintenance costs, are related to the general management of the company.

Operating and Net Income
Operating income compares the gross profit from operations against operating expenses. This calculation for Google ($9.94 billion – $4.86 billion) reveals an operating income, or income before taxes, of $5.08 billion. Subtracting income taxes from operating income ($5.08 billion – $0.88 billion)

reveals **net income (net profit or net earnings)**. Google's net income for the year was $4.20 billion (rounded).

The step-by-step information in an income statement shows how a company obtained its net income for the period, making it easier for shareholders and other stakeholders to evaluate the firm's financial health.

Statements of Cash Flows

Some companies prepare only balance sheets and income statements. However, the SEC requires all firms whose stock is publicly traded to issue a third report, the **statement of cash flows**, which shows the effects on cash of three aspects of a business: *operating activities*, *investing activities*, and *financing activities*. Google's 2007 statement of cash flows is reproduced in Figure 14.3.

COST OF REVENUES costs that a company incurs to obtain revenues from other companies

COST OF GOODS SOLD costs of obtaining materials for making the products sold by a firm during the year

GROSS PROFIT a preliminary, quick-to-calculate profit figure calculated from the firm's revenues minus its cost of revenues (the direct costs of getting the revenues)

OPERATING EXPENSES costs, other than the cost of revenues, incurred in producing a good or service

OPERATING INCOME gross profit minus operating expenses

NET INCOME (NET PROFIT, NET EARNINGS) gross profit minus operating expenses and income taxes

STATEMENT OF CASH FLOWS financial statement describing a firm's yearly cash receipts and cash payments

---

Figure 14.3
Google's Statement of Cash Flows[14]

Google, Inc.
Summary of Statement of Cash Flows (condensed)
as of December 31, 2007
Increase (Decrease) in Cash
(in millions)

Net cash provided by operating activities		**$5,775.41**
Cash flows from investment activities:		
Payment for purchase of property, equipment, and securities	(3,681.59)	
Net cash used in investing activities		**(3,681.59)**
Cash flows from financing activities:		
Proceeds from sale of stock (IPO)	23.86	
Other	419.24	
Net cash provided by financing activities		**443.10**
Net increase in cash		2,536.92
Cash at beginning of year		3,544.67
Cash at end of year		**$6,081.59**

Google's statement of cash flows for year ended December 31, 2007. The final entry shows year-end cash position resulting from operating activities, investing activities, and financing activities.

Figure 14.4
Perfect Posters' Sales Budget

BUDGET detailed statement of estimated receipts and expenditures for a future period of time

■ **Cash Flows from Operations.** This first section of the statement concerns main operating activities: cash transactions involved in buying and selling goods and services. For the Google example, it reveals how much of the year's cash balance results from the firm's main line of business—sales of advertising and Web-search services.

<table>
<tr><td colspan="5">**Perfect Posters, Inc.**
555 RIVERVIEW, CHICAGO, IL 60606</td></tr>
<tr><td colspan="5">Perfect Posters, Inc.
Sales Budget
First Quarter, 2009</td></tr>
<tr><th></th><th>January</th><th>February</th><th>March</th><th>Quarter</th></tr>
<tr><td>Budgeted sales (units)</td><td>7,500</td><td>6,000</td><td>6,500</td><td>20,000</td></tr>
<tr><td>Budgeted selling price per unit</td><td>$3.50</td><td>$3.50</td><td>$3.50</td><td>$3.50</td></tr>
<tr><td>**Budgeted sales revenue**</td><td>**$26,250**</td><td>**$21,000**</td><td>**$22,750**</td><td>**$70,000**</td></tr>
<tr><td>Expected cash receipts:</td><td></td><td></td><td></td><td></td></tr>
<tr><td>From December sales</td><td>$26,210</td><td></td><td></td><td>$26,210</td></tr>
<tr><td>From January sales</td><td>17,500</td><td>$8,750</td><td></td><td>26,250</td></tr>
<tr><td>From February sales</td><td></td><td>14,000</td><td>$7,000</td><td>21,000</td></tr>
<tr><td>From March sales</td><td></td><td></td><td>15,200</td><td>15,200</td></tr>
<tr><td>**Total cash receipts:**</td><td>**$43,710**</td><td>**$22,750**</td><td>**$22,200**</td><td>**$88,660**</td></tr>
</table>

■ **Cash Flows from Investing.** The second section reports net cash used in or provided by investing. It includes cash receipts and payments from buying and selling stocks, bonds, property, equipment, and other productive assets. These sources of cash are not the company's main line of business. A cash outflow is shown in parentheses.

■ **Cash Flows from Financing.** The third section reports net cash from all financing activities. It includes cash inflows from borrowing or issuing stock, as well as outflows for payment of dividends and repayment of borrowed money.

The overall change in cash from these three sources is added to or subtracted from the beginning cash (year-end cash from the 2006 balance sheet) to arrive at the end-of-year cash position. When creditors and stockholders know how a firm obtained and used funds during the course of a year, it's easier for them to interpret year-to-year changes in the balance sheet and income statement.

The Budget: An Internal Financial Statement

For planning, controlling, and decision making, the most important internal financial statement is the **budget**—a detailed report on estimated receipts and expenditures for a future period of time. Although that period is usually one year, some companies also prepare three- or five-year budgets, especially when

considering major capital expenditures. The budget differs from the other statements we have discussed in that budgets are not shared outside the company; hence the "internal financial statement" title.

Although the accounting staff coordinates the budget process, it needs input from many areas regarding proposed activities and required resources. Figure 14.4 is a sales budget for a hypothetical wholesaler, Perfect Posters. In preparing the budget, accounting must obtain from the sales group projections for units to be sold and expected expenses for the coming year. Then, accounting draws up the final budget and, throughout the year, compares the budget to actual expenditures and revenues. Discrepancies signal potential problems and spur action to improve financial performance.

Reporting Standards and Practices

Accountants follow standard reporting practices and principles when they prepare external reports. The common language dictated by standard practices and spelled out in GAAP is designed to give external users confidence in the accuracy and meaning of financial information. Forensic accountants such as PricewaterhouseCoopers's Al Vondra watch for deviations from GAAP as indicators of possible fraudulent practices.

Revenue Recognition and Activity Timing The reporting of revenue inflows, and the timing of other transactions, must abide by accounting principles that govern financial statements. **Revenue recognition**, for example, is the formal recording and reporting of revenues at the appropriate time. Although a firm earns revenues continuously as it makes sales, earnings are not reported until the *earnings cycle* is completed. This cycle is complete under two conditions:

1 The sale is complete and the product delivered.

2 The sale price has been collected or is collectible (accounts receivable).

The end of the earnings cycle determines the timing for revenue recognition in a firm's financial statements. Suppose a toy company in January signs a sales contract to supply $1,000 of toys to a retail store, with delivery scheduled in February. Although the sale is completed in January, the $1,000 revenue should not then be recognized because the toys have not been delivered and the sale price is not yet collectible, so the earnings cycle is incomplete. Revenues are recorded in the accounting period—February—in which the product is delivered and collectible (or collected).

Full Disclosure To help users better understand the numbers in a firm's financial statements, GAAP requires that financial statements also include management's interpretations and explanations of those numbers. This is known as the **full disclosure** principle. Because they know about events inside the company, managers prepare additional information to explain certain events or transactions or to disclose the circumstances behind certain results.

> **REVENUE RECOGNITION** formal recording and reporting of revenues at the appropriate time
>
> **FULL DISCLOSURE** guideline that financial statements should not include just numbers but should also furnish management's interpretations and explanations of those numbers

Entrepreneurship and New Ventures

Reaping the Rewards of Innovation

What do Entrepreneurial Advisory Services, the PKF Academy, and FromGregsHead.com have in common? They are three of the initiatives developed by Pannell Kerr Forster of Texas, P.C. (PKF Texas) that have helped the Houston-based accounting firm capture seven consecutive Practice Innovation Awards. These awards are given by *Practical Accountant* magazine "to public accounting firms that take the lead in developing a new service area, improving services to their clients, or promoting efficiency in the practice of public accounting."

PKF Texas's most recent win, in 2007, was for The Entrepreneur's Playbook, a series of business tips that air weekly on a Houston-area radio station and are posted on a blog run by the company's director of consulting solutions, Gregory Price. (The blog, FromGregsHead.com, won a Practice Innovation Award in 2006.) The tips cover such fundamental accounting matters as preparing a budget and cost analysis, as well as more topical concerns such as "going green" and competing in a global marketplace. Readers and listeners are invited to respond and share their own tips with the community.

According to Kenneth Guidry, president of PKF Texas and himself a certified public accountant, "The Entrepreneur's Playbook has proven to be an effective tool for business owners. We're excited by the feedback from the marketplace that these tips are greatly appreciated." This appreciation has come in forms other than awards. For its continuous efforts to innovate and improve, PKF Texas has grown to be the fourth-largest accounting firm in the Southwest, with revenues in 2007 approaching $20 million.[15]

Analyzing Financial Statements

Financial statements present a lot of information in the form of data. This data, when applied to various *ratios* (comparative numbers), reveals trends that can be used to evaluate a firm's financial health, its progress, and its prospects for the future.

Ratios are normally grouped into three major classifications:

1 Solvency ratios for estimating short-term and long-term risk

2 Profitability ratios for measuring potential earnings

3 Activity ratios for evaluating management's use of assets

Depending on the decisions to be made, a user may apply none, some, or all of these ratios.

Solvency Ratios: Borrower's Ability to Repay Debt

What are the chances that a borrower will be able to repay a loan and the interest due? Solvency ratios provide measures of a firm's ability to meet its debt obligations.

The Current Ratio and Short-Term Solvency **Short-term solvency ratios** measure a company's liquidity and its ability to pay immediate debts. The most commonly used of these is the **current ratio**, or "banker's ratio." This measures a firm's ability to generate cash to meet current obligations through the normal, orderly process of selling inventories and collecting revenues from customers. It is calculated by dividing current assets by current liabilities. The higher a firm's current ratio, the lower the risk to investors.

As a rule, a current ratio is satisfactory at 2:1 or higher—that is, if current assets more than double current liabilities. A smaller ratio may indicate that a firm will have trouble paying its bills.

How does Google measure up? Look again at the balance sheet in Figure 14.1. Judging from current assets and current liabilities at the end of 2007, we see that

$$\frac{\text{Current assets}}{\text{Current liabilities}} = \frac{\$17.29 \text{ billion}}{\$2.04 \text{ billion}} = 8.5$$

The industry average for companies that provide business services is 1.4. Google's current ratio of 8.5 indicates the firm is a good short-run credit risk.

Long-Term Solvency A firm that can't meet its long-term debt obligations is in danger of collapse or takeover—a risk that makes creditors and investors quite cautious. To evaluate a company's risk of running into this problem, creditors turn to the balance sheet to see the extent to which a firm is financed through borrowed money. Long-term solvency is calculated by dividing **debt**—total liabilities—by owners' equity. The lower a firm's debt, the lower the risk to investors and creditors. Companies with more debt may find themselves owing so much that they lack the income needed to meet interest payments or to repay borrowed money.

Leverage Sometimes, high debt can be not only acceptable, but also desirable. Borrowing funds gives a firm **leverage**—the ability to make otherwise unaffordable investments. In *leveraged buyouts*, firms have willingly taken on sometimes huge debts to buy out other

"It's up to you now, Miller. The only thing that can save us is an accounting breakthrough."

companies. If owning the purchased company generates profits above the cost of borrowing the purchase price, leveraging often makes sense. Unfortunately, many buyouts have caused problems because profits fell short of expected levels or because rising interest rates increased payments on the buyer's debt.

Profitability Ratios: Earnings Power for Owners

It's important to know whether a company is solvent in both the long and the short term, but risk alone is not an adequate basis for investment decisions. Investors also want some indication of the returns they can expect. Evidence of earnings power is available from profitability ratios, such as *earnings per share*.

Earnings per Share Defined as net income divided by the number of shares of common stock outstanding, **earnings per share** determines the size of the dividend

that a firm can pay shareholders. As the ratio goes up, stock value increases because investors know that the firm can better afford to pay dividends. Naturally, stock loses market value if financial statements report a decline in earnings per share. For Google, we can use the net income total from the income statement in Figure 14.2, together with the number of outstanding shares of stock, to calculate earnings per share as follows:

$$\frac{\text{Net income}}{\text{Number of common shares outstanding}} = \frac{\$4{,}203.7 \text{ million}}{313.3 \text{ million shares of stock}} = \frac{\$13.42}{\text{per share}}$$

This means that Google had net earnings of $13.42 (rounded) for each share of stock during 2007. In

---

Say What You Mean

Technically Speaking

The general manager began the meeting by asking for a report on the budget. The head of accounting replied: "On a static-budget basis, unfavorable variances were realized for variable expenses and total expenses. Favorable budget variances were realized for units sold, sales revenues, and operating income. However, on a flexible-budget basis, unfavorable variances were realized on variable expenses, fixed expenses, total expenses, and operating income."

At this point, you might find yourself wishing that the head of accounting would speak "in plain English." The key obstacle to your comprehending the report is specialization. Accountants and other specialists tend to develop their own languages to communicate with each other efficiently and clearly. These "languages" contain technical terms and jargon that may be confusing to those outside the field, a problem that led the U.S. Securities and Exchange Commission (SEC) to develop *A Plain English Handbook*. The SEC

strongly encourages companies to follow the handbook's guidelines when composing disclosure documents and other financial reports intended for investors. As former SEC Chairman Arthur Levitt argues in the handbook's introduction, "Companies that communicate successfully with their investors form stronger relationships with them."

The situation may be more complicated, however. In a 2006 paper, Feng Li of the University of Michigan's Stephen M. Ross School of Business analyzed the relationship between a company's earnings and the readability of its financial reports. He discovered that poorly performing firms were more likely to issue reports that are difficult to read. This led him to conclude that "managers may be opportunistically choosing the readability of annual reports to hide adverse information from investors." All of which serves to underscore Levitt's words about successful communication—we are more likely to trust what we understand.[16]

contrast, Time Warner's recent earnings were $1.08 per share, while Microsoft earned $1.70.

Activity Ratios: How Efficiently Is the Firm Using Its Resources?

The efficiency with which a firm uses resources is linked to profitability. As a potential investor, you want to know which company gets more mileage from its resources. Information obtained from the income statement can be used for *activity ratios* to measure this efficiency. For example, two firms use the same amount of resources or assets to perform a particular activity, such as advertising or inventory management. If Firm A generates greater profits or sales, it has used its resources more efficiently and so enjoys a better activity ratio. It means that Firm A is getting more bang for the buck.

Bringing Ethics into the Accounting Equation

• •

The purpose of ethics in accounting is to maintain public confidence in business institutions, financial markets, and the products and services of the accounting profession. Without ethics, all of accounting's tools and methods

Table 14.3 **Overview of the Code of Ethics for CPAs[17]**

Membership in the American Institute of Certified Public Accountants is voluntary. By accepting membership, a certified public accountant assumes an obligation of self-discipline above and beyond the requirements of laws and regulations.	
Responsibilities	In carrying out their responsibilities as professionals, members should exercise sensitive professional and moral judgments in all their activities.
The Public Interest	Members should accept the obligation to act in a way that will serve the public interest, honor the public trust, and demonstrate commitment to professionalism.
Integrity	To maintain and broaden public confidence, members should perform all professional responsibilities with the highest sense of integrity.
Objectivity and Independence	A member should maintain objectivity and be free of conflicts of interest in discharging professional responsibilities. A member in public practice should be independent in fact and appearance when providing auditing and other attestation services.
Due Care	A member should observe the profession's technical and ethical standards, strive continually to improve competence and the quality of services, and discharge professional responsibility to the best of the member's ability.
Scope and Nature of Services	A member in public practice should observe the Principles of the Code of Professional Conduct in determining the scope and nature of services to be provided.

would be meaningless because their usefulness depends, ultimately, on veracity in their application.

Why Accounting Ethics?

Amidst a flurry of unscrupulous activity, ethics remains an area where one person who is willing to "do the right thing" can make a difference—and people do, every day. Refusing to turn a blind eye to unethical accounting around her at Enron, Lynn Brewer tried to alert people inside about misstatements of the company's assets. When that failed, she, along with colleagues Sherron Watkins and Margaret Ceconi, talked with the U.S. Committee on Energy and Commerce to voice concerns about Enron's condition. To Brewer, maintaining personal and professional integrity was an overriding concern, and she acted accordingly.

AICPA's Code of Professional Conduct The **code of professional conduct** for public accountants in the United States is maintained and enforced by the AICPA.

Table 14.4 **Examples of Unethical and Illegal Accounting Actions[18]**

Corporation	Accounting Violation
AOL Time Warner	America Online (AOL) inflated ad revenues to keep stock prices high before and after merging with Time Warner.
Cendant	Inflated income in financial statements by $500 million through fraud and errors.
HCA, Columbia/HCA	Defrauded Medicare, Medicaid, and TRICARE through false cost claims and unlawful billings (must pay $1.7 billion in civil penalties, damages, criminal fines, and penalties).
Tyco	CEO Dennis Kozlowski illegally used company funds to buy expensive art for personal possession (he received an 8- to 25-year prison sentence).
Waste Management	Overstated income in financial statements (false and misleading reports) by improperly calculating depreciation and salvage value for equipment.
WorldCom	Hid $3.8 billion in expenses to show an inflated (false) profit instead of loss in an annual income statement.

The institute identifies six ethics-related areas—listed in Table 14.3—with which accountants must comply to maintain certification. Comprehensive details for compliance in each area are spelled out in the AICPA Code of Professional Conduct. The IMA maintains a similar code to provide ethical guidelines for the management accounting profession.

In reading the AICPA's Code, you can see that it forbids misrepresentation and fraud in financial statements. Deception certainly violates the call for exercising moral judgments (in "Responsibilities"), is contrary to the public interest (by deceiving investors) and does not honor the public trust (in "The Public Interest"). Misleading statements destroy the public's confidence in the accounting profession and in business in general. While the Code prohibits such abuses, its success depends, ultimately, on its acceptance and use by the professionals it governs.

Violations of Accounting Ethics and GAAP
Unethical and illegal accounting violations have dominated the popular press in recent years. Some of the more notorious cases, listed in Table 14.4, violated the public's trust, ruined retirement plans for thousands of employees, and caused shutdowns and lost jobs. As you read each case, you should be able to see how its violation relates to the presentation of balance sheets and income statements in this chapter. In each case, adversity would have been prevented if employees had followed the code of professional conduct. In each case, nearly all of the code's six ethics-related areas were violated. And in every case, "professionals" willingly participated in unethical behavior. Such was the impetus for Sarbox.

> **For additional topics related to this material and end-of-chapter exercises and practices, please visit www.mybizlab.com.**

Questions for Review

1. Who are the users of accounting information, and for what purposes do they use it?

2. Identify the three types of services performed by CPAs.

3. Explain the ways in which financial accounting differs from managerial (management) accounting.

4. Discuss the activities and services performed by forensic accountants.

5. What are the three basic financial statements, and what major information does each contain?

6. Explain how financial ratios allow managers to gain additional information from financial statements.

Questions for Analysis

7. If you were planning to invest in a company, which of the three types of financial statements would you most want to see? Why?

8. Suppose that you, as the manager of a company, are making changes to fully comply with provisions of the Sarbanes-Oxley Act. Your company traditionally has relied on CPA firms for auditing, tax services, and management services. What major changes will your company need to make?

Application Exercises

9. Interview an accountant at a local firm. How does the firm use budgets? How does budgeting help managers plan business activities? How does budgeting help them control activities? Give examples.

10. Interview the manager of a local retailer, wholesale business, or manufacturing firm about the role of ethics in that company's accounting practices. Is ethics in accounting an important issue to the manager? If the firm has its own private accountants, what measures are taken for ensuring ethical practices internally? What steps, if any, does the company take to maintain ethical relationships in its dealings with CPA firms?

chapter 15

Money and Banking

part VI Financial Issues

After reading this chapter, you should be able to:

1 Define *money* and identify the different forms that it takes in the nation's money supply.

2 Describe the different kinds of financial institutions that compose the U.S. financial system and explain the services they offer.

3 Explain how financial institutions create money, and describe the means by which they are regulated.

4 Discuss the functions of the Federal Reserve System and describe the tools that it uses to control the money supply.

5 Identify three important ways in which the money and banking system is changing.

6 Discuss some of the institutions and activities in international banking and finance.

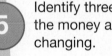

Going with the Currency

Players in today's global economy often convert money from one currency into another. As currency values change, the best currency choice for your money changes too. At any one time, some currencies are "strong"—selling at a higher price and worth more—while others are "weak." A "strong" currency may seem preferable, but in an international context, it turns out to be a "good news–bad news" situation.

Consider the euro's rising strength against the dollar. As a citizen of one of the 15 Eurozone countries—for example, France—you chose wisely in delaying that U.S. vacation until 2008, when each euro paid for about $1.55 of the trip but would have covered only $0.92 in 2000. The stronger euro means more purchasing power against the weaker dollar. The bad news for French innkeepers, though, is that Americans avoid expensive European travel—€1 costs them $1.55, up from $0.92 eight years earlier. Simply put, that $0.92 cup of coffee at a French sidewalk café in 2000 now costs American travelers $1.55. The purchasing power of the American traveler has declined as the dollar has weakened against the euro, and that French innkeeper is paying the price.

Additionally, Eurozone businesses are less competitive against their global counterparts: exports remain less competitive, while European imports markets are more competitive. However, fearing overinflation, the European Central Bank (ECB) refuses to cut interest rates to increase the supply of euros, decrease the price of euros, and stimulate Europe's economy. The U.S. Federal Reserve, on the other hand, has opted to address the threat of a recession by slashing rates seven times from September 2007 to April 2008, despite inflation concerns. As pressures mount, some observers expect the ECB, too, will concede by cutting interest rates to weaken the euro.[1]

What's in It for Me?

Dealing in matters of money is vastly more complicated than counting the cash and coins in your pocket, especially when technology and globalization come into play. It's also not an area in which you want to make many mistakes. This chapter will give you a solid understanding of the different forms of money and how its supply is created and controlled by different kinds of financial institutions and government regulations.

What Is Money?

When someone asks you how much money you have, do you count the dollar bills and coins in your pockets? Do you include your checking and savings accounts? What about stocks and bonds? Do you count your car? Taken together, the value of all these combined is your personal wealth. Not all of it, however, is "money." This section considers more precisely what *money* is and does.

The Characteristics of Money

Modern money generally takes the form of stamped metal or printed paper issued by governments. Theoretically, however, just about anything *portable*, *divisible*, *durable*, and *stable* can serve as **money**. To appreciate these qualities, imagine using something that lacks them—for example, a 1,000-pound cow used as a unit of exchange in ancient agrarian economies.

- **Portability.** Try lugging 1,000 pounds of cow from shop to shop. In contrast, modern currency is light and easy to handle.

- **Divisibility.** How would you divide your cow if you wanted to buy a hat, a book, and a radio from three different stores? Is a pound of head worth as much as a pound of leg? Modern currency is easily divisible into smaller parts with fixed values—for example, a dollar for ten dimes.

- **Durability.** Your cow will lose value every day (and eventually die). Modern currency, however, neither dies nor spoils, and if it wears out, it can be replaced. It is also hard to counterfeit—certainly harder than cattle breeding.

- **Stability.** If cows were in short supply, you might be able to make quite a deal for yourself. In the middle of an abundant cow year, however, the market would be flooded with cows, so their value would fall. The value of our paper money also fluctuates, but it is considerably more stable and predictable.

The Functions of Money

Imagine a successful cow rancher who needs a new fence. In a *barter economy*—one in which goods are exchanged directly for one another—he or she would have to find someone who is willing to exchange a fence for a cow (or parts of it). If no fence maker wants a cow, the rancher must find someone else—for example, a wagon maker—who does want a cow. Then, the rancher must hope that the fence maker will trade for a new wagon. In a money economy, the rancher would sell his or her cow, receive money, and exchange the money for such goods as a new fence.

Money serves three functions:

1. **It is a medium of exchange.** Like the rancher "trading" money for a new fence, money is used to buy and sell things. Without money, we would be bogged down in a system of barter.

2. **It is a store of value.** Pity the rancher whose cow gets sick on Monday and who wants to buy some clothes on the following Saturday, by which time the cow may have died and lost its value. In the form of currency, however, money can be used for future purchases and "stores" value.

3. **It is a measure of worth.** Money lets us measure the relative values of goods and services. It acts as a measure of worth because all products can be valued and accounted for in terms of money. For example, the concepts of $1,000 worth of clothes or $500 in labor costs have universal meaning.

Cattle are not portable, divisible, durable, or stable, making them an unsuitable medium of exchange in the modern, monetized economy.

Instead of using a modern monetary system, traders like Muhammed Essa in Quetta, Pakistan, transfer funds through handshakes and code words. The ancient system is called *hawala*, which means *trust* in Arabic. The worldwide *hawala* system, though illegal in most countries, moves billions of dollars past regulators annually and is alleged to be the system of choice for terrorists because it leaves no paper trail.

M-1: The Spendable Money Supply

For money to serve its basic functions, both buyers and sellers must agree on its value, which depends in part on its *supply*—how much money is in circulation. When the money supply is high, the value of money drops. When it is low, that value increases.

Unfortunately, there is no single agreed-upon measure of the supply of money. The oldest and most basic measure, **M-1**, counts only the most liquid, or spendable, forms of money—cash, checks, and checking accounts.

■ Paper money and metal coins are **currency (cash)** issued by the government and widely used for small exchanges. Law requires creditors to accept it in payment of debts.

■ A **check** is essentially an order instructing a bank to pay a given sum to a payee. Checks are usually, but not always, accepted because they are valuable only to specified payees and can be exchanged for cash.

■ **Checking accounts**, or **demand deposits**, are money because their funds may be withdrawn at any time on demand.

These are all noninterest-bearing or low–interest-bearing forms of money. As of May 2008, M-1 in the United States totaled $1.36 trillion.[2]

M-2: M-1 Plus the Convertible Money Supply

M-2, a second measure of the money supply, is often used for economic planning by businesses and government agencies. **M-2** includes everything in M-1 plus other forms of money that are not quite as liquid—short-term investments that are easily converted to spendable forms—including *time deposits*, *money market mutual funds*, and *savings accounts*. Totaling $7.68 trillion in May 2008, M-2 accounts for most of the nation's money supply.[3] As this overall level increases, more money is available for consumer purchases and business investments. When the supply is tightened, less money is available; financial transactions, spending, and business activity slow down.

Unlike demand deposits, **time deposits**, such as certificates of deposit (CDs), have a fixed term, are intended to be held to maturity, cannot be transferred by check, and pay higher interest rates. Time deposits in M-2 include only accounts of less than $100,000 that can be redeemed on demand, with penalties for early withdrawal.

With **money market mutual funds**, investment companies buy a collection of short-term, low-risk financial securities. Ownership of and profits (or

M-1 measure of the money supply that includes only the most liquid (spendable) forms of money

CURRENCY (CASH) government-issued paper money and metal coins

CHECK demand deposit order instructing a bank to pay a given sum to a specified payee

CHECKING ACCOUNT (DEMAND DEPOSIT) bank account funds, owned by the depositor, that may be withdrawn at any time by check or cash

M-2 measure of the money supply that includes all the components of M-1 plus the forms of money that can be easily converted into spendable forms

TIME DEPOSIT bank funds that have a fixed term of time to maturity and cannot be withdrawn earlier or transferred by check

MONEY MARKET MUTUAL FUND fund of short-term, low-risk financial securities purchased with the pooled assets of investor-owners

losses) from the sale of these securities are shared among the fund's investors.

Figure 15.1 shows how M-1 and M-2 have grown since 1969. For many years, M-1 was the traditional measure of liquid money. Because it was closely related to gross domestic product, it served as a reliable predictor of the nation's economic health. This situation changed in the early 1980s, with the introduction of new types of investments and the easier transfer of money among investment funds to gain higher interest returns. As a result, M-2 today is regarded as a more reliable measure than M-1.

The U.S. Financial System

Many forms of money depend on the existence of financial institutions that provide money-related services to both individuals and businesses. The sections that follow explain their role as creators of money and discuss the regulation of the U.S. banking system.

Financial Institutions

The main function of financial institutions is to ease the flow of money from users with surpluses to those with deficits by attracting funds into checking and savings accounts. Incoming funds will be loaned to individuals and businesses and perhaps invested in government securities. U.S. consumers have access to more than 89,000 U.S. branches and offices of *commercial banks*, *savings institutions*, *credit unions*, and various *nondeposit institutions*.

Commercial Banks Federally insured **commercial banks** accept deposits, make loans, earn profits, and pay interest and dividends. Commercial banks range from the very largest institutions in New York, such as Citigroup, Bank of America, and JPMorgan Chase, to tiny banks dotting the rural landscape. Bank liabilities—holdings owed to others—include checking accounts and savings accounts.

Savings Institutions Savings institutions include mutual savings banks and savings and loan associations. They are also called *thrift institutions* because they were established decades ago to promote the idea of savings among the general population.

Savings and Loan Associations Like commercial banks, **savings and loan associations (S&Ls)** accept deposits, make loans, and are owned by investors. Most S&Ls were created to encourage savings habits and provide financing for homes; they did not offer check services. Many have ventured into a variety of other investments.

Mutual Savings Banks In a **mutual savings bank**, all depositors are considered owners of the bank. All profits are divided proportionately among depositors, who receive dividends. Some 1,200 U.S. mutual savings banks attract most of their funds in the form of savings deposits, and funds are loaned out in the form of mortgages.

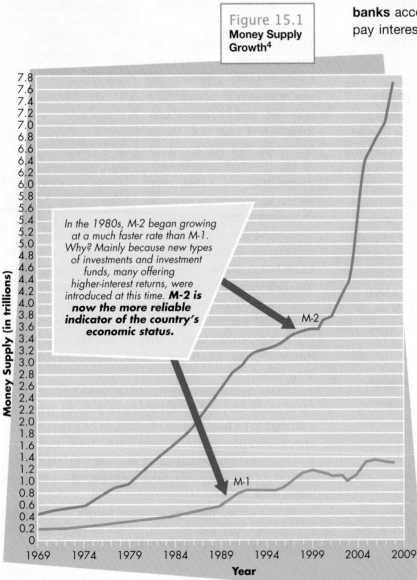

Figure 15.1
Money Supply Growth[4]

*In the 1980s, M-2 began growing at a much faster rate than M-1. Why? Mainly because new types of investments and investment funds, many offering higher-interest returns, were introduced at this time. **M-2 is now the more reliable indicator of the country's economic status.***

M-2

M-1

Money Supply (in trillions)

Year

Credit Unions A **credit union** is a nonprofit, cooperative financial institution owned and run by its members. Its purpose is to promote *thrift*—careful management of one's money or resources—and to provide members with a safe place to save and borrow at reasonable rates. Members pool their funds to make loans to one another. Each credit union decides whom it will serve, such as a group of employees, people in a particular community, or members of an association. Most universities, for example, have credit unions, as does the U.S. Navy.

Nondeposit Institutions A variety of other organizations take in money, provide interest or other services, and make loans. Unlike commercial banks, these *nondeposit institutions* use inflowing funds for purposes other than earning interest for depositors. Four of the most important are *pension funds*, *insurance companies*, *finance companies*, and *securities investment dealers*.

1 A **pension fund** is a pool of funds that is managed to provide retirement income for its members. *Public pension funds* include Social Security and $3 trillion in retirement programs for state and local government employees. *Private pension funds*, operated by employers, unions, and other private groups, cover about 40 million people and have total assets of $15 trillion.[5]

2 **Insurance companies** accumulate money from premiums charged for coverage. They invest these funds in stocks, real estate, and other assets. Earnings pay for insured losses, such as death benefits, automobile damage, and healthcare expenses.

3 **Finance companies** specialize in making loans to businesses and consumers. *Commercial finance companies* lend to businesses needing capital or long-term funds. *Consumer finance companies* devote most of their resources to providing small noncommercial loans to individuals.

4 **Securities investment dealers (brokers)**, such as Merrill Lynch and A. G. Edwards & Sons, buy and sell stocks and bonds for client investors. They also invest in securities—they buy stocks and bonds for their own accounts in hopes of reselling them later at a profit. These companies hold large sums of money for transfer between buyers and sellers. (We discuss the activities of brokers and investment bankers more fully in Chapter 16.)

CREDIT UNION nonprofit, cooperative financial institution owned and run by its members, usually employees of a particular organization

PENSION FUND nondeposit pool of funds managed to provide retirement income for its members

INSURANCE COMPANY nondeposit institution that invests funds collected as premiums charged for insurance coverage

FINANCE COMPANY nondeposit institution that specializes in making loans to businesses and consumers

SECURITIES INVESTMENT DEALER (BROKER) financial institution that buys and sells stocks and bonds both for investors and for its own accounts

PRIME RATE interest rate available to a bank's most creditworthy customers

The Growth of Financial Services

The finance business today is highly competitive. No longer is it enough for commercial banks to accept deposits and make loans. Most, for example, also offer bank-issued credit cards, safe-deposit boxes, ATMs, and electronic money transfer. In addition, many offer pension, trust, international, and brokerage services and financial advice.

The Prime Rate

Every bank receives a major portion of its income from interest paid on loans by borrowers. As long as terms and conditions are clearly revealed to borrowers, banks may set their own interest rates, within limits set by each state. Traditionally, banks only offered the lowest rate, or **prime rate**, to their most creditworthy commercial customers. Most commercial loans are set at markups over prime, like prime + 1, which means 1 percent over the prime rate. However, borrowers can now get funds less expensively from other sources, including foreign banks that set lower interest rates. To remain competitive, U.S. banks now offer some commercial loans at rates below prime. Figure 15.2 shows the changes in the prime rate since 1996.

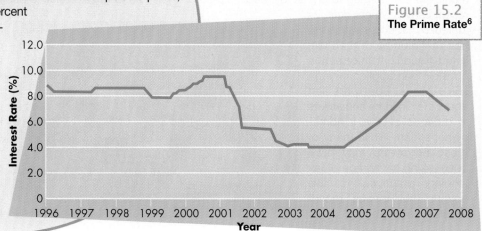

Figure 15.2
The Prime Rate[6]

Pension and Trust Services

Individual retirement accounts (IRAs) are tax-deferred pension funds that wage earners and their spouses can set up to supplement other retirement funds. Advantages and drawbacks to various kinds of IRAs—*traditional, Roth, and Education*—are discussed in Appendix III.

Many commercial banks offer **trust services**—the management of funds left in the bank's trust. In return for a fee, the trust department will perform such tasks as making your monthly bill payments and managing your investment portfolio. Trust departments also manage the estates of deceased persons.

International Services Suppose a U.S. company wants to buy a product from a Japanese supplier. For a fee, it can use one or more of three services offered by its bank:

① *Currency Exchange:* It can exchange U.S. dollars for Japanese yen to pay the supplier.

"*And, hey, don't kill yourself trying to pay it back. You know our motto—'What the hell, it's only money.'*"

② *Letters of Credit:* It can pay its bank to issue a **letter of credit**—a promise by the bank to pay the Japanese firm a certain amount if specified conditions are met.

③ *Banker's Acceptances:* It can pay its bank to draw up a **banker's acceptance**, which promises that the bank will pay some specified amount at a future date.

A banker's acceptance requires payment by a particular date. Letters of credit are payable only after certain conditions are met. The Japanese supplier, for example,

---

Say What You Mean

Liars and Lenders

The consequences of miscommunication in matters of money and banking, whether intentional or not, continue to be sorely felt by millions of people in the United States and worldwide in 2008. The subprime mortgage crisis that has devastated both borrowers and lenders in recent years can be partially attributed to a lack of truthful communication. According to one study, nearly 70 percent of recent early-payment defaults (defaults that occur within the first few months of the loan) listed fraudulent information on their loan applications. In some cases, borrowers lied about their income and assets in order to secure a home-owner's loan. While many of these borrowers may have been taking advantage of lax lending practices to live beyond their means, recent reports suggest that some

dishonesty on loan applications can be attributed to the desire of parents to move to areas with better schools for their children.

Other misinformation can be attributed to mortgage brokers eager to get otherwise unqualified borrowers approved for loans. Some mortgage brokers went so far as to have a relative pose as a borrower's fake employer and falsify W-2 forms to gain approval. These problems were compounded further by those within the banking and finance system who knew that rampant fraud was occurring but looked the other way as long as profits kept rolling in. It is clear from this crisis that greater transparency is needed in communication between borrowers, brokers, and lenders in order to avoid similar financial disasters in the future.[7]

may not be paid until shipping documents prove that the merchandise has been shipped from Japan.

Financial Advice and Brokerage Services Many banks, both large and small, help their customers manage their money. Depending on the customer's situation, the bank, in its role as financial advisor, may recommend different investment opportunities. The recommended mix might include CDs, mutual funds, stocks, and bonds. Many banks also serve as securities intermediaries, using their own stockbrokers to buy and sell securities and their own facilities to hold them.

Electronic Funds Transfer **Electronic funds transfer (EFT)** provides for payments and collections by transferring financial information electronically. Consumers using debit cards instead of writing personal checks enjoy EFT's convenience and speed at the checkout. In addition, EFT systems provide automatic payroll deposit, ATM transactions, bill payment, and automatic funds transfer. Such systems can help a businessperson close an important business deal by transferring money from San Francisco to Miami within a few seconds. The U.S. Treasury reports that it costs $0.83 to issue a check payment, but only $0.08 to issue an EFT payment.[8]

Automated Teller Machines **Automated teller machines (ATMs)** allow customers to withdraw money, make deposits, transfer funds between accounts, and access information on their accounts. About 400,000 machines are located in U.S. bank buildings and other locations.[9] Increasingly, ATMs have become multilingual global fixtures. As Figure 15.3 shows, among the world's more than 1.5 million ATMs, most are located outside the United States, and many U.S. banks now offer international ATM services.

Financial Institutions as Creators of Money

Financial institutions provide a special service to the economy: they create money. They don't mint bills and coins, but by taking in deposits and making loans, they expand the money supply.

As Figure 15.4 shows, the money supply expands because banks are allowed to loan out most (although not all) of the money they take in from deposits. If you deposit $100 in your bank and banks are allowed to loan out 90 percent of all their deposits, then your bank will hold $10 in reserve and loan $90 of your money to borrowers. (You

still have $100 on deposit.) Meanwhile, a borrower—or the people paid—will deposit the $90 loan in a bank. The borrower's bank will then have $81 (90 percent of $90) available for new loans. The banks, therefore, have turned your original $100 into $271 ($100 + $90 + $81). The chain continues, with borrowings from one bank becoming deposits in the next.

Regulation of the Banking System

Because commercial banks are essential to the creation of money, the government regulates them to ensure a sound and competitive financial system. Federal and state agencies regulate banks to ensure that the failure of some will not cause the public to lose faith in the banking system itself.

Federal Deposit Insurance Corporation The **Federal Deposit Insurance Corporation (FDIC)** supervises banks and insures deposits in banks and thrift institutions. The FDIC is a government agency, created by President Franklin D. Roosevelt to restore public confidence in banks during the Depression era. More than 99 percent of the nation's commercial banks and savings institutions pay fees for membership in the FDIC. In return, the FDIC guarantees the safety of all deposits of every account owner up to the current maximum of $100,000. If a bank collapses, the FDIC promises to pay each depositor for losses up to $100,000. A person with more money can establish accounts in more than one bank to protect sums in excess of $100,000. (A handful of the nation's 8,500 commercial

Figure 15.3
Global Dispersion of ATMs

- Asia — 31%
- North America — 25%
- Western Europe — 8%
- Latin America — 4%
- Other — 32%

Figure 15.4
How Banks Create Money

Deposit	Money Held in Reserve by Bank	Money to Lend	Total Supply
$100.00	$10.00	$90.00	**$190.00**
90.00	9.00	81.00	**271.00**
81.00	8.10	72.90	**343.90**
72.90	7.29	65.61	**409.51**
65.61	6.56	59.05	**468.56**

banks are insured by states rather than by the FDIC.) To insure against multiple bank failures, the FDIC maintains the right to examine the activities and accounts of all member banks.

The Federal Reserve System

Perched atop the U.S. financial system and regulating many aspects of its operation is the **Federal Reserve System (the Fed)**, the nation's central bank, established by Congress in 1913. This section describes the structure of the Fed, its functions, and the tools it uses to control the nation's money supply.

The Structure of the Fed

The Fed consists of a board of governors, a group of reserve banks, and member banks. As originally established by the Federal Reserve Act of 1913, the system consisted of 12 relatively autonomous banks and a seven-member committee whose powers were limited to coordinating the activities of those banks. By the 1930s, however, both the structure and function of the Fed had changed dramatically.

The Board of Governors The Fed's board of governors consists of seven members appointed by the president for overlapping terms of 14 years. The chair of the board serves on major economic advisory committees and works actively with the administration to formulate economic policy. The board plays a large role in controlling the money supply. It alone determines the reserve requirements, within statutory limits, for depository institutions. It also works with other members of the Fed to set discount rates and handle the Fed's sale and purchase of government securities.

Reserve Banks The Fed consists of 12 districts, as shown in Figure 15.5. Each Federal Reserve Bank holds reserve deposits from and sets the discount rate for commercial banks in its geographic region. Reserve Banks also play a major role in the nation's check-clearing process.

Open Market Committee The Federal Open Market Committee is responsible for formulating the Fed's monetary policies to promote economic stability and growth by managing the nation's money supply. Its members include the Board of Governors, the president of the Federal Reserve Bank of New York, and the presidents of four other Reserve Banks, who serve on a rotating basis.

Member Banks All nationally chartered commercial banks and some state-chartered banks are members of the

Devout Muslims can't pay or receive interest—a fact that tends to complicate banking operations. Because money has to work in order to earn a return, institutions like the Shamil Bank in Bahrain invest deposits directly in such ventures as real estate and pay back profit shares rather than interest.

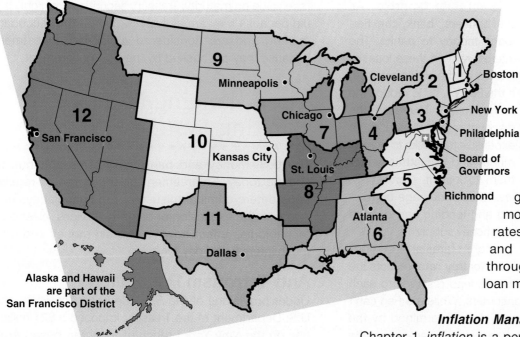

Alaska and Hawaii are part of the San Francisco District

Figure 15.5
The Twelve Federal Reserve Districts[10]

Fed. The accounts of all member bank depositors are automatically covered by the FDIC.

Other Depository Institutions Although many state-chartered banks, credit unions, and S&Ls do not belong to the Fed, they are subject to its regulations, pay deposit insurance premiums, and are covered by the FDIC.

The Functions of the Fed

In addition to chartering national banks, the Fed serves as the federal government's bank and the "bankers' bank," regulating a number of banking activities. Most importantly, it controls the money supply.

The Government's Bank The Fed produces the nation's paper currency and decides how many bills to produce and destroy. It also lends money to the government by buying bonds issued by the Treasury Department to help finance the national deficit.

The Bankers' Bank Individual banks can borrow from the Fed and pay interest on the loans. In addition, the Fed provides storage for commercial banks, which are required to keep funds on reserve at a Federal Reserve Bank.

Controlling the Money Supply The Fed is responsible for the conduct of U.S. **monetary policy**—the management of the nation's economic growth by managing the money supply and interest rates to influence the ability and willingness of banks throughout the country to loan money.

Inflation Management As defined in Chapter 1, *inflation* is a period of widespread price increases throughout an economic system. It occurs if the money supply grows too large. Demand for goods and services increases, and the prices of everything rise. (In contrast, too little money means that an economy will lack the funds to maintain high levels of employment.) Because commercial banks are the main creators of money, much of the Fed's management of the money supply takes the form of regulating the supply of money through commercial banks.

The Tools of the Fed

According to the Fed's original charter, its primary duties were to supervise banking and to manage the nation's currency. The duties of the Fed have evolved to include an emphasis on the broad economic goals as discussed in Chapter 1, especially growth and stability. The Fed's role in controlling the nation's money supply stems from its role in setting policies to help reach these goals. To control the money supply, the Fed uses *reserve requirements*, *interest rate controls*, and *open-market operations*.

Reserve Requirements The **reserve requirement** is the percentage of its deposits that a bank must hold, in cash or on deposit, with a Federal Reserve Bank. High requirements mean that banks have less money to lend and the money supply is reduced. Conversely, low requirements permit the supply to expand.

Check Clearing

The Fed also clears checks, some 100 million of them each day, for commercial banks.[11] Checks received by banks are sent (electronically) to the Fed to ensure that cash is deducted from the check writer's bank account and deposited into the check receiver's account.

Interest Rate Controls As the bankers' bank, the Fed loans money to banks. The interest rate on these loans is known as the **discount rate**. If the Fed wants to reduce the money supply, it increases the discount rate, making it more expensive for banks to borrow money and less attractive for them to loan it. Conversely, low rates encourage borrowing and lending and expand the money supply.

More familiar to consumers, the **federal funds rate** (or **key rate**) reflects the rate at which commercial banks lend reserves to each other and, therefore, to consumers. While the Fed can't actually control this rate, which is determined by the supply and demand of bank reserves, it can control the supply of those reserves to create the desired rate. By instructing its bond traders to buy fewer government bonds, the supply of reserves was decreased, resulting in a series of key rate increases—from a historic low of 1 percent in 2004 up to 5.25 percent in 2006—to slow a booming U.S. economy. The Fed then reversed its policy as the economy lost momentum, cutting the target rate down to 2.00 percent in early 2008 to boost the economy and avoid a recession.[12] In May 2008, Federal Reserve Chairman Ben Bernanke requested that Congress give the Fed the authority to pay interest on commercial bank reserves. Doing so would pump money into the struggling economy by allowing banks to make money off the reserves they are legally required to bank with the Fed.[13]

Open-Market Operations **Open-market operations** refer to the Fed's sale and purchase of securities (usually U.S. Treasury notes and bonds) in the open market, as directed by the open-market committee. Open-market operations are particularly effective because they act quickly and predictably on the money supply. The Fed buys securities from a dealer, whose bank account is credited for the transaction. Its bank has more money to lend, so this transaction expands the money supply.

The opposite happens when the Fed sells securities. Selling treasury securities to investors allows the U.S. government to raise money and contract the money supply. These securities are usually bought at a price below face value and mature to face value within a few weeks to a year for T-bills, between 2 and 10 years for T-notes, and in 30 years for T-bonds. T-bills are known as discount bonds because they do not pay interest periodically but are sold at a discount and pay out the face value on maturity. Treasury securities are highly liquid because they are actively traded on the secondary market, and are considered a risk-free investment because they are backed by the U.S. government.[14]

The Changing Money and Banking System

The U.S. money and banking systems continue to change today. Enforcement of anti-terrorism regulations deters criminal misuse of the financial system. And with the expansion of banking services, electronic technologies affect how you obtain money and how much interest you pay for it.

Anti-Terrorism Regulations

Under provisions of the *Bank Secrecy Act (BSA)*, the U.S. Department of the Treasury imposed a $24 million fine on the New York branch of a Jordan-based Arab Bank for failing to implement required monitoring and record-keeping methods to deter funding of crimes. The enforcement of BSA regulations—enacted in 1970 and reawakened by the 9/11 tragedy—includes tracking and reporting on suspicious transactions, such as a sudden increase in wire transfers or cash transactions exceeding $10,000, to cut off funding of terrorist activities.

The *USA PATRIOT Act*, passed in 2001 and designed to reduce terrorism risks, requires banks to obtain and verify every customer's name, address, date of birth, and Social Security (or tax identification) number. They must also implement a *customer identification program (CIP)* to verify identities, keep records of customer activities, and compare identities of new customers with government terrorist lists.[15]

The Impact of Electronic Technologies

Banks are increasingly adopting technology to improve efficiency and customer service. In addition to EFT systems, banks offer telephone, TV, and Internet banking, which allow customers to make around-the-clock transactions. Each business day, more than $4 trillion exists in and among banks and other financial institutions in purely electronic form. Each year, the Fed's Fedwire funds transfer system—the world's largest electronic payments system—processes about $800 trillion in transactions for some 9,300 financial institutions.

Check 21: Making the Paper Check Go Away The *Check Clearing for the 21st Century Act (Check 21)*, which became federal law in 2004, allows a receiving bank to make an electronic image of a paper check and electronically send the image to the paying bank for instant payment instead of waiting days for the paper check to wind its way back to the sender. The result, when fully implemented by U.S. banks, will be less paper handling, reduced reliance on physical transportation, faster collection times, and elimination of expensive float. The days of writing a check, mailing it, and having several days to put money in the account to cover it are numbered, so check writers need to be prepared for faster check clearing.[16]

Blink Credit Card "Blink" technology uses a computer chip that sends radio-frequency signals in place of the magnetic strips that have been embedded in credit cards for the past 30 years. The "contactless" payment system lets consumers wave the card in front of a merchant's terminal, at a gas pump or in a department store, without waiting to swipe and sign. Radio-frequency identification, while new to credit cards, is familiar on toll roads with electronic passes that allow drivers to avoid waiting in line to pay.

Debit Cards Unlike credit cards, **debit cards** do not increase the funds at an individual's disposal but allow users only to transfer money between accounts to make retail purchases. Debit cards are used as payment for more than 30 percent of all U.S. consumer transactions, as compared with 21 percent for credit-card payments.[22]

Many stores use **point-of-sale (POS) terminals** to communicate relevant purchase information with a customer's bank. A customer inserts a card, and the bank automatically transfers funds from the customer's account to the store's account.

Smart Cards A **smart card** has an embedded computer chip that can be programmed with "electronic money." Also known as *electronic purses* or *stored-value cards*, smart cards have existed for more than a decade. They are most popular in gas-pump payments, followed by prepaid phone service, ATMs, self-operated checkouts, vending machines, and automated banking services.[23]

DEBIT CARD plastic card that allows an individual to transfer money between accounts

POINT-OF-SALE (POS) TERMINAL electronic device that transfers funds from the customer's bank account to pay for retail purchases

SMART CARD credit-card-sized plastic card with an embedded computer chip that can be programmed with electronic money

Entrepreneurship and New Ventures

E-Banking: Easy and Eco-Friendly

Online banking has seen growing popularity in recent years largely because of the convenience it offers customers. Thirty-nine percent of Americans take advantage of online banking, a twelve percent increase over 2005.[17] Paperless banking saves banks and consumers money and has the added advantage of being environmentally friendly. As banks see the perks of these eco-friendly efforts, they are increasingly willing to adopt measures to support the movement in this direction.

Banks continue to improve and expand their online services, and customers are increasingly comfortable using them. With electronic checking, banks save on check-clearing costs, and with paperless statements and online bill paying, they save on printing and mailing. Staffing costs are also reduced as brick-and-mortar branch traffic slows. Corporate clients save on file-storage costs, and individuals reduce clutter in their homes. The immediacy of online banking transactions may also prevent customers from running out of paper checks or accruing late fees.

These endeavors may have their roots in speed and convenience, but they're also good for the environment. Less paper translates into saving trees and reducing wastewater and greenhouse gas emissions. Several banks have pushed these efforts even further. PNC Financial Services has committed to offering eco-friendly incentives for customers and creating Green Branches that use a majority of locally manufactured, recycled, or green building materials and significantly reduce energy and water usage.[18] By 2010, Wachovia plans to construct 300 green branches, which will use less energy and water, offer recycling, reduce the use of plastic and paper goods, and provide bike racks and priority parking for low-emission vehicles.[19] ShoreBank has an on-staff scientist to advise clients on environmental concerns, and Wells Fargo allows customers to purchase carbon-offset credits with their rewards points.[20] These endeavors are not only socially responsible and cost-effective, but they also serve as a powerful marketing strategy to attract an increasingly eco-conscious public.[21]

E-Cash Electronic money, **e-cash**, moves via digital transmissions on the Internet and outside the established network of banks, checks, and paper currency overseen by the Fed. Traditional currency is used to buy electronic funds, which are downloaded onto a PC or portable "electronic wallet" that can store and transmit e-cash. E-cash is purchased from any company that issues (sells) it, including Mondex, Citicorp, and other financial institutions. Instead of using checks, credit cards, or online banking to transfer cash, consumers and businesses can use e-cash to purchase goods and services electronically from any merchant that accepts e-cash. It flows from the buyer's into the seller's e-cash funds, which are instantaneously updated and stored on a microchip. Unlike smart cards, e-cash can be converted back into dollars in the customer's conventional banking account. Although e-cash transactions are cheap and convenient, they are a largely unregulated and unprotected system and are vulnerable to hackers and computer crashes.

International Banking and Finance

Electronic technologies permit nearly instantaneous financial transactions around the globe. The *international payments process* that moves money between buyers and sellers on different continents is not subject to any worldwide policy system beyond loosely structured agreements among countries.

The International Payments Process

Financial settlements between buyers and sellers in different countries are simplified through services provided by banks. For example, payments from U.S. buyers start at a local bank that converts them from dollars into the seller's currency—for example, into euros to be sent to a seller in Greece. At the same time, payments and currency conversions from separate transactions also are flowing between Greek businesses and U.S. sellers in the other direction.

If trade between the two countries is in balance—if money inflows and outflows are equal for both countries—then *money does not actually have to flow between the two countries*. If inflows and outflows are not in balance at the U.S. bank (or at the Greek bank), then a flow of money—either to Greece or to the United States—is made to cover the difference.

International Bank Structure

There is no worldwide banking system comparable, in terms of policy making and regulatory power, to the system of any industrialized nation. Worldwide banking stability relies on a loose structure of agreements among individual countries or groups of countries.

Two United Nations agencies, the World Bank and the International Monetary Fund, help to finance international trade. Unlike true banks, the **World Bank** (technically the International Bank for Reconstruction and Development) provides only a very limited scope of services. For instance, it funds national improvements by making loans to build roads, schools, power plants, and hospitals. The resulting improvements eventually enable borrowing countries to increase productive capacity and international trade.

Tellers at the Bank of Baghdad in the capital's Karrada neighborhood work with customers to convert Iraqi dollars into euros for sending payments from Iraq to a French seller.

Another U.N. agency, the **International Monetary Fund (IMF)**, is a group of some 150 nations that have combined resources for the following purposes:

■ To promote the stability of exchange rates

■ To provide temporary, short-term loans to member countries

■ To encourage members to cooperate on international monetary issues

■ To encourage development of a system for international payments

The IMF makes loans to nations suffering from temporary negative trade balances. By making it possible for these countries to continue buying products from other countries, the IMF facilitates international trade. However, some nations have declined IMF funds rather than accept the economic changes that the IMF demands. For example, some developing countries reject the IMF's requirement that they cut back social programs and spending in order to bring inflation under control.

For additional topics related to this material and end-of-chapter exercises and practices, please visit www.mybizlab.com.

Questions for Review

1. Explain the four characteristics of money.

2. What are the components of M-1 and M-2?

3. Explain the roles of commercial banks, savings and loan associations, credit unions, and nondeposit institutions in the U.S. financial system.

4. Describe the structure of the Federal Reserve System.

5. Show how the Fed uses the discount rate to manage inflation in the U.S. economy.

Questions for Analysis

6. Do you think credit cards should be counted in the money supply? Why or why not? Support your argument by using the definition of *money*.

7. Should commercial banks be regulated, or should market forces be allowed to determine the kinds of loans and the interest rates for loans and savings deposits? Why?

8. Customers who deposit their money in online-only checking and savings accounts can expect to get much higher interest rates than at brick-and-mortar banks. Why do you think that online banks can offer these rates? What might be some drawbacks to online-only banking?

Application Exercises

9. Start with a $1,000 deposit and assume a reserve requirement of 15 percent. Now trace the amount of money created by the banking system after five lending cycles.

10. Interview the manager of a local commercial bank. Identify the ways in which the bank has implemented requirements of the Bank Secrecy Act and the USA PATRIOT Act. What costs has the bank incurred to implement the federal requirements?

Managing Finances

After reading this chapter, you should be able to:

1 Explain the concept of the time value of money and the principle of compound growth.

2 Identify the investment opportunities offered by mutual funds and exchange-traded funds.

3 Describe the role of securities markets, and identify the major stock exchanges and stock markets.

4 Explain how securities markets are regulated and tracked.

5 Describe the risk-return relationship, and discuss the use of diversification and asset allocation for investments.

6 Describe the various ways that firms raise capital and identify the pros and cons of each method.

7 Identify the reasons a company might make an initial public offering of its stock, and explain how stock value is determined.

Investing In Green

Traders are accustomed to using financial markets for investing in just about everything, ranging from pig bellies to movie production, in hopes of gaining a profit. New financial markets for commodities known as carbon credits, however, are driven, not just by profit motive, but by a sense of social responsibility. The economic incentives of emissions trading (ET) bring together both environmental polluters and green investors in an effort to both turn a profit and save the planet.

Here's how it works—regulators in various countries are setting limits on the amounts of industrial pollutants that can be released, including carbon dioxide (CO_2), sulfur dioxide, and mercury. A leading example, the European Union's Emissions Trading Scheme (ETS), was started by the European Commission in 2005 to meet the EU's obligations for carbon reductions in accordance with the Kyoto Protocol on Climate Change. The ETS annually sets a cap for the total amount of CO_2 emissions allowed for each EU member state and company. The state totals and the EU total cannot exceed the caps.

Companies are issued a permit containing a number of "credits" (or certificates) representing the right to emit a certain amount of CO_2. Any company producing below its CO_2 cap can sell its surplus credits to other, more pollution-prone companies that need more credits to keep operating. That's where trading comes into play—it's like a stock exchange that quickly matches up buyers and sellers of emissions credits.

With emissions trading, environmentally oriented companies (so-called green companies) sell unneeded emissions allowances and gain a financial return on past investments for reducing pollution. Such companies view environmental cleanup not as an expense, but as a responsible investment. Other companies, finding it cheaper to avoid such investments, are facing higher costs as they bid for others' unused carbon credits. The trading scheme is adding a new financial incentive for cleaner industries that reduce carbon emissions and other greenhouse gases.[1]

What's in It for Me?

Emissions trading is just one of countless activities drawing investors of every kind to the world's financial markets. Businesses from all over the world, representing every industry, converge there each day, seeking funds that can be used to finance their endeavors and pay off their debts. Individual investors gather as well, in person or—increasingly—online, looking to make their money "work" for them. This chapter will help you understand the various ways this is possible, whether your goals are short- or long-term, whether you are motivated by the desire for profit or security, or simply because you enjoy the challenges inherent in the successful raising and investing of capital.

TIME VALUE OF MONEY principle that invested money grows, over time, by earning interest or some other form of return

COMPOUND GROWTH the compounding of interest over time—with each additional time period, interest returns accumulate

STOCK a portion of ownership of a corporation

COMMON STOCK the most basic form of ownership, including voting rights on major issues, in a company

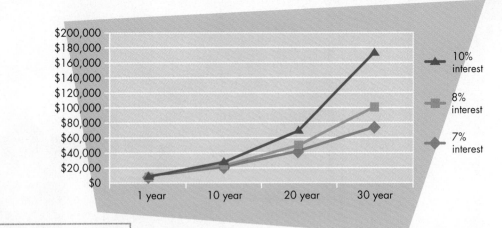

Figure 16.1
Amount to Which an Initial $10,000 Investment Grows

Maximizing Capital Growth

Wise investments are the key to growing your money, especially if you are seeking to build capital to start your own business. In searching for investment opportunities, a number of concepts come into play for evaluating alternative investments and sorting out the good from the bad.

The Time Value of Money

The **time value of money**, perhaps the single most important concept in business finance, recognizes the basic fact that, while it's invested, money grows by earning interest or yielding some other form of return. Time value stems from the principle of **compound growth**—the compounding of interest paid to the investor over given time periods. With each additional time period, interest payments accumulate and earn more interest, thus multiplying the earning capacity of the investment.

Making Better Use of Your Time Value What if you invested $10,000 at seven percent interest for one year? You would earn $700 on your $10,000 investment. If you re-invested the principal amount plus the interest you earned during the first year for another 4 years, you'd end up with $14,025. Now, if you were planning for retirement and reinvested that money at the same interest rate for another 25 years, you could

retire with $76,122—almost eight times the amount you started with!

Figure 16.1 illustrates how the returns from an initial investment of $10,000 accumulate substantially over longer periods of time. Notice that the gains for the last 10 years are much greater than for the first 10 years, illustrating the power of compound growth. Each year, the interest rate is applied to a larger sum. Notice also the larger gains from higher interest rates. Even a seemingly small change in interest rates, from 7% to 8%, results in much larger accumulations.

Common Stock

As you can see from Figure 16.1, the best way to take advantage of the time value of money is to obtain a high rate of return on your investment. One way to achieve a high rate of return is to invest in the stock market. A **stock** is a portion of the ownership of a corporation. The company's total ownership is divided into small parts, called *shares*, that can be bought and sold to determine how much of the company (how many shares of stock) is owned by each shareholder.

While several types of stock exist, common stock is the most prominent. A share of **common stock** is the most basic form of ownership in a company. Individuals and other companies purchase a firm's common stock in the hope that it will increase in value and provide dividend income; in addition, each common share has a vote on major issues that are brought before the shareholders.

The Rule of 72

How long does it take to double an investment? A handy rule of thumb is called the "Rule of 72." You can find the number of years needed to double your money by dividing the annual interest rate (in percent) into 72. If, for example, you re-invest annually at 8 percent, you'll double your money in about 9 years:

$$\frac{72}{8} = 9 \text{ years to double the money}$$

The Rule of 72 can also calculate how much interest you must get if you want to double your money in a given number of years: Simply divide 72 by the desired number of years. If you want to double your money in 10 years, you need to get 7.2 percent:

$$\frac{72}{10} = 7.2 \text{ percent interest needed to double the money}$$

The lesson for the investor is clear: seek *higher* interest rates because money will double more frequently.

Stock values are usually expressed in two different ways: as market value and book value.

1 A stock's real value is its **market value**—the current price of a share in the stock market. Market value reflects the amount that buyers are willing to pay for a share of the company's stock.

2 The **book value** for a share of common stock is determined as the firm's owners' equity (from the balance sheet) divided by the number of common shares owned by all shareholders. Book value is used as a comparison indicator because the market value for successful companies is usually greater than its book value. Thus, when market price falls to near book value, some profit-seeking investors buy the stock on the principle that it is underpriced and will increase in the future.

Investment Traits of Common Stock Common stocks are among the riskiest of all investments. Uncertainties about the stock market itself can quickly change a given stock's value. Furthermore, when companies have unprofitable years, or when economic conditions go sour, potential investors become wary of future stock values, so share price drops. On the upside, however, common stocks offer high growth potential; when a company's performance brightens, because of public acceptance of a hot new product, for example, share price can sharply increase.

Dividends A **dividend** is a payment to shareholders, on a per-share basis, from the company's earnings. Dividend payments are optional and variable—the corporation's board of directors decides whether and when a dividend will be paid, as well as the amount that is best for the future of the company and its shareholders. Many companies distribute between 30 and 70 percent of their profits to shareholders. However, some firms, especially fast-growing companies, do not pay dividends; instead, they use cash earnings for expanding the company so that future earnings can grow even faster. What's more, any company can have a bad year and decide to reduce or omit dividend payments to stockholders.

Mutual Funds and Exchange-Traded Funds

As an alternative to buying stock, mutual funds and exchange-traded funds are popular because they offer attractive investment opportunities for various financial objectives and often do not require large sums of money for entry. In addition, the simple and easy transaction process makes them accessible to the public.

Mutual funds are created by companies such as T. Rowe Price and Vanguard that pool cash investments from individuals and organizations to purchase a portfolio of stocks, bonds, and other securities. The portfolio is expected to appreciate in market value and otherwise produce income for the mutual fund and its investors.

Reasons for Investing It's relatively easy to open a mutual fund account by e-mail or phone. There are numerous funds that meet any chosen financial objective. Three of the most common objectives are financial stability, conservative growth, and aggressive growth.

■ **Stability and Safety**
Funds stressing safety seek only modest growth with little fluctuation in principal value regardless of economic conditions. They include *money market mutual funds* and other funds that preserve the fund holders' capital and reliably pay current income. Typical assets of these funds include lower-risk

---

MARKET VALUE current price of a share of stock in the stock market

BOOK VALUE value of a common stock expressed as the firm's owners' equity divided by the number of common shares

DIVIDEND payment to shareholders, on a per-share basis, out of the company's earnings

MUTUAL FUND company that pools cash investments from individuals and organizations to purchase a portfolio of stocks, bonds, and other securities

PROSPECTUS registration statement filed with the SEC, containing information for prospective investors about a security to be offered and the issuing company

INSIDER TRADING illegal practice of using special knowledge about a firm for profit or gain

---

The Securities and Exchange Commission

The U.S. Securities and Exchange Commission (SEC) is the regulation and enforcement agency that oversees the markets' activities, including the ways securities are issued. The SEC was created in 1934 to prevent the kinds of abuses that led to the stock market crash of 1929. The SEC regulates the public offering of new securities by requiring that all companies file prospectuses before proposed offerings commence. To protect investors from fraudulent issues, a **prospectus** contains pertinent information about both the offered security and the issuing company. False statements are subject to criminal penalties.

The SEC also enforces laws against **insider trading**—the use of special knowledge about a firm for profit or gain. It is illegal, for example, for an employee of a firm to tell others about an anticipated event that may affect the value of that firm's stock, such as an acquisition or a merger, before news of that event is made public. Those in possession of such insider knowledge would have an unfair advantage over other investors.

U.S. corporate bonds, U.S. government bonds, and other safe short-term securities that provide stable income from interest and dividends.

- **Conservative Capital Growth** Mutual funds that stress preservation of capital and current income, but also seek some capital appreciation, are called *balanced funds.* Typically, these funds hold long-term municipal bonds, corporate bonds, and common stocks with good dividend-paying records and potential for market appreciation (higher market value), though there is always the risk of price declines if the general stock market falls.

- **Aggressive Growth** *Aggressive growth funds* seek maximum long-term capital growth. They sacrifice current income and safety by investing in stocks of new (and even troubled) companies, firms developing new products and technologies, and other high-risk securities. They are designed for investors who can accept the risk of loss inherent in common stock investing with severe price fluctuations, but also the potential for superior returns over time.

Most Mutual Funds Don't Match the Market Many, but not all, mutual funds are managed by "experts" who select the fund's stocks and other securities that provide the fund's income. Unfortunately, some estimates indicate that up to 80% of these managed funds do not perform as well as the average return of the overall stock market, due to costly management expenses and underperforming stocks.[2] This underperformance disadvantage has resulted in the emergence of passively managed mutual funds such as index funds, which nearly match the performance of a particular market. The selection of which stocks to purchase in an index fund is relatively automatic—it holds many of the same stocks as the market it tracks—and requires little human input, thus reducing management expenses.

Exchange-Traded Funds As with an index mutual fund, an **exchange-traded fund (ETF)** is a bundle of stocks (or bonds) that are in an index that tracks the overall movement of a market; unlike a mutual fund, however, an ETF can be traded like a stock. Each share of an ETF rises and falls as market prices change continuously for the market being tracked.

Founded in 1792 and located at the corner of Wall and Broad Streets in New York City, the New York Stock Exchange sees billions of shares change hands each day.

Advantages of ETFs ETFs offer three areas of advantage over mutual funds: They can be traded throughout the day like a stock, they have low operating expenses, and they do not require high initial investments. Because they are traded on stock exchanges (hence, "exchange traded"), ETFs can be bought and sold—priced continuously—any time throughout the day. This *intraday trading* means you can time your transaction during the day to buy or sell when (or if) the market reaches a desired price. Mutual fund shares, in contrast, are priced once daily, at the end of the day. Thus, when you buy or sell during the day, you don't find out the share price until after the day has ended.

Whereas many mutual funds pass the costs of expensive active management onto shareholders, an ETF is bound by a rule that specifies what stocks will be purchased and when; once the rule is established, little or no active human decisions are involved. The *lower annual operating expenses* mean that, for the buy-and-hold investor, annual fees for ETFs are as low as 0.09 percent of assets; annual fees for mutual funds average 1.4 percent.[3]

Finally, unlike mutual funds, ETFs require no minimum investment, meaning they offer *ease of entry* for investors getting started without much money.[4] On the other hand, because ETFs must be bought and sold through a broker, they require payment of a brokerage commission (transaction fees). Traders who buy and sell frequently can end up paying more in transactions fees, even surpassing a mutual fund's high management expenses.[5]

The Business of Trading Securities

Stocks, bonds, and mutual funds are known as **securities** because they represent *secured,* or financially valuable claims on the part of investors. The markets in which stocks and bonds are sold are called **securities markets**. Mutual funds, on the other hand, are not bought and sold on securities markets, but are managed by financial professionals in the investment companies that create, buy, and sell the funds.

Primary and Secondary Securities Markets In **primary securities markets**, new stocks and bonds are bought and sold by firms and governments. Sometimes, new securities are sold to single buyers or small groups of buyers. These so-called *private placements* are desirable because they allow issuers to keep their plans confidential.

Most new stocks and some bonds are sold on the wider public market. To bring a new security to market, the issuing firm must get approval from the U.S. **Securities and Exchange Commission (SEC)**—the government agency that regulates U.S. securities markets. The firm also needs the services of an **investment bank**—a financial institution such as Merrill Lynch or Goldman Sachs that specializes in issuing and reselling new securities. Such investment banking firms provide three important services:

1 They advise companies on the timing and financial terms of new issues.

2 They *underwrite*—that is, assume liability for—new securities, thus providing the issuing firms with 100% of the money (less commission). The inability to resell the securities is a risk that the banks must bear.

3 They create distribution networks for moving new securities through groups of other banks and brokers into the hands of individual investors.

New securities, however, represent only a small portion of traded securities. *Existing* stocks and bonds are sold in the much larger **secondary securities market**, which is handled by such familiar bodies as the New York Stock Exchange and, more recently, by online trading with electronic communication networks.

Stock Exchanges

Most of the buying and selling of stocks, historically, has been handled by organized stock exchanges. A **stock exchange** is an organization of individuals coordinated to provide an institutional auction setting in which stocks can be bought and sold.

The Trading Floor Each exchange regulates the places and times at which trading may occur. The most important difference between traditional exchanges and the electronic market is the geographic location of the trading activity. Brokers at an exchange trade face-to-face on the *trading floor* (also referred to as an *outcry market*). The electronic market, on the other hand, conducts trades electronically among thousands of dealers in remote locations around the world.

Trading floors today are equipped with vast arrays of electronic communications equipment for displaying buy and sell orders or confirming completed trades. A variety of news services furnish up-to-the-minute information about world events and business developments. Any change in these factors, then, may be swiftly reflected in share prices.

The Major Stock Exchanges Among the stock exchanges that operate on trading floors in the United States, the New York Stock Exchange is the largest. Today it faces stiff competition from both the electronic market in the United States—NASDAQ—and large foreign exchanges, such as those in London and Tokyo.

The New York Stock Exchange For many people, "the stock market" means the *New York Stock Exchange (NYSE)*. Founded in 1792, the NYSE is the model for exchanges worldwide. Only firms meeting certain minimum requirements—earning power, total value of outstanding stock, and number of shareholders—are eligible for listing on the NYSE.[6]

Today's NYSE is a *hybrid market* that utilizes both floor and electronic trading. When a client places an order through a brokerage house or online, it is transmitted to a broker on the NYSE floor. Floor brokers who want to trade that stock meet together to agree upon a trading price based on supply and demand, and the order is executed. Alternatively, buyers can use the NYSE's Direct+ service to automatically execute trades electronically.

Other, smaller, U.S. exchanges include the American Stock Exchange (AMEX), also located in New York City, and several regional stock exchanges organized over a century ago to serve investors in places other than New York—including Chicago, Los Angeles, San Francisco, Cincinnati, and Spokane.

Global Stock Exchanges As recently as 1980, the U.S. market accounted for more than half the value of the world market in traded stocks. Market activities, however, have shifted as the value of shares listed on foreign exchanges continues to grow. Table 16.1 identifies several stock exchanges and the volume of shares traded each day. Relatively new exchanges are also flourishing in cities from Shanghai to Warsaw.

> **PRIMARY SECURITIES MARKET** market in which new stocks and bonds are bought and sold by firms and governments
>
> **SECURITIES AND EXCHANGE COMMISSION (SEC)** government agency that regulates U.S. securities markets
>
> **INVESTMENT BANK** financial institution that specializes in issuing and reselling new securities
>
> **SECONDARY SECURITIES MARKET** market in which existing (not new) stocks and bonds are sold to the public
>
> **STOCK EXCHANGE** an organization of individuals to provide an institutional auction setting in which stocks can be bought and sold

The NASDAQ Market The **National Association of Securities Dealers Automated Quotation (NASDAQ) system**, the world's oldest electronic stock market, was established in 1971. Whereas buy and sell orders to the NYSE are gathered on the trading floor, NASDAQ orders are gathered and executed on a computer network connecting 350,000 terminals worldwide. Currently, NASDAQ is working with officials in an increasing number of countries in replacing the trading floors of traditional exchanges with electronic networks like NASDAQ's.

The stocks of some 3,300 companies, both emerging and well known, are traded by NASDAQ. Although the volume of shares traded surpasses that of the New York Stock Exchange, the total market value of NASDAQ's U.S. stocks is less than that of the NYSE.

International Consolidation and Cross-Border Ownership A wave of technological advances, along with regulatory and competitive factors, is propelling the consolidation of stock exchanges and the changeover from physical to electronic trading floors across international borders. Electronic communication networks have opened the door to around-the-clock and around-the-globe trading. Every major European stock exchange had gone electronic by the close of the twentieth century, and the United States is catching up. Stock exchanges that don't have enough savvy with electronic technologies to stay competitive are merging or partnering with those having more advanced trading systems. The intensified competition among stock exchanges is resulting in speedier transactions and lower transaction fees for investors.[8]

Non-Exchange Trading: Electronic Communication Networks

The SEC in 1998 authorized the creation of **electronic communication networks (ECNs)**—electronic trading systems that bring buyers and sellers together outside of traditional stock exchanges by automatically matching buy and sell orders at specified prices. ECNs have gained rapid popularity because the trading procedures are fast and efficient, often lowering transactions costs per share to mere pennies. They also allow after-hours

Table 16.1 **Selected Global Stock Exchanges and Markets[7]**

Country	Stock Exchange	Average Daily Trading Volume (millions of shares)
Australia	Australian Stock Exchange	1,200
Brazil	Sao Paulo Bovespa	18,000
Canada	Toronto Stock Exchange	272
France	Paris Bourse Stock Market	55
Hong Kong	Hong Kong Stock Exchange	7,000
Japan	Tokyo Stock Exchange	1,400
United Kingdom	London Stock Exchange	370
United States	New York Stock Exchange	1,400

trading (after traditional markets have closed for the day) and protect traders' anonymity.[9]

ECNs must register with the SEC as broker-dealers. The ECN then provides service to subscribers, that is, other broker-dealers and institutional investors. Subscribers can view all orders at any time on the system's Web site to see information on what trades have taken place and at what times.[10] Individual investors must open an account with a subscriber (a broker-dealer) before they can send buy or sell orders to the ECN system.

Individual Investor Trading

Some of the many individual investors who buy and sell securities are novices who seek the advice of experienced professionals, or brokers. Investors who are well informed and experienced, however, often prefer to invest independently without outside guidance.

Stock Brokers **Stock brokers** earn commissions by executing buy and sell orders for outside customers. Although they match buyers with sellers, brokers do not own the securities. They earn commissions from the individuals and organizations for whom they place orders.

Discount Brokers Like many products, brokerage assistance can be purchased at either discount or at full-service prices. Discount brokers offer well-informed individual investors who know what they want to buy or sell a fast, low-cost way to participate in the market. Sales personnel receive fees or salaries, not commissions. Unlike many full-service brokers, they do not offer in-depth investment advice or person-to-person sales consultations. They do, however, offer automated online services, such as stock research, industry analysis, and screening for specific types of stocks.

Full-Service Brokers Despite the growth in online investing, full-service brokers remain an important resource, both for new, uninformed investors and for experienced investors who don't have time to keep up with all the latest developments. Full-service firms such as Merrill Lynch offer clients consulting advice in personal financial planning, estate planning, and tax strategies, along with a wider range of investment products. In addition to delivering and interpreting information, financial advisors can point clients toward investments that might otherwise be lost in an avalanche of online financial data.

Online Investing   The popularity of online trading stems from convenient access to the Internet, fast, no-nonsense transactions, and the opportunity for self-directed investors to manage their own investments while paying low fees for trading.

Online investors buy into and sell out of the stocks of thousands of companies daily. Consequently, keeping track of who owns what at any given time has become a monumental burden. Relief has come from **book-entry ownership**. Historically, shares of stock have been issued as physical paper certificates; now they are simply recorded in the companies' books, thereby eliminating the costs of storing, exchanging, and replacing certificates.

Tracking the Market Using Stock Indexes

For decades investors have used stock indexes to measure market performance and to predict future movements of stock markets. Although not indicative of the status of individual securities, **market indexes** provide useful summaries of overall price trends, both in specific industries and in the stock market as a whole. Market indexes, for example, reveal bull and bear market trends. **Bull markets** are periods of rising stock prices, generally lasting 12 months or longer; investors are motivated to buy, confident they will realize capital gains. Periods of falling stock prices, usually 20% off peak prices, are called **bear markets**; investors are motivated to sell, anticipating further falling prices.

As Figure 16.2 shows, the past three decades have been characterized primarily by bull markets, including the longest in history, from 1981 to the beginning of 2000. In contrast, the period 2000 to 2003 was characterized by a bear market, as was 2008. The data that characterize such periods are drawn from three leading market indexes: the Dow Jones, Standard & Poor's, and NASDAQ Composite.

BOOK-ENTRY OWNERSHIP procedure that holds investors' shares in book-entry form, rather than issuing a physical paper certificate of ownership

MARKET INDEX statistical indicator designed to measure the performance of a large group of stocks or track the price changes of a stock market

BULL MARKET period of rising stock prices, lasting 12 months or longer, featuring investor confidence for future gains and motivation to buy

BEAR MARKET period of falling stock prices marked by negative investor sentiments with motivation to sell ahead of anticipated losses

---

Say What You Mean

An Insider on Trial

In July 2007, Joseph P. Nacchio, the former CEO of Qwest Communications, was sentenced to serve 6 years in prison following his conviction on 19 counts of insider trading. He was also ordered to pay a fine of $19 million—$1 million per count, the maximum financial penalty allowed by law—and turn over the $52 million from gains he had earned from the illegal trading.

Nacchio had steered Qwest to the top of the telecommunications industry, riding the Internet bubble of the late-1990s. By 2001, however, the bubble had burst, and Qwest seemed increasingly unlikely to hit its aggressive earnings targets. Nacchio chose not to inform investors of these concerns, instead publicly pronouncing favorable growth prospects for the company. At the same time, he accelerated his sale of more than $100 million worth of

Qwest common stock, ultimately making $52 million in violation of insider trading laws.

Nearly a year after Nacchio's conviction, however, an appeals court overturned the guilty verdict, ruling that the trial judge had erred in refusing to allow an expert witness to testify on Nacchio's behalf. The appeals court did, however, find sufficient evidence of insider trading to warrant retrying the case, and the lead prosecutor has vowed to keep fighting, an indication of the seriousness with which insider trading is viewed in the wake of the corporate scandals that marked the early 2000s. Furthermore, this case illustrates the dangers of using insider information to mislead the public.[11]

Figure 16.2
Bull and Bear Markets

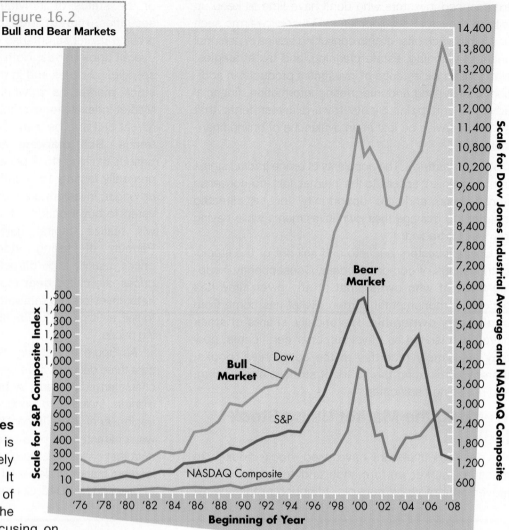

The Dow The **Dow Jones Industrial Average (DJIA)** is the oldest and most widely cited U.S. market index. It measures the performance of the industrial sector of the U.S. stock markets by focusing on just 30 blue-chip, large-cap companies as reflectors of the economic health of the many similar U.S. firms. The Dow is an average of the stock prices for these 30 large firms, and traders and investors use it as a traditional barometer of the market's overall movement.

Over the decades, the Dow has been revised and updated to reflect the changing composition of U.S. companies and industries. The most recent modification occurred in 2004, when three companies were added—insurance giant American International Group, pharmaceuticals goliath Pfizer, telecom titan Verizon—replacing AT&T, Eastman Kodak, and International Paper. These changes better reflect today's information-based economy and the increasing prominence of financial services and pharmaceuticals.

The S&P 500 Because it considers very few firms, the Dow is a limited gauge of the overall U.S. stock market. The **S&P 500** is a broader report, considered by many to be the best single indicator of the U.S. equities market. It consists of 500 large-cap stocks, including companies from various sectors—such as information

technology, energy, industrials, financials, health care, consumer staples, and telecommunications—for a balanced representation of the overall large-cap equities market.

The NASDAQ Composite Because it considers more stocks, some Wall Street observers regard the **NASDAQ Composite Index** as one of the most useful of all market indexes. Unlike the Dow and the S&P 500, all NASDAQ-listed companies, not just a selected few, are included in the index for a total of some 3,200 firms (mostly domestic, and about 300 foreign). However, it includes a high proportion of technology companies, including small-company stocks, and a smaller representation of other sectors—financial, consumer products, and industrials.

The Russell 2000 Investors in the U.S. small-cap market are interested in the **Russell 2000 Index**—a specialty index that measures the performance of the smallest U.S. companies based on market capitalization. As the most quoted index focusing on the small-cap portion of the U.S. economy, its stocks represent a range of sectors such as financials, consumer discretionary, health care, technology, materials, and utilities.

Index-Matching ETFs Countless other specialty indexes exist for specific industries, countries, and economic sectors to meet investors' diverse needs. Additionally, many exchange-traded funds are available to investors for duplicating (or nearly duplicating) the market performance of popular stock-market indexes. For example, one ETF, Standard & Poor's Depository Receipts (SPDRS, known as *Spiders*), owns a portfolio of stocks that matches the composition of the S&P 500 index. Similarly the Fidelity® NASDAQ Composite Index® Tracking Stock holds a portfolio of equities for tracking the NASDAQ Composite Index.

The Risk-Return Relationship

Each type of investment has a **risk–return (risk-reward) relationship**: Whereas safer investments tend to offer lower returns, riskier investments tend to offer higher returns (rewards).

Figure 16.3 shows the general risk–return relationship for various financial instruments, along with the types of investors they attract. Thus, conservative investors, who have a low tolerance for risk, will opt for no-risk U.S. Treasury Bills, or even intermediate-term high-grade corporate bonds that rate low in terms of risk on future returns, but also low on the size of expected returns. The reverse is true of aggressive investors who prefer the higher risks and potential returns from long-term junk bonds and common stocks.

Investment Dividends (or Interest), Appreciation, and Total Return

In evaluating potential investments, investors look at returns from dividends (or from interest),

returns from price appreciation, and total return.

Dividends The returns from stock dividends are commonly referred to as the **current dividend yield** (or, in the case of interest from a loan, the **interest dividend yield**), and are figured by dividing the yearly dollar amount of dividend income by the investment's current market value. In 2008, for example, each share of GE stock was receiving annual dividends payments of $1.24. If, on a particular day, the share price was $33.82, the current yield would be 3.66% ($1.24/$33.82 × 100). This dividend can then be compared against current yields from other investments. Larger dividend yields, of course, are preferred to smaller returns.

Price Appreciation Another source of returns depends on whether the investment is increasing or decreasing in dollar value. **Price appreciation** is an increase in the dollar value of an investment. Suppose, for example, you purchased a share of GE stock for $33.82, then sold it one year later for $36.50. The price appreciation

RISK-RETURN (RISK-REWARD) RELATIONSHIP principle that safer investments tend to offer lower returns whereas riskier investments tend to offer higher returns (rewards)

CURRENT/INTEREST DIVIDEND YIELD yearly dollar amount of income divided by the investment's current market value, expressed as a percentage

PRICE APPRECIATION increase in the dollar value of an investment at two points in time (the amount by which the price of a security increases)

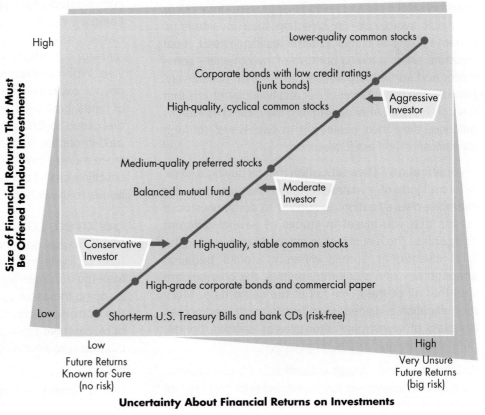

Figure 16.3
Uncertainty About Financial Returns on Investments[12]

Uncertainty About Financial Returns on Investments

is $2.68 ($36.50 – 33.82). This profit, realized from the increased value of an investment, is known as a **capital gain**.

Total Return The sum of an investment's current dividend (interest) yield and capital gain is referred to as its total return. Total return cannot be accurately evaluated until it's compared to the investment that was required to get that return. Total return as a percentage of investment is calculated as follows:

Total return (%) = (Current dividend payment + Capital gain)/Original investment × 100.

To complete our GE example, the total return as a percentage of our one-year investment would be 11.59% [($1.24 + $2.68)/$33.82 × 100]. Note that larger total returns are preferred to smaller ones.

Reducing Risk with Diversification and Asset Allocation

Investors seldom take an extreme approach—total risk or total risk avoidance—in selecting their investments. Extreme positions attract extreme results; instead, most investors select a mixed portfolio of investments—some riskier and some more conservative—that, collectively, provides the overall level of risk and financial returns that feel comfortable. After determining the desired *risk-return* balance, they then achieve it in two ways: through *diversification* and *asset allocation*.

Diversification
Diversification means buying several different kinds of investments rather than just one. For example, diversification as applied to common stocks means that you invest in stocks of several different companies. The risk of loss is reduced by spreading the total investment across different stocks because although any one stock may tumble, the chances are less that all of them will fall at the same time. More diversification is gained when assets are spread across a variety of investment alternatives—stocks, bonds, mutual funds, real estate, and so on.

Asset allocation
Asset allocation is the proportion—the relative amounts—of funds invested in (or allocated to) each of the investment alternatives. You may decide for

example, to allocate 50% of your funds to common stocks, 25% to a money market mutual fund, and 25% to a U.S. Treasury bond mutual fund. Ten years later, with more concern for financial safety, you may decide on a less risky asset allocation of 20%, 40%, and 40% in the same investment categories, respectively.

Performance Differences for Different Portfolios
Once an investment objective with acceptable risk level is chosen, the tools of diversification and asset allocation are put to use in the investor's portfolio. A **portfolio** is the combined holdings of all the financial investments—stocks, bonds, mutual funds, real estate—of any company or individual.

Just like investors, investment funds have different investment objectives—ranging from aggressive growth/high risk to stable income/low volatility—and their holdings are diversified accordingly among hundreds of company stocks, corporate bonds, or government bonds that provide the desired orientation. The money in a diversified portfolio is allocated in different proportions among a variety of funds; if all goes according to plan, most of these funds will meet their desired investment objectives and the overall portfolio will increase in value.

Financing the Business Firm

If you invest wisely, you may earn enough money to start your own firm—but that's only the first step in the complicated process of financing a business. Every company needs cash to function. Although a business owner's savings may be enough to get a firm up and running, businesses depend on sales revenues to survive. When current sales revenues are insufficient to pay for expenses, firms tap into various other sources of funds, typically starting with the owners' savings—as discussed in Chapter 14, owners contribute funds, or paid-in capital, from their own pockets. If a firm needs more money, they can turn to borrowing from banks, soliciting cash from private outside investors, or selling bonds to the public.

Secured Loans for Equipment

Money to purchase new equipment often comes in the form of loans from commercial banks. In a **secured loan** the borrower guarantees repayment of the loan by pledging the asset as **collateral** to the lender. That is, if the borrower defaults, or fails to repay the loan, the bank can take possession of his or her assets and sell them to recover the outstanding debt.

Principal and Interest Rates
The amount of money that is loaned and must be repaid is called the **loan principal**. However, borrowers also pay the lender an

additional fee, called **interest**, for the use of the borrowed funds. The amount of interest owed depends on an **annual percentage rate (APR)** that is agreed upon between the lender and borrower. The interest amount is found by multiplying the APR by the loan principal.

Working Capital and Unsecured Loans from Banks

Firms need more than just fixed assets for daily operations; they need current, liquid assets available to meet short-term operating expenses such as employee wages and marketing expenses. The firm's ability to meet these expenses is measured by its working capital:

Working capital = Current assets − Current liabilities

Positive working capital means the firm's current assets are large enough to pay off current liabilities (see Chapter 14). Negative working capital means the firm's current liabilities are greater than current assets, so it may need to borrow money from a commercial bank. With an **unsecured loan**, the borrower does not have to put up collateral. In many cases, however, the bank requires the borrower to maintain a *compensating balance*—the borrower must keep a portion of the loan amount on deposit with the bank in a non–interest-bearing account.

Firms with bad credit scores typically cannot get unsecured loans. Because access to such loans requires a good credit history, many firms establish a relationship with a commercial bank and, over time, build a good credit record by repaying loan principal and interest on time.

Angel Investors and Venture Capital

Once a business has been successfully launched it needs additional capital for growth. Outside individuals who provide such capital are called **angel investors**. In return for their investment, angel investors typically expect a sizable piece of ownership in the company (up to 50 percent of its equity). They may also want a formal say in how the company is run. If the firm is bought by a larger company or if it sells its stock in a public offering, the angel may receive additional payments.

Angel investors help many firms grow rapidly by providing what is known as **venture capital**—private funds from wealthy individuals or companies (see Chapter 3) that seek investment opportunities in new

INTEREST fee paid to a lender for the use of borrowed funds; like a rental fee

ANNUAL PERCENTAGE RATE (APR) one-year rate that is charged for borrowing, expressed as a percentage of the borrowed principal

UNSECURED LOAN a loan for which collateral is not required

ANGEL INVESTORS outside investors who provide new capital for firms in return for a share of equity ownership

VENTURE CAPITAL private funds by wealthy individuals seeking investment opportunities in new growth companies

---

Entrepreneurship and New Ventures

An Online Community for People 50 and Older

The social networking site Facebook began specifically for college students, and over 90 percent of its users remain under the age of 35. That's one reason Kelly and Jeff Lantz founded *55-Alive!*, a social networking site for users over 50 years old. Launched in 2005, the company's revenues for 2006 were a meager $5,000. The following year they jumped to $30,000, as the site's activities expanded into instant messaging, blogging, and chat rooms for member-created groups. Among its livelier activities is the *55-Alive! Battle of the Boomer Bands*, an online competition for musicians born before 1964.

So what's next? Financed to date with their own money, and with just one part-time employee, Kelly and Jeff project a need for at least $250,000 of outside funding to expand the site's content and to hire someone to help with sales ads. Despite its early success, *55-Alive!* still only receives 100,000 visits per month, just a small fraction of Facebook's 115 million monthly users.[13]

CORPORATE BOND a formal pledge obligating the issuer (the company) to pay interest periodically and repay the principal at maturity

BOND INDENTURE legal document containing complete details of a bond issue

MATURITY DATE (DUE DATE) future date when repayment of the bond is due from the bond issuer (borrower)

FACE VALUE (PAR VALUE) amount of money that the bond buyer (lender) lent the issuer, and that the lender will receive upon repayment

DEFAULT failure of the borrower to make payment when due to lenders

BONDHOLDERS' CLAIM request for court enforcement of a bond's terms of payment

BANKRUPTCY court-granted permission for a company to not pay some or all debts

INITIAL PUBLIC OFFERING (IPO) first sale of a company's stock to the general public

Table 16.2 Bond Rating Systems

Rating System	High Grades	Medium Grades (Investment Grades)	Speculative	Poor Grades
Moody's	Aaa, Aa	A, Baa	Ba, B	Caa to C
Standard & Poor's	AAA, AA	A, BBB	BB, B	CCC to D

growth companies. In most cases, the growth firm turns to venture capital sources because they have not yet built enough credit history to get a loan from commercial banks or other lending institutions.

Sale of Corporate Bonds

Corporations can raise capital by issuing bonds. A **corporate bond** is a formal pledge (an IOU) obligating the issuer to pay interest periodically and repay the principal at maturity (a preset future date) to the lender. The federal government also issues bonds to finance projects and meet obligations, as do state and local governments (called *municipal bonds*).

Characteristics of Corporate Bonds The bondholder (the lender) has no claim to ownership of the company and does not receive dividends. However, interest payments and repayment of principal are financial obligations; payments to bondholders have priority over dividend payments to stockholders in cases of financial distress.

Each new bond issue has specific terms and conditions spelled out in a **bond indenture**—a legal document identifying the borrower's obligations and the financial returns to lenders. One of the most important details is the **maturity date** (or **due date**), when the firm must repay the bond's **face value** (also called **par value**, or the amount purchased) to the lender.

Corporate bonds have been traditionally issued to fund outstanding debts and major projects for various lengths of time. Short-term bonds mature in less than five years after they are issued. Bonds with 5- to 10-year lives are considered intermediate term, while anything over 10 years is considered long term. Longer-term corporate bonds are somewhat riskier than shorter-term bonds because they are exposed to greater unforeseen economic conditions that may lead to default.

Default and Bondholders' Claim A bond is said to be in **default** if the borrower fails to make payment when due to lenders. Bondholders may then file a **bondholders' claim**—a request for court enforcement of the bond's terms of payment. When a financially distressed company cannot pay bondholders, it may seek relief by filing for **bankruptcy**—the court-granted permission not to pay some or all debts.

Risk Ratings To aid investors in making purchase decisions, several services measure the default risk of bonds. Table 16.2, for example, shows the rating systems of two well-known services, Moody's and Standard & Poor's. The highest grades are AAA and Aaa, and the lowest are C and D. Low-grade bonds are usually called *junk bonds*. Negative ratings do not necessarily keep issues from being successful. Rather, they raise the interest rates that issuers must offer to attract lenders.

Becoming a Public Corporation

• •

Initial public offerings (IPOs)—the first sale of a company's stock to the general public—are a major source of funds that fuel continued growth for many firms, as well as introduce numerous considerations and complexities inherent in running a public company.

Going Public Means Selling off Part of the Company

Private owners lose some control of the company when shares are sold to the public. Common shareholders usually have voting rights in corporate governance, so they elect the board of directors and vote on major issues put forth at the company's annual shareholders' meeting. Anyone owning a large proportion of the company's shares gains a powerful position in determining who runs the corporation and how.

With an initial public offering in 2004, Google began selling its stock to the public, thus creating additional funds that were needed for expansion. The IPO raised proceeds of $1.9 billion from selling 22.5 million shares at $85 per share.

At an extreme, a **corporate raider**—an investor conducting a type of hostile (unwanted) takeover—buys shares on the open market, attempting to seize control of the company and its assets. The raider then sells off those assets at a profit, resulting in the company's disappearance.

A company is ripe for raiding when its stock price falls so shares can be cheaply bought, although its assets still have high value.

Stock Valuation

There are many factors that affect a stock's value, which in turn affect the value of the business. In addition, different investors measure value differently, and their measurements may change according to circumstance. Because of the uncertainties involved in stock prices, investment professionals believe day-to-day prices to be a generally poor indicator of any stock's real value. Instead, a long-run perspective considers the company's financial health, past history of results and future forecasts, its record for managerial performance, and overall prospects for competing successfully in the coming years. Accordingly, any stock's value today looks

beyond the current price and is based on expectations of the financial returns it will provide to shareholders during the long run.

Why Shares Are Different Prices In June 2008 the price of Google Inc. was about $570 per share on the New York Stock Exchange, while GE shares traded at about $29, and Delta Airlines shares were priced at about $5.30. Berkshire Hathaway shares traded for $127,000.[14]

Why such differences? One reason is supply and demand for each company's shares; another is because some corporations want the shares to sell within a particular price range, say between $20 and $80, believing it will attract a larger pool of investors. If the price gets too high, the company can restore it to the desired range by a **stock split**—a stock dividend paid in additional shares to shareholders. Here's how it works. Suppose company X has 100,000 common shares outstanding that are trading at $100 per share, but the company wants it priced in the $20 to $80 range. X can declare a 2-for-1 stock split, meaning the company gives shareholders one additional share for each share they own. Now X has 200,000 shares outstanding but its financial performance has not changed, so the stock price immediately falls to $50 per share. Every shareholder's investment value, however, is unchanged: they previously owned one share at $100, and now they own two shares at $50 each.

Market Capitalization

A widely used measure of corporate size and value is known as **market capitalization (market cap)**—the total dollar value of all the company's outstanding

CORPORATE RAIDER an investor conducting a type of hostile corporate takeover against the wishes of the company

STOCK SPLIT stock dividend paid in additional shares to shareholders, thus increasing the number of outstanding shares

MARKET CAPITALIZATION (MARKET CAP) the total dollar value of all the company's outstanding shares

"Our stock just went up ten points on the rumor that I was replacing you all with burlap sacks stuffed with straw."

DEBT FINANCING long-term borrowing from sources outside a company

EQUITY FINANCING using the owners' funds from inside the company as the source for long-term funding

shares, calculated as the current stock price multiplied by the number of shares outstanding. As indicated in Table 16.4, the investment industry categorizes firms according to size of capitalization.

Investors typically regard larger market caps as less risky, and firms with small market caps (small-cap firms) as being particularly risky investments.

In early 2008 Exxon Mobil's share price was $86.10, and there were 5,454 million common shares outstanding. Its market cap was over $469 billion, making it the largest company in the world.

Choosing Equity versus Debt Capital

Firms can meet their capital needs through two sources: debt financing (from outside the firm) or equity financing (putting the owners' capital to work).

Pros and Cons for Debt Financing

Long-term borrowing from sources outside the company—**debt financing**—via loans or the sale of corporate bonds is a major component in most U.S. firms' financial planning.

Long-Term Loans Long-term loans are attractive for several reasons:

- Because the number of parties involved is limited, loans can often be arranged very quickly.

- The firm need not make public disclosure of its business plans or the purpose for which it is acquiring the loan. (In contrast, the issuance of corporate bonds requires such disclosure.)

Long-term loans also have some disadvantages. Borrowers, for example, may have trouble finding lenders to supply large sums. Long-term borrowers may also face restrictions as conditions of the loan. For example, they may have to pledge long-term assets as collateral or agree to take on no more debt until the loan is paid.

Corporate Bonds Bonds are attractive when firms need large amounts for long periods of time. The issuing company gains access to large numbers of lenders through nationwide bond markets. On the other hand, bonds entail high administrative and selling costs. They may also require stiff interest payments, especially if the issuing company has a poor credit rating. Bonds

Comparing Prices of Different Stocks

Consider a recent day when PepsiCo's share price was $70, while Coca-Cola was $58 per share. Does the price difference mean that PepsiCo is a better company than Coca-Cola, because its shares are more expensive? Or does it mean that Coke shares are a better value because they can be bought at a lower price than PepsiCo's? In fact, neither of these two reasons is correct. Share prices alone do not provide enough information to determine which is the better investment. Table 16.3 can help us make a better comparison.

First, earnings per share (EPS) are greater for PepsiCo. Even though you pay more to own a PepsiCo share, earnings per dollar of investment are greater as well ($3.42 earnings/$70 investment = $0.049; versus $2.16 earnings/$58 investment = $0.037): PepsiCo's earnings were nearly 5 cents for each dollar of its share price, whereas Coca-Cola earned less than 4 cents. PepsiCo generated more earnings power for each dollar of shareholder investment.

Now consider annual dividends paid to shareholders. The dividend yield from Coca-Cola was 2.32%. That is, the dividend payment amounted to a 2.32% return on the shareholder's $58 investment, or $1.35 ($58 × 2.32%). PepsiCo's dividend payment was about $1.50 ($70 × 2.14%), though this represents a somewhat smaller return (yield) on shareholder investment than Coca-Cola.

Based on this limited information, it's not clear which of the two companies is the better investment. A more complete evaluation would compare historical performance consistency over a period of several years, along with indicators of each firm's prospects for the future.

Table 16.3 **Financial Comparison: Coca-Cola and PepsiCo[15]**

	Coca-Cola	PepsiCo
Recent price	$58	$70
EPS	$2.16	$3.42
Dividend yield	2.32%	2.14%

Table 16.4 **Corporation Sizes Based on Capitalization**

Capitalization Category	Range of Capitalization
Micro-Cap	below $250 million
Small-Cap	$250–$2 billion
Mid-Cap	$2 billion–$10 billion
Large-Cap	over $10 billion

also impose binding obligations on the firm, in many cases for up to 30 years, to pay bondholders a stipulated sum of annual or semiannual interest, even in times of financial distress. If the company fails to make a bond payment, it goes into default.

Pros and Cons for Equity Financing

Although debt financing often has strong appeal, **equity financing**—looking inside the company for long-term funding—is sometimes preferable. Equity financing includes either issuing common stock or retaining the firm's earnings.

The Expense of Common Stock The use of equity financing by means of common stock can be expensive because paying dividends is more expensive than paying bond interest. Interest paid to bondholders is a business expense and therefore a tax deduction for the firm. Payments of cash dividends to shareholders are not tax deductible.

Retained Earnings as a Source of Capital As presented in Chapter 14, *retained earnings* are net profits retained for the firm's use rather than paid out in dividends to stockholders. If a company uses retained earnings as capital, it will not have to borrow money and pay interest. If a firm has a history of reaping profits by reinvesting retained earnings, it may be very attractive to some investors. Retained earnings, however, mean smaller dividends for shareholders. This practice may decrease the demand for—and the price of—the company's stock.

For additional topics related to this material and end-of-chapter exercises and practices, please visit www.mybizlab.com.

Questions for Review

1 Explain the concept of the *time value of money*.

2 What do mutual funds and exchange-traded funds offer, and how do they work?

3 Identify the various characteristics of corporate bonds.

4 How does the market value of a stock differ from the book value of a stock?

5 How do firms meet their needs through debt financing and equity financing?

Questions for Analysis

6 After researching several stocks online, you notice that they have continually fluctuated in price. What might be the reason for this? Is a higher-priced stock a better investment than a lower-priced stock? What factors would you consider in purchasing stocks?

7 Which type of fund do you think you would invest in, a mutual fund or an exchange traded fund? What is the difference, and why would you favor one over the other?

8 Suppose that you are a business owner and you need new equipment and immediate funds to meet short-term operating expenses. From what sources could you gain the capital you need, and what are some of the characteristics of these sources?

Application Exercises

9 Go to http://www.sec.gov to research how a new security is approved by the Securities and Exchange Commission. What is the process involved and how long would it take? Next, contact a financial institution such as Merrill Lynch and request information about their procedures for issuing or reselling new securities. Share this information with your classmates.

10 If you are not currently involved in investing, imagine that you are analyzing potential investments to build your portfolio. Create a mock portfolio with the investments you would obtain. How would you apply diversification and asset allocation to assure that your risk-return balance is at a point at which you are comfortable?

RISK uncertainty about future events

SPECULATIVE RISK risk involving the possibility of gain or loss

PURE RISK risk involving only the possibility of loss or no loss

RISK MANAGEMENT the process of conserving the firm's earning power and assets by reducing the threat of losses due to uncontrollable events

RISK AVOIDANCE the practice of avoiding risk by declining or ceasing to participate in an activity

RISK CONTROL the practice of minimizing the frequency or severity of losses from risky activities

RISK RETENTION the practice of covering a firm's losses with its own funds

RISK TRANSFER the practice of transferring a firm's risk to another firm

Risk Management

In this appendix, we describe other types of risks that businesses face, and analyze some of the ways in which they typically manage them.

Coping With Risk

Businesses constantly face two basic types of **risk**—uncertainty about future events. **Speculative risks**, such as financial investments, involve the possibility of gain or loss. **Pure risks** involve only the possibility of loss or no loss. Designing and distributing a new product, for example, is a speculative risk—the product may fail, or it may succeed and earn high profits. In contrast, the chance of a warehouse fire is a pure risk.

For a company to survive and prosper, it must manage both types of risk in a cost-effective manner. We can define the process of **risk management** as conserving the firm's earning power and assets by reducing the threat of losses due to uncontrollable events. In every company, each manager must be alert for risks to the firm and their impact on profits.

The risk-management process usually involves five steps:

Step 1: Identify Risks and Potential Losses Managers analyze a firm's risks to identify potential losses.

Step 2: Measure the Frequency and Severity of Losses and Their Impact To measure the frequency and severity of losses, managers must consider both history and current activities. How often can the firm expect the loss to occur? What is the likely size of the loss in dollars?

Step 3: Evaluate Alternatives and Choose the Techniques That Will Best Handle the Losses Having identified and measured potential losses, managers are in a better position to decide how to handle them. They generally have four choices:

- A firm opts for **risk avoidance** by declining to enter or by ceasing to participate in a risky activity.

- When avoidance is not practical or desirable, firms can practice **risk control**—the use of loss-prevention techniques to minimize the frequency or severity of losses.

- When losses cannot be avoided or controlled, firms must cope with the consequences. When such losses are manageable and predictable, the firm may decide to cover them out of company funds. The firm is said to assume or retain the financial consequences of the loss; hence, the practice is known as **risk retention**.

- When the potential for large risks cannot be avoided or controlled, managers often opt for **risk transfer** to another firm—namely, an insurance company—to protect itself.

Step 4: Implement the Risk-Management Program The means of implementing risk-management decisions depend on both the technique chosen and the activity being managed.

- Risk avoidance for certain activities can be implemented by purchasing those activities from outside providers.

- Risk control might be implemented by training employees and designing new work methods and equipment for on-the-job safety.

- For situations in which risk retention is preferred, reserve funds can be set aside from revenues.

- When risk transfer is needed, implementation means selecting an insurance company and buying the appropriate policies.

Step 5: Monitor Results New types of risks emerge with changes in customers, facilities, employees, and products. Insurance regulations change, and new types of insurance become available. Consequently, managers must continuously monitor a company's risks, reevaluate the methods used for handling them, and revise them as necessary.

Insurance as Risk Management

To deal with some risks, both businesses and individuals may choose to purchase insurance. Insurance is purchased by paying **insurance premiums**—payments to an insurance company to buy a policy and keep it active. In return, the insurance company issues an **insurance policy**—a formal agreement to pay the policyholder a specified amount in the event of certain losses. In some cases, the insured party must also pay a **deductible**, an agreed-upon amount of the loss that the insured must absorb prior to reimbursement. Buyers find insurance appealing because they are protected against large, potentially devastating losses in return for a relatively small sum of money.

With insurance, individuals and businesses share risks by contributing to a fund from which those who suffer losses are paid. Insurance companies are willing to accept these risks because they make profits by taking in more premiums than they pay out to cover policyholders' losses. Although many policyholders are paying for protection against the same type of loss, by no means will all of them suffer such a loss.

Insurable Versus Uninsurable Risks Like every business, insurance companies must avoid certain risks. Insurers divide potential sources of loss into *insurable risks* and *uninsurable risks*. They issue policies only for insurable risks. Although there are some exceptions, an insurable risk must meet the following four criteria:

1 *Predictability*: The insurer must be able to use statistical tools to forecast the likelihood of a loss. This forecast also helps insurers determine premiums charged to policyholders.

2 *Casualty*: A loss must result from an *accident,* not from an intentional act by the policyholder. To avoid paying in cases of fraud, insurers may refuse to cover losses when they cannot determine whether policyholders' actions contributed to them.

3 *Unconnectedness*: Potential losses must be random and must occur independently of other losses. No insurer can afford to write insurance when a large percentage of those who are exposed to a particular kind of loss are likely to suffer such a loss. By carefully choosing the risks that it will insure, an insurance company can reduce its chances of a large loss or insolvency.

4 *Verifiability*: Insured losses must be verifiable as to cause, time, place, and amount.

Special Forms of Insurance for Business Businesses have special insurable concerns—*liability, property, business interruption, key person insurance*, and *business continuation agreements.*

Liability Insurance Liability means responsibility for damages in case of accidental or deliberate harm to individuals or property. **Liability insurance** covers losses resulting from damage to people or property when the insured party is judged liable.

A business is liable for any injury to an employee when the injury arises from activities related to the occupation. When workers are permanently or temporarily disabled by job-related accidents or disease, employers are required by law to provide **workers' compensation coverage** for medical expenses, loss of wages, and rehabilitation services.

Property Insurance A firm purchases **property insurance** to cover injuries to itself resulting from physical damage to or loss of real estate or personal property. Property losses may result from fire, lightning, wind, hail, explosion, theft, vandalism, or other destructive forces.

Business Interruption Insurance In some cases, loss to property is minimal in comparison to loss of income. If a firm is forced to close down for an extended time, it will not be able to generate income. During this time, however, certain expenses—such as taxes, insurance premiums, and salaries for key personnel—may

---

INSURANCE PREMIUM fee paid to an insurance company by a policyholder for insurance coverage

INSURANCE POLICY a formal agreement to pay the policyholder a specified amount in the event of certain losses

DEDUCTIBLE an amount of the loss that the insured must absorb prior to reimbursement

LIABILITY INSURANCE insurance covering losses resulting from damage to people or property when the insured party is judged liable

WORKERS' COMPENSATION COVERAGE coverage provided by a firm to employees for medical expenses, loss of wages, and rehabilitation costs resulting from job-related injuries or disease

PROPERTY INSURANCE insurance covering losses resulting from physical damage to or loss of the insured's real estate or personal property

continue. To cover such losses, a firm may buy **business interruption insurance**.

Key Person Insurance

Many businesses choose to protect themselves against loss of the talents and skills of key employees, as well as the recruitment costs to find a replacement and training expenses once a replacement is hired. **Key person insurance** is designed to offset both lost income and additional expenses.

Business Continuation Agreements

Who takes control of a business when a partner or associate dies? Surviving partners are often faced with the possibility of having to accept an inexperienced heir as a management partner. This contingency can be handled in **business continuation agreements**, whereby owners make plans to buy the ownership interest of a deceased associate from his or her heirs. The value of the ownership interest is determined when the agreement is made. Special policies can also provide survivors with the funds needed to make the purchase.

In this appendix, we describe the basic tenets of U.S. law and show how these principles work through the court system. We'll also survey a few major areas of business-related law.

The U.S. Legal and Judicial Systems

Laws are the codified rules of behavior enforced by a society. In the United States, laws fall into three broad categories according to their origins: *common*, *statutory*, and *regulatory*.

Types of Law

Law in the United States originated primarily with English common law. U.S. law includes the U.S. Constitution, state constitutions, federal and state statutes, municipal ordinances, administrative agency rules and regulations, executive orders, and court decisions.

Common Law   Court decisions follow *precedents*, or the decisions of earlier cases. Following precedent lends stability to the law by basing judicial decisions on cases anchored in similar facts. This principle is the keystone of **common law**—the body of decisions handed down by courts ruling on individual cases.

Statutory Law   Laws created by constitutions or by federal, state, or local legislative acts constitute **statutory law**. Under the U.S. Constitution, federal statutes take precedence over state and local statutes.

Regulatory Law   Statutory law and common law have long histories. Relatively new is **regulatory (or administrative) law**—law made by the authority of administrative agencies.

Although Congress retains control over the scope of agency action, regulations have the force of statutory law once passed. Government regulatory agencies act as a secondary judicial system, determining whether regulations have been violated and then imposing penalties.

Much agency activity consists of setting standards for safety or quality and monitoring the compliance of businesses.

Congress has created many new agencies in response to pressure to address social issues. In some cases, agencies were established in response to public concern about corporate behavior. The activities of these agencies have sometimes forced U.S. firms to consider the public interest almost as routinely as they consider their own financial performance.

> **LAWS** codified rules of behavior enforced by a society
>
> **COMMON LAW** body of decisions handed down by courts ruling on individual cases
>
> **STATUTORY LAW** law created by constitution(s) or by federal, state, or local legislative acts
>
> **REGULATORY (ADMINISTRATIVE) LAW** law made by the authority of administrative agencies
>
> **DEREGULATION** elimination of rules that restrict business activity

Keeping an Eye on Business   Today a host of agencies regulate U.S. business practices, including:

- Equal Employment Opportunity Commission (EEOC)
- Environmental Protection Agency (EPA)
- Food and Drug Administration (FDA)
- Federal Trade Commission (FTC)
- Occupational Safety and Health Administration (OSHA)

The Move Toward Deregulation   Although government regulation has benefited U.S. business in many ways, it is not without its drawbacks. Businesspeople complain—with some justification—that government regulations require too much costly paperwork. Many people in both business and government support broader **deregulation**—the elimination of rules that restrict business activity. Deregulation, they argue, is a primary incentive to innovation; deregulated industries are forced to innovate in order to survive in fiercely competitive industries. Those firms that are already conditioned to compete by being more creative will outperform firms that have been protected by regulatory climates in their home countries.

The U.S. Judicial System

Much of the responsibility for law enforcement falls to the courts. Litigation is a significant part of contemporary life, and we have given our courts a voice in a wide range of issues, some touching personal concerns, some ruling on matters of public policy that affect all our lives.

The Court System There are three levels in the U.S. judicial system—*federal*, *state*, and *local*. Federal courts hear cases on questions of constitutional law, disputes relating to maritime laws, and violations of federal statutes. They also rule on regulatory actions and on such issues as bankruptcy, postal law, and copyright or patent violation. Both the federal and most state systems embody a three-tiered system of *trial*, *appellate*, and *supreme courts*.

Trial Courts At the lowest level of the federal court system are the **trial courts**, the general courts that hear cases not specifically assigned to another court. Every state has at least one federal trial court, called a *district court*.

Trial courts also include special courts and administrative agencies. Special courts hear specific types of cases, such as cases involving tax evasion, fraud, international disputes, or claims against the U.S. government. Within their areas of jurisdiction, administrative agencies also make judgments much like those of courts.

Courts in each state deal with the same issues as their federal counterparts. However, they may rule only in areas governed by state law. For example, a state special court would hear a case involving state income tax laws. Local courts in each state system also hear cases on municipal ordinances, local traffic violations, and similar issues.

Appellate Courts A losing party may disagree with a trial court ruling. If that party can show grounds for review, the case may go before a federal or state **appellate court**. These courts consider questions of law, such as possible errors of legal interpretation made by lower courts. They do not examine questions of fact.

Supreme Courts Cases still not resolved at the appellate level can be appealed to the appropriate state supreme courts or to the U.S. Supreme Court. If it believes that an appeal is warranted or that the outcome will set an important precedent, the U.S. Supreme Court also hears cases appealed from state supreme courts.

Business Law

Most legal issues confronted by businesses fall into one of six basic areas: *contract*, *tort*, *property*, *agency*, *commercial*, or *bankruptcy law*. These areas cover a wide range of business activity.

Contract Law

A **contract** is any agreement between two or more parties that is enforceable in court. As such, it must meet six conditions. If all these conditions are met, one party can seek legal recourse from another if the other party breaches, or violates, the terms of the agreement.

1 *Agreement.* Agreement is the serious, definite, and communicated offer and acceptance of the same terms.

2 *Consent.* A contract is not enforceable if any of the parties has been affected by an honest mistake, fraud, or pressure.

3 *Capacity.* To give real consent, both parties must demonstrate legal **capacity** (competence). A person under legal age (usually 18 or 21) cannot enter into a binding contract.

4 *Consideration.* An agreement is binding only if it exchanges **considerations**—items of value. Note that items of value do not necessarily entail money. Contracts need not be rational, nor must they provide the best possible bargain for both sides. They need only include legally sufficient consideration. The terms are met if both parties receive what the contract details.

5 *Legality.* A contract must be for a lawful purpose and must comply with federal, state, and local laws and regulations.

6 *Proper form.* A contract may be written, oral, or implied from conduct. It must be written, however, if it involves the sale of land or goods worth more than $500. It must be written if the agreement requires more than a year to fulfill. All changes to written contracts must also be in writing.

Breach of Contract

Contract law offers a variety of remedies designed to protect the reasonable expectations of the parties and, in some cases, to compensate them for actions taken to enforce the agreement. As the injured party to a breached contract, any of the following actions might occur:

- You might cancel the contract and refuse to live up to your part of the bargain.
- You might sue for damages up to the amount that you lost as a result of the breach.
- If money cannot repay the damage you suffered, you might demand specific performance, or require the other party to fulfill the original contract.

Tort Law

Tort law applies to most business relationships *not governed by contracts*. A **tort** is a *civil*—that is, noncriminal—injury to people, property, or reputation for which compensation must be paid. Trespass, fraud, defamation, invasion of privacy, and even assault can be torts, as can interference with contractual relations and wrongful use of trade secrets. There are three classifications of torts: *intentional*, *negligence*, and *product liability*.

Intentional Torts

Intentional torts result from the deliberate actions of another person or organization. To remedy torts, courts will usually impose **compensatory damages**—payments intended to redress an injury actually suffered. They may also impose **punitive damages**—fines that exceed actual losses suffered by plaintiffs and are intended to punish defendants.

Negligence Torts

Most suits involve charges of **negligence**—conduct that falls below legal standards for protecting others against unreasonable risk.

Product Liability Torts

In cases of **product liability**, a company may be held responsible for injuries caused by its products.

Strict Product Liability Since the early 1960s, businesses have faced a number of legal actions based on the relatively new principle of **strict product liability**—the principle that liability can result not from a producer's negligence but from a defect in the product itself. An injured party need only show the following:

1. The product was defective.
2. The defect was the cause of injury.
3. The defect caused the product to be unreasonably dangerous.

Because plaintiffs need not demonstrate negligence or fault, these suits have a good chance of success.

Property Law

Property is anything of value to which a person or business has sole right of ownership. Legally speaking, the right of ownership is itself property.

Within this broad general definition, we can divide property into four categories:

1. **Tangible real property** is land and anything attached to it.
2. **Tangible personal property** is any movable item that can be owned, bought, sold, or leased.
3. **Intangible personal property** cannot be seen but exists by virtue of written documentation.
4. **Intellectual property** is created through a person's creative activities.

Protection of Intellectual Rights The U.S. Constitution grants protection to intellectual property by means of copyrights, trademarks, and patents. Copyrights and patents apply to the tangible expressions of an idea, not to the ideas themselves.

Copyrights Copyrights give creators exclusive ownership rights to their intellectual property. Copyrights extend to creators for their entire lives and to their estates for 70 years thereafter.

Trademarks Because the development of products is expensive, companies must

TORT civil injury to people, property, or reputation for which compensation must be paid

INTENTIONAL TORT tort resulting from the deliberate actions of a party

COMPENSATORY DAMAGES monetary payments intended to redress injury actually suffered because of a tort

PUNITIVE DAMAGES fines imposed over and above any actual losses suffered by a plaintiff

NEGLIGENCE conduct that falls below legal standards for protecting others against unreasonable risk

PRODUCT LIABILITY tort in which a company is responsible for injuries caused by its products

STRICT PRODUCT LIABILITY principle that liability can result not from a producer's negligence but from a defect in the product itself

PROPERTY anything of value to which a person or business has sole right of ownership

TANGIBLE REAL PROPERTY land and anything attached to it

TANGIBLE PERSONAL PROPERTY any movable item that can be owned, bought, sold, or leased

INTANGIBLE PERSONAL PROPERTY property that cannot be seen but that exists by virtue of written documentation

INTELLECTUAL PROPERTY property created through a person's creative activities

COPYRIGHT exclusive ownership right belonging to the creator of a book, article, design, illustration, photo, film, or musical work

TRADEMARK exclusive legal right to use a brand name or symbol

PATENT exclusive legal right to use and license a manufactured item or substance, manufacturing process, or object design

EMINENT DOMAIN principle that the government may claim private land for public use by buying it at a fair price

AGENT individual or organization acting for and in the name of another party

PRINCIPAL individual or organization authorizing an agent to act on its behalf

EXPRESS AUTHORITY agent's authority, derived from written agreement, to bind a principal to a certain course of action

IMPLIED AUTHORITY agent's authority, derived from business custom, to bind a principal to a certain course of action

APPARENT AUTHORITY agent's authority, based on the principal's compliance, to bind a principal to a certain course of action

UNIFORM COMMERCIAL CODE (UCC) body of standardized laws governing the rights of buyers and sellers in transactions

WARRANTY seller's promise to stand by its products or services if a problem occurs after the sale

EXPRESS WARRANTY warranty whose terms are specifically stated by the seller

prevent other firms from using their brand names. Often, they must act to keep competitors from seducing consumers with similar or substitute products. A producer can apply to the U.S. government for a **trademark**—the exclusive legal right to use a brand name.

Trademarks are granted for 20 years and may be renewed indefinitely if a firm continues to protect its brand name. If a firm allows the brand name to lapse into common usage, it may lose protection. Common usage takes effect when a company fails to use the ® symbol to indicate that its brand name is a registered trademark. It also takes effect if a company seeks no action against those who fail to acknowledge its trademark.

Patents Patents provide legal monopolies for the use and licensing of manufactured items, manufacturing processes, substances, and designs for objects. A patentable invention must be *novel*, *useful*, and *nonobvious*. Patents are valid for 20 years, with the term running from the date on which the application was *filed*, not the date on which the patent itself was *issued*.

Restrictions on Property Rights Property rights are not always absolute. For example, rights may be compromised under the following circumstances:

■ Utility companies typically have rights called *easements,* such as the right to run wire over private property or to lay cable or pipe under it.

■ Under the principle of **eminent domain**, the government may, upon paying owners fair prices, claim private land to expand roads or erect public buildings.

Agency Law

The transfer of property often involves agents. An **agent** is a person who acts for and in the name of another party, called the **principal**. Courts have ruled that both a firm's employees and its outside contractors may be regarded as its agents.

Authority of Agents Agents have the authority to bind principals to agreements. They receive that authority, however, from the principals themselves; they cannot create their own authority. An agent's authority to bind a principal can be **express**, **implied**, or **apparent**.

Responsibilities of Principals Principals have several responsibilities to their agents. They owe agents reasonable compensation, must reimburse them for related business expenses, and should inform them of risks associated with their business activities. Principals are liable for actions performed by agents *within the scope of their employment.* If agents make untrue claims about products or services, the principal is liable for making amends. Employers are similarly responsible for the actions of employees. Firms are often liable in tort suits because the courts treat employees as agents. Businesses are also increasingly being held accountable for *criminal* acts by employees. Court findings have argued that firms are expected to be aware of workers' negative propensities, to check their employees' backgrounds, and to train and supervise employees properly.

Commercial Law

Managers must be well acquainted with the most general laws affecting commerce. Specifically, they need to be familiar with the provisions of the **Uniform Commercial Code (UCC)**, which describes the rights of buyers and sellers in transactions. One key area of coverage by the UCC, contracts, was discussed earlier. Another key area is warranties.

A **warranty** is a seller's promise to stand by its products or services if a problem occurs after the sale. Warranties may be express or implied. The seller specifically states the terms of an **express warranty**, while an **implied warranty** is dictated by law. Implied warranties embody the principle that a product should (1) fulfill the promises made by advertisements and (2) serve the purpose for which it was manufactured and sold. It is important to note, however, that warranties, unlike most contracts, are easily limited, waived, or disclaimed. Consequently, they are the source of tort action more often, as dissatisfied customers seek redress from producers.

Bankruptcy Law

Both organizations and individuals can seek debt relief by filing for bankruptcy—the court-granted permission not to pay some or all incurred debts. Many individuals and businesses file for bankruptcy each year, and their numbers continue to increase. Three main factors account for the increase in bankruptcy filings:

1 The increased availability of credit

2 The "fresh-start" provisions in current bankruptcy laws

3 The growing acceptance of bankruptcy as a financial tactic

In some cases, creditors force an individual or firm into **involuntary bankruptcy** and press the courts to award them payment of at least part of what they are owed. Far more often, however, a person or business chooses to file for court protection against creditors. In general, individuals and firms whose debts exceed total assets by at least $1,000 may file for **voluntary bankruptcy**.

Business Bankruptcy   One of three plans resolves a business bankruptcy:

1 Under a *liquidation plan*, the business ceases to exist. Its assets are sold and the proceeds are used to pay creditors.

2 Under a *repayment plan*, the bankrupt company simply works out a new payment schedule to meet its obligations. The time frame is usually extended, and payments are collected and distributed by a court-appointed trustee.

3 *Reorganization* is the most complex form of business bankruptcy. The company must explain the sources of its financial difficulties and propose a new plan for remaining in business. Reorganization may include a new slate of managers and a new financial strategy. A judge may also reduce the firm's debts to ensure its survival.

Legislation passed since 1994 restricts how long a company can protect itself in bankruptcy while continuing to do business. Critics have charged that many firms have succeeded in operating for many months under bankruptcy protection. During that time, they were able to cut costs and prices, not only competing with an unfair advantage, but also dragging down overall industry profits. The new laws place time limits on various steps in the filing process. The intended effect is to speed the process and prevent assets from being lost to legal fees.

The International Framework of Business Law

Laws vary from country to country, and many businesses today have international markets, suppliers, and competitors. Managers need a basic understanding of the international framework of business law that affects the ways in which they can do business. Issues, such as pollution across borders, are matters of **international law**—the very general set of cooperative agreements and guidelines established by countries to govern the actions of individuals, businesses, and nations themselves.

International law has several sources. One source is custom and tradition. Among countries that have been trading with one another for centuries, many customs and traditions governing exchanges have gradually evolved into practice. Although some trading practices still follow ancient unwritten agreements, there has been a clear trend in more recent times to approach international trade within a more formal legal framework. Key features of that framework include a variety of formal trade agreements.

Another important source of international law is the formal trade treaties that nations negotiate with one another. Governing such entities as the WTO and the EU, for instance, also provide legal frameworks within which participating nations agree to abide.

IMPLIED WARRANTY warranty, dictated by law, based on the principle that products should fulfill advertised promises and serve the purposes for which they are manufactured and sold

INVOLUNTARY BANKRUPTCY bankruptcy proceedings initiated by the creditors of an indebted individual or organization

VOLUNTARY BANKRUPTCY bankruptcy proceedings initiated by an indebted individual or organization

INTERNATIONAL LAW general set of cooperative agreements and guidelines established by countries to govern the actions of individuals, businesses, and nations

FINANCIAL PLANNING
process of looking at
one's current financial
condition, identifying
one's goals, and
anticipating requirements
for meeting those goals

PERSONAL NET WORTH
value of one's total assets
minus one's total
liabilities (debts)

Dealing with personal finances is a lifelong job involving a crucial choice between two options:

1. Committing to the rational management of your personal finances by controlling them, helping them grow, and therefore enjoying greater personal satisfaction and financial stability.

2. Letting the financial chips fall where they may and hoping for the best (which seldom happens) and therefore inviting frustration, disappointment, and financial distress.

Personal finance management requires consideration of cash management, financial planning and control, investment alternatives, and risk. Let's start by looking at one key factor in success: the personal financial plan. We'll then discuss the steps in the planning process and show how you can make better decisions to manage your personal finances.

Building Your Financial Plan

• • • • • • • • • • • • • • • • •

Financial planning is the process of looking at your current financial condition, identifying your goals, and anticipating steps toward meeting those goals. Because your goals and finances will change as you get older, your plan should always allow for revision. Figure AIII.1 summarizes a step-by-step approach to personal financial planning.

Assessing Your Current Financial Condition

The first step in developing a personal financial plan is assessing your current financial position. Your **personal net worth** is the value of all your assets minus all your liabilities (debts) *at the present time.* The worksheet in Figure AIII.2 provides some sample calculations for developing your own personal "balance sheet." Because assets and liabilities change over time, updating your balance sheet not only allows you to monitor changes, but also provides more accurate information for realistic budgeting and planning.

Develop Your Financial Goals

Step 2 involves setting three different types of future goals: *immediate* (within one year), *intermediate* (within five years), and *long-term* (more than five years). The worksheet in Figure AIII.3 will help you establish these goals. By thinking about your finances in three different time frames, you'll be better able to

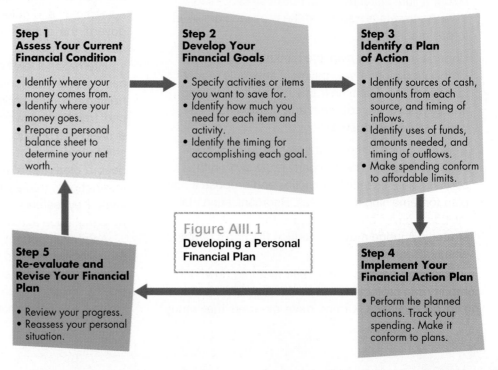

Step 1
Assess Your Current Financial Condition

- Identify where your money comes from.
- Identify where your money goes.
- Prepare a personal balance sheet to determine your net worth.

Step 2
Develop Your Financial Goals

- Specify activities or items you want to save for.
- Identify how much you need for each item and activity.
- Identify the timing for accomplishing each goal.

Step 3
Identify a Plan of Action

- Identify sources of cash, amounts from each source, and timing of inflows.
- Identify uses of funds, amounts needed, and timing of outflows.
- Make spending conform to affordable limits.

Step 5
Re-evaluate and Revise Your Financial Plan

- Review your progress.
- Reassess your personal situation.

Figure AIII.1
Developing a Personal Financial Plan

Step 4
Implement Your Financial Action Plan

- Perform the planned actions. Track your spending. Make it conform to plans.

Assets: What You Own	Example Numbers	Your Numbers
LIQUID ASSETS:		
1. Cash $	300	
2. Savings +	3,700	
3. Checking +	1,200	
INVESTMENTS:		
4. IRAs +	12,400	
5. Securities +	500	
6. Retirement Plan +	—	
7. Real Estate (other than primary residence) +	—	
HOUSEHOLD:		
8. Cars (market value) +	18,000	
9. House (market value) +	—	
10. Furniture +	3,400	
11. Personal Property +	6,600	
12. Other assets	—	
13. Total Assets (add lines 1-12)	**= $46,100**	
Liabilities (Dept): What You Owe		
CURRENT LIABILITIES:		
14. Credit card balance $	1,300	
15. Unpaid bills due +	1,800	
16. Alimony and child support +	—	
LONG-TERM LIABILITIES:		
17. Home mortgage +	—	
18. Home equity loan +	—	
19. Car loan +	4,100	
20. Student loan +	3,600	
21. Other liabilities +	2,400	
22. Total Liabilities (add lines 14-21)	**= $13,200**	
Net Worth		
23. Total Assets (line 13)	$46,100	
24. Less: Total Debt (line 22) –	13,200	
25. Results: Net Worth	**= $32,900**	

Figure AIII.2
Worksheet for Calculating Net Worth

set measurable goals and completion times, or to set priorities for rationing your resources if, at some point, you're not able to pursue all of your goals.

Because step 3 (identifying a plan of action) and step 4 (implementing your plan) will affect your assets and liabilities, your balance sheet will change over time. As a result, step 5 (reevaluating and revising your plan) needs periodic updating.

Making Better Use of the Time Value of Money

As discussed in Chapter 16, the value of time with any investment stems from the principle of compound growth—the compounding of interest received over several time periods. With each additional time period, interest receipts accumulate and earn even more interest, thus, multiplying the earning capacity of the investment. Whenever you make everyday purchases, you're giving up interest that you could have earned with the same money if you'd invested it instead. From a financial standpoint, "idle" or uninvested money, which could be put to work earning more money, is a wasted resource.

Planning for the Golden Years

The sooner you start saving, the greater your financial power will be—you will have taken advantage of the time value of money for a longer period of time. Consider co-workers Ellen and Barbara, who are both planning to retire in 25 years, as can be seen in Figure AIII.4. Over that period, each can expect a 10-percent annual return on investment (the U.S. stock market has averaged more than 10 percent for the past 75 years). Their savings strategies, however, are different: Barbara begins saving immediately, while Ellen plans to start later but invest larger sums. Barbara will invest $2,000 annually for each of the next 5 years (years 1 through 5), for a total investment of $10,000. Ellen, meanwhile, wants to live a little larger by spending rather than saving for the next 10 years. Then, for years 11 through 20, she'll start saving $2,000 annually, for a total investment of $20,000. They will both allow annual returns to accumulate until they retire in year 25. Ellen expects to have a larger retirement

Name the Goal	Financial Requirement (amount) for This Goal	Time Frame for Accomplishing Goal	Importance (1= highest, 5 = lowest)
Immediate Goals:			
Live in a better apartment	_____	_____	_____
Establish an emergency cash fund	_____	_____	_____
Pay off credit card debt	_____	_____	_____
Other	_____	_____	_____
Intermediate Goals:			
Obtain adequate life, disability, liability, property insurance	_____	_____	_____
Save for wedding	_____	_____	_____
Save to buy new car	_____	_____	_____
Establish regular savings program (5% of gross income)	_____	_____	_____
Save for college for self	_____	_____	_____
Pay off major outstanding debt	_____	_____	_____
Make major purchase	_____	_____	_____
Save for home remodeling	_____	_____	_____
Save for down payment on a home	_____	_____	_____
Other	_____	_____	_____
Long-Term Goals:			
Pay off home mortgage	_____	_____	_____
Save for college for children	_____	_____	_____
Save for vacation home	_____	_____	_____
Increase personal net worth to $___ in ___ years.	_____	_____	_____
Achieve retirement nest egg of $ __ in ___ years.	_____	_____	_____
Accumulate fund for travel in retirement	_____	_____	_____
Save for long-term care needs	_____	_____	_____
Other	_____	_____	_____

Figure AIII.3
Worksheet for Setting Financial Goals

fund than Barbara because she has contributed twice as much, but she is in for a surprise. Barbara's retirement wealth will be much larger—$90,364 versus Ellen's $56,468—even though she invested only half as much. Barbara's advantage lies in the length of her savings program. Her money is invested longer—over a period of 21 to 25 years—with interest compounding over that range of time. Ellen's earnings are compounded over a shorter period—6 to 15 years. Granted, Ellen may have had more fun in years 1 to 10, but Barbara's retirement prospects look brighter.

Time Value as a Financial-Planning Tool

A good financial plan takes into account future needs, the sources of funds for meeting those needs, and the time needed to develop those funds. When you begin your financial plan, you can use various time-based tables to take into account the time value of money.[1] Figure AIII.5 shows how much a $1.00 investment will grow over different lengths of time and at different interest rates.

A timetable like this can determine the factor at which your money will multiply over a given period of

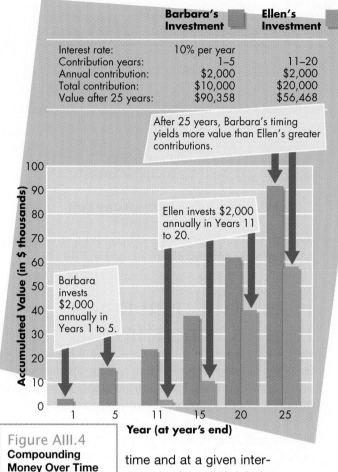

	Barbara's Investment	Ellen's Investment
Interest rate:	10% per year	
Contribution years:	1–5	11–20
Annual contribution:	$2,000	$2,000
Total contribution:	$10,000	$20,000
Value after 25 years:	$90,358	$56,468

After 25 years, Barbara's timing yields more value than Ellen's greater contributions.

Ellen invests $2,000 annually in Years 11 to 20.

Barbara invests $2,000 annually in Years 1 to 5.

Accumulated Value (in $ thousands)

Year (at year's end)

Figure AIII.4
Compounding Money Over Time

time and at a given interest rate. It can also help you determine how long and at what interest rate you will need to invest to meet your financial goals. For example, if you wanted to double your money in less than 10 years, you would have to find an interest rate of return of at least 8%. The catch is that to obtain a high interest rate, you will have to make riskier investments, such as buying stocks. Because higher interest rates carry greater risks, it is unwise to "put all your eggs in one basket." A sound financial plan will include more conservative investments, such as a bank savings account, to mitigate the risks of more speculative investments.

Conserving Money By Controlling It

A major pitfall in any financial plan is the temptation to spend too much, especially when credit is so easy to get. Because many credit-card issuers target college students and recent graduates with tempting offers appealing to the desire for financial independence, it is important that you arm yourself with a solid understanding of the financial costs entailed by credit cards. The same lessons apply equally to other loans—home mortgages, cars, and student financial aid.

Credit Cards: Keys to Satisfaction or Financial Handcuffs?

Although some credit cards don't charge annual fees, all of them charge interest on unpaid (outstanding) balances. Figure AIII.6 reprints part of a page from Bankrate.com's credit card calculator at **www.bankrate.com/brm/calc/MinPayment.asp**. Using the table as a guide, suppose you owe $5,000 for credit-card purchases, and your card company requires a minimum monthly payment (minimum payment due—or MPD) of five percent of the unpaid balance. The interest rate is 18 percent APR (annual percentage rate) on the outstanding balance.

If you only pay the monthly minimum, it will take you 115 months—over 9 1/2 years—to pay off your credit card debt. During this time you will pay $2,096.70 in interest, almost half again the principal balance! Repayment takes so long because you are

n	1%	2%	4%	6%	8%	10%
1	1.010	1.020	1.040	1.060	1.080	1.100
2	1.020	1.040	1.082	1.124	1.166	1.210
3	1.030	1.061	1.125	1.191	1.260	1.331
4	1.041	1.082	1.170	1.262	1.360	1.464
5	1.051	1.104	1.217	1.338	1.469	1.611
6	1.062	1.126	1.265	1.419	1.587	1.772
7	1.072	1.149	1.316	1.504	1.714	1.949
8	1.083	1.172	1.369	1.594	1.851	2.144
9	1.094	1.195	1.423	1.689	1.999	2.358
10	1.105	1.219	1.480	1.791	2.159	2.594
15	1.161	1.346	1.801	2.397	3.172	4.177
20	1.220	1.486	2.191	3.207	4.661	6.727
25	1.282	1.641	2.666	4.292	6.848	10.834
30	1.348	1.811	3.243	5.743	10.062	17.449

Note:
n = Number of time periods
% = Various interest rates

Figure AIII.5
Timetable for Growing $1.00

| Balance = $5,000 | MPD 3% | | MPD 5% | | MPD 10% | |
APR	Months	Costs	Months	Costs	Months	Costs
6%	144	$5,965.56	92	$5,544.58	50	$5,260.74
9%	158	$6,607.24	96	$5,864.56	51	$5,401.63
12%	175	$7,407.50	102	$6,224.26	53	$5,550.32
18%	226	$9,798.89	115	$7,096.70	55	$5,873.86
21%	266	$11,704.63	123	$7,632.92	57	$6,050.28

Note:
MPD = Minimum Payment Due
APR = Annual Percentage Rate

Figure AIII.6
Paying Off Credit Card Debt

Save Your Money: Lower Interest Rates and Faster Payments

Figure AIII.6 confirms two principles for saving money that you can apply when borrowing from any source, not just credit cards: look for lower interest rates and make faster repayments.

Seeking Lower Interest Rates Look again at Figure AIII.6 and compare the cost of borrowing $5,000 at 18 percent with the cost of borrowing it at 9 percent. If you assume the same 5-percent minimum monthly payment, a 9 percent APR will save you $1232.14 in interest during the repayment period—a nearly 59-percent savings.

Making Faster Payments Because money has a time value, lenders charge borrowers according to the length of time for which they borrow it. In general, longer lending periods increase the cost, while shorter periods are cheaper. Using Figure AIII.6, compare the costs of the 5 percent MPD with the faster 10 percent MPD. The faster schedule cuts the repayment period from 115 to 55 months and, at 18 percent APR, reduces interest costs by $1,222.84.

Combining both faster repayment and the lower interest rate cuts your total interest cost to $450.30—a savings of $1,695.07 over the amount you'd pay if you made slower repayments at the higher rate.

Declining Asset Value: A Borrower's Regret

Financially speaking, nothing's more disappointing than buying an expensive item only to discover that it's not worth what you paid. For example, if you buy a $5,000 used car with a credit card at 18 percent APR and make only the MPD, as in the example above, you'll end up spending a total of $7,407.50 over 9 1/2 years. By that time, however, the car you bought will be worth less than $1,000. Some of this loss in asset value can be avoided through realistic planning and spending—by knowing and staying within your financial means.

Financial Commitments of Home Ownership

Deciding whether to rent or buy a home involves a variety of considerations, including life stage, family needs, career, financial situation, and preferred lifestyle. If you decide to buy, you have to ask yourself what you can afford, and that requires asking yourself questions about your personal financial condition and your capacity for borrowing. Figure AIII.7 summarizes the key considerations in deciding whether to rent or buy.

How Much House Can You Afford?

Buying a home is the biggest investment most people ever make. Unfortunately, many make the mistake of buying a house that they can't afford. In addition, the typical demands of ownership—time and other resources for maintaining and improving a home—tend to cut into the money left over for recreation, eating out, taking vacations, and so on. You can reduce the financial pressure by calculating in advance a realistic price range—one that not only lets you buy a house but also lets you live a reasonably pleasant life once you're in it.

Most people need a loan to buy a house, apartment, or condominium. A **mortgage loan** is secured by the property—the home—being purchased. Because the size of a loan depends on the cost of the property, both borrowers and lenders want to know whether the buyer can afford the house he or she wants. To determine how much you can afford, one time-tested (though somewhat conservative) rule recommends keeping the price below 2 1/2 times

Renting	Buying
• No down payment to get started	• Must make payments for mortgage, property taxes, and insurance
• Flexibility to leave	• Equity builds up over time
• No obligation for upkeep or improvements	• More privacy
• No groundskeeping	• Value of property may increase
• Easy cash-flow planning (a single monthly payment)	• Lower income taxes: mortgage-interest and property tax payments reduce taxable income
• May provide access to recreation and social facilities	• Financial gains from selling house can be exempt from taxes
• Rental conditions may be changed by owner	• Greater control over use of property and improvements
• Timing for repairs controlled by owner	• The home can become a source of cash by refinancing with another mortgage loan or a home-equity loan

Figure AIII.7
To Buy or Not to Buy

your annual income. If your income is $48,000, look for a house priced below $120,000.

Any such calculation, however, will give you just a rough estimate of what you can afford. You should also consider how much money you have for a down payment and how much you can borrow. Lending institutions want to determine a buyer's borrowing capacity—the borrower's ability to meet the *recurring costs* of buying and owning.

PITI Every month, the homeowner must pay **p**rincipal (pay back some of the borrowed money), along with **i**nterest, **t**axes, and homeowner's **i**nsurance—PITI, for short. As Figure AIII.8 shows, the size of principal and interest payments depends on (1) the mortgage amount, (2) the length of the mortgage loan, and (3) the interest rate.

In evaluating loan applications, lenders use PITI calculations to estimate the buyer's ability to meet monthly payments. To determine how much someone is likely to lend you, calculate 28 percent of your gross monthly income (that is, before taxes and other deductions). If your PITI costs don't exceed that figure, your loan application probably will receive favorable consideration. With a monthly gross income of $4,000, for example, your PITI costs shouldn't exceed $1,120 (28 percent of $4,000). Additional calculations show a house price of $162,382 is the most this borrower can afford. Figure AIII.9

gives a sample calculation, and you should be able to make step-by-step computations by plugging your own numbers into the worksheet.

Other Debt In evaluating financial capacity, lenders also look at any additional outstanding debt, such as loans and credit-card bills. They will generally accept indebtedness (including PITI) up to 36 percent of gross income. Because PITI itself can be up to 28 percent, you might be allowed as little as 8 percent in other long-term debt. With your $4,000 monthly gross income, your total debt should be less than $1,440 ($1,120 for PITI and $320 for other debt). If your total debt exceeds $1,440, you may have to settle for a smaller loan than the one you calculated with the PITI method. Web sites such as **http://mortgages.interest.com** provide mortgage calculators for testing interest rates, lengths of loans, and other personal financial information.

Figure AIII.8
Monthly Payments on a $10,000 Loan

Interest Rate (%)	Length of Loan				
	3 Years	5 Years	10 Years	20 Years	30 Years
5.0	$299.71	$188.71	$106.07	$66.00	$53.68
6.0	304.22	193.33	111.02	71.64	59.96
6.5	306.49	195.66	113.55	74.56	63.21
7.0	308.77	198.01	116.11	77.53	66.53
8.0	313.36	202.76	121.33	83.65	73.38
9.0	318.00	207.58	126.68	89.98	80.47
10.0	322.67	212.47	132.16	96.51	87.76
11.0	327.39	217.42	137.76	103.22	95.24
12.0	332.14	222.44	143.48	110.11	102.86

Cashing Out From Tax Avoidance (Legally)

Personal expenditures always require cash outflows; some also reduce your tax bill and save you some cash. Individual retirement accounts (IRAs) and some education savings accounts have this effect. (Before you commit any money to these instruments or activities, check with an expert on tax regulations; they change from time to time.)

The IRA Tax Break

With a **traditional Individual Retirement Account (IRA)**, beginning in 2008 you can make an annual tax-deductible savings deposit of up to $5,000, depending on your income level. IRAs are long-term investments, intended to provide income after age 59 1/2. For distant future savings, an IRA boasts immediate cash advantages over a typical savings account because it reduces your current taxable income by the amount of your contribution.

Here's how it works: You're a qualified employee with a federal income tax rate of 20 percent in year 2008. If you contribute $4,000 to an IRA, you avoid $800 in income taxes (0.20 × $4,000 = $800). Your untaxed contributions and their accumulated earnings will be taxed later when you withdraw money from your IRA. The tax break is based on the assumption that, after you retire, you're likely to have less total income and will have to pay less tax on the money withdrawn as income from your IRA.

ASSUMPTIONS:

30-year mortgage
Closing costs (fees for property, survey, credit report, title search, title insurance, attorney, interest advance, loan origination) = $5,000
Funds available for closing costs and down payment = $25,000
Interest rate on mortgage = $6\frac{1}{2}$% per year
Estimated real estate taxes = $200 per month
Estimated homeowner's insurance = $20 month

Example Numbers / Your Numbers

1. Monthly income, gross (before taxes or deductions)........$4,000 _____
2. Apply PITI ratio (0.28 x amount on line 1) to determine
   borrower's payment capacity:
   0.28 x $4,000 = ...$1,120 _____
3. Determine mortgage payment (principal and interest)
   by subtracting taxes and insurance from
   PITI (line 2)...–$ 220 _____
4. **Result: Maximum mortgage payment (principal and interest)................................. $900** _____

5. Using Table Figure AIII.11, find the monthly mortgage payment
   on a $10,000 loan at $6\frac{1}{2}$% interest for
   30 years.. $63.21 _____
6. Since each $10,000 loan requires a $63.21 monthly payment,
   how many $10,000 loans can the borrower afford
   with the $900 payment capacity? The answer is
   determined as follows:
   $900.00/$63.21 =
   14.2382 loans of $10,000 each _____

7. **Result: Maximum allowable mortgage loan** [calculated
   as follows:
   14.2382 loans (from line 6 above)
   x $10,000 per loan] = ...**$142,382** _____

8. **Result: Maximum house price borrower can afford using PITI** (amount of house that can be bought with
   available funds):

   From loan..........................$142,382 _____
   From down payment............$ 25,000 _____
   Less clothing cost...............–$ 5,000 _____

   ....**$162,382** _____

IRA Risks If you underestimate your future cash requirements and have to withdraw money before you reach 59 1/2, you'll probably get hit with a 10 percent penalty. You can, however, make penalty-free withdrawals under certain circumstances: buying a first home, paying college expenses, and paying large medical bills.

The unpredictability of future income tax rates also poses a financial risk. If tax rates increase substantially, future IRA withdrawals may be taxed at higher rates, which may offset your original tax savings.

Roth IRA Versus Traditional IRA   The **Roth IRA** is the reverse of the traditional IRA in that contributions are not tax deductible, withdrawals on initial contribution are not penalized, and withdrawals on accumulated earnings after the age of 59 1/2 are not taxed.

Figure AIII.10 shows the significant advantage of this last feature. Accumulated earnings typically far outweigh the initial contribution, so although you pay an extra $1,285 in front-end taxes, you get $40,732 in additional cash at retirement—and even more if income-tax rates have increased.

IRAs and Education   Depending on your income level, you can contribute up to $2,000 annually to a Coverdell Education Savings Account (also known as an *Education IRA*) for each child under age 18. As with the Roth IRA, your initial contribution is not tax deductible, your earnings are tax-free, and you pay no tax on withdrawals to pay for qualified education expenses. However, the Education IRA requires that you use the money by the time your child reaches age 30. Funds that you withdraw but don't use for stipulated education expense are subject to taxation plus a 10 percent penalty.

Protecting Your Net Worth

With careful attention, thoughtful saving and spending, and skillful financial planning (and a little luck), you can build up your net worth over time. Every financial plan should also consider steps for preserving it. One approach involves the risk-return relationship discussed in Chapter 16. Do you prefer to protect your current assets, or are you willing to risk them in return for greater growth? At various life stages and levels of wealth, you should adjust your asset portfolio to conform to your risk and return preferences: conservative, moderate, or aggressive.

ROTH IRA provision allowing individual retirement savings with tax-free accumulated earnings

Why Buy Life Insurance?   You can think of life insurance as a tool for financial preservation. As explained in Appendix I, a life insurance policy is a promise to pay beneficiaries after the death of the insured party who paid the insurance company premiums during his or her lifetime.

What Does Life Insurance Do?   Upon the death of the policyholder, life insurance replaces income on which someone else is dependent. The amount of insurance you need depends on how many other people rely on your income. For example, while insurance makes sense for a married parent who is a family's sole source of income, a single college student with no financial dependents needs little or no insurance.

How Much Should I Buy?   The more insurance you buy, the more it's going to cost you. To estimate the amount of coverage you need, begin by adding up all of your annual expenses—rent, food, clothing, transportation, schooling, debts to be paid—that you pay for the dependents who'd survive you. Then multiply the total by the number of years that you want the insurance to cover

Figure AIII.10
Cash Flows: Roth IRA Versus Traditional IRA

Assumptions:
  Initial contribution and earnings average 10-percent growth annually.
  Initial contribution and earnings remain invested for 40 years.
  Income tax rate is 30 percent.

	Traditional IRA	Roth IRA
Initial cash contribution to IRA	$3,000	$3,000
Income tax paid initially: $4,285 income x 30% tax rate = $1,285 tax	0	1,285
Total initial cash outlay	**$3,000**	**$4,285**
Accumulated earnings (40 years)	$132,774	$132,774
Initial contribution	+ 3,000	+ 3,000
Total available for distribution after 40 years	= $135,774	= $135,774
Income tax at time of distribution	− $40,732	0
After-tax distribution (cash)	**= $95,042**	**= $135,774**

them. Typically, this sum will amount to several times—even 10 to 20 times—your current annual income.

Why Consider Term Insurance? *Term insurance* pays a predetermined benefit when death occurs during the stipulated policy term. If the insured outlives the term, the policy loses its value and simply ceases. Term-life premiums are significantly lower than premiums for whole-life insurance.

Unlike term life, *whole-life insurance*—also known as *cash-value insurance*—remains in force as long as premiums are paid. In addition to paying a death benefit, whole life accumulates cash value over time—a form of savings. Paid-in money can be withdrawn; however, whole-life savings earn less interest than most alternative forms of investment.

How Much Does It Cost? The cost of insurance depends on how much you buy, your life expectancy, and other statistical risk factors. To get the best match between your policy and your personal situation, you should evaluate the terms and conditions of a variety of policies. You can get convenient comparisons on Web sites such as **www.intelliquote.com**.

Notes, Sources, and Credits

REFERENCE NOTES

CHAPTER 1

[1] Energy Information Administration. "Short Term Energy Outlook," May 6, 2008, at **http://www.eia.doe.gov/steo**; "Why the World Is One Storm Away From Energy Crisis," *Wall Street Journal*, September 24, 2005, A1, A2; "Price of Oil Spurts to 42.90 a Barrel," *USA Today*, July 29, 2004, 1B; "Higher and Higher—Again: Gasoline Prices Set a Record," *USA Today*, May 25, 2004, 1B; Brad Foss, "Drivers Pay Price for Imported Gas," Associated Press Wire Story, May 22, 2004; Allan Sloan, "Why $2 Gas Isn't the Real Energy Problem," *Newsweek*, May 24, 2004, 40; "Who Wins and Loses When Gas Prices Skyrocket?" *Time*, May 8, 2006, 28.

[2] See Paul Heyne, Peter J. Boetke, and David L. Prychitko, *The Economic Way of Thinking*, 11th ed. (Upper Saddle River, NJ: Prentice Hall, 2005), 171–176.

[3] "100 Best Companies to Work For 2008," *Fortune*, February 4, 2008 (May 28, 2008), at **http://money.cnn.com/ magazines/fortune/bestcompanies/ 2008/snapshots/7.html**.

[4] See Karl E. Case and Ray C. Fair, *Principles of Economics*, 8th ed., updated (Upper Saddle River, NJ: Prentice Hall, 2007), 103–105.

[5] Adapted from Karl E. Case and Ray C. Fair, *Principles of Economics*, 8th ed., updated (Upper Saddle River, NJ: Prentice Hall, 2007).

[6] See Henry R. Cheeseman, *Business Law: Legal, E-Commerce, Ethical, and International Environments*, 7th ed. (Upper Saddle River, NJ: Prentice Hall, 2007), 920–923, 928–930.

[7] United States Department of Labor Bureau of Labor and Statistics. "National Employment Matrix," (May 2, 2008), at **http://www.bls.gov/oco/ocos285. htm#projections_data**.

[8] U.S. Department of Commerce Bureau of Economic Analysis, May 2008, **www. doc.gov**.

[9] Case and Fair, *Principles of Economics*, 432–433.

[10] The World Factbook: United States. (May 28, 2008), at **https://www.cia. gov/library/publications/the-world- factbook/print/us.html**.

[11] Ibid.

[12] Data obtained from U.S. Department of Commerce Bureau of Economic Analysis, **www.bea.gov/bea/dn/gdplev.xls**; U.S. Census Bureau, **www.census.gov/ popest/states/tables/NST-EST2005–01. xls**; **www.census.gov/popest/archives/ 1990s/**; National Economic Accounts, at **http://www.bea.gov/national/ nipaweb/TableView.asp#Mid**; From World Bank Development Indicators 2007–Feb 2008: International Comparison Program (May 29, 2008), at **http:// www.finfacts.com/biz10/ globalworldincomepercapita.htm**.

[13] See Olivier Blanchard, *Macroeconomics*, 4th ed. (Upper Saddle River, NJ: Prentice Hall, 2005), 24–26.

[14] Data obtained from Big Mac Index Review 2007 (May 29, 2008), at **http:// www.woopidoo.com/reviews/news/ big-mac-index.htm**.

[15] See Jay Heizer and Barry Render, Operations Management, 8th ed. (Upper Saddle River, NJ: Prentice Hall, 2006), 14.

[16] Data obtained from U.S. Census Bureau (June 19, 2008), at **www. census.gov/foreign-trade/balance/ c0004.html#2005**.

[17] This section is based on Paul Heyne, Peter J. Boetke, and David L. Prychitko, *The Economic Way of Thinking*, 11th ed. (Upper Saddle River, NJ: Prentice Hall, 2005), 491–493.

[18] This section follows Ronald M. Ayers and Robert A. Collinge, *Economics: Explore and Apply*, (Upper Saddle River, NJ: Prentice Hall, 2004), 163–167.

[19] See Heyne, Boetke, and Prychitko, *The Economic Way of Thinking*, 403–409, 503–504.

[20] See "The New Fed," *Business Week*, November 7, 2005, pp. 30–34.

CHAPTER 2

[1] "Oil company BP pleads guilty to environmental crime," *International Herald Tribune* (November 29, 2007), at **http://www.iht.com/articles/ap/2007/ 11/30/business/NA-FIN-US-BP- Settlement-Alaska.php?page=1**; Michael Hawthorne, "BP gets break on dumping in lake," *Chicago Tribune* (July 15, 2007), at **http://www.chicagotribune.com/ news/nationworld/chi-pollute_ 15jul15,1,386727**; Terry Macalister "Greenpeace calls BP's oil sands plan an environmental crime," *guardian.co.uk* (December 7, 2007), at **http://www. guardian.co.uk/business/2007/dec/07/ bp**; Sharon Epperson, "BP's Fundamental But Obscured Energy Contradiction," cnbc.com (May 21, 2008), at **http://www. cnbc.com/id/24758394**; Brad Hem, "10 plaintiffs in BP case will seek $950 million," *Houston Chronicle* (May 23, 2008), at **http://www.chron.com/disp/ story.mpl/headline/biz/5797579.html**.

[2] William G. Symonds, Geri Smith, "The Tax Games Tyco Played," *Business Week* (July 1, 2002), 40–41.

[3] "Tyco Votes to Stay Offshore," *BBC News* (March 6, 2003), at **http://news.bbc.co. uk/2/hi/business/2827683.stm**.

[4] Seib, Christine. "Volkswagen union boss Klaus Volkert jailed for two years," *Times Online* (February 22, 2008), at **http:/ /business.timesonline.co.uk/tol/ business/industry_sectors/ engineering/article3417994.ece**.

[5] This section follows the logic of Gerald F. Cavanaugh, *American Business Values: A Global Perspective*, 5th ed. (Upper Saddle River, NJ: Prentice Hall, 2006), Chapter 3.

[6] Manuel G. Velasquez, Business Ethics: Concepts and Cases, 6th ed. (Upper Saddle River, NJ: Prentice Hall, 2006), Chapter 2. See also John R. Boatright, *Ethics and the Conduct of Business*, 4th ed. (Upper Saddle River, NJ: Prentice Hall, 2003), 34–35, 57–59.

[7] Based on Gerald S. Cavanaugh, *American Business Values: With International Perspectives*, 4th ed. (Upper Saddle River, NJ: Prentice Hall, 1998) 71, 84.

[8] Jeffrey S. Harrison, R. Edward Freeman, "Stakeholders, Social Responsibility, and Performance: Empirical Evidence and Theoretical Perspectives," *Academy of Management Journal*, 1999, vol. 42, no. 5, 479–485. See also David P. Baron, *Business and Its Environment*, 5th ed. (Upper Saddle River, NJ: Prentice Hall, 2006), Chapter 18.

[9] http://bwnt.businessweek.com/interactive_reports/customer_satisfaction/index.asp, Accessed May 30, 2008.

[10] http://target.com/target_group/community_giving/index.jhtml, Accessed January 15, 2006.

[11] Starbucks About Us, at http://www.starbucks.com/aboutus/origins.asp, Accessed May 30, 2008; "Starbucks to Open Regional Farmer Support Center in Rwanda," (December 1, 2007), at http://www.csrwire.com/News/10275.html.

[12] Gerald Seib, "What Could Bring 1930s-Style Reform of U.S. Business?" *Wall Street Journal* (July 24, 2002), A1, A8.

[13] William G. Symonds, Geri Smith, "The Tax Games Tyco Played," *Business Week*, July 1, 2002, 40–41; "Tyco Titan Charged with Tax Violations," *CBSNews.com* (June 4, 2002), at www.cbsnew.com/stories/2002/06/04/national/main511051.shtm; Nicholas Varchaver, "CEOs Under Fire," *Fortune.com* (December 6, 2002), at www.fortune.com/fortune/ceo/articles/0,15114,442883,00.html; "Kozlowski Gets up to 25 Years," *money.cnn.com* (September 19, 2005).

[14] Based on Andrew C. Revkin, "Who Cares About a Few Degrees?" *New York Times*, December 12, 1997, F1.

[15] http://money.cnn.com/galleries/2007/fortune/0703/gallery.green_giants.fortune/index.html, Accessed May 30, 2008.

[16] Louise Story, "F.T.C. Asks if Carbon-Offset Money Is Well Spent," *New York Times* (January 8, 2008), at http://www.nytimes.com/2008/01/09/business/09offsets.html?_r=2&ei=5088&en=05dc8be5247f9737&ex=1357707600&oref=slogin&partner=rssnyt&emc=rss&pagewanted=print.

[17] Bob Sullivan, "FTC fines Xanga for violating kids' privacy," (September 7, 2006), at http://www.msnbc.msn.com/id/14718350.

[18] http://money.cnn.com/galleries/2007/fortune/0703/gallery.green_giants.fortune/7.html, Accessed

May 30, 2008; http://www.scjohnson.com/environment/growing_1.asp, Accessed May 30, 2008.

[19] http://www.nytimes.com/2008/01/09/business/09offsets.html?_r=1&ex=1357707600&en=05dc8be5247f9737&ei=5088&partner=rssnyt&emc=rss&oref=slogin, Accessed May 30, 2008.

[20] http://www.starbucks.com/csrnewsletter/winter06/csrEnvironment.asp, Accessed May 30, 2008.

[21] Alex Berenson, "Merck Agrees to Pay $4.85 Billion in Vioxx Claims," *New York Times,* (November 9, 2007), at http://www.nytimes.com/2007/11/09/business/09cnd-merck.html?ref=business; Rita Rubin, "How did Vioxx debacle happen?" *USA Today,* (October 12, 2004), at http://www.usatoday.com/news/health/2004-10-12-vioxx-cover_x.htm.

[22] "British Airways and Korean Air Lines Fined in Fuel Collusion," *New York Times* (August 2, 2007), at http://www.nytimes.com/2007/08/02/business/worldbusiness/02air.html?scp=2&sq=british+airways+price+fixing&st=nyt.

[23] Jerald Greenberg and Robert A. Baron, *Behavior in Organizations: Understanding and Managing the Human Side of Work*, 8th ed. (Upper Saddle River, NJ: Prentice Hall, 2003), 410–413.

[24] Greg Farrell, "Enron Law Firm Called Accounting Practices Creative," *USA Today*, January 2002, 1B.

[25] Cora Daniels, "It's a Living Hell," *Fortune* (April 15, 2002), 367–368.

[26] Henry R. Cheeseman, *Business Law: Legal, E Commerce, Ethical, and International Environments*, 5th ed. (Upper Saddle River, NJ: Prentice Hall, 2004), 128–129.

[27] http://www.usdoj.gov/usao/iln/pr/chicago/2008/pr0318_01.pdf, Accessed May 30, 2008; Jacob Goldstein, "CVS to Pay $37.5 Million to Settle Pill Switching Case," Wall Street Journal (March 18, 2008), at http://blogs.wsj.com/health/2008/03/18/cvs-to-pay-375-million-to-settle-pill-switching-case.

[28] http://foundationcenter.org/gainknowledge/research/pdf/keyfacts_corp_2007.pdf, Accessed May 30, 2008.

[29] Michael E. Porter and Mark R. Kramer, "Philanthropy's New Agenda: Doing Well

by Doing Good," *Sloan Management Review* (Winter 2000), 75–85.

CHAPTER 3

[1] Fred Vogelstein, "How Mark Zuckerberg Turned Facebook Into the Web's Hottest Platform," *Wired* (September 6, 2007), at http://www.wired.com/techbiz/startups/news/2007/09/ff_facebook?currentPage=3; Ellen McGirt, "Hacker. Dropout. CEO," *Fast Company* (May 2007), at http://www.fastcompany.com/magazine/115/open_features-hacker-dropout-ceo.html.

[2] See http://www.sba.gov/aboutsba.

[3] See http://www.sba.gov.

[4] Data from http://www.sba.gov, Accessed 3/6/2006, and U.S. Census Bureau, "Statistics About Business Size (including Small Business) from the U.S. Census Bureau," at http://www.census.gov/epcd/www/smallbus.html, Accessed 4/25/2007.

[5] U.S. Census Bureau, "Statistical Abstract of the United States," at http://www.census.gov/prod/www/statistical-abstract.html.

[6] "A New Generation Re-Writes the Rules," *Wall Street Journal* (May 22, 2002), R4; See also Mark Henricks, "Up to the Challenge," Entrepreneur (February 2006), 64–67.

[7] "Special Report—Stars of Asia," *BusinessWeek* (July 12, 2004), at http://www.businessweek.com/magazine/content/04_28/b3891412.htm?chan=search.

[8] "Special Report—Stars of Asia," *BusinessWeek* (July 12, 2004), at http://www.businessweek.com/magazine/content/04_28/b3891413.htm?chan=search.

[9] See Thomas Zimmerer and Norman Scarborough, *Essentials of Entrepreneurship and Small Business Management*, 5th ed. (Upper Saddle River, NJ: Prentice Hall, 2008).

[10] Ibid.

[11] "2008 Franchise 500 Rankings," Entrepreneur.com, http://www.entrepreneur.com/franchises/rankings/franchise500-115608/2008,.html, Accessed 6/3/2008.

[12] Kurt Badenhausen, Michael K. Ozanian, and Christina Settimi, "The Business of Football," Forbes.com (September 13, 2007), at http://www.forbes.com/home/business/2007/09/13/nfl-team-valuations-biz-07nfl_cz_kb_mo_cs_0913nfl_land.html.

13 U.S. Small Business Administration, "Finance Primer: A Guide to SBA's Loan Guaranty Programs," **http://app1.sba. gov/training/sbafp/**, Accessed 6/9/2008.

14 Ibid.

15 Zimmerer and Scarborough, 16.

16 Jim Hopkins, "The New Entrepreneurs: Americans Over 50," *USA Today* (January 18, 2005), 1A, 2A.

17 U.S. Census Bureau, "1997 Economic Census Surveys of Minority- and Women-Owned Business Enterprises," at **http:// www.census.gov/csd/mwb**.

18 Peter Hoy, "Minority- and Women-Owned Businesses Skyrocket," *Inc.* (May 1, 2006), at **http://www.inc.com/ news/articles/200605/census.html**.

19 Zimmerer and Scarborough, 20.

20 Ibid.

21 See U.S. Small Business Administration, "Frequently Asked Questions," at **http://app1.sba.gov/faqs/faqIndexAll. cfm?areaid=24**, Accessed 7/9/2008.

22 John Tozzi, "From Junkie to Software Success," *BusinessWeek* (May 12, 2008), at **http://www.businessweek.com/smallb iz/content/may2008/sb20080512_1338 43.htm?chan=search**.

23 Zimmerer and Scarborough.

24 See "Gladys Edmunds Biography," at **http://biography.jrank.org/pages/ 2404/Edmunds-Gladys.html**, Accessed 6/6/2008.

25 See Chris Penttila, "Keep it Simple," *Entrepreneur* (February 2006), 60–63.

26 Zimmerer and Scarborough, 161.

27 Ibid.

28 Emily Thornton, "A Little Privacy, Please," *BusinessWeek* (May 24, 2004), 74–75.

29 "Morgan Stanley Announces Record and Distribution Dates for Spin-off of Discover," Morgan Stanley Press Release (June 1, 2007), at **http://www. morganstanley.com/about/press/ articles/4984.html**.

CHAPTER 4

1 All box office data taken from **www. imdb.com**, Accessed May 14, 2008; Media By Numbers, "Full-Year Box-office & Attendance Since 1990" at **http://www. mediabynumbers.com/userfiles/file/ MEDIA%20BY%20NUMBERS% 20HISTORICAL%20AND%20YTD% 20BOX-OFFICE%20-%202008(10).pdf**, Accessed May 14, 2008; Box Office Mojo,

"2007 Worldwide Grosses" at **http://www. boxofficemojo.com/yearly/chart/? view2=worldwide&yr=2007&p=.htm**, Accessed May 14, 2008; Brooks Barnes, "Moviegoers in Seoul Will Love This Film," *The New York Times*, (January 27, 2008), at **http://www.nytimes.com/2008/01/27/ business/27steal.html?_r=1& pagewanted=print&oref=slogin**; Dave McNary, "Foreign box office hits record levels," *Variety* (January 1, 2008), at **http://www.variety.com/article/ VR1117978262.html?categoryid=1236& cs=1&query=%22resident+evil%22**; Ian Mohr, "Box office, admissions rise in 2006," *Variety* (March 6, 2007), at **http://www. variety.com/article/VR1117960597. html?categoryid=13&cs=1**; Edward Jay Epstein, "Send in the aliens," *Slate.com* (August 29, 2005), at **http://www.slate. com/id/2125153/**.

2 Ricky W. Griffin and Michael W. Pustay, International Business: A Managerial Perspective, 6th ed. (Upper Saddle River, NJ: Prentice Hall, 2009); The World Bank: Data & Statistics, at **http://web.worldbank.org/ WBSITE/EXTERNAL/DATASTATISTICS/ 0,,contentMDK:20420458~isCURL:Y~ menuPK:1277382~pagePK:64133150~ piPK:64133175~theSitePK:239419,00. html**, Accessed May 14, 2008.

3 Thomas Friedman, *The World Is Flat* (New York: Farrar, Straus, and Giroux, 2005).

4 Brian Love, "Weak dollar costs U.S. Economy its No. 1 Spot," (March 14, 2008), at **http://www.reuters.com/article/ idUSL1491971920080314**; International Monetary Fund (April 2008), at **http:// www.imf.org/external/pubs/ft/weo/ 2008/01/weodata/weorept.aspx?sy= 2006&ey=2013&scsm=1&ssd=1&sort= country&ds=.&br=1&c=924%2C158% 2C111&s=NGDP_R%2CNGDP_RPCH% 2CNGDP%2CNGDPD%2CPPPGDP&grp= 0&a=&pr.x=51&pr.y=14**.

5 Europe, at **http://europa.eu/abc/maps/ index_en.htm**, Accessed June 4, 2008.

6 World Trade Organization, at **http:// www.wto.org/English/thewto_e/ whatis_e/tif_e/org6_e.htm**, Accessed June 4, 2008.

7 Association of Southeast Asian Nations, at **http://www.aseansec.org/74.htm**, Accessed June 4, 2008.

8 U.S. Census Bureau: Foreign Trade Statistics, at **http://www.census.gov/ foreign-trade/statistics/highlights/top/ top0712.html**, Accessed May 14, 2008.

9 U.S. Census Bureau: Foreign Trade Statistics, at **http://www.census.gov/ foreign-trade/statistics/highlights/ annual.html**, Accessed May 14, 2008.

10 Ibid.

11 Griffin and Pustay, *International Business: A Managerial Perspective*, 125–127. See also Steven Husted and Michael Melvin, *International Economics*, 5th ed. (Boston: Addison Wesley Longman, 2001), 54–61; and Karl E. Case and Ray C. Fair, *Principles of Economics*, 8th ed. (Upper Saddle River, NJ: Prentice Hall, 2007), 700–708.

12 Ron Lieber, "Give Us This Day Our Global Bread," *Fast Company*, March 2001, 164–167; Poilâne: Our History, at **http://www.poilane.fr/pages/en/ company_univers_histoire.php**, Accessed May 14, 2008; "Les Boulangeries-Pâtisseries de Paris: Poilâne," (June 14, 2006), at **http://louisrecettes. blogspot.com/2006/06/les-boulangeries-ptisseries-de-paris.html**.

13 This section is based on Michael Porter, *The Competitive Advantage of Nations* (Boston: Addison Wesley Longman, 2001), 54–61; and Case and Fair, *Principles of Economics*, 669–677.

14 Lee J. Krajewski, Manoj Malhotra, and Larry P. Ritzman, *Operations Management: Processes and Value Chains*, 8th ed. (Upper Saddle River, NJ: Prentice Hall, 2007), 401–403.

15 *Hoover's Handbook of American Business 2006* (Austin, Texas: Hoover's Business Press, 2006), 432–433; Hershey Foods (HSY), at **http://www.wikinvest.com/stock/Hers hey_Foods_(HSY)**, Accessed May 14, 2008; The Hershey Company, at **http:/ /library.corporate-ir.net/library/11/ 115/115590/items/283950/10K_ Hershey%5b1%5d.pdf**, Accessed May 14, 2008.

16 Christopher Tkaczyk and David Goldman, "Fortune 500 - Big Business Battles It Out," *Fortune* (April 21, 2008), at **http://finance.yahoo.com/career-work/article/104864/Fortune-500-Big-Business-Battles-It-Out**.

17 "Fortune Global 500," *Fortune* (July 23, 2007), at **http://money.cnn.com/ magazines/fortune/global500/2007/ full_list/index.html**.

18 Cold Stone Creamery, at **http://www. coldstonecreamery.com/franchises/ international.html**, Accessed June 4, 2008.

[19] Louisa Schaefer, "World's Biggest Retailer Wal-Mart Closes Up Shop in Germany," *DW-World.de* (July 28, 2006), at **http://www.goethe-bytes.de/dw/ article/0,2144,21b12746,00.html**.

CHAPTER 5

[1] "The Business Week Top 50," *Business Week* (April 4, 2005), 92; "Best Managed Companies in America," *Forbes* (January 10, 2005), 150; Robert Berner, "Coach's Driver Picks Up the Pace," *Business Week* (March 29, 2004), 98–100; Julia Boorstin, "How Coach Got Hot," *Fortune* (October 28, 2003), 131–134; Marilyn Much, "Consumer Research Is His Bag," *Investor's Business Daily* (December 16, 2003); "S&P Stock Picks and Pans: Accumulate Coach," *Business Week* (October 22, 2003); Adrian Slywotzky, "The Upside of Strategic Risk," *Oliver Wyman Journal*, Fall 2007 (May 19, 2008), at **http://www.oliverwyman.com/ow/ pdf_files/OWJ23.pdf**.

[2] *Hoover's Handbook of American Business 2006* (Austin, Texas: Hoover's Business Press, 2006); "HP Reaches $100 Billion Revenue Mark for the Fiscal 2007," CBR Online (November 21, 2007), at **http://www.cbronline.com/article_ news.asp?guid=C4927745-C588-4832- B8A1-92C3B77DDFE0**.

[3] Jason Riley, "Movie Man," *Wall Streeet Journal Online* (February 9, 2008), at **http://online.wsj.com/article/ SB120251714532955425.html?mod= googlenews_wsj**.

[4] Richard D. Knabb, Jamie R. Rhome, and Daniel P. Brown, "Tropical Cyclone Report: Hurricane Katrina," National Hurricane Center (December 20, 2005), at **http://www.nhc.noaa.gov/pdf/ TCR-AL122005_Katrina.pdf**.

[5] "Sam Adams Beer to Expand Cincinnati Brewery," *USA Today* (January 6, 2005); Christopher Edmunds, "Bottom of the Barrel: Boston Beer's Winning Formula," RealMoney.com (March 5, 2003), **http:// www.thestreet.com/realmoney**; Gary Hamel, "Driving Grassroots Growth," *Fortune* (September 4, 2002), 173–187; Ronald Lieber, "Beating the Odds," *Fortune* (March 31, 2002), 82–90; The Boston Beer Company, Inc.: Investor Relations Center, "The Boston Beer Company Announces Agreement With Diageo to Acquire Pennsylvania Brewery," at **http://www.bostonbeer.com/**

phoenix.zhtml?c=69432&p=irol- newsArticle&ID=1035844&highlight, Accessed 6/18/2008; Income Statement for Boston Beer Co. Inc., Yahoo! Finance, at **http://finance.yahoo.com/q/is?s= SAM&annual**, Accessed 5/19/2008; Boston Beer Company - Company Profile, Information, Business Description, History, Background Information on Boston Beer Company, at **http://www. referenceforbusiness.com/history2/ 74/Boston-Beer-Company.html**, Accessed 5/19/2008.

[6] See Chipotle, "F.W.I," at **http://www. chipotle.com/#flash/fwi_story**; Income Statement for Chipotle Mexican Grill, Inc., Yahoo! Finance, at **http://finance.yahoo. com/q/is?s=CMG&annual**, Accessed 5/19/2008.

[7] Based on Stephen P. Robbins and Mary Coulter, *Management*, 9th ed. (Upper Saddle River, NJ: Prentice Hall, 2007), 199.

[8] See Blue Bell Creamery, "Our History," at **http://www.bluebell.com/The_ Little_Creamery/history.aspx**, Accessed 5/19/2008.

[9] Del Jones, "Next Time," *USA Today* (October 4, 2005), 1B, 2B.

CHAPTER 6

[1] Betsy Morris, "The Pepsi challenge," *Fortune*, February 19, 2008 (June 19, 2008), at **http://money.cnn.com/2008/ 02/18/news/companies/morris_nooyi. fortune/index.htm**; Flex News, "PepsiCo Unveils New Organizational Structure, Names CEOs of Three Principal Operating Units," May 11, 2007 (June 19, 2008), at **http://www.flex-news-food.com/ pages/12058/pepsi/pepsico-unveils- new-organizational-structure-names- ceos-three-principal-operating-units. html**; Diane Brady, "Indra Nooyi: Keeping Cool In Hot Water," *Business Week*, June 11, 2007 (June 19, 2008), at **http:// www.businessweek.com/magazine/ content/07_24/b4038067.htm**.

[2] Joann S. Lublin, "Place vs. Product: It's Tough to Choose a Management Model," *Wall Street Journal*, June 27, 2001, A1, A4; Joann Muller, "Ford: Why It's Worse Than You Think," *Business Week*, June 25, 2001, at **http://www.businessweek.com/ magazine/content/01_26/b3738001. htm**; "Can This Man Save the American Auto Industry?" *Time*, January 30, 2006, pp. 38–48.

[3] Amy Wrzesniewski and Jane Dutton, "Crafting a Job: Revisioning Employees as Active Crafters of Their Work," *Academy of Management Review*, 2001, 26 (2): 179–201.

[4] AllBusiness.com, "Kraft Foods North America Announces New Management Structure," September28, 2000 (June 19, 2008), at **http://www.allbusiness.com/ food-beverage/food-beverage-overview/ 6505848-1.html**.

[5] See Levi Strauss & Co., at **http://www. levistrauss.com/Company/ WorldwideRegions.aspx**.

[6] See Southern Company, **http:// investor.southerncompany.com/ governance.cfm**.

[7] Michael E. Raynor and Joseph L. Bower, "Lead From the Center," *Harvard Business Review*, May 2001, 93–102.

[8] Gary Hamel, "What Google, Whole Foods do best," *Fortune*, September 27, 2007 (June 19, 2008), at **http://money.cnn. com/2007/09/26/news/companies/ management_hamel.fortune/index.htm**.

[9] See **http://www.ea.com/**.

[10] *Hoover's Handbook of American Business 2006* (Austin, Texas: Hoover's Business Press, 2006); Brian Dumaine, "How I Delivered the Goods," *Fortune Small Business*, October 2002 (*quote); Charles Haddad, "FedEx: Gaining on the Ground," *Business Week*, December 16, 2002, 126–128; Claudia H. Deutsch, "FedEx Has Hit the Ground Running, but Will Its Legs Tire?" *New York Times*, October 13, 2002, BU7; **www.Forbes.com/finance** (February 16, 2006); PBS.org, "Who Made America" (June 19, 2008), at **http://www. pbs.org/wgbh/theymadeamerica/ whomade/fsmith_hi.html**.

[11] John Simons, "Prognosis looks good for J&J," *Fortune*, November 16, 2007 (June 19, 2008), at **http://money.cnn. com/2007/11/16/news/companies/ simons_JnJ.fortune/index.htm**; Johnson & Johnson, "Company Structure" (June 19, 2008), at **http://www.jnj.com/ connect/about-jnj/company-structure/**.

[12] "Wal-Mart Acquires Interspar," Management Ventures (July 20, 2001), at **http://www.mvi-insights.com/Index. aspx**; Kerry Capell et al., "Wal-Mart's Not- So-Secret British Weapon," *Business Week Online* (July 20, 2001), at **http://www. businessweek.com/2000/00_04/ b3665095.htm**; Brent Schlender,

"Wal-Mart's $288 Billion Meeting," *Fortune*, April 18, 2005, 90–106; see **http://walmartstores.com**.

[13] Thomas A. Stewart, "See Jack. See Jack Run," *Fortune*, September 27, 1999, 124–271; Jerry Useem, "America's Most Admired Companies," *Fortune*, March 7, 2005, 67–82; See GE.com, "Executive Leaders," at **http://www.ge.com/company/leadership/executives.html**.

[14] Leslie P. Willcocks and Robert Plant, "Getting from Bricks to Clicks," *Sloan Management Review*, Spring 2001, 50–60.

[15] "The Office Chart That Really Counts," *Business Week*, February 27, 2006, 48–49.

[16] Carol Loomis, "How the HP Board KO'd Carly," *Fortune*, March 7, 2005, 99–102.

[17] Lockheed Martin, "Skunk Works" (June 19, 2008), at **http://www.lockheedmartin.com/aeronautics/skunkworks/index.html**.

CHAPTER 7

[1] Bob Cox, "FAA knew of MD-80 wiring problem in 2003," *Airport Business* (April 14, 2008), at **http://www.airportbusiness.com/web/online/Top-News-Headlines/FAA-knew-of-MD-80-wiring-problem-in-2003/1$18873**; MSNBC News Services, "American Airlines grounds fleet of MD-80s," (March 26, 2008), at **http://www.msnbc.msn.com/id/23808772/**; MSNBC News Services, "American's MD-80s cleared to fly again," (April 14, 2008), at **http://www.msnbc.msn.com/id/24029455/**; Brent D. Bowen and Dean E. Headley, "2008 Airline Quality Rating," (April 2008), at **http://aqr.aero/aqrreports/2008aqr.pdf**; "Survey: Airline Complaints Sky High," *CBS News* (April 7, 2008), at **http://www.cbsnews.com/stories/2008/04/07/business/main3996989.shtml**.

[2] Invest and Deliver Every Day: GE Annual Report: 2007 (Fairfield, CT: General Electric Co., 2008).

[3] Terry Hill, *Manufacturing Strategy*, 3rd edition (Boston: Irwin McGraw-Hill, 2000), Chapters 2–4; James A. Fitzsimmons, Mona J. Fitzsimmons, *Service Management: Operations Strategy, Information Technology*, 6th edition (Boston: Irwin McGraw-Hill, 2008), 46–48.

[4] Photo-Kicks.com, at **http://photo-kicks.com/**, Accessed June 5, 2008; Inc.com 5000, at **http://www.inc.com/inc5000/2007/company-profile.html?id=200705920**, Accessed June 8, 2008.

[5] Gail Edmondson, Willam Boston, Andrea Zammert, "Detroit East," *BusinessWeek* (July 25, 2005), at **http://www.businessweek.com/print/magazine/content/05_30/b3944003.htm?chan=gl/**.

[6] "ASQ Glossary of Terms," American Society for Quality, **http://www.asq.org/glossary/q.html**, Accessed April 5, 2008.

[7] "Savoring Fine Chocolates," at **http://www.godiva.com/godivacollection/guideToGodiva.aspx**, Accessed April 5, 2008.

[8] Autropolis.com, at **http://www.autotropolis.com/wiki/index.php?title=Top_10_Best_Selling_Cars_for_2007**, Accessed June 6, 2008.

[9] Complaints.com (December 4, 2007), at **http://www.complaints.com/2007/december/4/Home_Depot_accuses_me_of_theft_155783.htm**; Consumer Affairs.com, at **http://www.consumeraffairs.com/homeowners/ge_service_contracts.htm**, Accessed June 6, 2008.

CHAPTER 8

[1] "Death by overwork in Japan," *The Economist*, December 19, 2007, (June 4, 2008), at **www.economist.com/world/asia/displaystory.cfm?story_id=10329261**.

[2] Smith, Tom W. "Job Satisfaction in the United States," April 17, 2007, (June 4, 2008), at **www.norc.org/NR/rdonlyres/2874B40B-7C50-4F67-A6B2-26BD3B06EA04/0/JobSatisfactionintheUnitedStates.pdf**.

[3] Mark Bolino and William Turnley, "Going the Extra Mile: Cultivating and Managing Employee Citizenship Behavior," *Academy of Management Executive*, 2003, vol. 17, no. 3, 60–70.

[4] See Carl Thoresen, Jill Bradley, Paul Bliese, and Joseph Thoresen, "The Big Five Personality Traits and Individual Job Performance," *Journal of Applied Psychology*, 2004, vol. 89, no. 5, 835–853.

[5] See Daniel Goleman, *Emotional Intelligence: Why It Can Matter More Than IQ* (New York: Bantam Books, 1995); see also Kenneth Law, Chi-Sum Wong, and Lynda Song, "The Construct and Criterion Validity of Emotional Intelligence and Its Potential Utility for Management Studies," *Journal of Applied Psychology*, 2004, vol 89, no. 3, 483–596.

[6] Daniel Goleman, "Leadership That Gets Results," *Harvard Business Review*, March–April 2000, 78–90.

[7] See Ricky W. Griffin and Gregory Moorhead, *Organizational Behavior*, 8th ed. (Boston: Houghton Mifflin Company), 2007.

[8] See Daniel Wren, *The History of Management Thought*, 5th ed. (New York: John Wiley & Sons), 2004.

[9] Ibid.

[10] Burke, Doris, Corey Hajim, John Elliott, Jenny Mero, and Christopher Tkaczyk. "The Top Ten Companies for Leaders," *Fortune*, October 1, 2007, (June 4, 2008), at **money.cnn.com/galleries/2007/fortune/0709/gallery.leaders_global_topten.fortune/index.html**.

[11] See Gallo, Carmine. "How Ritz-Carlton Maitains its Mystique," *BusinessWeek*, February 13, 2007, (June 4, 2008), at **www.businessweek.com/smallbiz/content/feb2007/sb20070213_171606.htm**; Gallo, Carmine. "Employee Motivation the Ritz-Carlton Way," BusinessWeek, February 29, 2008, (June 4, 2008), at **www.businessweek.com/smallbiz/content/feb2008/sb20080229_347490.htm?chan=search**.

[12] A. H. Maslow, *Motivation and Personality*, 2nd ed. (Upper Saddle River, NJ: Prentice Hall, 1970). Reprinted by permission of Prentice Hall Inc.

[13] Lyman Porter, Gregory Bigley, and Richard Steers, Motivation and Work Behavior, 7th ed. (New York: McGraw-Hill), 2003.

[14] Grant, Robert M. "AES Corporation: Rewriting the Rules of Management," Cotemporary Strategy Analysis (Hoboken: Wiley, John & Sons, 2007), (June 4, 2008), at **www.blackwellpublishing.com/grant/docs/17AES.pdf**.

[15] Gary P. Latham, "The Importance of Understanding and Changing Employee Outcome Expectancies for Gaining Commitment to an Organizational Goal," *Personnel Psychology*, 2001, vol. 54, 707–720.

[16] Russ Forrester, "Empowerment: Rejuvenating a Potent Idea," *Academy of Management Executive*, 2002, vol. 14, no. 1, 67–78.

[17] Ricky W. Griffin and Gary C. McMahan, "Motivation Through Job Design," in Jerald Greenberg (ed.), *Organizational Behavior: State of the Science* (New York: Lawrence Erlbaum and Associates, 1994), 23–44.

[18] Stephanie Armour, "Working 9-to-5 No Longer," *USA Today*, December 6, 2004, 1B, 2B.

[19] Foss, Brad. "Telecommuters tout perks of lifestyle," *Boston Globe*, March 14, 2006, (June 4, 2008), at **www.boston.com/ business/personalfinance/articles/ 2006/03/14/telecommuters_tout_ perks_of_lifestyle/?page=2**.

CHAPTER 9

[1] eBay Media Center (May 27, 2008), at **http://news.ebay.com/team.cfm**; "Meg Whitman to Step Down as President and CEO of eBay," January 23, 2008 (May 27, 2008), at **http://news.ebay.com/ releasedetail.cfm?ReleaseID=289314**; Jon Swartz, "EBay bids for durability in changing digital world," *USA Today*, March 31, 2008 (May 27, 2008), at **http:// www.usatoday.com/tech/techinvestor/ corporatenews/2008-03-30-ebay- donahoe_N.htm**; Brad Stone, "EBay's New Leader Moves Swiftly on a Revamping," *The New York Times*, January 24, 2008 (May 27, 2008), at **http://www.nytimes. com/2008/01/24/technology/24ebay. html?_r=2&ref=technology&oref= slogin&oref=slogin**; Brad Stone, "Stirring Up the Cubicles at eBay," *The New York Times*, February 21, 2007 (May 27, 2008), at **http://www.nytimes.com/2007/ 02/21/technology/21ebay.html? pagewanted=print**.

[2] See John Kotter, "What Leaders Really Do," *Harvard Business Review*, December 2001, 85–94.

[3] Reprinted by permission of The Free Press, a division of Simon & Schuster Adult Publishing Group, from *A Force for Change: How Leadership Differs From Management* by John P. Kotter. © 1990 by John P. Kotter, Inc. All rights reserved.

[4] Reprinted by permission of *Harvard Business Review*. Exhibit from 'How to Choose Leadership Patterns' by Robert Tannenbaum & Warren Schmidt, May–June 1973. © 1973 by the Harvard Business School Publishing Corporation. All rights reserved.

[5] David Gunzareth, "Murdoch, Rupert K.," The Museum of Broadcast Communications (May 27, 2008), at **http://www.museum. tv/archives/etv/M/htmlM/ murdochrupe/murdochrupe.htm**; Johnnie L. Roberts, "Murdoch, Ink.," *Newsweek*, April 28, 2008 (May 27, 2008), at **http://www.newsweek.com/id/132852**; BBC News, "Murdoch: I decide Sun's politics," November 24, 2007 (May 27, 2008), at **http://news.bbc.co.uk/2/hi/ uk_news/7110532.stm**; Mark Jurkowitz, "How Different Is Murdoch's New Wall Street Journal?" April 23, 2008 (May 27, 2008), at **http://journalism.org/node/ 10769**; Richard Siklos and Andrew Ross Sorkin, "Murdoch on Owning The Wall Street Journal," *The New York Times*, May 4, 2007 (May 27, 2008), at **http://www.nytimes. com/2007/05/04/business/media/ 04murdoch.html?pagewanted=print**.

[6] David A. Waldman and Francis J. Yammarino, "CEO Charismatic Leadership: Levels-of-Management and Levels-of- Analysis Effects," *Academy of Management Review*, 1999, vol. 24, no. 2, 266–285.

[7] Jane Howell and Boas Shamir, "The Role of Followers in the Charismatic Leadership Process: Relationships and Their Consequences," *Academy of Management Review*, January 2005, 96–112.

[8] J. Richard Hackman and Ruth Wageman, "A Theory of Team Coaching," *Academy of Management Review*, April 2005, 269–287.

[9] Clive Thompson, "The See-Through CEO," *Wired*, March 2007 (July 2, 2008), at **http://www.wired.com/wired/ archive/15.04/wired40_ceo.html**.

[10] "How Women Lead," *Newsweek*, October 24, 2005, 46–70.

[11] Steven Berglas, "What You Can Learn from Steve Jobs," **www.inc.com**; "Apple's Bold Swim Downstream," *Business Week*, January 24, 2006, 32–35; "The Seed of Apple's Innovation," *Business Week*, October 12, 2005, 86–87; Alan Deutschman, *The Second Coming of Steve Jobs* (New York: Broadway Publishing, 2001); Brent Schlender, "How Big Can Apple Get?" *Fortune*, February 21, 2005, 122–128; "Steve Jobs' Magic Kingdom," *Business Week*, February 6, 2006, 62–69 (source of quote); Lev Grossman, "Invention Of the Year: The iPhone," *Time*, October 31, 2007 (May 27, 2008), at **http://www.time.com/time/business/ article/0,8599,1678581,00.html**.

[12] Ricky W. Griffin, *Management*, 8th ed. (Boston: Houghton Mifflin Company, 2005), 282. Used with permission.

[13] Jerry Useem, "Boeing vs. Boeing," *Fortune*, October 2, 2000, 148–160; "Airbus Prepares to 'Bet the Company' As It Builds a Huge New Jet," *Wall Street Journal*, November 3, 1999, A1, A10.

[14] "Accommodating the A380," *Wall Street Journal*, November 29, 2005, B1; "Boeing Roars Ahead," *Business Week*, November 7, 2005, 44–45; "Boeing's New Tailwind," *Newsweek*, December 5, 2005, 45; Judith Crown, "Even More Boeing 787 Delays?" *Business Week*, April 4, 2008 (May 27, 2008), at **http://www.businessweek. com/bwdaily/dnflash/content/apr2008/ db2008043_948354.htm?campaign_id= rss_daily**; Aaron Karp, ATW Daily News, April 9, 2008 (May 27, 2008), at **http://www.atwonline.com/news/ story.html?storyID=12338**; "Airbus: New delays for A380 deliveries," CNNMoney. com, May 13, 2008 (May 27, 2008), at **http://money.cnn.com/2008/05/13/ news/international/airbus_delay.ap/ index.htm?postversion=2008051304**; "Airbus A380 delays not disclosed for months," MSNBC.com, May 29, 2007 (May 27, 2008), at **http://www.msnbc. msn.com/id/18918869/**.

[15] "Making Decisions in Real Time," *Fortune*, June 26, 2000, 332–334; see also Malcolm Gladwell, *Blink* (New York: Little, Brown, 2005).

[16] Charles P. Wallace, "Adidas—Back in the Game," *Fortune*, August 18, 1997, 176–182.

[17] Barry M. Staw and Jerry Ross, "Good Money After Bad," *Psychology Today*, February 1988, 30–33; D. Ramona Bobocel and John Meyer, "Escalating Commitment to a Failing Course of Action: Separating the Roles of Choice and Justification," *Journal of Applied Psychology*, vol. 79, 1994, 360–363.

[18] Gerry McNamara and Philip Bromiley, "Risk and Return in Organizational Decision Making," *Academy of Management Journal*, vol. 42, 1999, 330–339.

[19] See Brian O'Reilly, "What It Takes to Start a Startup," *Fortune*, June 7, 1999, 135–140, for an example.

CHAPTER 10

[1] Bill Breen, "Full House," *Fast Company* (December 2007), at **http://www. fastcompany.com/magazine/42/ pp_bellagio.html**.

[2] U.S. Small Business Association, at **http://app1.sba.gov/faqs/faqindex.cfm? areaID=24**, Accessed June 6, 2008; John S. DeMott, "A lifeline for lost data – computer data recovery," *BNET.com* (June 1995), at **http://findarticles.com/p/articles/ mi_m1154/is_n6_v83/ai_16928871/**; Sarah Lacy, "Marc Andreessen's New Gamble," *BusinessWeek* (May 16, 2008), at **http://www.businessweek.com/print/ technology/content/may2008/ tc20080516_232288.htm**; "How I Did It:

Jerome Boykin, Owner, JB Sweeping Service," *Inc. Magazine*, July 2007, at **http://www.inc.com/magazine/20070701/hidi-boykin_Printer_Friendly.html**.

[3] Lathryn Tyler, "Taking E-Learning to the Next Level," *HRMagazine*, February 2005, 56–61.

[4] "Some Employers Offer ID Theft Coverage," *USA Today*, September 12, 2005, 1B.

[5] "FedEx, Goodyear Make Big Pension Plan Changes," *Workforce Management* (March 1, 2007), at **http://www.workforce.com/section/00/article/24/77/95.html**.

[6] Henry R. Cheeseman, *Business Law: Ethical, International, and E-Commerce Environment*, 5th ed. (Upper Saddle River, NJ: Prentice Hall, 2004), Chapter 41.

[7] Gary Dessler, *Human Resource Management*, 9th ed. (Upper Saddle River, NJ: Prentice Hall, 2003), 31–32.

[8] Henry R. Cheeseman, *Business Law: Ethical, International, and E-Commerce Environment*, 5th ed. (Upper Saddle River, NJ: Prentice Hall, 2004), 806–810; Gary Dessler, *Human Resource Management*, 9th ed. (Upper Saddle River, NJ: Prentice Hall, 2003), 94–99.

[9] Texas Tech University: Health Sciences Center, at **http://www.ttuhsc.edu/hr/Employment/FAQs.aspx#usapa**, Accessed June 6, 2008; Richard S. Dunham, "The Patriot Act: Business Balks," *BusinessWeek*, (November 10, 2005), at **http://www.businessweek.com/bwdaily/dnflash/nov2005/nf20051110_9709_db016.htm**.

[10] U.S. Department of Labor, Bureau of Labor Statistics, at **http://www.bls.gov/news.release/union2.nr0.htm**, Accessed June 6, 2008.

[11] U.S. Department of Labor, Bureau of Labor Statistics, at **http://www.bls.gov/news.release/pdf/wkstp.pdf**, Accessed June 6, 2008.

CHAPTER 11

[1] Batman Film Series (May 23, 2008), at **en.wikipedia.org/wiki/Batman_%28film_series%29**; Claude Brodesser-Akner, "Hyping Joker–Without Exploiting Heath's Death," Advertising Age, (May 12, 2008), at **adage.com/article.php?article_id=126981**; Chungaiz, "New Batman Dark Knight Marketing Continues. Fantastic!" (December 13, 2007), at **www.altogetherdigital.com/20071213/new-batman-dark-knight-marketing-continues-fantastic**; Chris Lee, "The Dark Knight marketing blitz" (March 24, 2008), at **articles.latimes.com/2008/mar/24/entertainment/et-batmanviral24**; See also **batman.wikibruce.com/Timeline**; **www.42entertainment.com**; **whysoserious.com**.

[2] American Marketing Association, "Marketing Definitions" (January 14, 2008), at **www.marketingpower.com**.

[3] Philip Kotler and Gary Armstrong, *Principles of Marketing*, 12th ed. (Upper Saddle River, NJ: Prentice Hall, 2008), 7.

[4] "Financial Cards in Poland," Euromonitor International, (May 2004), at **http://www.euromonitor.com/**.

[5] "2008 Brand Keys Customer Loyalty Engagement Index," (March 18, 2008), at **www.brandkeys.com/awards/**.

[6] U.S. Department of Commerce, Statistical Abstract of the United States: 2008 (Washington, DC: Bureau of the Census, 2007), Tables No. 721, 723, and 455; David Dodson, "Minority Groups' Share of $10 Trillion U.S. Consumer Market is Growing Steadily," News & Announcements (Terry College of Business), (July 31, 2007), at www.terry.uga.edu/news/releases/2007/minority_buying_power_report. html.

[7] Ibid, Tables No. 422 and 455.

[8] "Packaged Goods See Record Number of New Products in 2006," Convenience Store News, (January 24, 2007), at www.allbusiness.com/retail-trade/food-stores/4490789-1.html.

[9] Adapted from Jay Heizer and Barry Render, Operations Management, 7th ed. (Upper Saddle River, NJ: Prentice Hall, 2004), 157.

[10] "Top 100 Global Brands Scoreboard: 2007," BusinessWeek Online (March 20, 2008), at **bwnt.businessweek.com/interactive_reports/top_brands**.

[11] Judy Strauss, Adel El-Ansary, and Raymond Frost, *E-Marketing*, 5th ed. (Upper Saddle River, NJ: Prentice Hall, 2007).

[12] "Netflix Updates First Quarter and Full Year 2008 Guidance," Netflix, (February 27, 2008), at **ir.netflix.com/**; Michael Liedtke, "Netflix Expands Internet Viewing Option," SFGate.com, January 13, 2008, at **www.sfgate.com/cgi-bin/article.cgifile=/n/a/2008/01/13/financial/f090113S93.DTL**; David B. Wilkerson, "Netflix, LG Team Up to Bring Movies Straight to HDTV,"

MarketWatch, January 3, 2008, accessed at **www.marketwatch.com/news/story/netflix-lg-team-up-bring/story.aspx?guid=%7b5**; Michael Liedtke, "Netflix's DVD Rental Pioneer has a Blockbuster Plan," *USA Today*, March 1, 2004, at **www.usatoday.com/tech/techinvestor/2004-03-01-reed-hastings_x.htm**.

CHAPTER 12

[1] Apple Inc. Form 10–Q (March 29, 2008), at **http://media.corporate-ir.net/media_files/irol/10/107357/AAPL_10Q_Q2FY08.pdf**.

[2] See "DoJ Probes Digital Music Pricing," *Techtree* (March 6, 2006), at **http://www.techtree.com/techtree/jsp/article.jsp?article_id=71743&cat_id=643**; Jim Dalrymple, "Apple now number 2 music retailer in the U.S.," *Network World* (February 26, 2008), at **http://www.networkworld.com/news/2008/022608-apple-now-number-2-music.html**; "iTunes Increasing Its Dominance," Telecom (April 30, 2008), at **http://web20.telecomtv.com/pages/?newsid=43081&id=e9381817-0593-417a-8639-c4c53e2a2a10&view=news**; "iTunes Store Top Music Retailer in the U.S." (April 3, 2008), at **http://www.apple.com/pr/library/2008/04/03itunes.html**; Chris Maxcer, "iTunes Tops Music Vendor Charts," *E-Commerce Times* (April 4, 2008), at **http://www.ecommercetimes.com/story/iTunes-Tops-Music-Vendor-Charts-62458.html**.

[3] Edward F. Moltzen, "HP Passes Dell as Top PC Maker Worldwide," *Information Week* (October 19, 2006), at **http://www.informationweek.com/news/personal_tech/showArticle.jhtml?articleID=193400624**.

[4] Lee S. Crane, "Seven Questions to Ask Before Running Your Next Reverse Auction," *Purchasing* (March 13, 2008), at **http://www.purchasing.com/article/CA6537987.html**; "MediaBids.com Adds Over 325 Newspapers & Magazines to Print Advertising Marketplace," MediaBids.com (March 4, 2008), at **http://express-press-release.net/47/MediaBids.comAddsOver325Newspapers&MagazinestoPrintAdvertisingMarketplace.php**.

[5] Parija Bhatnagar, "Not a mall, it's a lifestyle center," *CNN/Money* (January 12, 2005), at **http://money.cnn.com/2005/01/11/news/fortune500/retail_lifestylecenter/**;

Robert Preer, "Downtowns vs. lifestyle centers," *Boston Globe* (December 9, 2006), at **http://www.boston.com/realestate/ news/articles/2006/12/09/downtowns_ vs_lifestyle_centers?mode=PF**.

6 Plunkett Research, Ltd., "*Retail Industry Statistics: U.S. Retail Industry Overview (2004)*" (June 23, 2005), at **http://www. plunkettresearch.com/retail**.

7 *Avon 2006 Annual Report* (March 15, 2007), at **http://www.avoncompany. com/investor/annualreport/ 2006index.html**.

8 "Over 875 Million Consumers Have Shopped Online—the Number of Internet Shoppers Up 40% in Two Years," *Reuters* (January 27, 2008), at **http://www.reuters.com/article/press Release/idUS16394+28-Jan-2008+ PRN20080128**.

9 Melissa Dowling, "Online Sales Continue to Climb," Multichannel Merchant (March 1, 2008), at **http:// www.multichannelmerchant.com/ webchannel/marketing/online_sales_ continue**.

10 Associated Press, "Demand and prices rise for organic food, but supply falls," *Boston Globe* (January 30, 2008), at **http://www.boston.com/business/ articles/2008/01/30/demand_and_ prices_rise_for_organic_food_but_ supply_falls?mode=PF**; Diane Brady, "The Organic Myth," *BusinessWeek* (October 16, 2006), at **http://www.businessweek.com/ magazine/content/06_42/b4005001. htm?chan=search**.

11 "Facts for Features: Hispanic Heritage Month 2005," U.S. Census Bureau (August 9, 2007), at **http://www.census. gov/Press-Release/www/releases/ archives/cb05ff-14-3.pdf**; "Univision Announces 2007 Fourth Quarter and Full Year Results" (March 5, 2008), at **http:// u.univision.com/contentroot/uol/ 10portada/sp/pdf/corp_releases/2008/ NOMETA_03-05-2008-2en.pdf**; David Dodson, "Minority groups' share of $10 trillion U.S. consumer market is growing steadily, according to annual buying power study from Terry College's Selig Center for Economic Growth," (July 31, 2007), at **http://www.terry. uga.edu/news/releases/2007/ minority_buying_power_report.html**.

12 "100 Leading Advertisers," *Advertising Age* (June 20, 2007), at **http://adage.com/ datacenter/article?article_id=118652**.

13 Ibid.

14 "Ad Spending Totals By Media" and "Domestic Ad Spending By Category," *Advertising Age* (June 20, 2007), at **http:// adage.com/datacenter/article?article_ id=118652**.

15 Associated Press, "New Arrest in Wendy's Finger Case," MSNBC.com (May 19, 2005), at **http://www.msnbc. msn.com/id/7844274**.

16 Ron Insana, "Wendy's Knew from Start Story Was a Hoax," *USA Today* (June 5, 2005), at **http://www.usatoday.com/ money/companies/management/ 2005-06-05-insana-wendys_x.htm**.

CHAPTER 13

1 See **http://www.ponoko.com**; Ian Mount, "Manufacture and Sell Anything— in Minutes," *Wired* (March 24, 2008), at **http://www.wired.com/techbiz/it/ magazine/16-04/bz_instapreneur**.

2 Mark Long, "RIM's Blackberry Sales Soar, Along with Subscribers," Newsfactor.com (April 3, 2008), at **http://www. newsfactor.com/story.xhtml?story_id= 0120016HCCSO**.

3 See **http://www.xmnavtraffic.com**.

4 Donna Miles, "Joint Strike Fighter Testing, F35," TechNews (April 29, 2007), at **http:// www.technologynewsdaily.com/ node/6838**.

5 Alison Stein Wellner, "Into the Wild," *Inc.com* (October 2007), at **http://www. inc.com/magazine/20071001/into-the- wild.html**.

6 Andrea Cooper, "The Influencers," Entrepreneur.com (June 10, 2008), at **http://www.entrepreneur.com/ slideshow/190606.html**.

7 3D Systems, "3D Systems Helps Walter Reed Army Medical Center Rebuild Lives," at **http://www.3dsystems.com/ appsolutions/casestudies/walter_reed. asp**, Accessed 6/10/2008; "Hannah Hickey, "Camera in a pill offers cheaper, easier window on your insides," UWNews.org (January 24, 2008), at **http://uwnews.org/ article.asp?articleid=39292**.

8 See **http://www.internetworldstats. com/stats.htm**.

9 See University of Birmingham, "Internet map as of 16th January 2006," at **http:// www.eee.bham.ac.uk/com_test/dsnl. aspx**.

10 "An Intranet's Life Cycle," morebusiness. com (June 16, 1999), at **http://www. morebusiness.com/getting_started/ website/d928247851.brc**

11 Major modifications of diagrams at the BlackBerry Web site, modified from Research in Motion, Limited, technical images, at **http://www.blackberry.com/ images/technical/bes_exchange_ architecture.gif**.

12 Electronic Frontier Foundation, "How to Blog Safely (About Work or Anything Else)" (April 6, 2005), at **http://w2.eff.org/ Privacy/Anonymity/blog-anonymously. php**; Jonah Spangenthal-Lee, "Game Over," *The Stranger* (September 19, 2007), **http://www.thestranger.com/seattle/ Content?oid=322407**.

13 See **http://www.teradata.com/t/**; Mike Freeman, "Data company helps Wal-Mart, casinos, airlines analyze customers," *San Diego Union-Tribune* (February 24, 2006), at **http://archives. signonsandiego.com/uniontrib/ 20060224/news_1b24teradata.html**.

14 "Data Mining Examples & Testimonials," at **http://www.data-mining-software. com/data_mining_examples.htm**, Accessed 6/11/2008.

15 See **http://secondlife.com/whatis/ economy-market.php**; "Anshe Chung Becomes First Virtual World Millionaire" (November 26, 2006), at **http://www. anshechung.com/include/press/ press_release251106.html**; Toby Sterling, "'Second Life' 3-D digital world grows," *USA Today* (October 9, 2006), at **http://www. usatoday.com/tech/gaming/2006-10- 08-second-life_x.htm**; David Barboza, "Ogre to Slay? Outsource It to Chinese," *New York Times* (December 9, 2005), at **http://www.nytimes.com/2005/12/ 09/technology/09gaming.html? pagewanted=1&ei=5094&en= d5d225932e8ebecb&hp&ex= 1134190800&partner=homepage**.

16 "Designing a Better Future," The Post.ie: The Sunday Business Post Online (May 6, 2007), at **http://archives.tcm. ie/businesspost/2007/05/06/ story23327.asp**.

17 Alex Leary, "Wi-Fi Cloaks a New Breed of Intruder," *St. Petersburg Times* (July 4, 2005), at **http://www.sptimes.com/ 2005/07/04/State/Wi_Fi_cloaks_ a_new_br.shtml**.

18 Eliot Van Buskirk, "iTunes Store May Capture One-Quarter of Worldwide Music by 2012," *Wired* (April 27, 2008), at

http://www.wired.com/entertainment/music/news/2008/04/itunes_birthday; Christopher Burgess and Richard Power, "How to Avoid Intellectual Property Theft," CIO (July 10, 2006), at http://www.cio.com/article/22837; Hiawatha Bray, "Music Industry Aims to Send in Radio Cops," Boston Globe (November 15, 2004), at http://www.boston.com/business/articles/2004/11/15/music_industry_aims_to_send_in_radio_cops/.

[19] See http://www.webopedia.com/TERM/S/spyware.html.

[20] "Industry Statistics: The Cost of Spam, 2007," Ferris Research, at http://www.ferris.com/research-library/industry-statistics/, Accessed 3/31/2008.

[21] Brad Carlson, "Organizations Face New Records-Destruction Rule," Idaho Business Review (July 25, 2005), at http://www.idahobusiness.net/archive.htm/2005/07/25/Organizations-face-new-recordsdestruction-rule.

CHAPTER 14

[1] Jonathan Weil, "Wells Fargo Gorges on Mark-to-Make-Believe Gains," Bloomberg.com (August 22, 2007), at http://www.bloomberg.com/apps/news?pid=conewsstory&refer=conews&tkr=WFC:US&sid=aY8m0nta94GA#; Bhattiprolu Murti, "Goldman: Aug level 3 asset value $72.05B, 7% of total," MarketWatch.com (October 10, 2007), at http://www.marketwatch.com/news/story/goldmanaug-level-3-asset-value/story.aspx?guid=%7bA5F0CE1D-4004-448D-967B-895CC8213FD6%7d; Catherine Valenti, "Forensic Accounting Is Hot Job," ABCNews.com (April 10, 2008), at http://abcnews.go.com/Business/Story?id=87225&page=1; Adam Piore, "Fraud Scene Investigator," Portfolio (March 10, 2008), at http://www.portfolio.com/careers/job-of-the-week/2008/03/10/Forensic-Accountant-Al-Vondra.

[2] See Marshall B. Romney and Paul John Steinbart, Accounting Information Systems, 11th ed. (Upper Saddle River, NJ: Prentice Hall, 2009), Chapter 1.

[3] See Anthony A. Atkinson, Robert S. Kaplan, Ella Mae Matsumura, and S. Mark Young, Management Accounting, 5th ed. (Upper Saddle River, NJ: Prentice Hall, 2007), Chapter 1.

[4] See Walter T. Harrison and Charles T. Horngren, Financial Accounting and Financial Tips, 7th ed. (Upper Saddle River, NJ: Prentice Hall, 2007), Chapter 1.

[5] See Alvin A. Arens, Mark S. Beasley, and Randal J. Elder, Auditing and Assurance Services and ACL Software, 12th ed. (Upper Saddle River, NJ: Prentice Hall, 2008), Chapter 1.

[6] See Meg Pollard et al., Financial and Managerial Accounting Ch. 1–14 (Upper Saddle River, NJ: Prentice Hall, 2008), Chapter 1.

[7] Myra A. Thomas, "It's Not About Balance—It's About Reality," Jobs in the Money (November 30, 2007), at http://www.jobsinthemoney.com/news.php?articleID=513.

[8] Adapted from "CPA Vision Project: 2011 and Beyond" (September 24, 2002), at http://www.cpavision.org/final_report; Cynthia Bolt-Lee and Sheila Foster, "The Core Competency Framework: A New Element in the Continuing Call for Accounting Education Change in the United States," Accounting Education, vol. 12, issue 1, 2003, 33–47.

[9] D. Larry Crumbley, Lester E. Heitger, and G. Stevenson Smith, Forensic and Investigative Accounting, 3rd ed. (Chicago: CCH Incorporated, 2007), Chapter 1.

[10] "Executive Summary of the Sarbanes-Oxley Act of 2002 P.L. 107–204," Conference of State Bank Supervisors, at http://www.csbs.org/Content/NavigationMenu/LegislativeAffairs/Summaries/Executive_Summary_of.htm; "Summary of the Provisions of the Sarbanes-Oxley Act of 2002," AICPA, at http://thecaq.aicpa.org/Resources/Sarbanes+Oxley/Summary+of+the+Provisions+of+the+Sarbanes-Oxley+Act+of+2002.htm.

[11] Yahoo! Finance, at http://finance.yahoo.com/?fstype=ii&cid=694653, Accessed 6/9/2008; Yahoo! Finance, at http://finance.yahoo.com/q/bs?s=goog&annual, Accessed 6/9/2008.

[12] Yahoo! Finance, at http://finance.yahoo.com/q/bs?s=goog&annual, Accessed 6/10/2008.

[13] Yahoo! Finance, at http://finance.yahoo.com/q/is?s=GOOG&annual, Accessed 6/10/2008.

[14] Yahoo! Finance, at http://finance.yahoo.com/q/cf?s=GOOG&annual, Accessed 6/10/2008.

[15] PKF Texas: Awards and Special Honors, at http://www.pkftexas.com/pkf/Awards_and_Special_Honors.asp?SnID=1517489630, Accessed 6/9/2008; Greg Price, "From Greg's Head: The Entrepreneur's Playbook," at http://www.fromgregshead.com/archives/cat-pkf-texas-the-entrepreneurs-playbook.html, Accessed 6/9/2008; Greg Barr, "Weaver and Tidwell tops magazine ranking," Houston Business Journal (April 14, 2008), at http://www.bizjournals.com/houston/stories/2008/04/14/daily6.html; "Time to Submit an Entry for Practical Accountant's' Practical Innovation Awards," WebCPA.com (May 1, 2008), at http://www.webcpa.com/article.cfm?articleid=27511&pg=ros.

[16] U.S. Securities and Exchange Commission, A Plain English Handbook: How to create clear SEC disclosure documents (August 1998), at http://www.sec.gov/pdf/plaine.pdf; Feng Li, "Annual Report Readability, Current Earnings, and Earnings Persistence," University of Michigan at Ann Arbor–Stephen M. Ross School of Business, Paper No. 1028 (September 15, 2006), at http://papers.ssrn.com/sol3/papers.cfm?abstract_id=887382; D. Murali, "It pays to speak plain English," The Hindu Business Line (June 15, 2006), at http://www.thehindubusinessline.com/bline/2006/06/15/stories/2006061500371100.htm.

[17] "Code of Professional Conduct," AICPA, at http://www.aicpa.org.

[18] "The Corporate Scandal Sheet," Citizen Works (August 2004), at http://www.citizenworks.org/enron/corp-scandal.php; "Largest Health Care Fraud Case in U.S. History Settled," Department of Justice (June 26, 2003), at http://www.usdoj.gov/opa/pr/2003/June/03_civ_386.htm; "Waste Management, Inc. Founder and Three Other Former Top Officers Settle SEC Fraud Action for $30.8 Million," U.S. Securities and Exchange Commission, Litigation Release No. 19351 (August 29, 2005), at www.sec.gov/litigation/litreleases/lr19351.htm; "Kozlowski Is Found Guilty," TheStreet.com (June 17, 2005), at http://www.thestreet.com/story/10228619/1/kozlowski-is-found-guilty.html; "SEC Charges Time Warner with Fraud . . .," U.S. Securities and Exchange Commission, Release 2005–38 (March 21, 2005), at http://www.sec.gov/news/press/2005-38.htm.

CHAPTER 15

[1] "Open Market Operations," Federal Reserve Board, at http://www.federalreserve.gov/fomc/fundsrate.htm, Accessed 5/5/2008; Peter Ryan, "Fed signals possible end to rate cuts," ABC

News (May 5, 2008), at **http://www.abc. net.au/news/stories/2008/05/01/ 2232305.htm?section=justin**.

2 "Money Stock Measures," Federal Reserve, at **http://www.federalreserve. gov/releases/h6/hist/h6hist1.txt**, Accessed 6/16/2008.

3 Ibid.

4 Ibid.

5 "Global Pension Fund Assets Rise and Fall," Watson Wyatt Worldwide (January 30, 2008), at **http://www. watsonwyatt.com/news/press.asp?ID= 18579**; Anita Gallagher, "United Case Warns All U.S. Pensions Bankrupt," Executive Intelligence Review (May 27, 2005), at **http://www.larouchepub.com/other/ 2005/site_packages/strategic_ bankruptcy/3221pensions_gone.html**.

6 Federal Reserve Board, at **http://www. federalreserve.gov/releases/h15/data/ Annual/H15_PRIME_NA.txt**, Accessed 4/6/2008.

7 Richard Bitner, "Confessions of a Subprime Lender," *Newsweek* (March 12, 2008), at **http://www.newsweek.com/ id/121512/page/1**; Tyler Cowen, "So We Thought. But Then Again . . ." New York Times (January 13, 2008), at **http://www. nytimes.com/2008/01/13/business/ 13view.html?_r=2&scp=1&sq=Tyler+ Cowen&oref=login&oref=slogin**; Robert H. Frank, "Don't Blame All Borrowers," *Washington Post* (April 27, 2008), at **http://www.washingtonpost. com/wp-dyn/content/article/2008/04/ 25/AR2008042502783.html**.

8 "Electronic Funds Transfer" (January 2, 2006), at **http://fms.treas.gov/eft/ index.html**.

9 American Bankers Association, "ATM Fact Sheet," *2006 ABA Issue Summary* (April 6, 2008), at **http://www.aba.com**.

10 From **http://www.federalreserve. gov/otherfrb.htm**.

11 American Bankers Association, "Check Processing Facts," *2006 ABA Issue Summary* (April 6, 2008), at **http://www. aba.com**.

12 "Historical Changes of the Target Federal Funds and Discount Rates," Federal Reserve Bank of New York, at **http://www.newyorkfed.org/markets/ statistics/dlyrates/fedrate.html**, Accessed 4/7/2008; "Prime Rate, Fed Funds, COFI," Bankrate.com, at **http:// www.bankrate.com/brm/ratewatch/**

leading-rates.asp, Accessed 4/7/2008; Paul Heyne, Peter Boettke, and David Prychitko, *The Economic Way of Thinking* (Upper Saddle River, NJ: Prentice Hall, 2006).

13 Craig Torres, "Bernanke Wants Fed to Pay Interest on Bank Reserves," Bloomberg (May 7, 2008), at **http:// www.bloomberg.com/apps/news?pid= 20601087&sid=a4vkC.m1NdvI&refer= home**.

14 See **http://www.treasurydirect.gov**; **http://www.investopedia.com/ university/moneymarket**.

15 "U.S. Authorities Fine Arab Bank," *Al Bawaba* (August 18, 2005), 1; Paul R. Osborne, "BSA/AML Compliance Provides Opportunity to Improve Security and Enhance Customer Experience," *ABA Bank Compliance*, July/August 2005, 4.

16 Susan Ford, "New 'Check 21' Law to do Away with Float," *Toledo Business Journal* (February 1, 2005), 28; Tara Rice, "Implementing Check 21 Act: Potential Risks Facing Banks," *Chicago Fed Letter*, August 2005, 1; Sharon R. Cole, "Expect Checks to Stick Around," *Business Forms, Labels & Systems* (August 20, 2005), 28.

17 "Online Shopping," Pew Internet (February 13, 2008), at **http://www. pewinternet.org/press_release.asp? r=299**.

18 "PNC Expands Environmentally Friendly Practices with Retail Banking Customers," PRWeb (April 14, 2008), at **http://www. prweb.com/releases/2008/04/ prweb838094.htm**.

19 John Laumer, "Wachovia Bank To Open 300 'Green' Branches," *Treehugger* (July 10, 2007), at **http://www.treehugger.com/ files/2007/07/wachovia_bank_t.php**.

20 "Green Banking Lends Humanity a Sustainable Hand," Green Living Ideas, at **http://greenlivingideas.com/banking/ green-banking-lends-humanity-a- sustainable-hand.html**, Accessed 6/17/2008.

21 See **http://www.payitgreen.org**.

22 Jeremy Simon, "Paper to Plastic: Checks and Cash Losing to Debit and Credit," CreditCards.com (October 3, 2007), at **http://www.creditcards.com/credit- card-news/debit-credit-card-preferred- payment-1271.php**.

23 Estimated from "Statistics for Smart Cards," ePaynews.com (July 3, 2008), at **http://www.epaynews.com/statistics/ scardstats.html**.

CHAPTER 16

1 "Businesses Cash in on Carbon Cuts," *Columbia Daily Tribune*, August 20, 2007, page 6B, at **http://archive. columbiatribune.com/2007/aug/ 20070820busi007.asp**; Michael Specter, "Big Foot," *The New Yorker*, February 25, 2008, at **http://www.newyorker.com/ reporting/2008/02/25/080225fa_fact_ specter?printable=true**; "About Ecosystem Marketplace," The Katoomba Group's Ecosystem Marketplace, at **http:// ecosystemmarketplace.com/pages/ static/about.php**, Accessed June 13, 2008; Andrew T. Gillies, "Carbon Emissions: The Next Sarbox," *Forbes.com*, December 12, 2007, at **http://www.forbes.com/2007/ 12/06/greenhouse-carbon-inslee-biz- beltway-cz_atg_1206carbon.html**; Europa.eu, "Questions and Answers on the Commission's proposal to revise the EU Emissions Trading System," January 23, 2008, at **http://europa.eu/rapid/ pressReleasesAction.do?reference= MEMO/08/35&format=HTML&aged=0& language=EN&guiLanguage=en**.

2 "Advantages and Disadvantages of Mutual Funds," *The Motley Fool*, at **www. fool.com**, Accessed February 11, 2008.

3 "Why Exchange-Traded Funds?," *Yahoo!* Finance Exchange-Traded Funds Center, at **http://finance.yahoo.com/etf/ education/02**, on January 16 2008.

4 Katie Benner, "ETFs: A User's Guide," *Fortune*, February 19, 2007, page 112.

5 Walter Updegrave, "ETFs for the Long Run," February 8, 2007, *CNNMoney.com*, at **http://cnnmoney.com**.

6 New York Stock Exchange, August 7, 2007, at **www.nyse.com**.

7 Adapted from "World Markets," *StocksQuest: A Global Stock Market Game*, October 21, 2005, at **http://investsmart. coe.uga.edu/C001759/world/world_ nf.htm**.

8 "Chronology—Recent Consolidation Moves by Exchanges," *Reuters*, February 13, 2008, at **www.reuters.com**; Randy Grossman, "The Inevitable Stock Exchange Consolidation," *Finance Tech*, February 13, 2008, at **www.financetech.com**.

9 "Electronic Communication Networks (ECNs)," *U.S. Securities and Exchange Commission*, at **www.sec.gov/answers/ ecn.htm**, Accessed July 3, 2008; "Electronic Communication Network," *InvestorWords. com*, at **www.investorwords.com**, Accessed July 3, 2008.

[10] "Electronic Communication Networks (ECNs)," *U.S. Securities and Exchange Commission*, at **www.sec.gov/answers/ecn.htm**, Accessed July 3, 2008; "Island ECN—How Island Works," at **http://ecommerce.hostip.info/pages/636/Island-Ecn-HOW-ISLAND-WORKS.html**, Accessed January 16, 2008.

[11] Stephen Lawson, "Nacchio Appeals Insider-Trading Conviction," *IDG News Service*, October 10, 2007, at **http://www.itworld.com/Tech/4535/071010nacchio/**; U.S. Department of Justice, "Former Qwest Chief Executive Officer Joseph Nacchio Convicted on 19 Counts of Insider Trading," April 19, 2007, at **http://www.usdoj.gov/usao/co/press_releases/archive/2007/April07/4_19_07.html**; U.S. Department of Justice, "Former Qwest Chief Executive Officer Joseph Nacchio Sentenced to 72 Months in Prison for Insider Trading," July 27, 2007, at **http://www.usdoj.gov/usao/co/press_releases/archive/2007/July07/7_27_07.html**.

[12] Carl Beidelman, *The Handbook of International Investing* (Chicago, 1987), p. 133.

[13] Dalia Fahmy, "55-Alive! Wants to be MySpace for the Baby Boomer Set. Can It Raise $250,000?" *Inc. Magazine*, October 2007, page 50; "55-Alive! Announces 55-Alive Romance!" *PR Leap* (press release), June 7, 2007, at **www.prleap.com**; "55-Alive! Announces 55-Alive! Battle of the Boomer Bands," *PR.com* (press release), June 23, 2007, at **www.pr.com**; "55-Alive! Announces 55-AliveChat!(TM) for the Baby Boomer and 50+ Online Community, and the Launch of 55-Alive! Ask the Expert," *PR Newswire*, March 1, 2007, at **http://sev.prnewswire.com**; Michael Arrington, "Facebook No Longer The Second Largest Social Network," *Tech Crunch*, June 12, 2008, at **http://www.techcrunch.com/2008/06/12/facebook-no-longer-the-second-largest-social-network/**; iStrategyLabs, "Facebook Demographics Direct From Their System," October 22, 2007, at **http://www.istrategylabs.com/facebook-demographics-direct-from-their-system/**.

[14] New York Stock Exchange at **http://www.nyse.com/about/listed/lcddata.html?ticker=GOOG**; **http://www.nyse.com/about/listed/lcddata.html?ticker=GE**; **http://www.nyse.com/about/listed/lcddata.html?ticker=DAL**; **http://www.nyse.com/about/listed/lcddata.html?ticker=BRKA**, Accessed June 16, 2008.

[15] *CNN Money.com*, 12 February 2008.

SOURCES

CHAPTER 1

Figure 1.1: Adapted from Karl E. Case and Ray C. Fair, *Principles of Economics*, 8th ed., updated (Upper Saddle River, NJ: Prentice Hall, 2007). **Figure 1.2:** Data obtained from U.S. Department of Commerce Bureau of Economic Analysis, **www.bea.gov/bea/dn/gdplev.xls**; U.S. Census Bureau, **www.census.gov/popest/states/tables/NST-EST2005–01.xls**; **www.census.gov/popest/archives/1990s/**; National Economic Accounts, at **http://www.bea.gov/national/nipaweb/TableView.asp#Mid**; From World Bank Development Indicators 2007–Feb 2008: International Comparison Program (May 29, 2008), at **http://www.finfacts.com/biz10/globalworldincomepercapita.htm**. **Figure 1.3:** Data obtained from Big Mac Index Review 2007 (May 29, 2008), at **http://www.woopidoo.com/reviews/news/big-mac-index.htm**. **Figure 1.4:** Source: Data obtained from U.S. Census Bureau (June 19, 2008), at **www.census.gov/foreign-trade/balance/c0004.html#2005**.

CHAPTER 2

Figure 2.1: Based on Gerald S. Cavanaugh, *American Business Values: With International Perspectives*, 4th ed. (Upper Saddle River, NJ: Prentice Hall, 1998) 71, 84. **Figure 2.2:** Based on Andrew C. Revkin, "Who Cares About a Few Degrees?" *New York Times*, December 12, 1997, F1.

CHAPTER 3

Figure 3.1: Data from **http://www.sba.gov**, Accessed 3/6/2006, and U.S. Census Bureau, "Statistics About Business Size (including Small Business) from the U.S. Census Bureau," at **http://www.census.gov/epcd/www/smallbus.html**, Accessed 4/25/2007. **Figure 3.2:** U.S. Census Bureau, "Statistical Abstract of the United States," at **http://www.census.gov/prod/www/statistical-abstract.html**.

CHAPTER 4

Figure 4.1: Europe, at **http://europa.eu/abc/maps/index_en.htm**, Accessed June 4, 2008. **Figure 4.2:** Association of Southeast Asian Nations, at **http://www.aseansec.org/74.htm**, Accessed June 4, 2008. **Figure 4.3:** U.S. Census Bureau: Foreign Trade Statistics, at **http://www.census.gov/foreign-trade/statistics/highlights/annual.html**, Accessed May 14, 2008. **Figure 4.4:** Source: U.S. Census Bureau: Foreign Trade Statistics, at **http://www.census.gov/foreign-trade/statistics/highlights/annual.html**, Accessed May 14, 2008.

CHAPTER 5

Figure 5.2: Adapted from Stephen P. Robbins and Mary Coulter, *Management*, 9th ed. (Upper Saddle River, NJ: Prentice Hall, 2007), 199.

CHAPTER 8

Figure 8.2: A. H. Maslow, *Motivation and Personality*, 2nd ed. (Upper Saddle River, NJ: Prentice Hall, 1970). Reprinted by permission of Prentice Hall Inc.

CHAPTER 9

Figure 9.1: Reprinted by permission of *Harvard Business Review*. Exhibit from 'How to Choose Leadership Patterns' by Robert Tannenbaum & Warren Schmidt, May–June 1973. © 1973 by the Harvard Business School Publishing Corporation. All rights reserved. **Figure 9.2:** Ricky W. Griffin, *Management*, 8th ed. (Boston: Houghton Mifflin Company, 2005), 282. Used with permission.

CHAPTER 10

Figure 10.3a: **http://www.dol.gov/asp/media/reports/workforce2007/ADW2007_Full_Text.pdf**(p. 38). **Figure 10.3b:** U.S. Department of Labor, "America's Dynamic Workforce," (August 2007), p. 38, at **http://www.dol.gov/asp/media/reports/workforce2007/ADW2007_Full_Text.pdf**.

CHAPTER 11

Figure 11.2: Adapted from Jay Heizer and Barry Render, *Operations Management*, 7th ed. (Upper Saddle River, NJ: Prentice Hall, 2004), 157.

CHAPTER 13

Figure 13.2: Major modifications of diagrams at the BlackBerry Web site, modified from Research in Motion, Limited, technical images, at **http://www.blackberry.com/images/technical/bes_exchange_architecture.gif**.

CHAPTER 14

Figure 14.1: Yahoo! Finance, at **http://finance.yahoo.com/q/bs?s=goog&annual**, Accessed 6/10/2008.
Figure 14.2: Yahoo! Finance, at **http://finance.yahoo.com/q/is?s=GOOG&annual**, Accessed 6/10/2008.
Figure 14.3: Yahoo! Finance, at **http://finance.yahoo.com/q/cf?s=GOOG&annual**, Accessed 6/10/2008.

CHAPTER 15

Figure 15.2: **http://www.federalreserve.gov/releases/h15/data/annual/h15_prime_na.txt**.

CHAPTER 16

Figure 16.2: Dow Jones Industrial Average," *MSN.com*, at **http://moneycentral.msn.com/investor/charts/chartdl.aspx?PT=7&compsyms=&D4=1&DD=1&D5=0&DCS=2&MA0=0&MA1=0&CP=1&C5=1&C5D=1&C6=1976&C7=6&C7D=1&C8=2008&C9=-1&CF=0&D7=&D6=&showchartbt=Redraw+chart&symbol=%24indu&nocookie=1&SZ=0**, Accessed June 17, 2008; "Nasdaq Composite," *MSN.com*, at **http://moneycentral.msn.com/investor/charts/chartdl.aspx?PT=7&showchartbt=Redraw+chart&compsyms=&D4=1&DD=1&D5=0&DCS=2&MA0=0&MA1=0&CP=1&C5=1&C5D=1&C6=1976&C7=6&C7D=1&C8=2008&C9=-1&CF=0&D7=&D6=&symbol=%24COMPX&nocookie=1&SZ=0**, Accessed June 17, 2008; "S&P 500 Index; **http://moneycentral.msn.com/investor/charts/chartdl.aspx?PT=7&compsyms=&D4=1&DD=1&D5=0&DCS=2&MA0=0&MA1=0&CP=1&C5=1&C5D=1&C6=1976&C7=6&C7D=1&C8=2008&C9=-1&CF=0&D7=&D6=&showchartbt=Redraw+chart&symbol=%24INX&nocookie=1&SZ=0**, Accessed June 17, 2008. **Figure 16.3:** Carl Beidelman, *The Handbook of International Investing* (Chicago, 1987), p. 133.

CREDITS

CHAPTER 10

Page 134/135: MGM Mirage. Page 137: © Tom Brakefield/SuperStock, Inc. Page 138: Getty Images. Page 140: © David Zalubowski/AP Wide World Photos. Page 141: The Cartoon Bank. Page 142: Getty Images. Page 145: © Joyce Dopkeen/Redux Pictures.

CHAPTER 11

Page 148/149: Photofest. Page 151: Ting Shi. Page 152: Getty Images. Page 153: © James Leynse/Getty Images. Page 154: The Cartoon Bank. Page 158: Jill Connelly. Page 160: Heidi Cody. Page 161 (top): © Image Source/Corbis Royalty Free. Page 161 (bottom): © Todd Gipstein/CORBIS- NY. Page 162: Corbis. All Rights Reserved.

CHAPTER 12

Page 164/165: © Virginia Mayo/AP Wide World Photos. Page 166: © Ed Kashi/CORBIS- NY. Page 168: © Guillermo Granja/Corbis/Reuters America LLC.

Page 170: © Jim West/Jim West. Page 171: © Jerry S. Mendoza/AP Wide World Photos. Page 173: QVC, Inc. Page 174: © Tova R. Baruch/Tova R. Baruch. Page 175: © Hill Street Studios/Getty Images.

CHAPTER 13

Page 180/181: Pearson Business Publishing. Page 182: AGE Fotostock America, Inc. Page 184: Pearson Business Publishing. Page 185 (top): Corbis/Bettmann. Page 185 (bottom): Getty Images. Page 187: AP Wide World Photos. Page 188: © Image Source/CORBIS- NY. Page 189: © Porter Gifford/CORBIS- NY. Page 190: © Peter Zschunke/AP Wide World Photos. Page 191: Photo Researchers, Inc. Page 192: © Elizabeth Dalziel/AP Wide World Photos.

CHAPTER 14

Page 196/197: Photos.com. Page 199: © F. Carter Smith/Polaris Images. Page 202: © David McNew/Getty Images. Page 207: © George B. Diebold/CORBIS- NY. Page 208: The Cartoon Bank.

Page 209: © Comstock Images/Comstock Royalty Free Division.

CHAPTER 15

Page 212/213: Getty Images, Inc – Liaison. Page 214: Photos.com. Page 215: © Vincent Laforet/Redux Pictures. Page 218 (top): © The New Yorker Collection 1997 J. B. Handelsman from cartoonbank.com. All Rights Reserved. Page 218 (bottom): Comstock Royalty Free Division. Page 220: © Nikolai Ignatiev/arabianEye FZ LLC. Page 221: Jupiter Images. Page 223: Jupiter Images. Page 224: © Chris Hondros/Getty Images.

CHAPTER 16

Page 226/227: © Image 100/CORBIS- NY. Page 230: AP Wide World Photos. Page 233: © Rik Wilking/Reuters Limited. Page 237: Jose Luis Pelaez. Blend images/CORBIS- NY. Page 239 (top): Shaul Schwarz/CORBIS- NY. Page 239 (bottom): © The New Yorker Collection 2000 P.C. Vey from cartoonbank.com. All Rights Reserved. Page 240: © Benjamin Lowy/CORBIS- NY.

Glindex

Authority power to make the decisions necessary to complete a task [83]
    forms of, 83–84

Automated teller machine (ATM) electronic machine that allows bank customers to conduct account-related activities 24 hours a day, 7 days a week [219]

B

Bakke, Dennis, 116

Balance of payments flow of all money into or out of a country [52]

Balance of trade the economic value of all the products that a country exports minus the economic value of all the products it imports [15, 51]

Balance sheet financial statement that supplies detailed information about a firm's assets, liabilities, owners' equity [203–204]

Banana Republic, 11

Banker's acceptance bank promise, issued for a buyer, to pay a designated firm a specified amount at a future date [218–219]

Banking system, 219–220, 222–224

Bankruptcy permission granted by the courts to individuals and organization not to pay some or all of their debts [238]

Banks, 216

Bank Secrecy Act (BSA), 222

Barbato, Mark, 158

Bargain retailer retailer carrying a wide range of products at bargain prices [172]

BBVA, 112

Bear market period of falling stock prices [233, 234]

Behavioral approach to leadership focused on determining what behaviors are employed by leaders [123–124]

Behavioral theory, 112–114

Behavior modification, 115–116

Bellagio hotel and casino, 135

Benefits compensation other than wages and salaries [140–141, 146]

Bernanke, Ben, 16

Best Buy, 118

Bianchini, Gina, 137

Big business, relationship between small business and, 35

"Big five" personality traits five fundamental personality traits especially relevant to organizations [109–110]

Big Mac Index, 14

BlackBerry, 182, 187

"Blink" technology, 223

Blue Bell, 72

Board of directors governing body of a corporation that reports to its shareholders and delegates power to run its day-to-day operations while remaining responsible for sustaining its assets [44]

Boeing, 23, 130–131

Bondholders' claim request for court enforcement of a bond's terms of payment [238]

Bond indenture legal document containing complete details of a bond issue [238]

Bonds, 15, 238

Bonus individual performance incentive in the form of a special payment made over and above the employee's salary [139]

Bookkeeping recording of accounting transactions [198]

Book-entry ownership procedure that holds investors' shares in book-entry form, rather than issuing a physical paper certificate of ownership [233]

Book value value of a common stock expressed as total stockholders' equity divided by the number of shares of stock [229]

Boster, Adam, 96

Boston Beer, 70

Bowen, Brent, 91

Bowersox, Bob, 173

Boycott labor action in which workers refuse to buy the products of a targeted employer [146]

Boykin, Jerome, 137

BP, 20, 57

Branch office foreign office set up by an international or multinational firm [58]

Brand awareness extent to which a brand name comes to mind when the consumer considers a particular product category [159]

Brand competition competitive marketing that appeals to consumer perceptions of benefits of products offered by particular companies [152]

Branding process of using symbols to communicate the qualities of a product made by a particular producer [159–160]

Brand loyalty pattern of regular consumer purchasing based on satisfaction with product [155]

Brand names, 160

Brazil, 21, 55

Breakeven analysis for a particular selling price, assessment of the sellers costs versus revenues at various sales volumes [167]

Breakeven point sales volume at which the seller's total revenue from sales equals total costs (variable and fixed) with neither profit nor loss [167]

Bribery, 21

British Airways, 27

Broker independent intermediary who matches numerous sellers and buyers as needed, often without knowing in advance who they will be [169–170]

Brokerage services, 219

Budget detailed statement of estimated receipts and expenditures for a future period of time [206]

Bulgaria, 49

Bull market period of rising stock prices [233, 234]

Business organization that provides goods or services to earn profits [4]
    benefits of, 4
    buying existing, 38
    entertainment and, 12
    external environments of, 4–5

Business (competitive) strategy strategy, at the business-unit or product-line level, focusing on improving a firm's competitive position [71]

Business continuation agreement special form of business insurance whereby owners arrange to buy the interests of deceased associates from their heirs [244]

Business culture, risk taking and, 7

Business cycle short-term pattern of economic expansions and contractions [13]

Business ethics ethical or unethical behaviors by employees in the context of their jobs [20]
    company practices and, 23

Business financing, 236–238, 240–241

Business forms
    cooperatives, 42
    corporations, 41, 43–45
    partnerships, 41–42
    sole proprietorships, 41

Business goals, setting, 69–71

Business interruption insurance insurance covering income lost during times when a company is unable to conduct business [244]

Business management. *See* Management

Business plan document in which the entrepreneur summarized her or his business strategy for the proposed new venture and how that strategy will be implemented [37]

Business practice law law of regulation governing business practices in given countries [60, 61]

Business process reengineering the rethinking and radical redesign of business processes to improve performance, quality, and productivity [103]

Business strategy, as driver of operations, 94–96

Buyers, organizational, 156

Buzz marketing a promotional method that relies on work of mouth to create buzz about products and ideas [160]

C

Cabot Creamery, 42

Cafeteria benefits plan benefit plan that sets limits on benefits per employee, each of whom may choose form a variety of alternative benefits [141]

Calvin Klein, 27

Canada, 48

CAN-SPAM Act, 194–195

Capacity amount of a product that a company can produce under normal conditions [96]

Capacity competence required of individuals entering into a binding contract [246]

Capacity planning, 96–97

Capital funds needed to create and operate a business enterprise [6]
    lack of, in start-ups, 40–41
    paid-in, 204

Capital gains the earnings, reflecting changed in market value, from buying and selling a share of stock [236]

Capital growth, 228–235

Capitalism system that sanctions the private ownership of the factors of production and encourages entrepreneurship by offering profits as incentive [7–8]

Capital item expensive, long-lasting, infrequently purchased industrial good, such as a building, or industrial services, such as building maintenance [157, 158]

Carbon dioxide emissions, 25

Carbon offsets, 26

Carbon trading, 227

Caring, 22

Cartel association of producers whose purpose is to control supply and prices [60, 61]

Cash flows, 206

Catalog showroom bargain retailer to which customers place order for catalog items to be picked up at on-premises warehouses [172]

Cendant, 210

Centralized organization organization in which most decision-making authority is held by upper-level management [81]

Certificates of deposit (CDs), 215

Certified Development Company (504) program, 39

Certified Fraud Examiner (CFE) professional designation administered by the association of Certified Fraud Examiners in recognition of qualifications for a specialty area within forensic accounting [201]

Certified management accountant (CMA) professional designation awarded by the Institute of Management Accountants in recognition of management accounting qualifications [200]

Certified public accountant (CPA) accountant licensed by the state and offering services to the public [198–200]

Chain of command reporting relationships within a company [78]

Chambers, John, 39

Chamitoff, Ken, 96

Change management, 74–75

Chaparral Steel, 79

Charismatic leadership type of influence based on the leader's personal charisma [125–126]

Check demand deposit order instructing a bank to pay a given sum to a specified payee [215]

Check Clearing for the 21st Century Act, 222–223

Checking account bank account funds, owned by the depositor, that may be withdrawn at any time by check or cash [215]

Chenault, Kenneth, 64

Chevron, 57

Chief executive officer (CEO) top manager who is responsible for the overall performance of a corporation [44, 45, 127]

Chief financial officer (CFO), 67

Chief information officer (CIO), 67

Children's Online Privacy Protection Act, 26

China
    communism in, 7
    emergence of, 49
    free enterprise in, 7
    oil demand in, 3
    private ownership in, 8
    trade balance in, 51

Chinese Petroleum, 49

Chipotle Mexican Grill, 71

Chiquita, 60

Cisco, 39

Citigroup, 24

Civil Rights Act, 141

Clark Equipment, 83, 84

Classical theory of motivation theory holding that workers are motivated solely by money [111–112]

Clayton Act, 12

Clean Harbors, 41

Client relationships, 118

Clients, 186

Client-server network a common business network in which clients make requests for information or resources and servers provide the services [186]

Climate change, 25–26

Closely held (private) corporation corporation whose stock is held by only a few people and is not available for sale to the general public [43, 44]

Coach, 63

Coaches, leaders as, 127

Coalition an informal alliance of individuals or groups formed to achieve a common goal [132]

Coca-Cola, 67, 161, 240

Codes of conduct, 23, 210

Code of professional conduct the code of ethics for CPAs as maintained and enforced by the AICPA [210]

Collaboration, 182–183

Collateral an asset pledged for the fulfillment of paying a loan [236]

Collective bargaining process by which labor and management negotiate conditions of employment for union-represented workers [145–147]

Collectivism, 128

Collusion illegal agreement between two or more companies to commit a wrongful act [27]

Commercial bank company that accepts deposits that it used to make loans, earn profits, pay interest to depositors, and pay dividends to owners [216]

Commitment, escalation of, 132

Committee and team authority authority granted to committees or teams involved in a firm's daily operations [83–84]

Common law body of decisions handed down by courts ruling on individual cases [245]

Common stock the most basic form of ownership, including voting rights in major issues, in a company [228–229, 241]

Communication, of corporate culture, 74–75

Communication mix, 176

Communication networks, 185–186

Communism political system in which the government owns and operates all factors of production [7]

Comparative advantage the ability to produce some products more efficiently than others [55]

Compensation, 139–140, 146

Compensation system total package of rewards that organizations provide to individuals in return for their labor [139]

Compensatory damages monetary payments intended to redress injury actually suffered because of a tort [247]

Competition vying among businesses for the same resources or customers [10]
    brand, 152
    degrees of, 11
    international, 152
    in market economy, 10–12
    monopolistic, 11
    oligopoly, 11–12
    perfect, 11
Competitive advantage, forms of, 54–55
Competitive environment, 152

Competitive product analysis process by which a company analyzes a competitor's products to identify desirable improvements [102–103]

Complaints.com, 99

Compound growth how a sum of money grows by paying interest on the principal of an investment, as well as paying interest on previously earned interest, over several time periods [228]

Computer-aided design (CAD) IS with software that helps knowledge workers design products by simulating them and displaying then in three-dimensional graphics [191]

Computer-based scheduling, 100

Computer network a group of two or more computers linked together by some form of cabling or by wireless technology to share data or resources, such as a printer [186]

Computer viruses, 193, 194

Conceptual skills abilities to think in the abstract, diagnose and analyze different situations, and see beyond the present situation [68]

Confidentiality, 21

Conflict of interest, 21

ConocoPhillips, 57

Conscientiousness, 109

Consideration any item of value exchanged between parties to create a valid contract [246]

Consistency a dimension of quality that refers to sameness of product quality from unit to unit [98]

Construction, small business, 35

ConsumerAffairs.com, 99

Consumer behavior study of the decision process by which people buy and consume products [154]
    influences on, 154–155
    understanding, 154–155
Consumer Bill of Rights, 27
Consumer buying process, 155
Consumer choice, 4, 8–9
Consumer complaints, 161
Consumer demand, 17

Consumer goods physical products purchased by consumers for personal use [150]

Consumerism form of social activism dedicated to protecting the rights of consumers in their dealings with businesses [26]

Consumer price index (CPI) a measure of the prices of typical products purchased by consumers living in urban areas [16]

Consumer products, categories of, 157
Consumer rights, 26–27
Contests, 177
Continental Airlines, 66, 117–118

Contingency planning identifying aspects of a business or its environment that might entail changes in strategy [73]

Contingent workers employee hired on something other than a full-time basis to supplement an organization's permanent workforce [144–145]

Contract agreement between two or more parties enforceable in court [246]

Contract issues, 145–146

Controller person who manages all of a firm's accounting activities (chief accounting officer) [198]

Controlling management process of monitoring an organization's performance to ensure that it is meeting its goals [66]

Control process, 66
Control systems, weak, 40

Convenience goods and services inexpensive good or service purchased and consumed rapidly and regularly [157]

Convenience store retail store offering easy accessibility, extended hours, and fast service [172]

Cooperative form of ownership in which a group of sole proprietorships and/or partnerships agree to work together for common benefits [42]

Copyright exclusive ownership right belonging to the creator of a book, article, design, illustration, photo, film, or musical work [247]

Core competencies for accounting the combination of skills, technology, and knowledge that will be necessary for the future CPA [200]

Corporate bond bond issued by a company as a source of long-term funding [238]

Corporate culture the shared experiences, stories, beliefs, and norms that characterize an organization [74–75]

Corporate foundations, 30

Corporate governance roles of shareholders, directors, and other managers in corporate decision making and accountability [44–45]

Corporate ownership, issues in, 45

Corporate raider an investor conducting a type of hostile corporate takeover against the wishes of the company [239]

Corporate scandals, 24, 25, 197

Corporate strategy strategy for determining the firm's overall attitude toward growth and the way it will manage its businesses or product lines [71]

Corporation business that is legally considered an entity separate from its owners and is liable for its own debts; owners' liability extends to the limits of their investments [42]
    advantages of a, 43
    characteristics, 41, 43
    disadvantages of a, 43
    going public, 238–240
    management, 44–45
    types of, 43–44

Cost of goods sold costs of obtaining materials for making the products sold by a firm during the year [205]

Cost-of-living adjustment (COLA) labor contract clause tying future raises to changes in consumer purchasing power [146]

Cost of revenues costs that a company incurs to obtain revenues from other companies [205]

Cost-oriented pricing pricing that considers the firm's desire to make a profit and its need to cover production costs [166–167]

Costs, 167

Counterproductive behaviors behaviors that detract from organizational performance [108–109]

Coupon sales promotion technique in which a certificate is issued entitling the buyer to a reduced price [177]
CPA Vision Project, 199–200
Creative selling personal selling task in which salespeople try to persuade buyers to purchase products by providing information about their benefits [177]
Credit cards, 223
Creditor nations, 15
Credit Suisse First Boston, 24
Credit union nonprofit, cooperative financial institution owned and run by its members, usually employees of a particular organization [217]
Crisis management organization's methods for dealing with emergencies [73]
Cross-cultural leadership, 128
Cultural differences
    in communication, 142
    global business and, 58, 59, 88
    in leadership styles, 128
Cultural forces, shaping business, 36
Currency (cash) government-issued paper money and metal coins [215]
Currency exchange, 218
Currency trading, 213
Current asset asset that can or will be converted into cash within a year [203]
Current dividend/interest yield yearly dollar amount of income divided by the investment's current market value, expressed as a percent [235]
Current liability debt that must be paid within one year [204]
Current ratio financial ratio for measuring a company's ability to pay current debts out of current assets [208]
Curves, 38
Customer contact, 94
Customer departmentalization dividing an organization to offer products and meet needs for identifiable customer groups [80–81]
Customer identification program (CIP), 222
Customers, 24
    closeness with, 103
    presence of in operations process, 93–94
    responsibility toward, 26–27
Customer satisfaction, 112, 150
Customer service, improving, 98–99
Customization, 183, 184
Cybermall Collection of virtual storefronts (business Web sites) representing a variety of products and product lines on the Internet [173]
Cyclical unemployment, 17

D

Daewoo, 49
DaimlerChrysler, 57
Dark Knight (film), 149
Data raw facts and figures that, by themselves, may not have much meaning [189]
Data mining the application of electronic technologies for searching, sifting, and reorganizing pools of data to uncover useful information [151, 189–190]
Data warehousing the collection, storage, and retrieval of data in electronic files [151, 189–190]
Debit card plastic card that allows an individual to transfer money between accounts [223]
Debt a company's total liabilities [208]
    national, 15
Debt financing long-term borrowing from sources outside a company [240–241]
Debtor nations, 15
Decentralized organization organization in which a great deal of decision-making authority is delegated to levels of management at points below the top [81–82]
Decision making choosing one alternative from among several options [130]
    behavioral aspects of, 131–133
    political forces in, 132
    rational, 130–131
    steps in process of, 130–131
Decision-making hierarchy, 81–84
Decision-making skills skills in defining problems and selecting the best courses of action [68]
Decision support system (DSS) interactive system that creates virtual business models for a particular kind of decision and tests them with different data to see how they respond [192]
Deductible an amount of the loss that the insured must absorb prior to reimbursement [243]
Default failure of the borrower to make payment when due to lenders [238]
Defensive stance approach to social responsibility by which a company meets only minimum legal requirements in its commitments to groups and individuals in its social environment [29]
Delegation process through which a manager allocates work to subordinates [82, 83]
Dell, Michael, 34
Dell Computer, 34, 38, 59, 166
Delphi Automotive Systems, 170

Demand the willingness and ability of buyers to purchase a good or service [9]
    consumer, 17
    international, 56
    law of, 9–10
    in market economy, 8–10
Demand and supply schedule assessment of the relationships among different levels of demand and supply at different price levels [9, 10]
Demand conditions, 55
Demand curve graph showing how many units of a product will be demanded (bought) at different prices [9, 10]
Demand deposits, 215
Demographic segmentation, 154
Demographic variables characteristics of populations that may be considered in developing a segmentation strategy [154]
Denial of service (DoS) attacks, 192
Departmentalization process of grouping jobs into logical units [80–81]
Department store large product-line retailer characterized by organization into specialized departments [171]
Depreciation accounting method for distributing the cost of an asset over its useful life [203]
Depression a prolonged and deep recession [16, 17]
Deregulation elimination of rules that restrict business activity [245]
Detailed schedule a schedule showing daily work assignments with start and stop times for assigned jobs [99]
Differentiation strategies, 11
Digital transmission, 174
Direct channel distribution channel in which a product travels from producer to consumer without intermediaries [169]
Direct-response retailing form of nonstore retailing by direct interaction with customers to inform them of products and to receive sales orders [172]
Direct selling form of nonstore retailing typified by door-to-door sales [172]
Discount broker, 232
Discount house bargain retailer that generates large sales volume by offering goods at substantial price reductions [172]
Discount rate interest rate at which member banks can borrow money from the Fed [222]
Discounts price reduction offered as an incentive to purchase [169]
Discover Financial Services, 45
Discrimination, employment, 28

Discrimination law, 142–143

Discriminatory harassment, 109

Disney, Walt, 65, 79

Distribution part of the marketing mix concerned with getting products from producers to consumers [153]
international, 162
as marketing strategy, 175–176
physical, 174–176
small business, 163

Distribution channel network of interdependent companies through which a product passes from producer to end user [169–170]

Distribution mix the combination of distribution channels by which a firm gets its products to end users [169–170]

Diversification purchase of several different kinds of investments rather than just one [236]

Divestiture strategy whereby a firm sells one or more of its business units [44, 45]

Dividends a payment to shareholders, on a per share basis, out of the company's earnings [229, 235]

Divisional structure organizational structure in which corporate divisions operate as autonomous businesses under the larger corporate umbrella [84–86]

Divisions department that resembles a separate business in that it produces and markets its own products [84]

Dole, 60

Domestic business environment the environment in which a firm conducts its operations and derives its revenues [4, 5]

Donahoe, John, 121

Double taxation situation in which taxes may be payable both by a corporation on its profits and by shareholders on dividend incomes [43]

Dow Jones Industrial Average (DJIA) market index based on the prices of 30 of the largest industrial firms listed on the NYSE [234]

Downsizing, 111

DriveSavers, 137

Drug tests, 138

Due date, 238

Duke Energy, 73

Dumping practice of selling a product abroad for less than the cost of production [60, 61]

Duncan, David, 24

Dynamic pricing, 168

E

Earnings cycle, 207

Earnings per share profitability ratio measuring the net profit that the company earns for each share of outstanding stock [209–210]

Eastern Europe, 49

eBay, 121, 159, 168

E-cash electronic money that moves between consumers and businesses via digital electronic transmissions [224]

E-catalog nonstore retailing in which the Internet is used to display products [172–173]

E-commerce the use of the Internet and other electronic means for retailing and business-to-business transactions [182]
emergence of, 39
in Europe, 49

Economic differences, 59

Economic environment relevant conditions that exist in the economic system in which a company operates [5, 151–152]

Economic growth, 12–15

Economic impact, of multinationals, 57

Economic indicator a statistic that helps assess the performance of an economy [12–17]

Economic stability, 15–17

Economic system a nation's system for allocating its resources among its citizens [5–8]
factors of production, 5–6
market economy, 7–8
mixed market economy, 8
planned economy, 6–7
types of, 6–8

Economy, global, 48–55

Edmunds, Gladys, 41

Edmunds Travel Consultants, 41

E-intermediary Internet distribution channel member that assists in delivering products to customers or that collects information about various sellers to be presented to consumers [172–174]

Electric companies, 12

Electronic Arts, 82, 107

Electronic banking, 222–224

Electronic communication network (ECN) electronic trading system that brings buyers and sellers together outside traditional stock exchanges [232]

Electronic conferencing IT that allows groups of people to communicate simultaneously from various locations via e-mail, phone, or video [186]

Electronic funds transfer (EFT) communication of fund-transfer information over wire, cable, or microwave [219]

Electronic retailing (online retailing) nonstore retailing in which information about the seller's products and services is connected to consumers' computers, allowing consumers to receive the information and purchase the products in the home [172–174]

Electronic storefront commercial Web site in which customers gather information about products, buying opportunities, placing orders, and paying for purchases, [173]

Ells, Steve, 71

E-mail
management of, 68
privacy issues, 24

Embargo government order banning exportation and/or importation of a particular product or all products from a particular country [59]

Eminent domain principle that the government may claim private land for public use by buying it at a fair price [248]

Emissions Trading Scheme (ETS), 227

Emission trading (ET), 227

Emotional intelligence the extent to which people are self-aware, can manage their emotions, can motivate themselves, express empathy for others, and possess social skills [110]

Emotionality, 109

Emotional motives reasons for purchasing a product that are based on nonobjective factors [155]

Emotional quotient (EQ) the extent to which people are self-aware, can manage their emotions, can motivate themselves, express empathy for others, and possess social skills [110]

Empathy, 110

Employee behavior the pattern of actions by the members of an organization that directly or indirectly influences the organization's effectiveness [108–109]

Employee e-mails, 24

Employee-focused leader behavior leader behavior focusing on satisfaction, motivation, and well-being of employees [123]

Employee information system computerized system containing information on each employee's education, skills, work experiences, and career aspirations [136–137]

Employee Retirement Income Security Act, 142

Employees
behavior toward, 20–21
compensation and benefits for, 139–141
individual differences among, 109–110
matching to jobs, 110–111
motivation of, 111–119
performance appraisals, 139
responsibility toward, 27–28
selection of, 137–138
as stakeholders, 24
training of, 138

Employment at will principle, increasingly modified by legislation and judicial decision, that organizations should be able to retain or dismiss employees at their discretion [143]
Employment discrimination, 28
Empowerment, employee, 116–117

Encryption software software that assigns an e-mail message to a unique code number (digital fingerprint) for each computer so only that computer, not others, can open and read the message [194]
Enron, 24, 28, 197
Enterprise, 4
Enterprise resource planning (ERP), 183
Entertainment, merging of business with, 12

Entrepreneur individual who accepts the risk and opportunities involved in creating and operating a new business venture [6, 36–37]

Entrepreneurship the process of seeking businesses opportunities under conditions of risk [36]
Environment, responsibility toward, 25–26

Environmental analysis process of scanning the business environment for threats and opportunities [72]
Environmental management system, 103

Equal employment opportunity legally mandated nondiscrimination in employment on the basis of race, creed, sex, or national origin [141–142]

Equal Employment Opportunity Commission (EEOC) federal agency enforcing several discrimination-related laws, 141
Equal Pay act, 141

Equilibrium price profit-maximizing price at which the quantity of goods demanded and the quantity of goods supplied are equal [9, 10]

Equity financing the use of owners' funds from inside the company as the source of long-term funding [240, 241]
Equity Marketing, 158
Equity theory, 114–115

Escalation of commitment condition in which a decision maker becoming so committed to a course of action that she or he stays with it even when it appears to have been wrong [132]

Ethical behavior behavior conforming to generally accepted social norms concerning beneficial and harmful actions [20]
assessing, 22–23

Ethical leadership leader behaviors that reflect high ethical standards [129]
Ethical norms, 22

Ethics beliefs about what is right and wrong or good and bad in actions that affect others [20]
accounting, 210–211
advertising, 27
company practices and, 23
individual, 20
international, 21
managerial, 20–21
Ethics programs, 23

Euro a common currency shared among most of the members of the European Union (excluding Denmark, Sweden, and the United Kingdom) [53, 213]
Europe, 49
European Central Bank (ECB), 213

European Union (EU) agreement among major Western European nations to eliminate or make uniform most trade barriers affecting group members [49, 50]

Exchange rate rate at which the currency of one nation can be exchanged for the currency of another nation [53–54]

Exchange-traded fund (ETF) a bundle of stocks or bonds that are in an index that tracks the overall movement of a market but, unlike a mutual fund, can be traded like a stock [230, 235]

Expectancy theory theory of motivation holding that people are motivated to work toward rewards that they want and that they believe they have a reasonable chance of obtaining [114]

Expense item industrial product purchased and consumed rapidly and regularly for daily operations [157, 158]

Export product made or grown domestically but shipped and sold abroad [48]

Exporter firm that distributes and sells products to one or more foreign countries [56]

Express authority agent's authority, derived from written agreement, to bind a principal to a certain course of action [248]

Express warranty warranty whose terms are specifically stated by the seller [248]

External environment everything outside an organization's boundaries that might affect it [4–5]

External recruiting attracting persons outside the organization to apply for jobs [137]

Extranet a system that allows outsiders limited access to a firm's internal information network [186]
Extraversion, 109
ExxonMobil, 23, 56, 57, 82, 240

F

Facebook, 33, 237

Face value (par value) amount of money that the bond buyer (lender) lent the issuer, and that the lender will receive upon repayment [238]

Factors of production resources used in the production of goods and services— labor, capital, entrepreneurs, physical resources, and information resources [5–6]
capital, 6
competitive advantage and, 55
entrepreneur, 6
information resources, 6
labor, 5–6
physical resources, 6

Factory outlet bargain retailer owned by the manufacturer whose products it sells [172]
Fair and Accurate Credit Transactions Act (FACTA), 194
Fair Labor Standards Act, 142
False Claims Act, 28
Favoritism, 21
Federal Aviation Administration (FAA), 91
Federal Contract Compliance Programs (OFCCP), 141

Federal Deposit Insurance Corporation (FDIC) federal agency that guarantees the safety of deposits up to $100,000 in the financial institutions that it insures [219–220]
Federal Emergency Management Agency (FEMA), 65–66

Federal funds rate interest rate at which commercial banks lend reserve to each other, usually overnight [222]
Federal Open Market Committee, 220

Federal Reserve System (the Fed) central bank of the United States, which acts as the government's bank, serves member commercial banks, and controls the nation's money supply [16, 17, 220–222]
functions of, 221

types of, 71
using, to motivate behavior, 116
Goal setting, 69–71
Godiva, 98
Gold farming, 190

Goods operations (goods production)
activities producing tangible products,
such as radios, newspapers, buses, and
textbooks [92]
   vs. service operations, 93–94
Goods production processes, 94

Goodwill amount paid for an existing
business above the value of its other
assets [204]
Goodyear, 140–141
Google, 23, 36, 159, 184, 203, 204,
   205, 208
Gordon, Gil, 119
Government regulation, 25

Green marketing the marketing of
environmentally friendly goods [26, 27]
Green policies, 26

Greenwashing using advertising to
project a green image without adopting
substantive environmentally friendly
changes [26]

Gross domestic product (GDP) total
value of all goods and services produced
within a given period by a national
economy through domestic factors of
production [13–14]
   nominal, 14
   per capita, 13, 14
   real, 13–14
Gross national product (GNP), 13

Gross profit a preliminary, quick-to-
calculate profit figure calculated from the
firm's revenues minus its cost of
revenues (the direct costs of getting the
revenues) [205]
Groupware, 188–189
Growth, specialization and, 79
Grubman, Jack, 24
Guidry, Kenneth, 207

H

Hacker cybercriminal who gains
unauthorized access to a computer or
network, either to steal information, money,
or property or to tamper with data [192]
Hagan, Jay, 137
Halliburton, 140
Handheld computers, 188

Hardware the physical components of a
computer network, such as keyboards,
monitors, system units, and printers [188]
Hastings, Reed, 65, 162
Hawala, 215

Hawthorne effect tendency for
productivity to increase when workers
believe they are receiving special attention
from management [112]
HCA, 210
Helton, Todd, 140
Henderson, Jill, 111
Hershey, 56
Herzberg, Frederick, 113
Hesse, Dan, 74
Hewlett-Packard (HP), 65, 78, 89, 160

Hierarchy of human needs model
theory of motivation describing five levels
of human needs and arguing that basic
needs must be fulfilled before people
work to satisfy higher-level needs [113]

High-contact system level of customer
contact in which the customer is part of
the system during service delivery [94]
High-income countries, 48
Hiring process, 137–138
Hispanics, as business owners, 39
Hollywood, 47
Home country, 5
Honda, 26
Honesty, 21
Hong Kong, 49
Horizon Software International, 40

Hostile work environment form of
sexual harassment deriving from off-color
jokes, lewd comments, and so forth [143]

Human relations skills skills in
understanding and getting along with
people [68]

Human resource management (HRM)
set of organizational activities directed at
attracting, developing, and maintaining an
effective workforce
   challenges for, 143–145
   compensation and benefits, 139–141
   foundations of, 136–137
   legal context of, 141–143
   organized labor and, 145–147
   staffing the organization, 137–138
   strategic importance of, 136
Human resource manager, 66
Human resource planning, 136–137
Human resources, 5–6
Human resources model, 112–113
Human resource supply and demand,
   136, 137
Hungary, 49
Hurricane Katrina, 20, 65–66, 73

Hypertext transfer protocol (HTTP)
the communications protocol used for the
World Wide Web, in which related pieces
of information on separate Web pages are
connected using hyperlinks [185]
Hyundai, 49

I

IBM, 30, 56
IBP, 29

Identity theft unauthorized stealing of
personal information (such as social
security number and address) to get loans,
credit cards, or other monetary benefits by
impersonating the victim [192–193, 194]
Identity Theft Resource Center, 194
ImClone, 29

Implied authority agent's authority,
derived from business custom, to bind a
principal to a certain course of action [248]

Implied warranty warranty, dictated by
law, based on the principle that products
should fulfill advertised promises and
serve the purposes for which they are
manufactured and sold [249]

Import product made or grown abroad
but sold domestically [48]

Importer firm that buys products in
foreign markets and then imports them for
resale in its home country [56]
Import-export balances, 50–52

Incentive program special compensation
program designed to motivate high
performance [139–140]
Income
   net, 205
   operating, 205
   per capita, 48

Income statement financial statement
listing a firm's annual revenues and
expenses so that a bottom line shows
annual profit or loss [204–205]

Independent agent foreign individual or
organization that agrees to represent an
exporter's interests [57]
Index-matching ETFs, 235
India, 51
Individualism, 128

Individual differences personal
attributes that vary from one person to
another [109–110]
Individual ethics, 20
Individual investor trading, 232–233

Individual retirement accounts (IRAs)
tax-deferred pension fund that wage
earners set up to supplement retirement
funds [218]

Industrial goods physical products
purchased by companies to produce other
products [150]

Industrial market organizational market
consisting of firms that buy goods that are
either converted into products or used
during production [156]

Industrial products, 157, 158

Inflation occurs when widespread price increases occur throughout an economic system [16, 221]

Informal groups, 89

Informal organization network, unrelated to the firm's formal authority structure, of everyday social interactions among company employees [88, 89]

Information the meaningful, useful interpretation of data [189]

Information manager, 67

Information overload, 151

Information resources data and other information used by businesses [6]

Information seeking, 155

Information system (IS) a system that uses IT resources to convert data into information and to collect, process, and transmit that information for use in decision making [189–192]
  accounting, 198
  decision support system, 192
  knowledge, 191
  management, 191
  types of, 190–192

Information systems managers managers who operate the systems used for gathering, organizing, and distributing information [189]

Information technology (IT) the various appliances and devices for creating, storing, exchanging, and using information in diverse modes, including visual images, voice, multimedia, and business data
  impact of, 182–184
  protection measures, 194–195
  resources, 185–189
  risks and threats, 192–194

Infosys Technologies, 112

Initial public offering (IPO), 238

Innovation, 34–35

Insider trading illegal practice of using special knowledge about a firm for profit or gain [29, 229, 233]

Instapreneur, 181

Institutional market organizational market consisting of such nongovernmental buyers of goods and services as hospitals, churches, museums, and charitable organizations [156]

Insurance, small businesses in, 35

Insurance company nondeposit institution that invests funds collected as premiums charged for insurance coverage [217]

Insurance premium fee paid to an insurance company by a policyholder for insurance coverage [243]

Insurance policy a formal agreement to pay the policyholder a specified amount in the event of certain losses [243]

Intangibility, 93

Intangible asset nonphysical asset, such as a patent or trademark, that has economic value in the form of expected benefit [203–204]

Intangible personal property property that cannot be seen, but exists by virtue of written documentation [247]

Intangibles, 94

Intellectual property something produced by the that has commercial value [193]

Intellectual property property created through a person's creative activities [247]

International law general set of cooperative agreements and guidelines established by countries to govern the actions of individuals, businesses, and nations [249]

Intentional tort tort resulting from the deliberate actions of a party [247]

Interactive marketing nonstore retailing that uses a Web site to provide real-time sales and customer service [173]

Interest fee paid to a lender for the use of borrowed funds; like a rental fee [237]

Interest rate controls, 222

Intermediaries individual or firm that helps to distribute a product [169]

Intermediate goal goal set for a period of one to five years into the future [71]

Internal recruiting considering present employees as candidates for openings [137]

International banking and finance, 224–225

International business
  cultural forces shaping, 36
  levels of involvement, 56–57
  management, 55–59
  practices, 21

International competition competitive marketing of domestic products against foreign products [152]

International demand, 56

International distribution, 162

International firm firm that conducts a significant portion of its business in foreign countries [56]

International law general set of cooperative agreements and guidelines established by countries to govern the actions of individuals, businesses, and nations [249]

International marketing mix, 161–162

International Monetary Fund (IMF) U.N. agency consisting of about 150 nations that have combined resources to promote stable exchange rates, provide temporary short-term loans, and serve other purposes [224–225]

International operations, decision making about, 55–56

International organizational structures approaches to organizational structure developed in response to the need to manufacture, purchase, and sell in global markets [57–59, 86–87]

International payments process, 224

International pricing, 162

International products, 161

International stakeholders, 25

International trade
  barriers to, 59–61
  competitive advantage and, 54–55
  exchange rates, 53–54
  import-export balances, 50–52
  scope of, 48
  trade agreements, 49–50

Internet a gigantic system of interconnected computers; more than 100 million computers in over 100 countries [185]

Internet start-ups, 49

Interviews, 138

Intraday trading, 230

Intranet an organization's private network of internally linked Web sites accessible only to employees [185–186]

Intrapreneuring process of creating and maintaining the innovation and flexibility of a small-business environment within the confines of a large organization [88]

Intuition an innate belief about something, often without conscious consideration [132]

Inventory control receiving, storing, handling, and counting of all raw materials, partly finished goods, and finished goods [101]

Investigative accounting, 200

Investment bank financial institution engaged in issuing and reselling new securities [231]

Investments
  exchange-traded funds, 230
  mutual funds, 229–230
  risk-return relationship, 235–236
  stock, 228–229
  time value of money, 228

Investors, 24, 28–29

Involuntary bankruptcy bankruptcy proceedings initiated by the creditors of an indebted individual or organization [249]

Ireland, 49

ISO 14000 certification program attesting to the fact that a factory, laboratory, or office has improved its environmental performance [103]

ISO 9000 Program certifying that a factory, laboratory, or office has met the quality management standards set by the International Organization for Standardization [103]

iTunes, 72, 165

J

Japan, 7, 49
    cultural conditions in, 58
    leadership styles in, 128
Jargon, 209
JB Sweeping Service, 137
J. C. Penney, 74
Jeitinho, 21
JetBlue, 12

Job analysis systematic analysis of jobs within an organization [136]
Job applicants, screening, 137–138
Job creation, 34

Job description description of the duties and responsibilities of a job, its working conditions, and the tools, materials, equipment, and information used to perform it [136]

Job enrichment method of increasing job satisfaction by adding one or more motivating factors to job activities [117–118]
Job interviews, 138

Job redesign method of increasing job satisfaction by designing a more satisfactory fit between workers and their jobs [118]
Job rotation, 117
Jobs, matching people to, 110–111
Jobs, Steve, 75, 129

Job satisfaction degree of enjoyment that people derive from performing their jobs [107, 110]
Job security, 146
Job shops, 97

Job specialization the process of identifying the specific jobs that need to be done and designating the people who will perform them [79]

Job specification description of the skills, abilities, and other credentials and qualifications required by a job [136]
John Deere, 116
Johnson & Johnson, 23, 85

Joint venture strategic alliance in which the collaboration involves joint ownership of the new venture [44, 45]

Jung, Andrea, 128
Junk bonds, 238
Justice, 22

Just-in-time (JIT) production a type of lean production system that brings together all materials at the precise time they are required at each production stage [101]

K

Karlgaard, Richard, 107
Kautzman, Frank, 158
Kelleher, Herb, 65
Kelman, Glenn, 127
Kennedy, John F., 26

Key Person Insurance special form of business insurance designed to offset expenses entailed by the loss of key employees [244]
Key rate, 222
KFC, 58

Knowledge information system information system that supports knowledge workers by providing resources to create, store, use, and transmit new knowledge for useful applications [191]

Knowledge workers employees who are of value because of the knowledge they possess [144, 191]
Koch, James, 70
Korean Air Lines, 27
Kozlowski, Dennis, 25
Kraft Foods, 80
Kroc, Ray, 38

L

Labels, 175

Labor (human resources) physical and mental capabilities of people as they contribute to economic production [5–6]

Labor relations process of dealing with employees who are represented by a union [145]

Labor union group of individuals working together to achieve shared job-related goals, such as higher pay, shorter working hours, more job security, greater benefits, or better working conditions [145]
Language differences, 58, 59
Latin America, 58, 60, 88

Law of demand principle that buyers will purchase (demand) more of a product as its price drops and less as its price increases [9–10]

Law of supply principle that producers will offer (supply) more of a product for sale as its price rises and less as its price drops [9–10]

Laws codified rules of behavior enforced by a society [245]
Lay, Kenneth, 28
Layout planning, 97–98
Leaders, as coaches, 127

Leadership the processes and behaviors used by someone, such as a manager, to motivate, inspire, and influence the behaviors of others [122]
    behavioral approach to [123–124]
    changing nature of, 127–128
    charismatic, 125–126
    cross-cultural, 128
    decision making and, 130–133
    early approaches to, 122–124
    emerging issues in, 128–130
    ethical, 129
    gender and, 127–128
    vs. management, 122
    nature of, 122
    situational approach to, 124
    special issues in, 126
    strategic, 128
    trait approaches to, 122–123
    transactional, 125
    transformational, 124–125
    virtual, 129–130
Leadership continuum, 124

Leadership neutralizers factors that may render leader behaviors ineffective [126]

Leadership substitutes individual, task, and organizational characteristics that tend to outweigh the need for a leader to initiate or direct employee performance [126]

Leading management process of guiding and motivating employees to meet an organization's objectives [65–66]
Lean organizations, 182

Lean production system a production system designed for smooth production flows that avoid inefficiencies, eliminate unnecessary inventories, and continuously improve production processes [101]
Learning organization, 88
Legal issues
    affecting international business, 59–61
    in human resource management, 141–143
Lesar, David, 140

Letter of credit bank promise, issued for a buyer, to pay a designated firm a certain amount of money if specified conditions are met [218]

Leverage ability to finance an investment through borrowed funds [208–209]
Leveraged buyouts, 208–209
Levi Strauss, 67, 117
Lexus, 24

Liability debt owed by a firm to an outside organization or individual [202]
    current, 204
    limited, 43
    long-term, 204
    unlimited, 41, 42

Liability insurance insurance covering losses resulting from damage to people or property when the insured party is judged liable [243]

Licensed brand brand-name product for whose name the seller has purchased the right from an organization or individual [160]

Licensing arrangement arrangement in which firms choose foreign individuals or organizations to manufacture or market their products in another country [57–58]
Lifestyle centers, 171

Limited liability legal principle holding investors liable for a firm's debts only to the limits of their personal investments in it [43]

Limited liability corporation (LLC) hybrid of a publicly held corporation and a partnership in which owners are taxed as partners but enjoy the benefits of limited liability [43, 44]

Limited partner partner who does not share in a firm's management and is liable for its debts only to the limits of said partner's investment [42]

Limited partnership type of partnership consisting of limited partners and a general (or managing) partner [42]
Lincoln, Abraham, 123

Line authority organizational structure in which authority flows in a direct chain of command from the top of the company to the bottom [83]

Line department department directly linked to the production and sales of a specific product [83]

Liquidity ease with which an asset can be converted into cash [203]
Livermore, Ann, 65

Loan principal the amount of money that is loaned and must be repaid [236]
Loans, 39, 237–238
Lobbyists, 132

Local area network (LAN) computers that are linked in a small area, such as all of a firm's computers within a single building [186]
Local communities, 24

Local content law law requiring that products sold in a particular country be at least partly made there [60–61]

Location planning, 97
Lockheed Martin, 183

Lockout management tactic whereby workers are denied access to the employer's workplace [146]
Logan Aluminum, 99
Lombardi, Vince, 126

Long-term goal goal set for an extended time, typically five years or more into the future [71]

Long-term liability debt that is not due for at least one year [204]

Low-contact system level of customer contact in which the customer need not be part of the system to receive the service [94]
Lower middle-income countries, 48
Low-income countries, 48
Lufthansa, 27

M

M-1 measure of the money supply that includes only the most liquid (spendable) forms of money [215, 216]

M-2 measure of the money supply that includes all the components of M-1 plus the forms of money that can be easily converted into spendable forms [215–216]

Mail order (catalog marketing) form of nonstore retailing in which customers place orders for catalog merchandise received through the mail [172]

Make-to-order operations activities for one-of-a-kind or custom-made production [94]
Make-to-order shops, 97

Make-to-stock operations activities for producing standardized products for mass consumption [94]

Management process of planning, organizing, leading, and controlling an organizations's resources to achieve its goals [64]
    areas of, 66–67
    corporate culture and, 74–75
    crisis, 73
    vs. leadership, 122
    levels of, 66, 67
    materials, 100, 101
    operations, 93
    participative, 116–117
    process, 64–66, 183
    scientific, 112
    strategic, 69–72
    team, 117

Management accountant private accountant who provides financial services to support managers in various business activities within a firm [200]

Management advisory services assistance provided by CPA firms in areas such as financial planning, information systems design, and other areas of concern for client firms [199]

Management by objective (MBO) set of procedures involving both managers and subordinates in setting goals and evaluating progress [116]

Management information system (MIS) computer system that supports managers by providing information—reports, schedules, plans, and budgets—that can be used for making decisions [191]
Management skills, 67–69

Managerial accounting field of accounting that serves internal users of a company's financial information [198]

Managerial ethics standards of behavior that guide individual managers in their work [20–21]
Managerial incompetence, 40
Managers
    information systems, 189
    leadership by, 65–66
    marketing, 152
    operations, 93
    role of, 64, 64–66
    types of, 66–67
Manufacturing, small businesses in, 35
Manufacturing operations, 93–94

Market mechanism for exchange between buyers and sellers of a particular good or service [7]
Marketable securities, 203

Market capitalization the total dollar value of all the company's outstanding shares [239–240]

Market economy economy in which individuals control production and allocation decisions through supply and demand [7–8]
    competition in, 10–12
    demand and supply in, 8–10

Market index summary of price trends in a specific industry and/or the stock market as a whole [233]

Marketing a set of processes for creating, communicating, and delivering value to customers and for managing customer relationships in ways that benefit the organization and its stakeholders
    buzz, 160

distribution as, 175–176
environment, 151–152
interactive, 173
international, 161–162
online, 161
organizational, 155–156
overview, 150–153
relationship, 151
target, 153
video, 173–174
viral, 160

Marketing manager manager who plans and implements the marketing activities that result in the transfer of products from producer to consumer [67, 152]

Marketing mix the combination of product, pricing, promotion, and distribution strategies used to market products [152–153]
international, 161–162
small business and, 162–163

Marketing plan detailed strategy for focusing marketing efforts on consumer needs and wants [152]

Market price profit-maximizing price at which the quantity of goods demanded and the quantity of goods supplied are equal [9, 10]

Market segmentation process of dividing a market into categories of customer types [153–154]
Market share objectives, 166
Market systems, economics of, 8–12

Market value current price of a share of stock in the stock market [229]

Markup amount added to an item's purchase cost to sell it at a profit [166–167]
Martha Stewart Living Omnimedia, 86, 87
Marx, Karl, 7
Maslow, Abraham, 113

Mass-customizaton a principle in which companies produce in large volumes, but each unit features the unique options the customer prefers [183, 184]

Master limited partnership form of ownership that sells shares to investors who receive profits and that pays taxes on income from profits [42]

Master production schedule schedule showing which products will be produced, and when, in upcoming time periods [99]

Materials management planning, organizing, and controlling the flow of materials from sources of supply through distribution of finished goods [100, 101]

Matrix structure organizational structure created by superimposing one form of structure onto another [86]

Maturity date (due date) future date when repayment of the bond is due from the bond issuer (borrower) [238]
Matz, Jack, 36
Maytag, 105
McDonald's, 30, 38, 54, 58, 81, 97
McEwan, Terry, 171
McGregor, Douglas, 112
McKim, Alan, 41
MediaBids.com, 168

Media mix combination of advertising media chosen to carry a message about a product [177]

Mediation method of resolving a labor dispute in which a third party suggests, but does not impose, a settlement [146, 147]
Medical advances, 184
Meetings, 68
Mellinger, Doug, 40
Merchandise inventory, 203
Merck, 26–27, 67

Merger the union of two corporations to form a new corporation [44, 45]
Mergers and acquisitions (M&As), 45

Merit salary system individual incentive linking compensation to performance in nonsales jobs [139]
Merkel, Angela, 128
Merrill Lynch, 111
Methods improvement, 98–99
Methods planning, 98–99
Mexico, 48–49
Micro-loan programs, 39
Microsoft, 38, 58–59

Middle manager manager responsible for implementing the strategies and working toward the goals set by top managers [66, 67]
Millennials, 153
Minimum wage, 142
Minorities, opportunities for, 39
Minority enterprise small-business investment companies (MESBICs), 39

Missionary selling personal selling task in which salespeople promote their firms and products rather than try to close sales [177]

Mission statement organization's statement of how it will achieve its purpose in the environment in which it conducts its business [70]

Mixed market economy economic system featuring characteristics of both planned and market economies [8]

Monetary policy management of the nation's economic growth by managing the money supply and interest rates [16, 17, 221]

Money any object that is portable, divisible, durable, and stable and that serves as a medium of exchange, a store of value, and a measure of worth
characteristics of, 214
functions of, 214
M-1, 215, 216
M-2, 215–216

Money market mutual fund fund of short-term, low-risk financial securities purchased with the pooled assets of investor-owners [215–216]
Money supply, 216

Monopolistic competition market or industry characterized by numerous buyers and relatively numerous sellers trying to differentiate their products from those of competitors [11]

Monopoly market or industry in which there is only one producer, which can therefore set the prices of its products [11, 12]
Monsanto, 67
Morgan, J.P., 25
Morgan Stanley, 45
Mortgage brokers, 218

Mortgage loan loan secured by property (the home) being purchased [254]

Motivation the set of forces that cause people to behave in certain ways [111, 115–119]
Motivational theories, 111–115

Multinational corporation form of corporation spanning national boundaries [43, 44]

Multinational firm firm that designs, produces, and markets products in many nations [56–57]
Murdoch, Rupert, 125

Mutual fund company that pools cash investments from individuals and organizations to purchase a portfolio of stocks, bonds, and other securities [229–231]

Mutual savings bank financial institution whose depositors are owners sharing in its profits [216]

N

Nacchio, Joseph P., 233
NASA, 86
NASCAR, 160

NASDAQ Composite Index value-weighted market index that includes all NASDAQ-listed companies, both domestic and foreign [234]

National Association of Securities Dealers Automated Quotation (NASDAQ) System world's oldest electronic stock market consisting of dealers who buy and sell securities over a network of electronic communications [232]

National brand brand-name product produced by, widely distributed by, and carrying the name of a manufacturer [160]

National competitive advantage international competitive advantage stemming from a combination of factor conditions, demand conditions, related and supporting industries, and firm strategies, structures, and rivalries [55]

National debt the amount of money the government owes its creditors [15]

National Semiconductor, 175–176

Natural monopoly industry in which one company can most efficiently supply all needed goods or services [12]

Natural Resource Defense Council, 19

Nature Conservancy, 27

Negligence conduct that falls below legal standards for protecting others against unreasonable risk [247]

Nestlé, 49, 56

Netflix.com, 162

Netherlands, 8, 49

Net income gross profit minus operating expenses and income taxes [205]

Networks, 186–187

Net worth, 202

Newington, Tim, 24

News Corp., 125

Newsweek magazine, 27

New ventures, 36

New York Giants, 67

New York Stock Exchange (NYSE), 231

Ning, 137

Nippon Steel, 49

Nissan, 80

Nominal GDP gross domestic product (GDP) measured in current dollars or with all components valued at current prices [14]

Noncertified public accountants, 199

Noncorporate business ownership, 41

Nondeposit institutions, 217

Nondirect distribution, 170

Nondisclosure agreements, 21

Nonstore retailing, 172

Nooyi, Indra, 77

North America, 48–49

North American Free Trade Agreement (NAFTA) agreement to gradually eliminate tariffs and other trade barriers among the United States, Canada, and Mexico [50]

North Korea, 7

O

Objectives, on business plan, 37

Obstructionist stance approach to social responsibility that involves doing as little as possible and may involve attempts to deny or cover up violations [29]

Occupational Safety and Health Act (OSHA) federal law setting and enforcing guidelines for protecting workers from unsafe conditions and potential health hazards in the workplace [142]

Ocean Spray, 42

Odd-even pricing psychological pricing tactic based on the premise that customers prefer prices not stated in even dollar amounts [169]

Officers, 44, 45

Offshoring the practice of outsourcing to foreign countries [56]

Off-the-job training training conducted in a controlled environment away from the work site [138]

Oligopoly market or industry characterized by a handful of (generally large) sellers with the power to influence the prices of their products [11–12]

Olis, Jamie, 199

Omniva Policy Systems, 24

Online anonymity, 188

Online banking, 223

Online distribution, 172–174

Online investing, 233

Online marketing, 161

Online pricing, 168

Online retailers, 173

Online retail spending, 39

On-the-job training training, sometimes informal, conducted while an employee is at work [138]

Open Market Committee, 220

Open-market operations the Fed's sales and purchases of securities in the open market [222]

Openness, 109

Operating expenses costs, other than the cost of revenues, incurred in producing a good or service [205]

Operating income gross profit minus operating expenses [205]

Operational plan plan setting short-term targets for daily, weekly, or monthly performance [65, 72]

Operations capability an activity or process that production does especially well with high proficiency [95–96]

Operations control process of monitoring production performance by comparing results with plans and taking corrective action when needed [100–102]

Operations planning, 96–99
   capacity planning, 96–97
   layout planning, 97–98
   location planning, 97
   methods planning, 98–99
   quality planning, 98

Operations process set of methods and technologies used to produce a good or a service [94]

Operations (production) activities involved in making products—goods and services—for customers [92]
   business strategy as driver of, 94–96
   goods, 92
   service, 92
   services vs. goods manufacturing, 93–94
value creation through, 92–94

Operations (production) management systematic direction and control of the processes that transform resources into finished products that create value for and provide benefits to customers [93]

Operations (production) managers managers responsible for ensuring that operations processes create value and provide benefits to customers [66–67, 93]

Operations scheduling, 99–100

Opportunity, 4, 183–184

Order processing personal selling task in which salespeople receive orders and see to their handling and delivery [177]

Organic foods, 175

Organizational analysis process of analyzing a firm's strengths and weaknesses [72]

Organizational buyer behavior, 156

Organizational citizenship positive behaviors that do not directly contribute to the bottom line [108]

Organizational commitment an individual's identification with the organization and its mission [110]

Organizational marketing, 155–156

Organizational markets, 156

Organizational stakeholders those groups, individuals, and organizations that are directly affected by the practices of an organization and who therefore have a stake in its performance [23]

Organizational structure specification of the jobs to be done within an organization and the ways in which they relate to one another [78]
   building blocks of, 79–81
   decision-making hierarchy, 81–84
   determinants of, 78
   forms of, 84–88
   in twenty-first century, 87–88

Organization chart diagram depicting a company's structure and showing employees where they fit into its operations [65, 78]

Organization of Petroleum Exporting Countries (OPEC), 61

Organized labor, 145–147

Organizing management process of determining how best to arrange an organization's resources and activities into a coherent structure [65]

Outcry market, 231

Outsourcing the practice of paying suppliers and distributors to perform certain business processes or to provide needed materials or services [56, 104–105]

Overwork, 107

Owners' equity amount of money that owners would receive if they sold all of a firm's assets and paid all of its liabilities [202, 204]

Ownership utility, 150

P

Pacific Asia, 49

Packaging physical container in which a product is sold, advertised, or protected [161]

Packaging reduction, 26

Paid-in capital money that is invested in a company by its owners [204]

Pannell Kerr Forster, 207

Paperwork, 68

Participative management and empowerment method of increasing job satisfaction by giving employees a voice in the management of their jobs and the company [116–117]

Partnerships, 41–42

Par value, 238

Patent exclusive legal right to use and license a manufactured item or substance, manufacturing process, or object design [248]

PATRIOT Act, 143, 222

Pay-for-knowledge plan incentive plan to encourage employees to learn new skills or become proficient at different jobs [140]

Pay for performance (variable pay) individual incentive that rewards a manager for especially productive output [140]

Penetration pricing setting an initially low price to establish a new product in the market [168]

Pension fund nondeposit pool of funds managed to provide retirement income for its members [217]

Pension services, 218

People's Republic of China. *See* China

PepsiCo, 77, 240

Per-capita income, 48

Perfect competition market or industry characterized by numerous small firms producing an identical product [11]

Performance a dimension of quality that refers to how well a product does what it is supposed to do [98]

Performance appraisals evaluation of an employee's job performance in order to determine the degree to which the employee is performing effectively [139]

Performance behaviors the total set of work-related behaviors that the organization expects employees to display [108]

Personality the relatively stable set of psychological attributes that distinguish one person from another [109–110]

Personal net worth value of one's total assets minus one's total liabilities (debts) [250]

Personal selling promotional tool in which a salesperson communicates one-to-one with potential customers [177]

Person-job fit the extent to which a person's contributions and the organization's inducements match one another [111]

Pharming, 193

Phishing, 193

Photo-Kicks, 96

Physical distribution activities needed to move a product efficiently from manufacturer to consumer [174–176]

Physical exams, 138

Physical resources tangible items organizations use in the conduct of their businesses [6]

Picketing labor action in which workers publicize their grievances at the entrance to an employer's facility [146]

Pipelines, 175

Piracy, 192

Pizza Hut, 58

Place (distribution) part of the marketing mix concerned with getting products from producers to consumers [153]

Place utility, 92, 150

Plain English Handbook (SEC), 209

Planes, 174

Planned economy economy that relies on a centralized government to control all or most factors of production and to make all or most production and allocation decisions [6–7]

Planning management process of determining what an organization needs to do and how best to get it done [64–65]

Plans, hierarchy of, 72

Poag & McEwan, 171

Poilâne, Lionel, 54

Point-of-sale (POS) display sales promotion technique in which product displays are located in certain areas to stimulate purchase or to provide information on a product [178]

Point-of-sale (POS) terminal electronic device that allows customers to pay for retail purchases with debit cards [223]

Poland, 7, 49

Political action committees (PACs), 151

Political issues
    affecting international business, 59–61
    in decision making, 132

Political-legal environment the relationship between business and government [5, 151]

Polygraph tests, 138

Ponoko, 181

Portable devices, 182

Portfolio the combined holdings of all the financial assets of any company or individual [236]

Positioning process of establishing an identifiable product image in the minds of consumers [176]

Positive reinforcement reward that follows desired behaviors [115–116]

Post office protocol (POP) one of the basic communications protocols used to receive e-mail [185]

Postpurchase evaluation, 155

Premium sales promotion technique in which offers of free or reduced-price items are used to stimulate purchases [177]

President, 45

Price, market (equilibrium), 9, 10

Price appreciation increase in the dollar value of an investment at two points in time (the amount of which the price of a security increases) [235–236]

Price fixing, 27

Price gouging, 27

Price indexes, 16

Priceline.com, 168

Price lining setting a limited number of prices for certain categories of products [168–169]

Price-setting tools, 166–167

Price skimming setting an initially high price to cover new product costs and generate a profit [168]

Pricing process of determining what a company will receive in exchange for its products [153]
- cost-oriented, 166–167
- determining, 166–169
- international, 162
- penetration, 168
- psychological, 169
- small business, 163
- strategies and tactics, 168–169
- unfair, 27

Pricing objectives goals that sellers hope to attain in pricing products for sale [166]

Primary securities market market in which new stocks and bonds are bought and sold [231]

Prime rate interest rate available to a bank's most creditworthy customers [217]

Principal individual or organization authorizing an agent to act on its behalf [248]

Private accountant salaried accountant hired by a business to carry out its day-to-day financial activities [200]

Private brand (private label) brand-name product that a wholesaler or retailer has commissioned from a manufacturer [160]

Private enterprise economic system that allows individuals to pursue their own interests without undue governmental restriction [10]

Private placements, 231

Private property rights, 10

Private warehouse warehouse owned by and providing storage for a single company [174]

Privatization process of converting government enterprises into privately owned companies [8]

Problem/need recognition, 155

Process departmentalization dividing an organization according to production processes used to create a good or service [80]

Process flowchart, 98

Process flows, 98

Process layout physical arrangement of production activities that groups equipment and people according to function [97]

Procter & Gamble, 67, 160

Product good, service, or idea that is marketed to fill consumer needs and wants [152]
- branding, 159–160
- classification, 157, 158
- identification, 159–161
- international, 161

mortality rates, 157–158
- packaging, 161
- small business, 163
- speed to market, 158
- value package, 156–157

Product departmentalization dividing an organization according to specific products or services being created [80, 81]

Product development, 157–159

Product differentiation creation of a product feature or product image that differs enough from existing products to attract consumers [11, 153]

Product features tangible and intangible qualities that a company builds into a product [156]

Production

See also Operations
- just-in-time, 101

Production capability, 95–96

Production processes
- goods, 94
- green, 26
- service, 94

Productivity a measure of economic growth that compares how much a system produces with the resources needed to produce it [14–15]

Product layout physical arrangement of production activities designed to make one type of product in a fixed sequence according to its production requirements [97–98]

Product life cycle (PLC) series of stages in a product's commercial life [158–159]

Product liability tort in which a company is responsible for injuries caused by its products [247]

Product line group of products that are closely related because they function in a similar manner or are sold to the same customer group who will use them in similar ways [157]

Product-line retailers, 171–172

Product mix group of products that a firm makes available for sale [157]

Product modification, 26

Product placement a promotional tactic for brand exposure in which characters in television, film, music, magazines, or video games use a real product with its brand visible to viewers [159–160]

Professional corporation form of ownership allowing professionals to take advantage of corporate benefits while granting them limited business liability and unlimited professional liability [43, 44]

Profitability, 167

Profitability ratio financial ratio for measuring a firm's potential earnings [208, 209–210]

Profit-and-loss statement. *See* Income statement

Profit center separate company unit responsible for its own costs and profits [80]

Profit-maximizing objectives, 166

Profits difference between a business's revenues and its expenses [4, 10, 205]

Profit-sharing plan incentive plan for distributing bonuses to employees when company profits rise above a certain level [140]

Project scheduling, 100

Promotion aspect of the marketing mix concerned with the most effective techniques for communicating information about a product [153, 176–179]
- international, 162
- small business, 163

Promotional mix combination of tools used to promote a product [176–179]

Property anything of value to which a person or business has sole right of ownership [247]

Property insurance insurance covering losses resulting from physical damage to or loss of the insured's real estate or personal property [243]

Property rights, 10

Prospectus registration statement filed with the SEC before the issuance of a new security [229]

Protected class set of individuals who by nature of one or more common characteristics is protected under the law from discrimination on the basis of that characteristic [141]

Protectionism practice of protecting domestic business against foreign competition [60]

Protectionist tariff, 59

PRT Group, 40

Psychographic variables consumer characteristics, such as lifestyles, opinions, interests, and attitudes, that may be considered in developing a segmentation strategy [154]

Psychological contract set of expectations held by an employee concerning what he or she will contribute to an organization (referred to as contributions) and what the organization will in return provide the employee (referred to as inducements) [110–111]

Psychological pricing pricing tactic that takes advantage of the fact that consumers do not always respond rationally to stated prices [169]

Publicity promotional tool in which information about a company, a product, or an event is transmitted by the general mass media to attract public attention, [178–179]

Publicly held (public) corporation corporation whose stock is widely held and available for sale to the general public [43, 44]

Public offerings, 238–240

Public relations company-influenced information directed at building goodwill with the public or dealing with unfavorable events [178–179]

Public Utility Regulatory Policy Act, 116

Public warehouse independently owned and operated warehouse that stores goods for many firms [174]

Punishment unpleasant consequences of an undesirable behavior [116]

Punitive damages fines imposed over and above any actual losses suffered by a plaintiff [247]

Purchase decision, 155

Purchasing acquisition of the materials and services that a firm needs to produce its products [101]

Purchasing power parity the principle that exchange rates are set so that the prices of similar products in different countries are about the same [14]

Pure risk risk involving only the possibility of loss or no loss [242]

Q

Quality the combination of characteristics of a product or service that bear on its ability to satisfy stated or implied needs [98]

Quality circles, 103

Quality control the action of ensuring that operations produce products that meet specific quality standards [102]

Quality improvement teams TQM tool in which collaborative groups of employees from various work areas work together to improve quality by solving commonly shared production problems [103]

Quality ownership principle of total quality management that holds that quality belongs to each person who creates it while performing a job [102]

Quality planning, 98

Quid pro quo harassment form of sexual harassment in which sexual favors are requested in return for job-related benefits [143]

Quinlan, Mary Lou, 107
Quinn, Ann, 145

Quota restriction on the number of products of a certain type that can be imported into a country [59–60]

QVC, 173

R

Radio frequency identification, 223
Railroads, 175
Ralph Lauren, 11
Rational decision making, 130–131

Rational motives reasons for purchasing a product that are based on a logical evaluation of product attributes [155]

Ratios, 208–210

Real GDP gross domestic product (GDP) adjusted to account for changes in currency values and price changes [13–14]

Real growth rate, 13

Recession a period during which aggregate output, as measured by GDP, declines [16, 17]

Recruiting process of attracting qualified persons to apply for jobs an organization is seeking to fill [137]

Redfin, 127
Reengineering, 103, 104
Reese, Jerry, 67
Reference checks, 138

Regulatory (administrative) law law made by the authority of administrative agencies [245]

Relationship marketing marketing strategy that emphasizes lasting relationships with customers and suppliers [151]

Reliant Energy, 73
Remote deliveries, 182

Replacement chart list of each management position, who occupies it, how long that person will likely stay in the job, and who is qualified as a replacement [136]

Reporting relationships, 78
Research in Motion (RIM), 187

Reseller market organizational market consisting of intermediaries that buy and resell finished goods [156]

Reserve banks, 220

Reserve requirement percentage of its deposits that a bank must hold in cash or on deposit with the Fed [221]

Responsibility duty to perform an assigned task [82]

Retail distribution, 169

Retailers intermediary who sells products directly to consumers [169]

Retailing, 171–172
   electronic, 172–174
   nonstore, 172
   small business, 35
Retail outlets, 171–172

Retained earnings earnings retained by a firm for its use rather than paid out as dividends [204, 241]

Retirement plans, 140–141

Revenue recognition formal recording and reporting of revenues at the appropriate time [207]

Revenues funds that flow into a business from the sale of goods or services [204]

Revenue tariff, 59
Reverse auction, 168
Revised Uniform Limited Partnership Act, 42
Rights, 22

Risk uncertainty about future events [242]

Risk avoidance the practice of avoiding risk by declining or ceasing to participate in an activity [242]

Risk control the practice of minimizing the frequency or severity of losses from risky activities [242]

Risk management the process of conserving the firm's earning power and assets by reducing the threat of losses due to uncontrollable events [242]

Risk propensity extent to which a decision maker is willing to gamble when making a decision [132, 133]

Risk ratings, 238

Risk retention the practice of covering a firm's losses with its own funds [242]

Risk-return relationship the principle that safer investments tend to offer lower returns, while riskier investments tend to offer higher returns [235–236]

Risk taking, 7, 37

Risk transfer the practice of transferring a firm's risk to another firm [242]

Rockefeller, John D., 25
Romania, 49
Ronald McDonald House program, 30
Roosevelt, Eleanor, 123

Roth IRA provision allowing individual retirement savings with tax-free accumulated earnings [257]

Router, 194
Royal Dutch Shell, 57
Rule of 72, 228

Russell 200 Index specialty index that uses 2000 stocks to measure the performance of the smallest U.S. companies [234–235]

Russia, 7, 49

S

S&P 500 market index of U.S. equities based on the performance of 500 large-cap stocks representing various sectors of the overall equities market [234]

Sabotage, 109

Salary compensation in the form of money paid for discharging the responsibilities of a job [139]

Sales agent independent intermediary who generally deals in the related product lines of a few producers and forms long-term relationships to represent those producers and meet the needs of many customers [169–170]

Sales forecasting, 37

Sales promotion short-term promotional activity designed to encourage consumer buying, industrial sales, or cooperation from distributors [177–178]

Samples, 177

Samsung, 49

Sant, Roger, 116

Sarbanes-Oxley Act enactment of federal regulations to restore public trust in accounting practices by imposing new requirements on financial activities in publicly traded corporations [29, 201]

Save-A-Lot, 95

Savings and loan association (S&L) financial institution accepting deposits and making loans primarily for home mortgages [216]

Savings institutions, 216

Scandinavia, 49

Scardino, Marjorie, 64

Scheduling
    operations, 99–100
    project, 100

Schultz, Howard, 6

Scientific management, 112

S.C. Johnson, 26

S corporation hybrid of a closely held corporation and a partnership, organized and operated like a corporation but treated as a partnership for tax purposes [43, 44]

Sears, 80–81

Secondary securities market market in which existing stocks and bonds are traded [231]

Second Life, 190

Secured loan loan for which the borrower must provide collateral [236]

Securities stocks, bonds, and mutual funds representing secured, or asset-based, claims by investors against issuers [230–231]

Securities and Exchange Commission (SEC) federal agency that administers U.S. securities laws to protect the investing public and maintain smoothly functioning markets [229, 231]

Securities investment dealer (broker) financial institution that buys and sells stocks and bonds both for investors and for its own accounts [217]

Securities markets the markets in which stocks and bonds are sold [230–231]

Security policy, 194

Self-awareness, 110

Self-motivation, 110

Servers, 186

Service Corps of Retired Executives (SCORE), 39

Service operations (service production) activities producing intangible and tangible products, such as entertainment, transportation, and education [92, 93–94]

Service production processes, 94

Services products having nonphysical features, such as time, expertise, or an activity that can be purchased [35, 150]

Sexual harassment making unwelcome sexual advances in the workplace [143]

Shamil Bank, 220

Shell, 30

Shell Oil, 88

Sherman Antitrust Act, 12

Shinohara, Yoshiko, 37

Shopping agent (e-agent) e-intermediary (middleman) in the Internet distribution channel that assists users in finding products and prices but that does not take possession of products [172, 173]

Shortage situation in which quantity demanded exceeds quantity supplied [9–10]

Short-term goal goal set for the very near future [71]

Short-term solvency ratio financial ratio for measuring a company's ability to pay immediate debts [208]

Simple message transfer protocol (SMTP) the basic communications protocol used to send e-mail [185]

Sinegal, James, 64

Situational approach to leadership assumes that appropriate leader behavior varies from one situation to another [124]

Skills inventories [136–137]

Slovakia, 97

Small business independently owned business that has relatively little influence in its market [34]

    factors in success of, 41

    failures, 39, 40–41

    financing, 38–39

    importance of, in U.S. economy, 34–35

    marketing mix and, 162–163

    popular areas for, 35–36

    social responsibility and, 31

    starting and operating, 37–39

    trends in, 39–40

Small Business Administration (SBA) government agency charged with assisting small businesses [34, 39]

Small Business Development Center (SBDC) SBA program designed to consolidate information from various disciplines and make it available to small businesses [39]

Small-business investment companies (SBICs) government-regulated investment company that borrows money from the SBA to invest in or lend to a small business [39]

Smart card credit-card-sized plastic card with an embedded computer chip that can be programmed with electronic money [223]

Smith, Fred, 85

Social audit systematic analysis of a firm's success in using funds earmarked for meeting its social responsibility goals [30, 31]

Social consciousness, 25

Socialism planned economic system in which the government owns and operates only selected major sources of production [7, 8]

Social networking, 161, 237

Social responsibility, 19

Social responsibility the attempt of a business to balance its commitments to groups and individuals in its environment, including customers, other businesses, employees, investors, and local communities [23]

    approaches to, 29–30

    areas of, 25–29

    management of, 30–31

    program implementation, 29–31

    small business and, 31

    social consciousness, 25

    stakeholder model of, 23–25

    toward customers, 26–27

    toward employees, 27–28

    toward environment, 25–26

    toward investors, 28–29

Sociocultural environment the customs, norms, values, and demographic characteristics of the society in which an organization functions [5, 151]

Software programs that tell the computer's hardware what resources to use and how to use them [188–189]

Sole proprietorship business owned and usually operated by one person who is responsible for all of its debts [41]

Solvency ratio financial ratio, either short- or long-term, for estimating the borrower's ability to repay debt [208, 209]

SONY, 27

South America, 88

South Korea, 49, 55

Southwest Airlines, 91

Soviet Union, 7

Spain, 49

Spam junk e-mail sent to a mailing list or a newsgroup [193–195]

Spamhaus Project, 195

Span of control number of people supervised by one manager [82, 83]

Specialization, 79

Special purpose loans, 39

Specialty goods and services expensive, rarely purchased good or service [157]

Specialty store retail store carrying one product line or category of related products [171]

Speculative risk risk involving the possibility of gain or loss [242]

Speed to market strategy of introducing new products to respond quickly to customer or market changes [158]

Spin-off strategy of setting up one or more corporate units as new, independent corporations [44, 45]

Sprint Nexel, 74

Spyware program unknowingly downloaded by users that monitors their computer activities, gathering e-mail addresses, credit card numbers, and other information that it transmits to someone outside the host system [193, 194–195]

Sreekanti, Kumar, 24

Stability, 15–17

Stabilization policy government economic policy intended to smooth out fluctuations in output and unemployment and to stabilize prices [16, 17]

Staff authority authority based on expertise that usually involves counseling and advising line managers [83]

Staff members advisers and counselors who help line departments in making decisions but who do not have the authority to make final decisions [83]

Staff schedule assigned working times in upcoming days for each employee on each work shift [100]

Stakeholders, 38
   customers, 24
   employees, 24
   international, 25
   investors, 24
   local communities, 24
   organizational, 23
   suppliers, 24

Standard of living the total quantity and quality of goods and services people can purchase with the currency used in their economic system [13, 15]

Starbucks, 6, 12, 24, 26, 131–132

Start-ups, 36, 38, 137
   Internet, 49
   trends in, 39–40

Starvu, 70

Statement of cash flows financial statement describing a firm's yearly cash receipts and cash payments [205–206]

Statutory law law created by constitution(s) or by federal, state, or local legislative acts [245]

Stewart, Martha, 29

Stock a portion of ownership of a corporation [228–229]

Stock broker individual or organization that receives and executes buy and sell orders on behalf of outside customers in return for commission [232–233]

Stock exchange organization of individuals formed to provide an institutional setting in which stock can be traded [231–232]

Stockholder (shareholder) owner of shares of stock in a corporation [44]

Stock indexes, 233–234

Stock options, 140

Stock ownership, 44

Stock split stock dividend paid in additional shares to shareholders, thus increasing the number of outstanding shares [239]

Stock valuation, 239

Strategic alliance strategy in which two or more organizations collaborate on a project for mutual gain [44, 45, 58–59]

Strategic goal goal derived directly from a firm's mission statement [71]

Strategic leadership leader's ability to understand the complexities of both the organization and its environment and to lead change in the organization so as to enhance its competitiveness [128]

Strategic management process of helping an organization maintain an effective alignment with its environment [69–72]

Strategic plan plan reflecting decisions about resource allocations, company priorities, and steps needed to meet strategic goals [72]

Strategy broad set of organizational plans for implementing the decisions made for achieving organizational goals [69, 71]

Strategy formulation creation of a broad program for defining and meeting an organization's goals [71–72]

Strict product liability principle that liability can result not from a producer's negligence but from a defect in the product itself [247]

Strike labor action in which employees temporarily walk off the job and refuse to work [146]

Strikebreaker worker hired as a permanent or temporary replacement for a striking employee [146]

Subprime mortgage crisis, 218

Subsidy government payment to help a domestic business compete with foreign firms [60]

Substitute product product that is dissimilar from those of competitors but that can fulfill the same need [152]

Supermarket large product-line retailer offering a variety of food and food-related items in specialized departments [171]

Suppliers, 24, 190

Supplier selection process of finding and choosing suppliers from whom to buy [101]

Supply the willingness and ability of producers to offer a good or service for sale
   law of, 9–10
   in market economy, 8–10

Supply chain management (SCM) principle of looking at the supply chain as a whole to improve the overall flow through the system [104]

Supply chain (value chain) flow of information, materials, and services that starts with raw-materials suppliers and continues adding value through other stages in the network of firms until the product reaches the end customer [104]
   global, 104–105
   reengineering, 104

Supply curve graph showing how many units of a product will be supplied (offered for sale) at different prices [9, 10]

Surplus situation in which quantity supplied exceeds quantity demanded [9]

Sustainability, 26

Suzuki, 49

SWOT Analysis identification and analysis of organizational strengths and weaknesses and environmental opportunities and threats as part of strategy formulation [71–72]
System software, 188

T

Taco Bell, 97

Tactical plan generally short-term plan concerned with implementing specific aspects of a company's strategic plans [65, 72]
Taiwan, 49

Tall organizational structure characteristic of centralized companies with multiple layers of management [82, 83]

Tangible personal property any movable item that can be owned, bought, sold, or leased [247]

Tangible real property land and anything attached to it [247]
Target, 11, 25, 151
Target audience, 176

Target market group of people that has similar wants and needs and that can be expected to show interest in the same products [153]

Tariff tax levied on imported products [59–60]

Task-focused leader behavior leader behavior focusing on how tasks should be performed in order to meet certain goals and to achieve certain performance standards [123]
Tax rates, 17

Tax services assistance provided by CPAs for tax preparation and tax planning [199]
Taylor, Frederick, 111–112
Team management, 117
Team organization, 87

Technical skills skills needed to perform specialized tasks [68]

Technological environment all the ways by which firms create value for the constituents [4–5, 151]
Technology, infrastructure, 49
Technology skills, 69

Telecommuting form of flextime that allows people to perform some or all of a job away from standard office settings [118–119]

Telemarketing form of nonstore retailing in which the telephone is used to sell directly to consumers [172]
Telephone calls, 68
Temporary workers, 144–145
Tempstaff, 37

Tender offer offer to buy shares made by a prospective buyer directly to a target corporation's shareholders, who then make individual decisions about whether to sell [43]
Tests, 138
Texas Instruments, 23
Theft, 109

Theory X theory of motivation holding that people are naturally lazy and uncooperative [113]

Theory Y theory of motivation holding that people are naturally energetic, growth-oriented, self-motivated, and interested in being productive [113]
Thrift institutions, 216
Timbuk2, 183

Time deposit bank funds that have a fixed term of time to maturity and cannot be withdrawn earlier or transferred by check [215]

Time management skills skills associated with the productive use of time [68]
Time utility, 92, 150

Time value of money principle that invested money grows by earning interest or yielding some other form of return [228]
TNT Post Group N.V., 8
Tobacco companies, 29

Top manager manager responsible for a firm's overall performance and effectiveness [66, 67]

Tort civil injury to people, property, or reputation for which compensation must be paid [247]
Toshiba, 49

Total quality management (TQM) the sum of all activities involved in getting high-quality goods and services into the marketplace [102–103]
Total return, 236
Toyota, 49, 57, 94–95, 98
Trade agreements, 49–50
Trade balances, 50–52
Trade barriers, 59–61

Trade deficit situation in which a country's imports exceed its exports, creating a negative balance of trade [15, 51–52]

Trade show sales promotion technique in which various members of an industry gather to display, demonstrate, and sell products [178]

Trade surplus situation in which a country's exports exceed its imports, creating a positive balance of trade [51]

Trademark exclusive legal right to use a brand name or symbol [248]
Trading floor, 231

Traditional Individual Retirement Account (IRA) provision allowing individual tax-deferred retirement savings [256]
Training, 138

Trait approach to leadership focused on identifying the essential traits that distinguished leaders [122–123]

Transactional leadership comparable to management, it involves routine, regimented activities [125]

Transformational leadership the set of abilities that allows a leader to recognize the need for change, to create a vision to guide that change, and to execute the change effectively [124–125]
Transnational corporation, 43
Transparency, 127

Transportation activities in transporting resources to the producer and finished goods to customers [36, 101]
Transportation operations, 174–175
Treaties, trade, 49–50

Trial court general court that hears cases not specifically assigned to another court [246]
Trojan horses, 193
Trucks, 174

Trust services bank management on behalf of an individual to manage an estate, investments, or other assets [218]

Turnover annual percentage of an organization's workforce that leaves and must be replaced [109]

Two-factor theory theory of motivation holding that job satisfaction depends on two factors, hygiene and motivation [113–114]
Tyco, 20, 25, 210
Tylenol, 23

U

Unemployment the level of joblessness among people actively seeking work in an economic system [16, 17]

Unethical behavior behavior that does not conform to generally accepted social norms concerning beneficial and harmful actions [20]

Uniform Commercial Code (UCC) body of standardized laws governing the rights of buyers and sellers in transactions [248]
Unilever, 59
Union. *See* Labor union
Union tactics, 146
United Kingdom, 49

United States
comparative advantages in, 55
GDP, 13
risk taking in, 7
trade deficit, 15, 51–52
trading partners of, 51
in world economy, 48

Unlimited liability legal principle holding owners responsible for paying off all debts of a business [41, 42]

Unsecured loan loan for which collateral is not required [237]

Unstorability, 93

Upper middle-income countries, 48

UPS, 24, 98

Urban Outfitters, 5, 82

U.S. dollar, 53

U.S. economy
management of, 17
role of small business in, 34–35

U.S. financial system, 216–220

U.S. Xpress Enterprises, 174

Utility ability of a product to satisfy a human want or need [22, 92, 150]

V

Value relative comparison of a product's benefits versus its costs [150]

Value-added analysis process of evaluating all work activities, materials flows, and paperwork to determine the value that they add for customers [103]

Value chain. *See* Supply chain

Value creation, through operations, 92–94

Value package product marketed as a bundle of value-adding attributes, including reasonable cost [156–157]

Vanderbilt, Cornelius, 25

Variable cost cost that changes with the quantity of a product produced or sold [167]

Variable pay, 140

Venture capital private funds by wealthy individuals seeking investment opportunities in new growth companies [237–238]

Venture capital company group of small investors who invest money in companies with rapid growth potential [39]

Vestibule training off-the-job training conducted in a simulated environment [138]

Vice-president, 45

Victoria's Secret, 27

Video marketing nonstore retailing to consumers via home television [173–174]

Vietnam, 7

Vioxx, 26–27

Viral marketing a promotional method that relies on word of mouth and the Internet to spread information like a "virus" from person-to-person about products and ideas [160]

Virgin, 27

Virtual leadership leadership in settings where leaders and followers interact electronically rather than in face-to-face settings [129–130]

Virtual organization, 87–88

Virtual reality, 190

Virtual storefront, 173

Viruses, 193, 194

Vlasic, 80

Volkert, Klaus, 20

Volkswagon, 26, 49, 59

Voluntary bankruptcy bankruptcy proceedings initiated by an indebted individual or organization [249]

Volvo, 59

Vondra, Al, 197

VSAT satellite communications a network of geographically dispersed transmitter-receivers (transceivers) that send signals to and receive signals from a satellite, exchanging voice, video, and data transmissions [186]

W

Wage reopener clause clause allowing wage rates to be renegotiated during the life of a labor contract [146]

Wages compensation in the form of money paid for time worked [16, 139]

Waksal, Sam, 29

Wal-Mart, 12, 25, 38, 57, 61, 74, 86, 97, 189

Walt Disney, 73, 74

Walton, Sam, 65

Warehousing physical distribution operation concerned with the storage of goods [101, 174]

Warranty seller's promise to stand by its products or services if a problem occurs after the sale [248]

Waste Management, 210

Water carriers, 174–175

Watkins, Sherron, 28

Wegmans Food Markets, 24

Weill, Sandy, 24

Wenner, Jann, 152

Whistle-blower employee who detects and tries to put an end to a company's unethical, illegal, or socially irresponsible actions by publicizing them [28]

Whitman, Meg, 121

Whole Foods Market, 26, 82, 151

Wholesale club bargain retailer offering large discounts on brand-name merchandise to customers who have paid annual membership fees [172]

Wholesale distribution, 169

Wholesalers intermediary who sells products to other businesses for resale to final consumers [169]

Wholesaling, 35, 170

Wide area network (WAN) computers that are linked over long distances through telephone lines, microwave signals, or satellite communications [186]

Wi-Fi technology using a wireless local area network [187]

Williamson, Bob, 40

WiMAX, 187

Wireless local area network (WLAN) a local area network with wireless access points for PC users [187]

Wireless mooching, 192

Wireless networks, 187

Wireless wide area network (WWAN) a network that uses airborne electronic signals instead of wires to link computers and electronic devices over long distances [187]

Women
as business owners, 39
as leaders, 127–128

Work attitudes, 110

Workers
contingent, 144–145
knowledge, 144, 191
temporary, 144–145

Worker safety regulations, 142

Workers' compensation coverage coverage provided by a firm to employees for medical expenses, loss of wages, and rehabilitation costs resulting from job-related injuries or disease [243]

Workers' compensation insurance legally required insurance for compensating workers injured on the job [140]

Work groups, 118

Workplace aggression and violence, 109

Workplace discrimination, 142–143

Workplace disputes, 142

Workplace diversity the range of workers' attitudes, values, beliefs, and behaviors that differ by gender, race, age, ethnicity, physical ability, and other relevant characteristics [143–144]

Work schedules, modified, 118–119

Work sharing method of increasing job satisfaction by allowing two or more people to share a single full-time job [118]

Work slowdown labor action in which workers perform jobs at a slower than normal pace [146]

Work teams groups of operating employees who are empowered to plan and organize their own work and to perform that work with a minimum of supervision [84]

World Bank U.N. agency that provides a limited scope of financial services, such as funding improvements in underdeveloped countries [48, 224]

WorldCom, 210
World marketplaces, 48–49
World of Warcraft, 190

World Trade Organization (WTO) organization through which member nations negotiate trading agreements and resolve disputes about trade policies and practices [50]

World Wide Web a standardized code for accessing information and transmitting data over the Internet; the common language that allows information sharing on the Internet [185]
Worms, 193

X

Xanga, 26
XM Radio, 12

Y

Yahoo!, 64–65, 159
Yifei, Li, 69

Z

Zenner, Jessica, 188
Zombori, Sandor, 107
Zuckerberg, Mark, 33